Camping
in State Parks
Eastern USA

Discover 1,634 Camping Areas at 955 Parks in 31 States

Published by:

Roundabout Publications
PO Box 569
LaCygne, KS 66040

Phone: 800-455-2207
Internet: www.RoundaboutPublications.com

Library of Congress Control Number: 2023941984

ISBN-10: 1-885464-92-4
ISBN-13: 978-1-885464-92-7

Table of Contents

Introduction

Huge portions of public lands, managed by a variety of government agencies, are available to the general public for recreational use. This book will guide you to 1,634 camping areas available at 955 parks in 31 eastern states. Additional information can be found online at state tourism and park websites. Please note that the camping areas accessible only by boat are not included in this guide.

Using This Guide

The guide is especially helpful when used along with Google Maps, Windows Maps, or a GPS device for locating and navigating to each camping area.

State Maps

A state map is provided to aid you in locating the camping areas. A grid overlay on each map is used when cross-referencing with each camping area.

Map Grid Chart & Alphabetical List

Following the state map is a chart showing the camping area ID number(s) located within a map grid. Following this chart is an alphabetical list of each camping area, which is especially helpful when you already know the name of an area. This list provides each location's ID number and map grid location.

Camping Area Details

Camping area details include information about each public camping area within the state. Preceding each location's name is the ID number and map grid location, which is used when referencing the state map.

Details for each camping area generally include the following information:

- Total number of sites or dispersed camping
- Number of RV sites
- Sites with electric hookups
- Full hookup sites, if available
- Water (central location or spigots at site)
- Showers
- RV dump station
- Toilets (flush, pit/vault, or none)
- Laundry facilities
- Camp store
- Maximum RV size limits (if any)
- Reservation information (accepted, not accepted, recommended or required)
- Generator use and hours (if limited)
- Operating season

- Camping fees charged
- Miscellaneous notes
- Length of stay limit
- Elevation in feet and meters
- Telephone number
- Nearby city or town
- GPS coordinates

The Ultimate Public Campground Project

Data for this publication is from The Ultimate Public Campground Project, which was established in 2008 to provide a consolidated and comprehensive source for public campgrounds of all types. Please note that despite our best efforts, there will always be errors to be found in the data. With over 45,000 records in our database, it is impossible to ensure that each one is always up-to-date.

Update: In 2022 The Ultimate Public Campground Project database was acquired by a GPS manufacturer. As a result, updated information for this book will no longer be available - this is the last edition.

Happy Camping!

Common Abbreviations Used

CCC	Civilian Conservation Corps
CG	Campground
CR	County Road
HP	Historical Park
HSP	Historical State Park
MP	Milepost
SFWMD	South Florida Water Management District
SHA	State Historic Area
SHP	State Historic Park
SHS	State Historic Site
SMP	State Marine Park
SP	State Park
SRP	State Resort Park
TC	Trail Camp
TH	Trail head

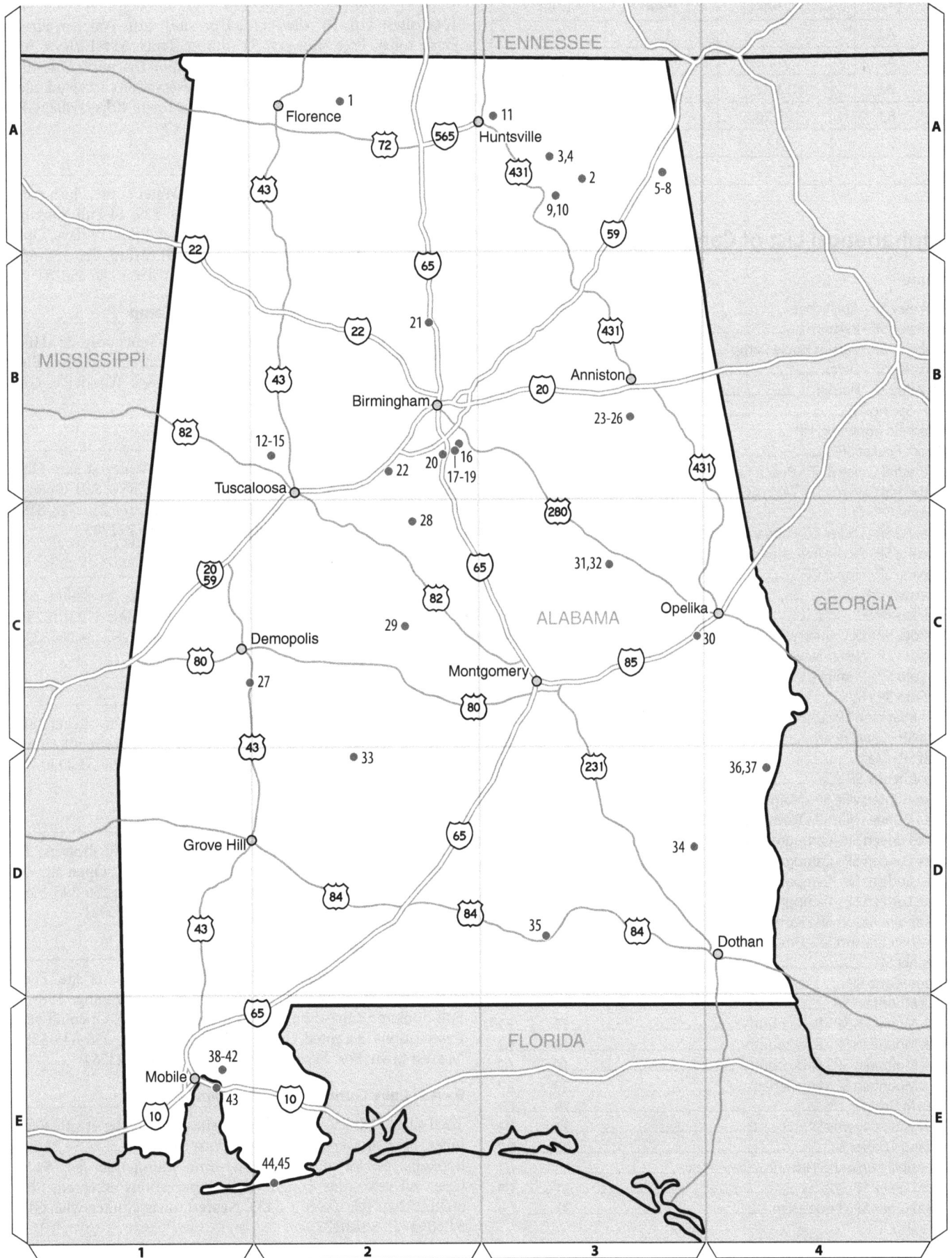

Alabama

TENNESSEE

Florence
1

11
Huntsville

3,4
2
5-8
9,10

Anniston

Birmingham

12-15
20
16
17-19
22

23-26

28

Tuscaloosa

29
31,32

Opelika
30

Demopolis
27

ALABAMA

Montgomery
85

33
36,37

Grove Hill
34

35
Dothan

MISSISSIPPI

GEORGIA

FLORIDA

38-42
Mobile
43

44,45

Map	ID	Map	ID
A2	1	C3	30-32
A3	2-11	D2	33
B2	12-22	D3	34-35
B3	23-26	D4	36-37
C1	27	E1	38-43
C2	28-29	E2	44-45

Alphabetical List of Camping Areas

1 • A2 | Joe Wheeler SP

Total sites: 116, RV sites: 116, Elec sites: 110, Water available, Flush toilet, Free showers, RV dump, Tents: $14-17/RVs: $35, Also cabins, 110 Full hookups, 15% Senior Discount, One-time transaction fee: $4.50, Open all year, Reservations accepted, Elev: 597ft/182m, Tel: 256-247-1184, Nearest town: Rogersville. GPS: 34.804913, -87.321467

2 • A3 | Buck's Pocket SP

Total sites: 34, RV sites: 23, Elec sites: 23, Water at site, Flush toilet, Free showers, RV dump, Tents: $17/RVs: $29, 14 Full hookups, Reservations only through park office, Stay limit: 14 days, Open all year, Reservations accepted, Elev: 699ft/213m, Tel: 256-659-6288, Nearest town: Grove Oak. GPS: 34.474365, -86.050781

3 • A3 | Cathedral Caverns SP - Beech Camp

Dispersed sites, No water, Vault/pit toilet, Tents only: $5, Hike-in, 3/4 mi, $5/person, Open all year, Reservations accepted, Elev: 971ft/296m, Tel: 256-728-8193, Nearest town: Woodville. GPS: 34.565751, -86.224016

4 • A3 | Cathedral Caverns SP - Main CG

Total sites: 20, RV sites: 13, Elec sites: 13, Water at site, Flush toilet, Free showers, No RV dump, Tents: $13/RVs: $20, Open all year, Reservations accepted, Elev: 787ft/240m, Tel: 256-728-8193, Nearest town: Woodville. GPS: 34.573267, -86.221305

5 • A3 | DeSoto SP - CCC Quarry

Dispersed sites, No water, Vault/pit toilet, Hike-to shelter: $17, 1.1 mi, Open all year, Reservations accepted, Elev: 1723ft/525m, Tel: 256-845-5380, Nearest town: Fort Payne. GPS: 34.506827, -85.626812

6 • A3 | DeSoto SP - Never-Never Land

Dispersed sites, No water, Vault/pit toilet, Hike-to shelter: $17, .75 mi, Open all year, Reservations accepted, Elev: 1660ft/506m, Tel: 256-845-5380, Nearest town: Fort Payne. GPS: 34.493036, -85.637432

7 • A3 | DeSoto SP - Primitive

Total sites: 21, Central water, Vault/pit toilet, No showers, No RV dump, Tents only: $15, 3 group sites available, Open all year, Reservations not accepted, Elev: 1823ft/556m, Tel: 256-845-5380, Nearest town: Fort Payne. GPS: 34.505139, -85.635921

8 • A3 | DeSoto SP - RV

Total sites: 94, RV sites: 94, Elec sites: 94, Water at site, Flush toilet, Free showers, RV dump, Tent & RV camping: $38, 94 Full hookups, One-time Convenience Fee: $4.50, Open all year, Reservations accepted, Elev: 1598ft/487m, Tel: 256-845-5380, Nearest town: Fort Payne. GPS: 34.501585, -85.623564

9 • A3 | Lake Guntersville SP - Main

Total sites: 318, RV sites: 318, Elec sites: 318, Water at site, Flush toilet, Free showers, RV dump, Tents: $14/RVs: $27-29, 23 Full hookups, Senior discount, One-time transaction fee: $4.50, Open all year, Max Length: 60ft, Reservations accepted, Elev: 663ft/202m, Tel: 256-571-5455, Nearest town: Guntersville. GPS: 34.403575, -86.201273

10 • A3 | Lake Guntersville SP - Town Creek

Dispersed sites, Central water, Flush toilet, Free showers, RV dump, Tent & RV camping: $14, One-time transaction fee: $4.25, Open all year, Reservations not accepted, Elev: 673ft/205m, Tel: 256-582-8352, Nearest town: Guntersville. GPS: 34.408729, -86.183371

11 • A3 | Monte Sano SP

Total sites: 100, RV sites: 82, Elec sites: 82, Water at site, Flush toilet, Free showers, RV dump, Tents: $14/RVs: $28-30, Also cabins, 18 Full hookups, 15% Senior Discount, One-time transaction fee: $4.50, Open all year, Reservations accepted, Elev: 1644ft/501m, Tel: 256-534-3757, Nearest town: Huntsville. GPS: 34.747598, -86.513394

12 • B2 | Lake Lurleen SP - Campground A

Total sites: 37, RV sites: 37, Elec sites: 37, Water at site, Flush toilet, Free showers, RV dump, Tent & RV camping: $31, Senior Discount Dec-Feb: $21 - Seniors $18, Jan A-Day Game: $37, One-time transaction fee: $4.50, Open all year, Reservations accepted, Elev: 331ft/101m, Tel: 205-339-1558, Nearest town: Coker. GPS: 33.299798, -87.676451

13 • B2 | Lake Lurleen SP - Campground B

Total sites: 8, RV sites: 8, Elec sites: 8, Water at site, Flush toilet, Free showers, RV dump, Tent & RV camping: $31, Senior Discount Dec-Feb: $21 - Seniors $18, Jan A-Day Game: $37, One-time transaction fee: $4.50, Open all year, Reservations accepted, Elev: 285ft/87m, Tel: 205-339-1558, Nearest town: Coker. GPS: 33.302214, -87.677409

14 • B2 | Lake Lurleen SP - Campground C

Total sites: 25, RV sites: 19, Elec sites: 19, Water at site, Flush toilet, Free showers, RV dump, Tent & RV camping: $31, Senior Discount Dec-Feb: $21 - Seniors $18, Jan A-Day Game: $37, One-time transaction fee: $4.50, Open all year, Reservations accepted, Elev: 259ft/79m, Tel: 205-339-1558, Nearest town: Coker. GPS: 33.308271, -87.675692

15 • B2 | Lake Lurleen SP - Campground D

Total sites: 27, RV sites: 27, Elec sites: 27, Water at site, Flush toilet, Free showers, RV dump, Tent & RV camping: $31, Senior Discount Dec-Feb: $21 - Seniors $18, Jan A-Day Game: $37, One-time transaction fee: $4.50, Open all year, Reservations accepted, Elev: 302ft/92m, Tel: 205-339-1558, Nearest town: Coker. GPS: 33.310322, -87.675994

16 • B2 | Oak Mountain SP

Total sites: 145, RV sites: 85, Elec sites: 85, Water at site, Flush toilet, Free showers, RV dump, Tents: $18/RVs: $27-31, Also cabins, 57 Full hookups, 15% Senior Discount, One-time transaction fee: $4.50, Nov-Feb monthly rate available, Open all year, Reservations accepted, Elev: 592ft/180m, Tel: 205-620-2520, Nearest town: Pelham. GPS: 33.363417, -86.710281

17 • B2 | Oak Mountain SP - Backcountry

Dispersed sites, No water, Vault/pit toilet, Tents only: $6, Hike-in, Fee is $6/person, One-time transaction fee: $4.50, No fires, Open all year, Reservations not accepted, Elev: 744ft/227m, Tel: 205-620-2520, Nearest town: Pelham. GPS: 33.343532, -86.724043

18 • B2 | Oak Mountain SP - Backcountry

Dispersed sites, No water, Vault/pit toilet, Tents only: $6, Hike-in, Fee is $6/person, One-time transaction fee: $4.50, No fires, Open all year, Reservations not accepted, Elev: 844ft/257m, Tel: 205-620-2520, Nearest town: Pelham. GPS: 33.334738, -86.732465

19 • B2 | Oak Mountain SP - Backcountry

Dispersed sites, No water, Vault/pit toilet, Tents only: $6, Hike-in, Fee is $6/person, One-time transaction fee: $4.50, No fires, Open all year, Reservations not accepted, Elev: 1248ft/380m, Tel: 205-620-2520, Nearest town: Pelham. GPS: 33.331976, -86.729854

20 • B2 | Oak Mountain SP - Equestrian

Total sites: 12, RV sites: 12, Elec sites: 12, Water at site, Flush toilet, Free showers, RV dump, Tents: $18-27/RVs: $27-33, Also cabins, 12 Full hookups, 15% Senior Discount, One-time transaction fee: $4.50, Nov-Feb monthly rate available, Open all year, Reservations accepted, Elev: 575ft/175m, Tel: 205-620-2520, Nearest town: Pelham. GPS: 33.321346, -86.779258

21 • B2 | Rickwood Caverns SP

Total sites: 13, RV sites: 9, Central water, Flush toilet, Free showers, RV dump, Tents: $16/RVs: $30, 15% Senior Discount Sun-Thu, One-time transaction fee: $4.50, Open all year, Reservations accepted, Elev: 810ft/247m, Tel: 205-647-9692, Nearest town: Warrior. GPS: 33.876709, -86.867676

22 • B2 | Tannehill Ironworks Historical State Park

Total sites: 295, RV sites: 195, Elec sites: 195, Flush toilet, Free showers, RV dump, Tents: $20/RVs: $25-30, 15% Senior Discount, Open all year, Reservations not accepted, Elev: 476ft/145m, Tel: 205-477-5711, Nearest town: McCalla. GPS: 33.250681, -87.067771

23 • B3 | Cheaha SP - CCC

Dispersed sites, Central water, Vault/pit toilet, No showers, No RV dump, Tents only: $15, Stay limit: 14 days, Generator hours: 0600-2200, Open all year, Reservations accepted, Elev: 1288ft/393m, Tel: 256-488-5111, Nearest town: Oxford. GPS: 33.474383, -85.823019

24 • B3 | Cheaha SP - Lower CG - Cheaha Lake

Total sites: 32, RV sites: 32, Elec sites: 32, Water at site, Flush toilet, Free showers, RV dump, Tent & RV camping: $31, 30 Full hookups, 15% Senior Discount, Stay limit: 14 days, Generator hours: 0600-2200, Open Apr-Dec, Reservations accepted, Elev: 1312ft/400m, Tel: 256-488-5111, Nearest town: Oxford. GPS: 33.472644, -85.824276

25 • B3 | Cheaha SP - Picnic Trail Sites

Total sites: 25, RV sites: 0, Elec sites: 25, Central water, Flush toilet, Free showers, No RV dump, Tents only: $19, Stay limit: 14 days, Generator hours: 0600-2200, Open all year, Reservations accepted, Elev: 2280ft/695m, Tel: 256-488-5111, Nearest town: Oxford. GPS: 33.487014, -85.810664

26 • B3 | Cheaha SP - Upper CG

Total sites: 40, RV sites: 40, Elec sites: 40, Water at site, Flush toilet, Free showers, RV dump, Tent & RV camping: $31, 40 Full hookups, Stay limit: 14 days, Generator hours: 0600-2200, Open all year, Reservations accepted, Elev: 2280ft/695m, Tel: 256-488-5111, Nearest town: Oxford. GPS: 33.487222, -85.812666

27 • C1 | Chickasaw SP

Total sites: 6, RV sites: 3, Elec sites: 6, Water at site, Flush toilet, No showers, No RV dump, Tents: $9/RVs: $18, Open all year, Reservations accepted, Elev: 174ft/53m, Tel: 334-295-8230, Nearest town: Gallion. GPS: 32.363635, -87.780627

28 • C2 | Brierfield Ironworks HP

Total sites: 12, RV sites: 5, Water at site, Flush toilet, Free showers, RV dump, Tents: $16/RVs: $24, Also cabins, Reservations not accepted, Elev: 381ft/116m, Tel: 205-665-1856, Nearest town: Montevallo. GPS: 33.040097, -86.948069

29 • C2 | Paul M Grist SP

Total sites: 11, RV sites: 11, Elec sites: 11, Water at site, Flush toilet, Free showers, RV dump, Tents: $13/RVs: $22-25, One-time transaction fee: $3, Discounts for Senior/100% Disabled, Open all year, Reservations accepted, Elev: 354ft/108m, Tel: 334-872-5846, Nearest town: Selma. GPS: 32.598060, -86.990830

30 • C3 | Chewacla SP

Total sites: 45, RV sites: 36, Elec sites: 36, Water at site, Flush toilet, Free showers, RV dump, Tents: $20/RVs: $25-33, Also cabins, 36 Full hookups, $5 Dump fee, 15% Senior Discount, Stay limit: 14 days, Open all year, Max Length: 60ft, Reservations accepted, Elev: 545ft/166m, Tel: 334-887-5621, Nearest town: Auburn. GPS: 32.553911, -85.477620

31 • C3 | Wind Creek SP

Total sites: 586, RV sites: 586, Elec sites: 586, Water at site, Flush toilet, Free showers, RV dump, Tent & RV camping: $23-26, 268 Full hookups, 16 horse sites, 15% Senior Discount Sun-Thu, One-time transaction fee: $4.50, Nov-Feb monthly rates available, Stay limit: 14 days, Open all year, Reservations accepted, Elev: 538ft/164m, Tel: 256-329-0845, Nearest town: Alexander City. GPS: 32.855872, -85.927299

32 • C3 | Wind Creek SP - Equestrian

Total sites: 20, RV sites: 20, Elec sites: 20, Water at site, Flush toilet, Tent & RV camping: $23-26, 15% Senior Discount Sun-Thu, One-time transaction fee: $4.50, Nov-Feb monthly rates available, Stay limit: 14 days, Reservations accepted, Elev: 527ft/161m, Tel: 256-329-0845, Nearest town: Alexander City. GPS: 32.857985, -85.927684

33 • D2 | Roland Cooper SP

Total sites: 60, RV sites: 47, Elec sites: 47, Water at site, Flush toilet, Free showers, RV dump, Tents: $19/RVs: $32, Also cabins, 47 Full hookups, Nov-Feb monthly rate available, Concessionaire, Open all year, Reservations accepted, Elev: 148ft/45m, Tel: 334-682-4838, Nearest town: Camden. GPS: 32.052795, -87.249393

34 • D3 | Blue Springs SP

Total sites: 50, RV sites: 50, Elec sites: 50, Water at site, Flush toilet, Free showers, RV dump, Tents: $15/RVs: $22-26, 7 Full hookups, 15% Senior/military/100% disabled discount Sun-Thu, One-time transaction fee: $3, Stay limit: 14 days, Open all year, Reservations

accepted, Elev: 322ft/98m, Tel: 334-397-4875, Nearest town: Clio. GPS: 31.661377, -85.507324

35 • D3 | Frank Jackson SP

Total sites: 40, RV sites: 32, Elec sites: 32, Water at site, Flush toilet, Free showers, RV dump, Tents: $19/RVs: $36, 32 Full hookups, 15% Senior Discount, Open all year, Reservations accepted, Elev: 292ft/89m, Tel: 334-493-6988, Nearest town: Opp. GPS: 31.298452, -86.277462

36 • D4 | Lakepoint Resort SP - Barbour/Clark Loops

Total sites: 64, RV sites: 64, Elec sites: 64, Water at site, Flush toilet, Free showers, RV dump, Tent & RV camping: $20-25, Also cabins, 15% senior weeknight discount, One-time transaction fee: $4.50, Oct-Apr monthly rate available, Open all year, Reservations accepted, Elev: 204ft/62m, Tel: 334-687-8011, Nearest town: Eufaula. GPS: 31.993093, -85.135696

37 • D4 | Lakepoint Resort SP - Deer Court

Total sites: 80, RV sites: 80, Elec sites: 80, Water at site, Flush toilet, Free showers, RV dump, Tent & RV camping: $25, Also cabins, 80 Full hookups, 15% senior weeknight discount, One-time transaction fee: $4.50, Oct-Apr monthly rate available, Open all year, Reservations accepted, Elev: 205ft/62m, Tel: 334-687-8011, Nearest town: Eufaula. GPS: 31.993278, -85.129105

38 • E1 | Blakeley SP - Apalachee

Total sites: 28, RV sites: 28, Elec sites: 28, Water at site, Flush toilet, Free showers, No RV dump, Tent & RV camping: $30, Full hookups sites, Open all year, Reservations accepted, Elev: 118ft/36m, Tel: 251-626-5581, Nearest town: Spanish Fort. GPS: 30.734145, -87.906568

39 • E1 | Blakeley SP - Bartram

Total sites: 8, RV sites: 0, Water at site, Flush toilet, Free showers, No RV dump, Tents only: $30, Stay limit: 5 days, Open all year, Reservations accepted, Elev: 64ft/20m, Tel: 251-626-5581, Nearest town: Spanish Fort. GPS: 30.735865, -87.907014

40 • E1 | Blakeley SP - Carson Horse Camp

Total sites: 3, RV sites: 3, Central water, Vault/pit toilet, No showers, No RV dump, Tent & RV camping: $30, Open all year, Reservations accepted, Elev: 64ft/20m, Tel: 251-626-5581, Nearest town: Spanish Fort. GPS: 30.732254, -87.910955

41 • E1 | Blakeley SP - Delta

Total sites: 8, RV sites: 0, Water at site, Flush toilet, Free showers, No RV dump, Tents only: $30, Stay limit: 5 days, Open all year, Reservations accepted, Elev: 74ft/23m, Tel: 251-626-5581, Nearest town: Spanish Fort. GPS: 30.742238, -87.915024

42 • E1 | Blakeley SP - Harper

Total sites: 8, RV sites: 8, Central water, Flush toilet, Free showers, No RV dump, Tent & RV camping: $20, Nothig larger than popup, Stay limit: 5 days, Open all year, Reservations accepted, Elev: 118ft/36m, Tel: 251-626-5581, Nearest town: Spanish Fort. GPS: 30.741185, -87.913921

43 • E1 | Meaher SP

Total sites: 71, RV sites: 61, Elec sites: 61, Water at site, Flush toilet, Free showers, RV dump, Tents: $24/RVs: $37, 61 Full hookups, 15% Senior Discount, Open all year, Reservations accepted, Elev: 52ft/16m, Tel: 251-626-5529, Nearest town: Spanish Fort. GPS: 30.666939, -87.933584

44 • E2 | Gulf SP - Canal Road

Total sites: 28, RV sites: 28, Elec sites: 28, Water at site, Flush toilet, Free showers, RV dump, Tent & RV camping: $57, Also cabins, 28 Full hookups, $63-$70 weekends Mar-Oct, 15% Senior Discount, Open all year, Reservations accepted, Elev: 11ft/3m, Tel: 251-948-7275, Nearest town: Gulf Shores. GPS: 30.256743, -87.649171

45 • E2 | Gulf SP - Main

Total sites: 479, RV sites: 468, Elec sites: 468, Water at site, Flush toilet, Free showers, RV dump, Tents: $20/RVs: $43-46, Also cabins, 496 Full hookups, $63-$70 weekends Mar-Oct, 15% Senior Discount, Open all year, Reservations accepted, Elev: 33ft/10m, Tel: 251-948-7275, Nearest town: Gulf Shores. GPS: 30.264182, -87.643236

Arkansas

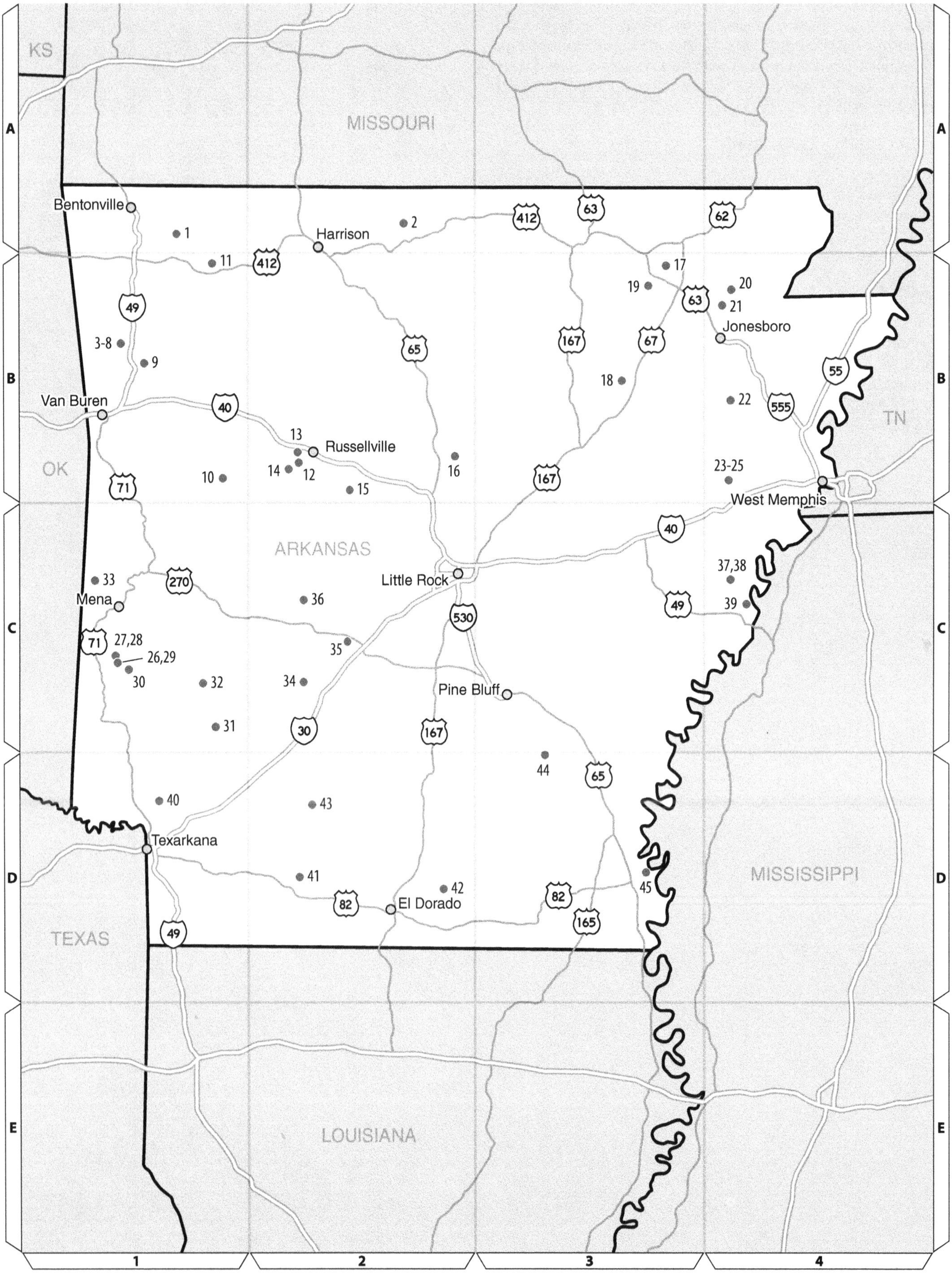

KS

MISSOURI

A

Bentonville

• 1

Harrison

• 2

412

63

62

• 11

412

17

49

19

20

3-8

63

21

• 9

Jonesboro

Van Buren

167

67

55

40

18

TN

OK

65

B

22

555

71

13

Russellville

23-25

10

14 12

16

167

West Memphis

• 15

167

ARKANSAS

40

33

270

Little Rock

37,38

Mena

36

49

39

71 27,28

530

26,29

35

30

44

32

34

65

31

30

167

Pine Bluff

40

43

MISSISSIPPI

Texarkana

41

45

82

42

El Dorado

82

TEXAS

49

165

LOUISIANA

Map	ID	Map	ID
A1	1	C1	26-35
A2	2	C2	34-36
B1	3-11	C4	37-39
B2	12-16	D1	40
B3	17-19	D2	41-43
B4	20-25	D3	44-45

Alphabetical List of Camping Areas

1 • A1 | Hobbs SP - Pigeon Roost TC

Dispersed sites, No water, Tents only: Free, Hike-in, 5 sites, Reservations not accepted, Elev: 1263ft/385m, Tel: 479-789-5000, Nearest town: Rogers. GPS: 36.300722, -93.939496

2 • A2 | Bull Shoals White River SP

Total sites: 102, RV sites: 82, Elec sites: 82, Water at site, Flush toilet, Free showers, RV dump, Tents: $14/RVs: $29-36, 34 Full hookups, Stay limit: 14 days, Open all year, Max Length: 75ft, Elev: 486ft/148m, Tel: 870-445-3629, Nearest town: Bull Shoals. GPS: 36.354817, -92.594016

3 • B1 | Devil's Den SP - CG A

Total sites: 24, RV sites: 24, Central water, Vault/pit toilet, No showers, RV dump, Tent & RV camping: $22, Stay limit: 14 days, Open all year, Max Length: 40ft, Reservations accepted, Elev: 1021ft/311m, Tel: 479-761-3325, Nearest town: West Fork. GPS: 35.783143, -94.245107

4 • B1 | Devil's Den SP - CG B

Total sites: 4, RV sites: 4, Central water, Flush toilet, Free showers, RV dump, Tent & RV camping: $22, Stay limit: 14 days, Open all year, Max Length: 35ft, Reservations accepted, Elev: 1055ft/322m, Tel: 479-761-3325, Nearest town: West Fork. GPS: 35.782713, -94.250886

5 • B1 | Devil's Den SP - CG D

Total sites: 6, RV sites: 6, Elec sites: 6, Central water, Vault/pit toilet, RV dump, Tent & RV camping: $22, Stay limit: 14 days, Open all year, Max Length: 20ft, Reservations accepted, Elev: 1082ft/330m, Tel: 479-761-3325, Nearest town: West Fork. GPS: 35.775786, -94.258192

6 • B1 | Devil's Den SP - CG E

Total sites: 44, RV sites: 44, Elec sites: 44, Water at site, Flush toilet, Free showers, RV dump, Tent & RV camping: $34, Full hookups sites, Stay limit: 14 days, Open all year, Max Length: 55ft, Reservations accepted, Elev: 996ft/304m, Tel: 479-761-3325, Nearest town: West Fork. GPS: 35.773696, -94.257897

7 • B1 | Devil's Den SP - CG F Horse Camp

Total sites: 43, RV sites: 43, Elec sites: 43, Water at site, Flush toilet, Free showers, RV dump, Tent & RV camping: $18, Stay limit: 14 days, Open all year, Max Length: 60ft, Reservations accepted, Elev: 1028ft/313m, Tel: 479-761-3325, Nearest town: West Fork. GPS: 35.773812, -94.263859

8 • B1 | Devil's Den SP - Hike-in

Total sites: 8, RV sites: 0, No water, Vault/pit toilet, Tents only: $13, Hike-in, Stay limit: 14 days, Open all year, Reservations accepted, Elev: 1043ft/318m, Tel: 479-761-3325, Nearest town: West Fork. GPS: 35.784934, -94.243132

9 • B1 | Lake Fort Smith SP

Total sites: 30, RV sites: 30, Elec sites: 30, Water at site, Flush toilet, Free showers, RV dump, Tent & RV camping: $22-34, Also cabins, 20 Full hookups, Stay limit: 14 days, Open all year, Max Length: 70ft, Reservations accepted, Elev: 1102ft/336m, Tel: 479-369-2469, Nearest town: Mountainburg. GPS: 35.696735, -94.114263

10 • B1 | Mount Magazine SP - Cameron Bluff

Total sites: 18, RV sites: 18, Elec sites: 18, Water at site, Flush toilet, Free showers, RV dump, Tents: $12/RVs: $30-34, Also cabins, 18 Full hookups, Stay limit: 14 days, Open all year, Max Length: 76ft, Reservations accepted, Elev: 2585ft/788m, Tel: 479-963-8502, Nearest town: Paris. GPS: 35.172017, -93.644669

11 • B1 | Withrow Springs SP

Total sites: 40, RV sites: 30, Elec sites: 30, Water at site, Flush toilet, Free showers, RV dump, Tents: $14/RVs: $32-36, Also walk-to sites, 30 Full hookups, Stay limit: 14 days, Open all year, Max Length: 65ft, Reservations accepted, Elev: 1417ft/432m, Tel: 479-559-2593, Nearest town: Huntsville. GPS: 36.164096, -93.720992

12 • B2 | Lake Dardanelle SP - Dardanelle Area

Total sites: 18, RV sites: 18, Elec sites: 18, Water at site, Flush toilet, Free showers, RV dump, Tent & RV camping: $22, Stay limit: 14 days, Open all year, Max Length: 60ft, Reservations accepted, Elev: 381ft/116m, Tel: 479-967-5516, Nearest town: Russellville. GPS: 35.253418, -93.213623

13 • B2 | Lake Dardanelle SP - Russellville Area

Total sites: 57, RV sites: 57, Elec sites: 57, Water at site, Flush toilet, Free showers, RV dump, Tent & RV camping: $22-34, 30 Full hookups, Stay limit: 14 days, Open all year, Max Length: 78ft, Reservations accepted, Elev: 360ft/110m, Tel: 479-967-5516, Nearest town: Russellville. GPS: 35.291867, -93.204317

14 • B2 | Mount Nebo SP

Total sites: 34, RV sites: 24, Elec sites: 24, Water at site, Flush toilet, Free showers, Tents: $13/RVs: $22, Also cabins, Stay limit: 14 days, Open all year, Max Length: 24ft, Reservations accepted, Elev: 1637ft/499m, Tel: 479-229-3655, Nearest town: Dardanelle. GPS: 35.222579, -93.251608

15 • B2 | Petit Jean SP

Total sites: 125, RV sites: 125, Elec sites: 125, Water at site, Flush toilet, Free showers, RV dump, Tent & RV camping: $22-34, Also cabins, 35 Full hookups, Stay limit: 14 days, Open all year, Max Length: 95ft, Reservations accepted, Elev: 919ft/280m, Tel: 501-727-5441, Nearest town: Morrilton. GPS: 35.126768, -92.914001

16 • B2 | Woolly Hollow SP

Total sites: 40, RV sites: 30, Elec sites: 30, Water at site, Flush toilet, Free showers, RV dump, Tent & RV camping: $13-34, 30 Full hookups, Stay limit: 14 days, Open all year, Max Length: 60ft, Reservations accepted, Elev: 551ft/168m, Tel: 501-679-2098, Nearest town: Greenbrier. GPS: 35.288306, -92.283988

17 • B3 | Davidsonville State Historic Park

Total sites: 49, RV sites: 24, Elec sites: 24, Water at site, Flush toilet, Free showers, RV dump, Tents: $13/RVs: $27-34, 23 Full hookups, Stay limit: 14 days, Open all year, Max Length: 60ft, Reservations accepted, Elev: 335ft/102m, Tel: 870-892-4708, Nearest town: Pocahontas. GPS: 36.158481, -91.055897

18 • B3 | Jacksonport SP

Total sites: 20, RV sites: 20, Elec sites: 20, Water at site, Flush toilet, Free showers, RV dump, Tent & RV camping: $27, Stay limit: 14 days, Open all year, Max Length: 46ft, Reservations accepted, Elev: 230ft/70m, Tel: 870-523-2143, Nearest town: Newport. GPS: 35.628087, -91.313935

19 • B3 | Lake Charles SP

Total sites: 56, RV sites: 56, Elec sites: 56, Water at site, Flush toilet, Free showers, RV dump, Tent & RV camping: $22-34, 22 Full hookups, Stay limit: 14 days, Open all year, Max Length: 62ft, Reservations accepted, Elev: 325ft/99m, Tel: 870-878-6595, Nearest town: Powhatan. GPS: 36.068514, -91.151062

20 • B4 | Crowley's Ridge SP

Total sites: 26, RV sites: 18, Elec sites: 18, Water at site, Flush toilet, Free showers, RV dump, Tents: $13/RVs: $22, Also cabins, Stay limit: 14 days, Open all year, Max Length: 68ft, Reservations accepted, Elev: 446ft/136m, Tel: 870-573-6751, Nearest town: Paragould. GPS: 36.041769, -90.663201

21 • B4 | Lake Frierson SP

Total sites: 7, RV sites: 4, Elec sites: 4, Central water, Flush toilet, Free showers, RV dump, Tent & RV camping: $13-22, Stay limit: 14 days, Open all year, Max Length: 48ft, Reservations accepted, Elev: 433ft/132m, Tel: 870-932-2615, Nearest town: Jonesboro. GPS: 35.972226, -90.717298

22 • B4 | Lake Poinsett SP

Total sites: 29, RV sites: 26, Elec sites: 26, Water at site, Flush toilet, Free showers, RV dump, Tents: $13-22/RVs: $22-27, Stay limit: 14 days, Open all year, Max Length: 65ft, Reservations accepted, Elev: 338ft/103m, Tel: 870-578-2064, Nearest town: Harrisburg. GPS: 35.531738, -90.686279

23 • B4 | Village Creek SP - Camp Area A

Total sites: 41, RV sites: 41, Elec sites: 41, Water at site, Flush toilet, Free showers, RV dump, Tent & RV camping: $23-29, Also cabins, Stay limit: 14 days, Open all year, Max Length: 100ft, Reservations accepted, Elev: 300ft/91m, Tel: 870-238-9406, Nearest town: Wynne. GPS: 35.164396, -90.709303

24 • B4 | Village Creek SP - Camp Area B

Total sites: 24, RV sites: 24, Elec sites: 24, Water at site, Flush toilet, Free showers, RV dump, Tent & RV camping: $32-36, Also cabins, 24 Full hookups, Stay limit: 14 days, Open all year, Max Length: 85ft, Reservations accepted, Elev: 407ft/124m, Tel: 870-238-9406, Nearest town: Wynne. GPS: 35.172102, -90.701375

25 • B4 | Village Creek SP - Equestrian Camp

Total sites: 31, RV sites: 31, Elec sites: 31, Water at site, Flush toilet, Free showers, RV dump, Tent & RV camping: $23-29, Also cabins, $10 mandatory stall fee - no high lines, Stay limit: 14 days, Open all year, Max Length: 120ft, Reservations accepted, Elev: 426ft/130m, Tel: 870-238-9406, Nearest town: Wynne. GPS: 35.176675, -90.697346

26 • C1 | Cossatot River SP - Cossatot Falls

Total sites: 7, RV sites: 0, Vault/pit toilet, Tents only: $15, Hike-in/boat-in, Stay limit: 14 days, Reservations not accepted, Elev: 649ft/198m, Tel: 870-385-2201, Nearest town: Wickes. GPS: 34.320828, -94.227163

27 • C1 | Cossatot River SP - Ed Banks Bridge Site 1

Total sites: 1, RV sites: 0, Vault/pit toilet, Tents only: $15, Hike-in/boat-in, Stay limit: 14 days, Reservations not accepted, Elev: 706ft/215m, Tel: 870-385-2201, Nearest town: Wickes. GPS: 34.339163, -94.250823

28 • C1 | Cossatot River SP - Ed Banks Bridge Site 2

Total sites: 1, RV sites: 0, Vault/pit toilet, Tents only: $15, Stay limit: 14 days, Reservations not accepted, Elev: 754ft/230m, Tel: 870-385-2201, Nearest town: Wickes. GPS: 34.343644, -94.250421

29 • C1 | Cossatot River SP - Sand Bar Bridge

Total sites: 15, RV sites: 0, Vault/pit toilet, Tents only: $15, Stay limit: 14 days, Open all year, Reservations not accepted, Elev: 659ft/201m, Tel: 870-385-2201, Nearest town: Wickes. GPS: 34.322103, -94.235257

30 • C1 | Cossatot River SP - US-278 Bridge

Dispersed sites, No water, Vault/pit toilet, Tents only: $15, Stay limit: 14 days, Reservations not accepted, Elev: 561ft/171m, Tel: 870-385-2201, Nearest town: Wickes. GPS: 34.295862, -94.175992

31 • C1 | Crater of Diamonds SP

Total sites: 52, RV sites: 47, Elec sites: 47, Water at site, Flush toilet, Free showers, RV dump, Tents: $13/RVs: $34, 47 Full hookups, Seek and keep diamonds! Senior discount, Stay limit: 14 days, Open all year, Max Length: 70ft, Reservations accepted, Elev: 433ft/132m, Tel: 870-285-3113, Nearest town: Murfreesboro,. GPS: 34.030521, -93.666411

32 • C1 | Daisy SP

Total sites: 103, RV sites: 82, Elec sites: 82, Water at site, Flush toilet, Free showers, RV dump, Tents: $13/RVs: $22-27, Stay limit: 14 days, Open all year, Max Length: 54ft, Reservations accepted, Elev: 630ft/192m, Tel: 870-398-4487, Nearest town: Kirby. GPS: 34.231937, -93.743501

33 • C1 | Queen Wilhelmina SP

Total sites: 41, RV sites: 35, Elec sites: 35, Water at site, Flush toilet, Free showers, RV dump, Tents: $13-17/RVs: $22-27, Also cabins, Stay limit: 14 days, Open all year, Max Length: 63ft, Reservations accepted, Elev: 2487ft/758m, Tel: 479-394-2863, Nearest town: Mena. GPS: 34.685537, -94.374362

34 • C2 | De Gray Lake Resort SP

Total sites: 113, RV sites: 113, Elec sites: 113, Water at site, Flush toilet, Free showers, RV dump, Tents: $14/RVs: $22-34, Also cabins, Stay limit: 14 days, Open all year, Max Length: 64ft, Reservations accepted, Elev: 505ft/154m, Tel: 501-865-5810, Nearest town: Bismarck. GPS: 34.249479, -93.162263

35 • C2 | Lake Catherine SP

Total sites: 69, RV sites: 69, Elec sites: 69, Water at site, Flush toilet, Free showers, RV dump, Tent & RV camping: $22-34, Also cabins, 44 Full hookups, Stay limit: 14 days, Open all year, Max Length: 50ft, Reservations accepted, Elev: 354ft/108m, Tel: 501-844-4176, Nearest town: Hot Springs. GPS: 34.434535, -92.913024

36 • C2 | Lake Ouachita SP

Total sites: 93, RV sites: 81, Elec sites: 58, Water at site, Flush toilet, Free showers, RV dump, Tent & RV camping: $13-34, Also cabins, 58 Full hookups, Stay limit: 14 days, Open all year, Max Length: 50ft, Reservations accepted, Elev: 623ft/190m, Tel: 501-767-9366, Nearest town: Mountain Pine. GPS: 34.618774, -93.176603

37 • C4 | Mississippi River SP - Beech Point

Total sites: 17, RV sites: 14, Elec sites: 14, Water at site, Flush toilet, Free showers, RV dump, Tents: $13/RVs: $34, Walk-to sites, 14 Full hookups, Stay limit: 14 days, Max Length: 70ft, Reservations accepted, Elev: 230ft/70m, Tel: 870-295-4040, Nearest town: Marianna. GPS: 34.710449, -90.695557

38 • C4 | Mississippi River SP - Lone Pine

Total sites: 14, RV sites: 14, Central water, Vault/pit toilet, No showers, No RV dump, Tent & RV camping: $13, Stay limit: 14 days, Max Length: 70ft, Reservations accepted, Elev: 272ft/83m, Tel: 870-295-4040, Nearest town: Marianna. GPS: 34.714881, -90.695809

39 • C4 | Mississippi River SP - Storm Creek Lake

Total sites: 12, RV sites: 12, Central water, Vault/pit toilet, No showers, No RV dump, Tent & RV camping: $13, Stay limit: 14 days, Open all year, Max Length: 80ft, Elev: 272ft/83m, Tel: 870-295-4040, Nearest town: West Helena. GPS: 34.600746, -90.612831

40 • D1 | Millwood SP

Total sites: 117, RV sites: 114, Elec sites: 114, Water at site, Flush toilet, Free showers, RV dump, Tents: $13/RVs: $22-34, 2 Full hookups, Stay limit: 14 days, Open all year, Max Length: 50ft, Reservations accepted, Elev: 302ft/92m, Tel: 870-898-2800, Nearest town: Ashdown. GPS: 33.682617, -93.983887

41 • D2 | Logoly SP

Total sites: 6, RV sites: 6, Central water, Flush toilet, Free showers, No RV dump, Tents only: $13, Groups have priority, Stay limit: 14 days, Open all year, Elev: 400ft/122m, Tel: 870-695-3561, Nearest town: McNeil. GPS: 33.347780, -93.184720

42 • D2 | Moro Bay SP

Total sites: 23, RV sites: 23, Elec sites: 23, Water at site, Flush toilet, Free showers, RV dump, Tent & RV camping: $34, Also cabins, Stay limit: 14 days, Open all year, Max Length: 60ft, Reservations accepted, Elev: 131ft/40m, Tel: 870-463-8555, Nearest town: Jersey. GPS: 33.300675, -92.345041

43 • D2 | White Oak Lake SP

Total sites: 45, RV sites: 41, Elec sites: 41, Water at site, Flush toilet, Free showers, RV dump, Tents: $14/RVs: $23-29, Stay limit: 14 days, Open all year, Max Length: 67ft, Reservations accepted, Elev: 216ft/66m, Tel: 870-685-2748, Nearest town: Bluff City. GPS: 33.689453, -93.114746

44 • D3 | Cane Creek SP

Total sites: 29, RV sites: 29, Elec sites: 29, Water at site, Flush toilet, Free showers, RV dump, Tent & RV camping: $23-29, Stay limit: 14 days, Open all year, Max Length: 95ft, Reservations accepted, Elev: 220ft/67m, Tel: 870-628-4714, Nearest town: Star City. GPS: 33.914999, -91.763618

45 • D3 | Lake Chicot SP

Total sites: 122, RV sites: 122, Elec sites: 122, Water at site, Flush toilet, Free showers, RV dump, Tent & RV camping: $22-34, Also cabins, 55 Full hookups, Stay limit: 14 days, Open all year, Max Length: 60ft, Elev: 128ft/39m, Tel: 870-265-5480, Nearest town: Lake Village. GPS: 33.372413, -91.196712

Connecticut

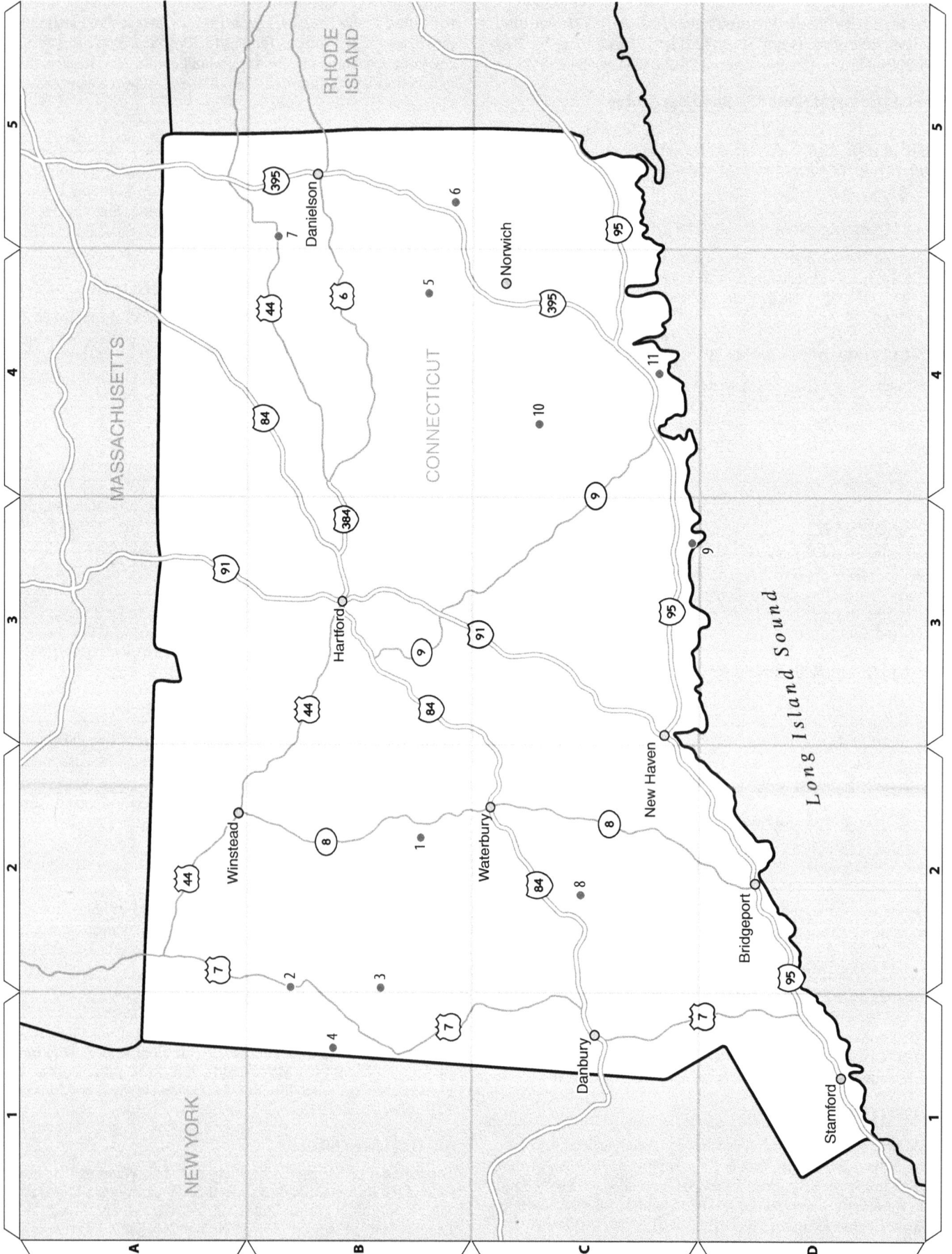

Map	ID	Map	ID
B1	1-4	C2	8
B4	5	C3	9
B5	6-7	C4	10-11

Alphabetical List of Camping Areas

1 • B1 | Black Rock SP

Total sites: 92, RV sites: 85, Central water, No toilets, No showers, RV dump, Tent & RV camping: $27, Also cabins, CT residents: $17, Stay limit: 14 days, Open Apr-Sep, Max Length: 35ft, Reservations accepted, Elev: 404ft/123m, Tel: 860-283-8088, Nearest town: Thomaston. GPS: 41.652841, -73.099706

2 • B1 | Housatonic Meadows SP

Total sites: 95, RV sites: 95, Central water, Flush toilet, Free showers, RV dump, Tent & RV camping: $27, Also cabins, CT residents: $17, No pets, Stay limit: 14 days, Open May-Oct, Max Length: 35ft, Reservations accepted, Elev: 525ft/160m, Tel: 860-672-6772, Nearest town: Sharon. GPS: 41.838408, -73.379507

3 • B1 | Lake Waramaug SP

Total sites: 78, RV sites: 78, Central water, Flush toilet, Free showers, RV dump, Tent & RV camping: $27, Also cabins, CT residents: $17, Stay limit: 14 days, Open May-Sep, Max Length: 35ft, Reservations accepted, Elev: 692ft/211m, Tel: 860-868-0220, Nearest town: Kent. GPS: 41.706813, -73.382724

4 • B1 | Macedonia Brook SP

Total sites: 51, RV sites: 51, Central water, Vault/pit toilet, No showers, No RV dump, Tent & RV camping: $24, CT residents: $14, No pets, Stay limit: 14 days, Open Apr-Sep, Max Length: 35ft, Reservations accepted, Elev: 866ft/264m, Tel: 860-927-4100, Nearest town: Kent. GPS: 41.776855, -73.493896

5 • B4 | Salt Rock SP

Total sites: 71, RV sites: 71, Elec sites: 23, Water at site, Flush toilet, Free showers, RV dump, Tent & RV camping: $45-52, CT residents: $33-$40, Stay limit: 14 days, Open May-Oct, Max Length: 35ft, Reservations accepted, Elev: 210ft/64m, Tel: 860-822-0884, Nearest town: Baltic. GPS: 41.642115, -72.093035

6 • B5 | Hopeville Pond SP

Total sites: 80, RV sites: 80, Central water, Flush toilet, Free showers, RV dump, Tent & RV camping: $27, Also cabins, CT residents: $17, Stay limit: 14 days, Open Apr-Sep, Max Length: 35ft, Reservations accepted, Elev: 174ft/53m, Tel: 860-376-0313, Nearest town: Griswold. GPS: 41.602208, -71.927481

7 • B5 | Mashamoquet Brook SP

Total sites: 20, RV sites: 20, Central water, Vault/pit toilet, No showers, No RV dump, Tent & RV camping: $24, CT residents: $14, No pets, Stay limit: 14 days, Open Apr-Oct, Max Length: 35ft, Reservations accepted, Elev: 479ft/146m, Tel: 860-928-6121, Nearest town: Pomfret. GPS: 41.859572, -71.987019

8 • C2 | Kettletown SP

Total sites: 68, RV sites: 68, Central water, Flush toilet, Free showers, RV dump, Tent & RV camping: $27, Also cabins, CT residents: $17, Open May-Sep, Max Length: 28ft, Reservations accepted, Elev: 216ft/66m, Tel: 203-264-5678, Nearest town: Southbury. GPS: 41.421143, -73.204834

9 • C3 | Hammonasset Beach SP

Total sites: 558, RV sites: 558, Central water, Flush toilet, Free showers, RV dump, Tent & RV camping: $30-45, Also cabins, CT residents: $20-$35, No pets, Stay limit: 21 days, Open May-Oct, Max Length: 35ft, Reservations accepted, Elev: 10ft/3m, Tel: 203-245-1817, Nearest town: Madison. GPS: 41.265137, -72.555908

10 • C4 | Devil's Hopyard SP

Total sites: 21, RV sites: 21, Central water, Vault/pit toilet, No showers, No RV dump, Tent & RV camping: $24, CT residents: $14, Stay limit: 14 days, Open Apr-Sep, Max Length: 35ft, Reservations accepted, Elev: 236ft/72m, Tel: 860-526-2336, Nearest town: East Haddam. GPS: 41.484611, -72.339982

11 • C4 | Rocky Neck SP

Total sites: 160, RV sites: 160, Central water, Flush toilet, Free showers, RV dump, Tent & RV camping: $30, CT residents: $20, No pets, Stay limit: 21 days, Open May-Sep, Max Length: 35ft, Reservations accepted, Elev: 23ft/7m, Tel: 860-739-1339, Nearest town: Niantic. GPS: 41.311629, -72.242147

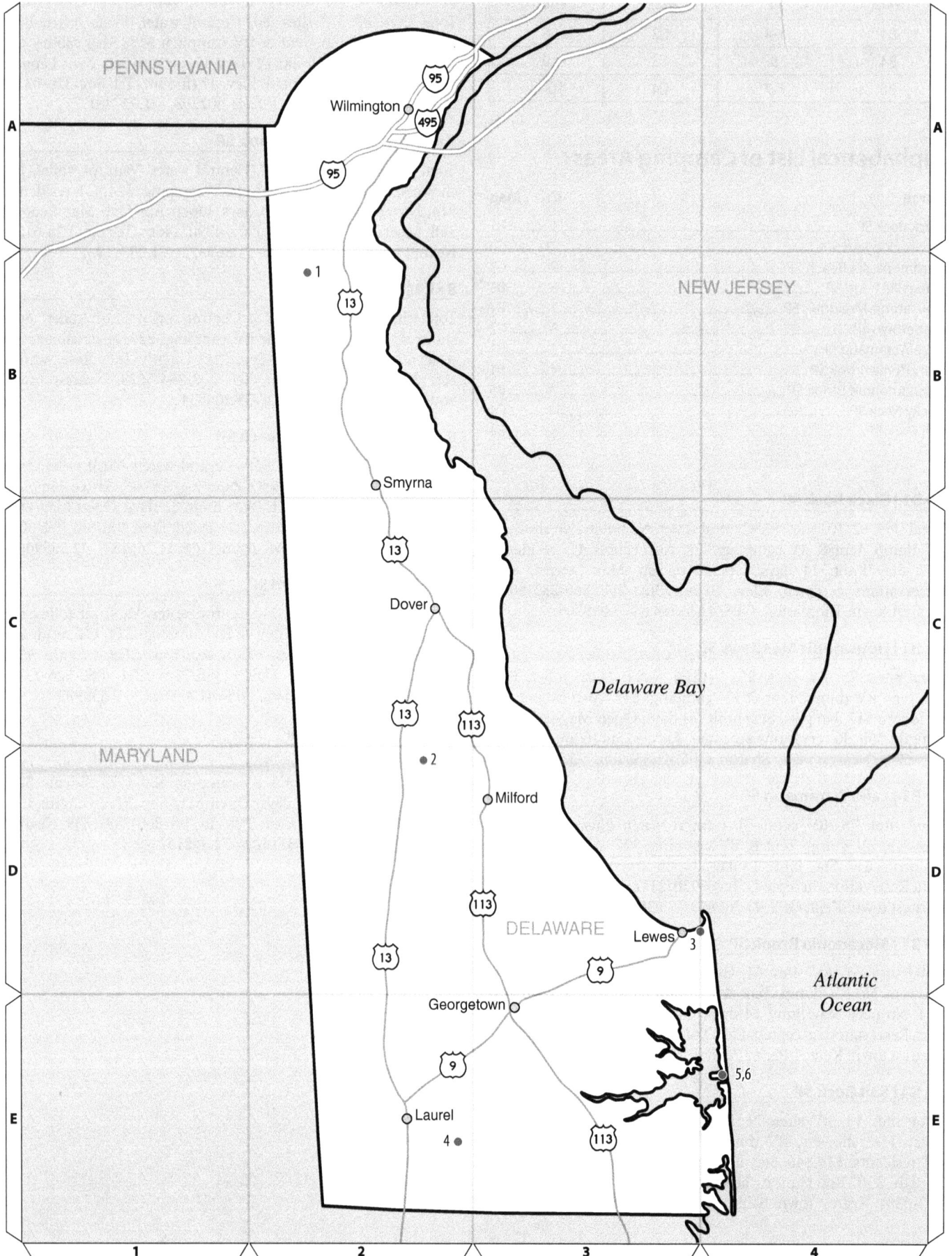

Delaware

PENNSYLVANIA

Wilmington

NEW JERSEY

• 1

Smyrna

Dover

MARYLAND

Delaware Bay

• 2

Milford

DELAWARE

Lewes • 3

Atlantic
Ocean

Georgetown

• 5,6

Laurel
4 •

Map	ID	Map	ID
B2	1	E2	4
D2	2	E3	5-6
D3	3		

Full hookups, Stay limit: 14 days, Open all year, Max Length: 45ft, Reservations accepted, Elev: 4ft/1m, Tel: 302-227-2800, Nearest town: Rehoboth Beach. GPS: 38.605102, -75.066252

Alphabetical List of Camping Areas

1 • B2 | Lums Pond SP

Total sites: 68, RV sites: 66, Elec sites: 66, Central water, Flush toilet, Free showers, RV dump, Tents: $15-32/RVs: $20-45, 4 horse sites, Stay limit: 14 days, Generator hours: 0700-2200, Open all year, Max Length: 40ft, Reservations accepted, Elev: 66ft/20m, Tel: 302-368-6989, Nearest town: Kirkwood. GPS: 39.550510, -75.718250

2 • D2 | Killens Pond SP

Total sites: 76, RV sites: 59, Elec sites: 59, Water at site, Flush toilet, Free showers, RV dump, Tents: $15-32/RVs: $20-37, Also cabins, Stay limit: 14 days, Open all year, Max Length: 40ft, Reservations accepted, Elev: 62ft/19m, Tel: 302-284-4526, Nearest town: Felton. GPS: 38.978536, -75.532731

3 • D3 | Cape Henlopen SP

Total sites: 165, RV sites: 165, Elec sites: 143, Water at site, Flush toilet, Free showers, RV dump, Tents: $20-45/RVs: $30-59, Also cabins, Lower off-peak rates, Stay limit: 14 days, Generator hours: 0700-2200, Open all year, Max Length: 106ft, Reservations accepted, Elev: 26ft/8m, Tel: 302-645-8983, Nearest town: Lewes. GPS: 38.775899, -75.097449

4 • E2 | Trap Pond SP

Total sites: 142, RV sites: 142, Elec sites: 130, Water at site, Flush toilet, Free showers, RV dump, Tents: $15-43/RVs: $20-37, Also cabins, Stay limit: 14 days, Generator hours: 0700-2200, Open all year, Max Length: 57ft, Reservations accepted, Elev: 69ft/21m, Tel: 302-875-2392, Nearest town: Laurel. GPS: 38.529426, -75.475981

5 • E3 | Delaware Seashore SP - North Inlet

Total sites: 82, RV sites: 82, Elec sites: 82, Water at site, Flush toilet, Free showers, RV dump, Tents: $20-45/RVs: $25-55, 82 Full hookups, Stay limit: 14 days, Open all year, Max Length: 45ft, Reservations accepted, Elev: 4ft/1m, Tel: 302-227-2800, Nearest town: Rehoboth Beach. GPS: 38.610111, -75.066074

6 • E3 | Delaware Seashore SP - South Inlet

Total sites: 273, RV sites: 240, Elec sites: 240, Water at site, Flush toilet, Free showers, RV dump, Tents: $20-45/RVs: $25-55, 151

Florida

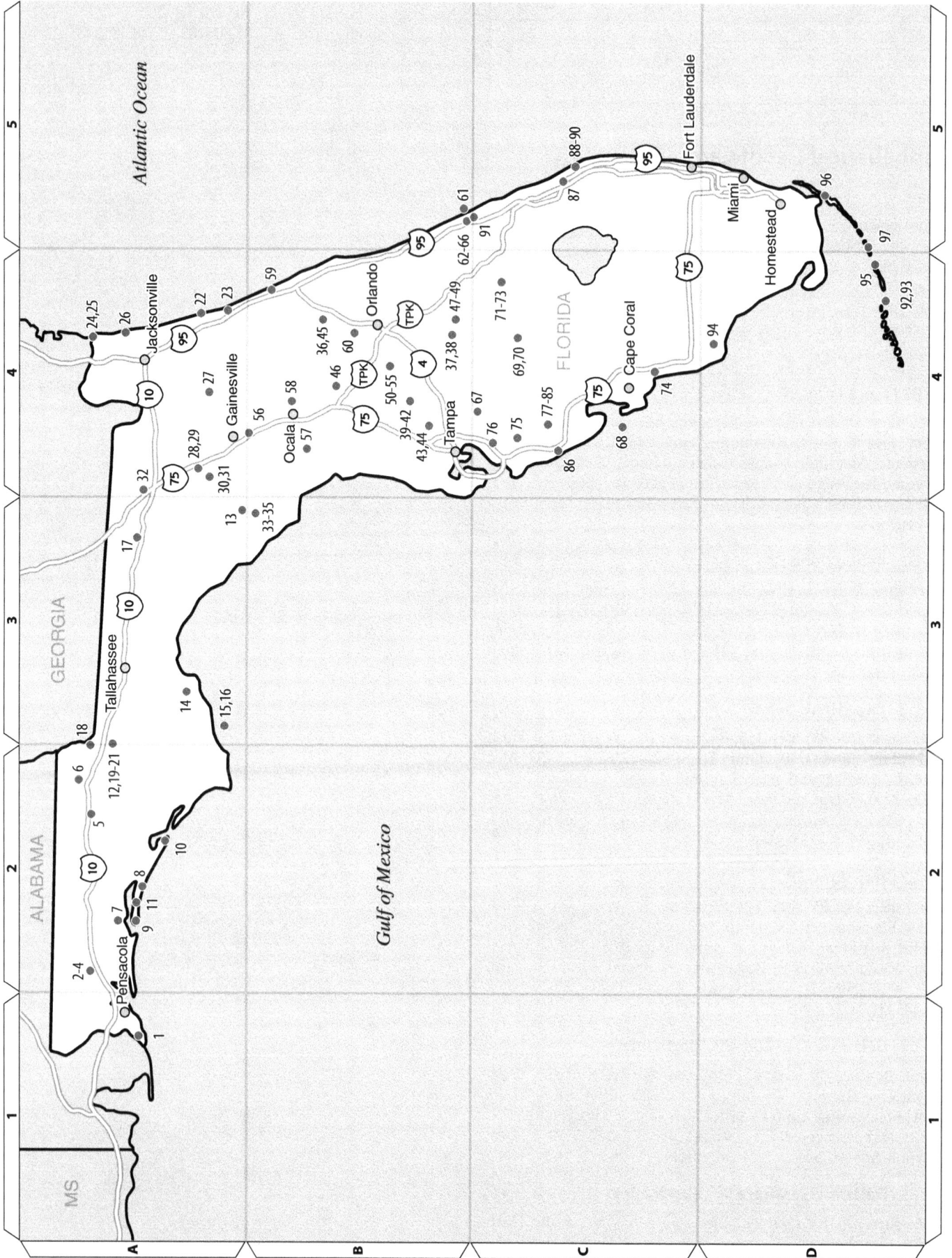

Map	ID	Map	ID
A1	1	B5	61-66
A2	2-12	C4	67-86
A3	13-21	C5	87-91
A4	22-32	D4	92-95
B3	33-35	D5	96-97
B4	36-60		

Alphabetical List of Camping Areas

Name	ID	Map
Alafia River SP	67	C4
Anastasia SP	22	A4
Atlantic Ridge Preserve SP/Halpatiokee RP - SFWMD	87	C5
Bahia Honda SP - Bayside	92	D4
Bahia Honda SP - Buttonwood	93	D4
Big Lagoon SP	1	A1
Blackwater River SP - Blackwater Beach	2	A2
Blackwater River SP - Boat Ramp	3	A2
Blackwater River SP - Main CG	4	A2
Blue Spring SP	36	B4
Catfish Creek Preserve SP - TC 1 - SFWMD	37	B4
Catfish Creek Preserve SP - TC 2 - SFWMD	38	B4
Cayo Costa SP	68	C4
Collier-Seminole SP	94	D4
Colt Creek SP - Equestrian	39	B4
Colt Creek SP - Main	40	B4
Colt Creek SP - Site 1	41	B4
Colt Creek SP - Site 2	42	B4
Curry Hammock SP	95	D4
Falling Waters SP	5	A2
Fanning Springs SP	13	A3
Faver-Dykes SP	23	A4
Florida Caverns SP	6	A2
Fort Clinch SP - Amelia River	24	A4
Fort Clinch SP - Atantic Beach	25	A4
Fred Gannon Rocky Bayou SP	7	A2
Grayton Beach SP	8	A2
Henderson Beach SP	9	A2
Highlands Hammock SP - Main	69	C4
Highlands Hammock SP - Wilderness Camp	70	C4
Hillsborough River SP	43	B4
Hillsborough River SP - Seminole TC	44	B4
Hontoon Island SP	45	B4
John Pennekamp Coral Reef SP	96	D5
Jonathan Dickinson SP - Horse Camp	88	C5
Jonathan Dickinson SP - Pine Grove	89	C5
Jonathan Dickinson SP - The River	90	C5
Kissimmee Prairie SP - Equestrian	71	C4
Kissimmee Prairie SP - Family	72	C4
Kissimmee Prairie SP - Trail Camp	73	C4
Koreshan SHS	74	C4
Lake Griffin SP	46	B4
Lake Kissimmee SP	47	B4
Lake Kissimmee SP - Buster Island	48	B4
Lake Kissimmee SP - Fallen Oaks	49	B4
Lake Louisa SP - Big Creek 1	50	B4
Lake Louisa SP - Big Creek 2	51	B4
Lake Louisa SP - Brantly Lake	52	B4
Lake Louisa SP - Dudes Lake	53	B4
Lake Louisa SP - Equestrian	54	B4
Lake Louisa SP - Main	55	B4
Lake Manatee SP	75	C4
Little Manatee River SP	76	C4
Little Talbot Island SP	26	A4
Long Key SP	97	D5
Manatee Springs SP - Hickory	33	B3
Manatee Springs SP - Magnolia 1	34	B3
Manatee Springs SP - Magnolia 2	35	B3
Mike Roess Gold Head Branch SP	27	A4
Myakka River SP - Bee Island	77	C4
Myakka River SP - Big Flats	78	C4
Myakka River SP - Honore	79	C4
Myakka River SP - Mossy Hammock	80	C4
Myakka River SP - Oak Grove	81	C4
Myakka River SP - Old Prairie	82	C4
Myakka River SP - Old Prairie/Palmetto Ridge	83	C4
Myakka River SP - Panther Point	84	C4
Myakka River SP - Prairie	85	C4
O'Leno SP - Dogwood	28	A4
O'Leno SP - Magnolia	29	A4
Ochlockonee River SP	14	A3
Oscar Scherer SP	86	C4
Paynes Prairie Preserve State Park - Puc Buggy	56	B4
Rainbow Springs SP	57	B4
River Rise Preserve SP	30	A4
Ruth B. Kirby Gilchrist Blue Springs SP	31	A4
Sebastian Inlet SP	61	B5
Silver Springs SP	58	B4
St Andrews SP	10	A2
St George Island SP	15	A3
St George Island SP - Gap Point	16	A3
St. Sebastian River Preserve SP - Eagle Camp	62	B5
St. Sebastian River Preserve SP - Mullen Camp	63	B5
St. Sebastian River Preserve SP - Pine Camp	64	B5
St. Sebastian River Preserve SP - Ranch	91	C5
St. Sebastian River Preserve SP - Storytelling Camp	65	B5
St. Sebastian River Preserve SP - Tree Frog Camp	66	B5
Stephen Foster SP	32	A4
Suwannee River SP	17	A3
Three Rivers SP	18	A3
Tomoka SP	59	B4
Topsail Hill Preserve SP	11	A2
Torreya SP - Challenge Primitive	19	A3
Torreya SP - Main CG	20	A3
Torreya SP - Rock Bluff Primitive	12	A2
Torreya SP - Rock Creek Primitive	21	A3
Wekiwa Springs SP	60	B4

1 • A1 | Big Lagoon SP

Total sites: 75, RV sites: 75, Elec sites: 75, Water at site, Flush toilet, Free showers, RV dump, Tents: $20/RVs: $27, Stay limit: 14 days, Open all year, Max Length: 45ft, Reservations accepted, Elev: 33ft/10m, Tel: 850-492-1595, Nearest town: Pensacola. GPS: 30.313882, -87.413999

2 • A2 | Blackwater River SP - Blackwater Beach

Dispersed sites, No water, No toilets, Tents only: $20, Walk-to sites, Stay limit: 14 days, Elev: 51ft/16m, Tel: 850-983-5363, Nearest town: Milton. GPS: 30.714081, -86.860099

3 • A2 | Blackwater River SP - Boat Ramp

Dispersed sites, No water, No toilets, Tents: $20/RVs: Fee unk, Stay limit: 14 days, Reservations not accepted, Elev: 51ft/16m, Tel: 850-983-5363, Nearest town: Milton. GPS: 30.710834, -86.866377

4 • A2 | Blackwater River SP - Main CG

Total sites: 30, RV sites: 30, Elec sites: 30, Water at site, Flush toilet, Free showers, RV dump, Tents: $20/RVs: $27, 30 Full hookups, Stay limit: 14 days, Open all year, Max Length: 50ft, Reservations accepted, Elev: 32ft/10m, Tel: 850-983-5363, Nearest town: Harold. GPS: 30.709449, -86.879132

5 • A2 | Falling Waters SP

Total sites: 24, RV sites: 24, Elec sites: 24, Water at site, Flush toilet, Free showers, RV dump, Tents: $18/RVs: $25, Open all year, Max Length: 40ft, Reservations accepted, Elev: 322ft/98m, Tel: 850-638-6130, Nearest town: Chipley. GPS: 30.731286, -85.532021

6 • A2 | Florida Caverns SP

Total sites: 35, RV sites: 32, Elec sites: 35, Water at site, Flush toilet, Free showers, RV dump, Tents: $20/RVs: $27, 26 Full hookups, Stay limit: 14 days, Open all year, Max Length: 40ft, Reservations accepted, Elev: 118ft/36m, Tel: 850-482-9598, Nearest town: Marianna. GPS: 30.819927, -85.242548

7 • A2 | Fred Gannon Rocky Bayou SP

Total sites: 42, RV sites: 42, Elec sites: 42, Water at site, Flush toilet, Free showers, RV dump, Tent & RV camping: $16, Stay limit: 14 days, Open all year, Reservations accepted, Elev: 7ft/2m, Tel: 850-833-9144, Nearest town: Niceville. GPS: 30.499118, -86.430205

8 • A2 | Grayton Beach SP

Total sites: 53, RV sites: 52, Elec sites: 34, Water at site, Flush toilet, Free showers, RV dump, Tent & RV camping: $30, Also cabins, 21 Full hookups, Stay limit: 14 days, Open all year, Max Length: 40ft, Reservations accepted, Elev: 16ft/5m, Tel: 850-267-8300, Nearest town: Santa Rosa Beach. GPS: 30.328730, -86.154450

9 • A2 | Henderson Beach SP

Total sites: 60, RV sites: 60, Elec sites: 60, Water at site, Flush toilet, Free showers, RV dump, Tents: $30/RVs: $37, Stay limit: 14 days, Open all year, Max Length: 45ft, Reservations accepted, Elev: 33ft/10m, Tel: 850-837-7550, Nearest town: Destin. GPS: 30.385671, -86.436289

10 • A2 | St Andrews SP

Total sites: 176, RV sites: 176, Elec sites: 176, Water at site, Flush toilet, Free showers, RV dump, Tents: $28/RVs: $35, Stay limit: 14 days, Open all year, Max Length: 45ft, Reservations accepted, Elev: 10ft/3m, Tel: 850-233-5140, Nearest town: Panama City. GPS: 30.137755, -85.738732

11 • A2 | Topsail Hill Preserve SP

Total sites: 178, RV sites: 156, Elec sites: 178, Water at site, Flush toilet, Free showers, RV dump, Tents: $24/RVs: $49, Also cabins, 156 Full hookups, Stay limit: 14 days, Open all year, Max Length: 45ft, Reservations accepted, Elev: 30ft/9m, Tel: 850-267-8330, Nearest town: Santa Rosa Beach. GPS: 30.368206, -86.274242

12 • A2 | Torreya SP - Rock Bluff Primitive

Total sites: 4, RV sites: 0, No water, Vault/pit toilet, Tents only: $5, Hike-in, Fee is per-person, Stay limit: 14 days, Open all year, Elev: 161ft/49m, Tel: 850-643-2674, Nearest town: Bristol. GPS: 30.563247, -84.961073

13 • A3 | Fanning Springs SP

Dispersed sites, Central water, Flush toilet, Free showers, No RV dump, Tents only: $5, Hike-in/boat-in/cabins, Outside cold showers, Stay limit: 14 days, Reservations accepted, Elev: 21ft/6m, Tel: 352-463-3420. GPS: 29.589173, -82.935869

14 • A3 | Ochlockonee River SP

Total sites: 30, RV sites: 30, Elec sites: 30, Water at site, Flush toilet, Free showers, RV dump, Tent & RV camping: $18, Open all year, Max Length: 40ft, Reservations accepted, Elev: 26ft/8m, Tel: 850-962-2771, Nearest town: Sopchoppy. GPS: 30.002383, -84.476822

15 • A3 | St George Island SP

Total sites: 60, RV sites: 60, Elec sites: 60, Water at site, Flush toilet, Free showers, RV dump, Tents: $24/RVs: $31, Stay limit: 14 days, Open all year, Max Length: 43ft, Reservations accepted, Elev: 10ft/3m, Tel: 850-927-2111, Nearest town: Appalachicola. GPS: 29.720465, -84.747083

16 • A3 | St George Island SP - Gap Point

Dispersed sites, No water, No toilets, Tents only: $5, Hike-in/boat-in, 2.5 mi, Reservations required, Elev: 3ft/1m, Nearest town: St George Island. GPS: 29.702162, -84.778093

17 • A3 | Suwannee River SP

Total sites: 30, RV sites: 30, Elec sites: 30, Water at site, Flush toilet, Free showers, RV dump, Tents: $22/RVs: $29, Also cabins, 30 Full hookups, Stay limit: 14 days, Open all year, Max Length: 55ft, Reservations accepted, Elev: 121ft/37m, Tel: 386-362-2746, Nearest town: Live Oak. GPS: 30.387660, -83.167370

18 • A3 | Three Rivers SP

Total sites: 30, RV sites: 30, Elec sites: 30, Water at site, Flush toilet, Free showers, RV dump, Tents: $16/RVs: $23, Also cabins, Stay limit: 14 days, Open all year, Max Length: 50ft, Reservations accepted, Elev: 108ft/33m, Tel: 850-482-9006, Nearest town: Sneads. GPS: 30.746941, -84.932856

19 • A3 | Torreya SP - Challenge Primitive

Total sites: 4, RV sites: 0, No water, Vault/pit toilet, Tents only: $5, Hike-in, Fee is per-person, Stay limit: 14 days, Open all year, Elev: 292ft/89m, Tel: 850-643-2674, Nearest town: Bristol. GPS: 30.569579, -84.908615

20 • A3 | Torreya SP - Main CG

Total sites: 30, RV sites: 30, Elec sites: 30, Water at site, Flush toilet, Free showers, RV dump, Tents: $16/RVs: $23, Stay limit: 14 days, Open all year, Max Length: 40ft, Reservations accepted, Elev: 253ft/77m, Tel: 850-643-2674, Nearest town: Bristol. GPS: 30.569282, -84.950251

21 • A3 | Torreya SP - Rock Creek Primitive

Total sites: 4, RV sites: 0, No water, Vault/pit toilet, Tents only: $5, Hike-in, Fee is per-person, Stay limit: 14 days, Open all year,

Elev: 131ft/40m, Tel: 850-643-2674, Nearest town: Bristol. GPS: 30.578886, -84.939743

22 • A4 | Anastasia SP

Total sites: 139, RV sites: 139, Elec sites: 139, Water at site, Flush toilet, Free showers, RV dump, Tents: $28/RVs: $35, Stay limit: 14 days, Open all year, Max Length: 40ft, Reservations accepted, Elev: 33ft/10m, Tel: 904-461-2033, Nearest town: Saint Augustine Beach. GPS: 29.872070, -81.278564

23 • A4 | Faver-Dykes SP

Total sites: 30, RV sites: 30, Elec sites: 30, Water at site, Flush toilet, Free showers, RV dump, Tents: $18/RVs: $25, Stay limit: 14 days, Open all year, Max Length: 30ft, Reservations accepted, Elev: 30ft/9m, Tel: 904-794-0997, Nearest town: Saint Augustine. GPS: 29.669807, -81.252093

24 • A4 | Fort Clinch SP - Amelia River

Total sites: 41, RV sites: 41, Elec sites: 41, Water at site, Flush toilet, Free showers, RV dump, Tents: $26/RVs: $33, Stay limit: 14 days, Open all year, Max Length: 40ft, Elev: 10ft/3m, Tel: 904-277-7274, Nearest town: Fernandina Beach. GPS: 30.702498, -81.458855

25 • A4 | Fort Clinch SP - Atantic Beach

Total sites: 20, RV sites: 20, Elec sites: 20, Water at site, Flush toilet, Free showers, RV dump, Tents: $26/RVs: $33, Stay limit: 14 days, Open all year, Reservations accepted, Elev: 7ft/2m, Tel: 904-277-7274, Nearest town: Fernandina Beach. GPS: 30.701541, -81.434113

26 • A4 | Little Talbot Island SP

Total sites: 40, RV sites: 40, Elec sites: 40, Water at site, Flush toilet, Free showers, RV dump, Tents: $24/RVs: $31, Stay limit: 14 days, Open all year, Max Length: 30ft, Reservations accepted, Elev: 20ft/6m, Tel: 904-251-2320, Nearest town: Jacksonville. GPS: 30.458345, -81.418178

27 • A4 | Mike Roess Gold Head Branch SP

Total sites: 73, RV sites: 73, Elec sites: 64, Water at site, Flush toilet, Free showers, RV dump, Tents: $20/RVs: $27, Also cabins, Stay limit: 14 days, Open all year, Reservations accepted, Elev: 156ft/48m, Tel: 352-473-4701, Nearest town: Keystone Heights. GPS: 29.830078, -81.950195

28 • A4 | O'Leno SP - Dogwood

Total sites: 30, RV sites: 30, Elec sites: 30, Water at site, Flush toilet, Free showers, RV dump, Tent & RV camping: $18, Open all year, Max Length: 50ft, Reservations accepted, Elev: 53ft/16m, Tel: 386-454-1853, Nearest town: High Springs. GPS: 29.920365, -82.601229

29 • A4 | O'Leno SP - Magnolia

Total sites: 31, RV sites: 31, Elec sites: 31, Water at site, Flush toilet, Free showers, RV dump, Tent & RV camping: $18, Also cabins, Open all year, Max Length: 40ft, Reservations accepted, Elev: 52ft/16m, Tel: 386-454-1853, Nearest town: High Springs. GPS: 29.913098, -82.584692

30 • A4 | River Rise Preserve SP

Total sites: 40, Vault/pit toilet, Tents only: $5, Hike-in, Ride-in

horse camp, Fee is per-person, Stay limit: 14 days, Reservations accepted, Elev: 47ft/14m, Tel: 386-454-1853, Nearest town: High Springs. GPS: 29.848049, -82.632983

31 • A4 | Ruth B. Kirby Gilchrist Blue Springs SP

Total sites: 23, RV sites: 15, Elec sites: 15, Water at site, Flush toilet, Free showers, RV dump, Tent & RV camping: $18, Stay limit: 14 days, Max Length: 40ft, Reservations accepted, Elev: 49ft/15m, Tel: 386-454-1369, Nearest town: High Springs. GPS: 29.829323, -82.683541

32 • A4 | Stephen Foster SP

Total sites: 45, RV sites: 45, Elec sites: 45, Water at site, Flush toilet, Free showers, RV dump, Tents: $20/RVs: $27, Also cabins, Park entrance: 30.330771 N, 82.761376 W, Open all year, Max Length: 45ft, Reservations accepted, Elev: 125ft/38m, Tel: 386-397-2733, Nearest town: White Springs. GPS: 30.333686, -82.771929

33 • B3 | Manatee Springs SP - Hickory

Total sites: 23, RV sites: 23, Elec sites: 23, Water at site, Flush toilet, Free showers, RV dump, Tent & RV camping: $20, Stay limit: 14 days, Open all year, Reservations accepted, Elev: 20ft/6m, Tel: 352-493-6072, Nearest town: Chiefland. GPS: 29.487806, -82.975488

34 • B3 | Manatee Springs SP - Magnolia 1

Total sites: 41, RV sites: 26, Elec sites: 41, Water at site, Flush toilet, Free showers, RV dump, Tent & RV camping: $20, 27 Full hookups, Stay limit: 14 days, Open all year, Max Length: 35ft, Reservations accepted, Elev: 21ft/6m, Tel: 352-493-6072, Nearest town: Chiefland. GPS: 29.485749, -82.975356

35 • B3 | Manatee Springs SP - Magnolia 2

Total sites: 18, RV sites: 18, Elec sites: 18, Water at site, Flush toilet, Free showers, RV dump, Tent & RV camping: $20, Stay limit: 14 days, Open all year, Reservations accepted, Elev: 22ft/7m, Tel: 352-493-6072, Nearest town: Chiefland. GPS: 29.486286, -82.977307

36 • B4 | Blue Spring SP

Total sites: 51, RV sites: 51, Elec sites: 51, Water at site, Flush toilet, Free showers, RV dump, Tent & RV camping: $24, Also cabins, Stay limit: 14 days, Open all year, Max Length: 40ft, Reservations accepted, Elev: 79ft/24m, Tel: 386-775-3663, Nearest town: Orange City. GPS: 28.946970, -81.334460

37 • B4 | Catfish Creek Preserve SP - TC 1 - SFWMD

Dispersed sites, No water, Tents only: $5, Hike-in, 1.7 mi, Free Special Use License required, Reservations required, Elev: 93ft/28m, Tel: 863-696-1112, Nearest town: Lake Wales. GPS: 27.973717, -81.483548

38 • B4 | Catfish Creek Preserve SP - TC 2 - SFWMD

Dispersed sites, No water, Tents only: $5, Hike-in, 2.3 mi, Free Special Use License required, Reservations required, Elev: 85ft/26m, Tel: 863-696-1112, Nearest town: Lake Wales. GPS: 27.962518, -81.484955

39 • B4 | Colt Creek SP - Equestrian

Dispersed sites, No water, No toilets, Tents only: $5, Reservations accepted, Elev: 92ft/28m, Tel: 863-815-6761, Nearest town: Lakeland. GPS: 28.275596, -82.037035

40 • B4 | Colt Creek SP - Main

Total sites: 35, RV sites: 29, Elec sites: 35, No water, No toilets, Tents: $24/RVs: $31, Reservations accepted, Elev: 95ft/29m, Tel: 863-815-6761, Nearest town: Lakeland. GPS: 28.289539, -82.041719

41 • B4 | Colt Creek SP - Site 1

Dispersed sites, No water, No toilets, Tents only: $5, Hike-in, Reservations accepted, Elev: 90ft/27m, Tel: 863-815-6761, Nearest town: Lakeland. GPS: 28.300155, -82.031656

42 • B4 | Colt Creek SP - Site 2

Dispersed sites, No water, No toilets, Tents only: $5, Hike-in, Reservations accepted, Elev: 89ft/27m, Tel: 863-815-6761, Nearest town: Lakeland. GPS: 28.312666, -82.044555

43 • B4 | Hillsborough River SP

Total sites: 112, RV sites: 112, Water at site, Flush toilet, Free showers, RV dump, Tents: $24/RVs: $31, Stay limit: 14 days, Open all year, Max Length: 50ft, Reservations accepted, Elev: 92ft/28m, Tel: 813-987-6771, Nearest town: Thonotosassa. GPS: 28.145054, -82.238431

44 • B4 | Hillsborough River SP - Seminole TC

Dispersed sites, No water, No toilets, Tents only: $5, Hike-in, Fee is per person, Stay limit: 14 days, Open all year, Elev: 102ft/31m, Tel: 813-987-6771, Nearest town: Thonotosassa. GPS: 28.149035, -82.246377

45 • B4 | Hontoon Island SP

Total sites: 12, RV sites: 0, Central water, Flush toilet, Free showers, No RV dump, Tents only: $18, Ferry access, Boat E/W hookups: $18, Stay limit: 14 days, Reservations accepted, Elev: 7ft/2m, Tel: 386-736-5309, Nearest town: Deland. GPS: 28.970595, -81.359607

46 • B4 | Lake Griffin SP

Total sites: 40, RV sites: 40, Elec sites: 40, Water at site, Flush toilet, Free showers, RV dump, Tents: $18/RVs: $25, 7 Full hookups, Stay limit: 14 days, Open all year, Max Length: 40ft, Reservations accepted, Elev: 92ft/28m, Tel: 352-360-6760, Nearest town: Fruitland Park. GPS: 28.859975, -81.901598

47 • B4 | Lake Kissimmee SP

Total sites: 60, RV sites: 60, Elec sites: 60, Water at site, Flush toilet, Free showers, RV dump, Tents: $20/RVs: $27, Stay limit: 14 days, Open all year, Max Length: 45ft, Reservations accepted, Elev: 89ft/27m, Tel: 863-696-1112, Nearest town: Lake Wales. GPS: 27.947252, -81.351426

48 • B4 | Lake Kissimmee SP - Buster Island

Total sites: 2, RV sites: 0, No water, No toilets, Tents only: $5, Hike-in, Stay limit: 14 days, Open all year, Reservations accepted, Elev: 72ft/22m, Tel: 863-696-1112, Nearest town: Lake Wales. GPS: 27.917108, -81.367821

49 • B4 | Lake Kissimmee SP - Fallen Oaks

Total sites: 2, RV sites: 0, No water, No toilets, Tents only: $5, Hike-in, Stay limit: 14 days, Open all year, Reservations accepted, Elev: 85ft/26m, Tel: 863-696-1112, Nearest town: Lake Wales. GPS: 27.954349, -81.378474

50 • B4 | Lake Louisa SP - Big Creek 1

Dispersed sites, No water, Vault/pit toilet, Tents only: $5, Hike-in, Stay limit: 14 days, Open all year, Reservations accepted, Elev: 103ft/31m, Tel: 352-394-3969, Nearest town: Clermont. GPS: 28.452924, -81.735345

51 • B4 | Lake Louisa SP - Big Creek 2

Dispersed sites, No water, Vault/pit toilet, Tents only: $5, Hike-in, Stay limit: 14 days, Open all year, Reservations accepted, Elev: 109ft/33m, Tel: 352-394-3969, Nearest town: Clermont. GPS: 28.436807, -81.741591

52 • B4 | Lake Louisa SP - Brantly Lake

Dispersed sites, No water, Vault/pit toilet, Tents only: $5, Hike-in, Stay limit: 14 days, Open all year, Reservations accepted, Elev: 108ft/33m, Tel: 352-394-3969, Nearest town: Clermont. GPS: 28.442968, -81.755804

53 • B4 | Lake Louisa SP - Dudes Lake

Dispersed sites, No water, Vault/pit toilet, Tents only: $5, Hike-in, Stay limit: 14 days, Open all year, Reservations accepted, Elev: 117ft/36m, Tel: 352-394-3969, Nearest town: Clermont. GPS: 28.436687, -81.751643

54 • B4 | Lake Louisa SP - Equestrian

Total sites: 5, RV sites: 5, No water, Vault/pit toilet, Tent & RV camping: $5, Also cabins, Stay limit: 14 days, Open all year, Reservations accepted, Elev: 109ft/33m, Tel: 352-394-3969, Nearest town: Clermont. GPS: 28.450409, -81.755941

55 • B4 | Lake Louisa SP - Main

Total sites: 60, RV sites: 60, Elec sites: 60, Water at site, Flush toilet, Free showers, RV dump, Tents: $24/RVs: $31, Also cabins, 11 Full hookups, Stay limit: 14 days, Open all year, Max Length: 115ft, Reservations accepted, Elev: 119ft/36m, Tel: 352-394-3969, Nearest town: Clermont. GPS: 28.434222, -81.724633

56 • B4 | Paynes Prairie Preserve State Park - Puc Buggy

Total sites: 45, RV sites: 31, Elec sites: 45, Central water, Flush toilet, Free showers, RV dump, Tent & RV camping: $18, Walk-to sites, 14 tent sites, Open all year, Reservations accepted, Elev: 77ft/23m, Tel: 352-466-3397, Nearest town: Micanopy. GPS: 29.528064, -82.294779

57 • B4 | Rainbow Springs SP

Total sites: 57, RV sites: 47, Elec sites: 57, Water at site, Flush toilet, Free showers, RV dump, Tent & RV camping: $30, 47 Full hookups, Stay limit: 14 days, Open all year, Max Length: 103ft, Reservations accepted, Elev: 52ft/16m, Tel: 352-465-8550, Nearest town: Dunnellon. GPS: 29.088460, -82.422200

58 • B4 | Silver Springs SP

Total sites: 59, RV sites: 59, Elec sites: 59, Water at site, Flush toilet, Free showers, RV dump, Tents: $24/RVs: $31, Also cabins, 12 Full hookups, Stay limit: 14 days, Open all year, Max Length: 50ft, Reservations accepted, Elev: 89ft/27m, Tel: 352-236-7148, Nearest town: Ocala. GPS: 29.197958, -82.035418

59 • B4 | Tomoka SP

Total sites: 100, RV sites: 100, Elec sites: 100, Water at site, Flush toilet, Free showers, RV dump, Tents: $24/RVs: $31, Stay limit: 14 days, Open all year, Max Length: 34ft, Reservations accepted, Elev: 20ft/6m, Tel: 386-676-4050, Nearest town: Ormond Beach. GPS: 29.337433, -81.081185

60 • B4 | Wekiwa Springs SP

Total sites: 60, RV sites: 60, Elec sites: 60, Water at site, Flush toilet, Free showers, RV dump, Tents: $24/RVs: $31, 28 Full hookups, Stay limit: 14 days, Open all year, Max Length: 50ft, Reservations accepted, Elev: 92ft/28m, Tel: 407-884-2008, Nearest town: Apopka. GPS: 28.711143, -81.464472

61 • B5 | Sebastian Inlet SP

Total sites: 51, RV sites: 51, Elec sites: 51, Water at site, Flush toilet, Free showers, RV dump, Tents: $28/RVs: $35, Stay limit: 14 days, Open all year, Max Length: 40ft, Reservations accepted, Elev: 13ft/4m, Tel: 321-984-4852, Nearest town: Melbourne Beach. GPS: 27.853313, -80.452437

62 • B5 | St. Sebastian River Preserve SP - Eagle Camp

Dispersed sites, No water, Tents only: Fee unk, Hike-in, Ride-in only, No pets, Reservations required, Elev: 24ft/7m, Tel: 321-953-5005, Nearest town: Fellsemere. GPS: 27.821614, -80.573396

63 • B5 | St. Sebastian River Preserve SP - Mullen Camp

Dispersed sites, No water, Tents only: Fee unk, Hike-in/boat-in, No pets, Reservations required, Elev: 16ft/5m, Tel: 321-953-5005, Nearest town: Fellsemere. GPS: 27.804176, -80.509123

64 • B5 | St. Sebastian River Preserve SP - Pine Camp

Dispersed sites, No water, No toilets, Tents only: Fee unk, Hike-in, Reservations required, Elev: 20ft/6m, Tel: 321-953-5004, Nearest town: Sebastian. GPS: 27.838509, -80.544481

65 • B5 | St. Sebastian River Preserve SP - Storytelling Camp

Dispersed sites, No water, Vault/pit toilet, Tents only: Fee unk, Hike-in, No pets, Reservations required, Elev: 22ft/7m, Tel: 321-953-5005, Nearest town: Fellsemere. GPS: 27.838486, -80.557378

66 • B5 | St. Sebastian River Preserve SP - Tree Frog Camp

Dispersed sites, No water, Tents only: Fee unk, Hike-in, No pets, Reservations required, Elev: 21ft/6m, Tel: 321-953-5005, Nearest town: Fellsemere. GPS: 27.796731, -80.534268

67 • C4 | Alafia River SP

Total sites: 30, RV sites: 30, Elec sites: 30, Water at site, Flush toilet, Free showers, RV dump, Tents: $22/RVs: $29, 12 equestrian sites, Stay limit: 14 days, Open all year, Max Length: 55ft, Reservations accepted, Elev: 104ft/32m, Tel: 813-672-5320, Nearest town: Lithia. GPS: 27.778339, -82.139294

68 • C4 | Cayo Costa SP

Total sites: 30, RV sites: 0, Central water, Flush toilet, Free showers, No RV dump, Tents only: $22, Walk-to/boat-in sites, Cold Showers, Boat camping: $20, No generators, Reservations accepted, Elev: 5ft/2m, Tel: 941-964-0375, Nearest town: Pine Island. GPS: 26.686321, -82.257783

69 • C4 | Highlands Hammock SP - Main

Total sites: 118, RV sites: 118, Elec sites: 118, Water at site, Flush

toilet, Free showers, RV dump, Tents: $22/RVs: $29, 4 Equestrian sites, CCC Museum, Stay limit: 14 days, Open all year, Max Length: 50ft, Reservations accepted, Elev: 141ft/43m, Tel: 863-386-6094, Nearest town: Sebring. GPS: 27.474542, -81.530728

70 • C4 | Highlands Hammock SP - Wilderness Camp

Dispersed sites, No water, No toilets, Tents only: $18, Stay limit: 14 days, Open all year, Reservations accepted, Elev: 131ft/40m, Tel: 863-386-6094, Nearest town: Sebring. GPS: 27.462328, -81.517551

71 • C4 | Kissimmee Prairie SP - Equestrian

Total sites: 14, RV sites: 14, Elec sites: 14, Water at site, Vault/pit toilet, No showers, Tents $16/RVs: $23, Stay limit: 14 days, Open all year, Reservations accepted, Elev: 61ft/19m, Tel: 863-462-5360, Nearest town: Okeechobee. GPS: 27.583662, -81.049706

72 • C4 | Kissimmee Prairie SP - Family

Total sites: 17, RV sites: 16, Elec sites: 17, Water at site, Flush toilet, Free showers, RV dump, Tents: $16/RVs: $23, Stay limit: 14 days, Open all year, Max Length: 50ft, Reservations accepted, Elev: 72ft/22m, Tel: 863-462-5360, Nearest town: Okeechobee. GPS: 27.583055, -81.043629

73 • C4 | Kissimmee Prairie SP - Trail Camp

Total sites: 3, RV sites: 0, No water, Vault/pit toilet, Tents only: $16, Hike-in, 2.5 mi, Stay limit: 14 days, Open all year, Elev: 56ft/17m, Tel: 863-462-5360, Nearest town: Okeechobee. GPS: 27.576645, -81.078012

74 • C4 | Koreshan SHS

Total sites: 60, RV sites: 48, Elec sites: 60, Water at site, Flush toilet, Free showers, RV dump, Tents: $26/RVs: $33, Stay limit: 14 days, Open all year, Max Length: 40ft, Reservations accepted, Elev: 30ft/9m, Tel: 239-992-0311, Nearest town: Estero. GPS: 26.436087, -81.817653

75 • C4 | Lake Manatee SP

Total sites: 60, RV sites: 60, Elec sites: 60, Water at site, Flush toilet, Free showers, RV dump, Tents: $22/RVs: $29, Stay limit: 14 days, Open all year, Max Length: 65ft, Reservations accepted, Elev: 72ft/22m, Tel: 941-741-3028, Nearest town: Bradenton. GPS: 27.480811, -82.346537

76 • C4 | Little Manatee River SP

Total sites: 34, RV sites: 34, Elec sites: 34, Water at site, Flush toilet, Free showers, RV dump, Tents: $22/RVs: $29, Stay limit: 14 days, Open all year, Max Length: 68ft, Elev: 56ft/17m, Tel: 813-671-5005, Nearest town: Wimauma. GPS: 27.670895, -82.383584

77 • C4 | Myakka River SP - Bee Island

Dispersed sites, No water, Vault/pit toilet, Tents only: $5, Hike-in, Fee is per-person, Stay limit: 14 days, Open all year, Elev: 35ft/11m, Tel: 941-361-6511, Nearest town: Sarasota. GPS: 27.252804, -82.253209

78 • C4 | Myakka River SP - Big Flats

Total sites: 26, RV sites: 26, Elec sites: 26, Water at site, Flush toilet, Free showers, RV dump, Tents: $26/RVs: $33, Also cabins, Stay limit: 14 days, Open all year, Reservations accepted, Elev: 19ft/

6m, Tel: 941-361-6511, Nearest town: Sarasota. GPS: 27.261933, -82.287419

79 • C4 | Myakka River SP - Honore

Dispersed sites, No water, Vault/pit toilet, Tents only: $5, Hike-in, Fee is per-person, Undependable water must be treated, Stay limit: 14 days, Open all year, Elev: 29ft/9m, Tel: 941-361-6511, Nearest town: Sarasota. GPS: 27.223686, -82.267528

80 • C4 | Myakka River SP - Mossy Hammock

Dispersed sites, No water, Vault/pit toilet, Tents only: $5, Hike-in, Fee is per-person, Stay limit: 14 days, Open all year, Elev: 45ft/14m, Tel: 941-361-6511, Nearest town: Sarasota. GPS: 27.276465, -82.242911

81 • C4 | Myakka River SP - Oak Grove

Dispersed sites, No water, Vault/pit toilet, Tents only: $5, Hike-in, Fee is per-person, Undependable water must be treated, Stay limit: 14 days, Open all year, Elev: 47ft/14m, Tel: 941-361-6511, Nearest town: Sarasota. GPS: 27.234274, -82.178592

82 • C4 | Myakka River SP - Old Prairie

Total sites: 22, RV sites: 22, Elec sites: 22, Water at site, Flush toilet, Free showers, RV dump, Tents: $26/RVs: $33, Also cabins, Stay limit: 14 days, Open all year, Elev: 25ft/8m, Tel: 941-361-6511, Nearest town: Sarasota. GPS: 27.244843, -82.313883

83 • C4 | Myakka River SP - Old Prairie/Palmetto Ridge

Total sites: 38, RV sites: 38, Elec sites: 38, Water at site, Flush toilet, Free showers, RV dump, Tents: $26/RVs: $33, Also cabins, 38 Full hookups, Stay limit: 14 days, Open all year, Elev: 22ft/7m, Tel: 941-361-6511, Nearest town: Sarasota. GPS: 27.245593, -82.315258

84 • C4 | Myakka River SP - Panther Point

Dispersed sites, No water, Vault/pit toilet, Tents only: $5, Hike-in, Fee is per-person, Undependable water must be treated, Stay limit: 14 days, Open all year, Elev: 32ft/10m, Tel: 941-361-6511, Nearest town: Sarasota. GPS: 27.215966, -82.223146

85 • C4 | Myakka River SP - Prairie

Dispersed sites, No water, Vault/pit toilet, Tents only: $5, Hike-in, Fee is per-person, Undependable water must be treated, Stay limit: 14 days, Open all year, Elev: 38ft/12m, Tel: 941-361-6511, Nearest town: Sarasota. GPS: 27.214862, -82.163262

86 • C4 | Oscar Scherer SP

Total sites: 98, RV sites: 98, Elec sites: 98, Water at site, Flush toilet, Free showers, RV dump, Tents: $26/RVs: $33, Open all year, Max Length: 36ft, Reservations accepted, Elev: 33ft/10m, Tel: 941-483-5956, Nearest town: Osprey. GPS: 27.171677, -82.466787

87 • C5 | Atlantic Ridge Preserve SP/Halpatiokee RP - SFWMD

Dispersed sites, No water, No toilets, Tents only: Free, Hike-in, Free Martin County permit required, Elev: 4ft/1m, Tel: 772-288-5690, Nearest town: Port Salerno. GPS: 27.091624, -80.243113

88 • C5 | Jonathan Dickinson SP - Horse Camp

Total sites: 5, RV sites: 5, Elec sites: 5, Water at site, Flush toilet, Free showers, RV dump, Tent & RV camping: $26, Also cabins, Stay limit: 14 days, Open all year, Elev: 23ft/7m, Tel: 772-546-2771, Nearest town: Stuart. GPS: 27.009308, -80.132138

89 • C5 | Jonathan Dickinson SP - Pine Grove

Total sites: 90, RV sites: 90, Elec sites: 90, Water at site, Flush toilet, Free showers, RV dump, Tent & RV camping: $26, Also cabins, 90 Full hookups, Stay limit: 14 days, Open all year, Max Length: 45ft, Reservations accepted, Elev: 43ft/13m, Tel: 772-546-2771, Nearest town: Stuart. GPS: 26.999605, -80.100734

90 • C5 | Jonathan Dickinson SP - The River

Total sites: 45, RV sites: 45, Elec sites: 45, Water at site, Flush toilet, Free showers, RV dump, Tent & RV camping: $26, Also cabins, Stay limit: 14 days, Open all year, Max Length: 45ft, Reservations accepted, Elev: 30ft/9m, Tel: 772-546-2771, Nearest town: Stuart. GPS: 26.990392, -80.142272

91 • C5 | St. Sebastian River Preserve SP - Ranch

Dispersed sites, No water, Tents only: Fee unk, Hike-in, No pets, Reservations required, Elev: 18ft/5m, Tel: 321-953-5005, Nearest town: Fellsmere. GPS: 27.779803, -80.527807

92 • D4 | Bahia Honda SP - Bayside

Total sites: 8, RV sites: 8, Water at site, No toilets, No showers, No RV dump, Tent & RV camping: $36, 6'8" height restriction, Stay limit: 14 days, Open all year, Elev: 10ft/3m, Tel: 305-872-2353, Nearest town: Big Pine Key. GPS: 24.661954, -81.272481

93 • D4 | Bahia Honda SP - Buttonwood

Total sites: 48, RV sites: 48, Elec sites: 48, Water at site, Flush toilet, Free showers, RV dump, Tent & RV camping: $36, Stay limit: 14 days, Open all year, Max Length: 40ft, Reservations accepted, Elev: 10ft/3m, Tel: 305-872-2353, Nearest town: Big Pine Key. GPS: 24.658526, -81.277369

94 • D4 | Collier-Seminole SP

Total sites: 104, RV sites: 82, Elec sites: 82, Water at site, Flush toilet, Free showers, RV dump, Tents: $22/RVs: $29, Home of the last existing Bay City Walking Dredge, Open all year, Max Length: 60ft, Reservations accepted, Elev: 36ft/11m, Tel: 239-394-3397, Nearest town: Naples. GPS: 25.992417, -81.595827

95 • D4 | Curry Hammock SP

Total sites: 28, RV sites: 28, Elec sites: 28, Water at site, Flush toilet, Free showers, RV dump, Tents: $36/RVs: $43, Stay limit: 14 days, Open all year, Max Length: 70ft, Reservations accepted, Elev: 13ft/4m, Tel: 305-289-2690, Nearest town: Marathon. GPS: 24.740827, -80.981948

96 • D5 | John Pennekamp Coral Reef SP

Total sites: 47, RV sites: 47, Elec sites: 47, Water at site, Flush toilet, Free showers, Tents: $36/RVs: $43, 47 Full hookups, Stay limit: 14 days, Open all year, Reservations accepted, Elev: 10ft/3m, Tel: 305-451-6300, Nearest town: Key Largo. GPS: 25.122889, -80.408187

97 • D5 | Long Key SP

Total sites: , Central water, Flush toilet, No showers, No RV dump, Tents only: $23, Walk-to sites, Open all year, Reservations accepted, Elev: 30ft/9m, Tel: 305-664-4815, Nearest town: Long Key. GPS: 24.810878, -80.828196

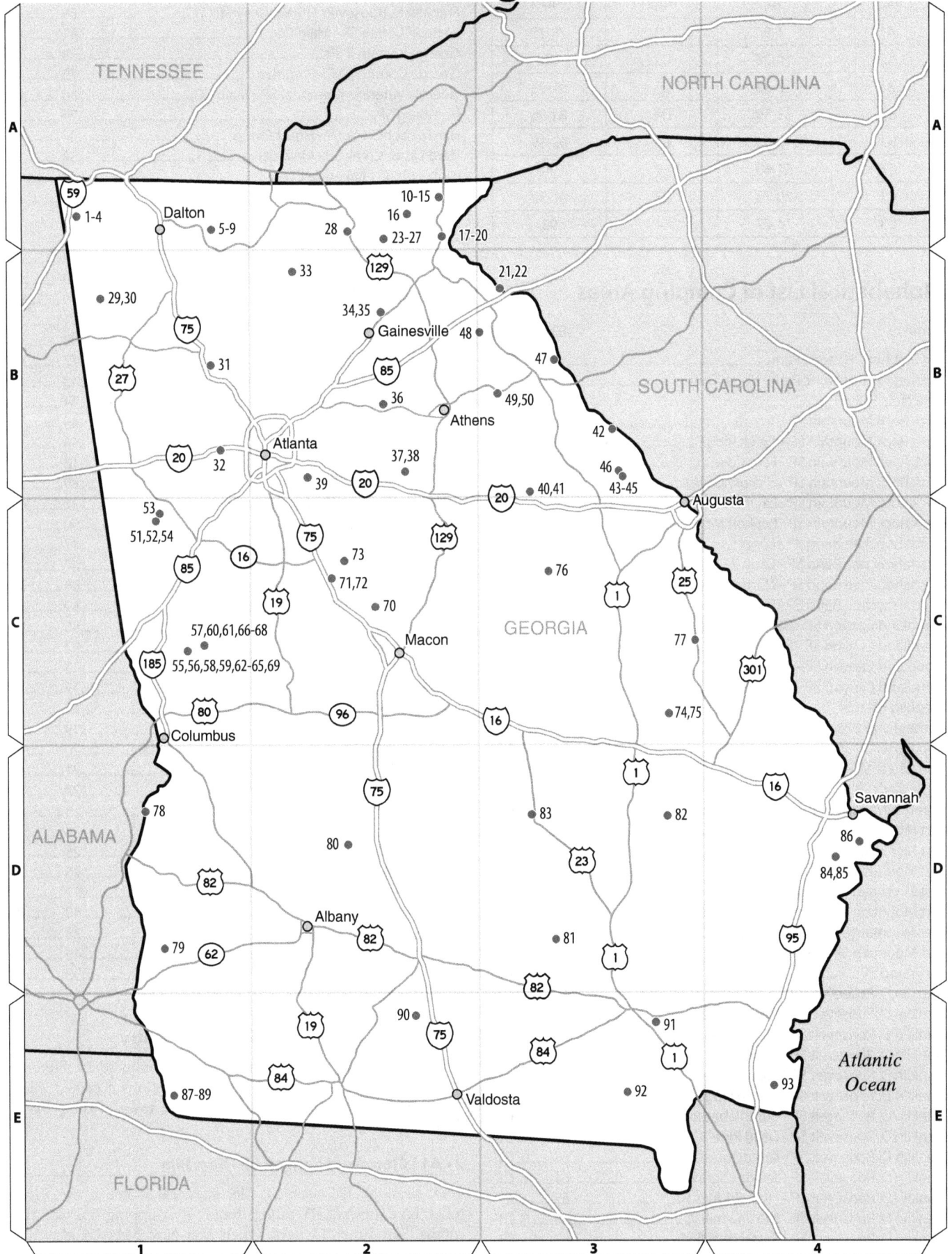

Georgia

TENNESSEE

NORTH CAROLINA

A

59

• 1-4

Dalton

• 5-9

• 10-15

• 16

28 •

• 23-27

17-20

129

• 33

21,22

29,30 •

34,35 •

75

Gainesville

48 •

47 •

SOUTH CAROLINA

B

27

85

31 •

36 •

49,50 •

Athens

42 •

Atlanta

20

32 •

37,38 •

46 •

43-45 •

39 •

20

20

40,41 •

Augusta

53 •

51,52,54

75

73 •

129

76 •

25

85

16

71,72 •

77 •

19

70 •

GEORGIA

301

C

57,60,61,66-68 •

185

55,56,58,59,62-65,69

Macon

1

80

74,75 •

96

Columbus

16

16

Savannah

75

86 •

78 •

84,85

ALABAMA

82 •

23

84,85

D

82

80 •

1

95

Albany

82

79 •

62

81 •

1

82

19

90 •

91 •

75

84

1

87-89 •

84

92 •

93 •

Valdosta

Atlantic Ocean

E

FLORIDA

1　　　　2　　　　3　　　　4

Map	ID	Map	ID
A1	1-9	D1	78-79
A2	10-28	D2	80
B1	29-32	D3	81-83
B2	33-39	D4	84-86
B3	40-50	E1	87-89
C1	51-69	E2	90
C2	70-73	E3	91-92
C3	74-77	E4	93

Alphabetical List of Camping Areas

Name	ID	Map
A H Stephens Historic Park	40	B3
A H Stephens Historic Park - Horse Camp	41	B3
Amicalola Falls SP	33	B2
Black Rock Mountain SP	10	A2
Black Rock Mountain SP - Creek Ridge	11	A2
Black Rock Mountain SP - Fern Cove	12	A2
Black Rock Mountain SP - Hickory Cove	13	A2
Black Rock Mountain SP - Laurel Ridge	14	A2
Black Rock Mountain SP - Lookoff Mt	15	A2
Chattahoochee Bend SP - Loop 1	51	C1
Chattahoochee Bend SP - Loop 2	52	C1
Chattahoochee Bend SP - North Camp	53	C1
Chattahoochee Bend SP - Platform West	54	C1
Cloudland Canyon SP - Back-Country	1	A1
Cloudland Canyon SP - East Rim	2	A1
Cloudland Canyon SP - Walk-in	3	A1
Cloudland Canyon SP - West Rim	4	A1
Crooked River SP	93	E4
Dames Ferry SP	70	C2
Don Carter SP - Main	34	B2
Don Carter SP - Primitive	35	B2
Elijah Clark SP	42	B3
Florence Marina SP	78	D1
Fort Mc Allister SP - Backcountry	84	D4
Fort McAllister SP	85	D4
Fort Mountain SP - Backcountry #1	5	A1
Fort Mountain SP - Backcountry #2	6	A1
Fort Mountain SP - Backcountry #3	7	A1
Fort Mountain SP - Backcountry #4	8	A1
Fort Mountain SP - Main CG	9	A1
Fort Yargo SP	36	B2
Franklin D. Roosevelt SP	55	C1
Franklin D. Roosevelt SP - Beech Bottom	56	C1
Franklin D. Roosevelt SP - Bethel Creek TC	57	C1
Franklin D. Roosevelt SP - Big Knot TC	58	C1
Franklin D. Roosevelt SP - Broken Tree TC	59	C1
Franklin D. Roosevelt SP - Brown Dog	60	C1
Franklin D. Roosevelt SP - Bumblebee Ridge	61	C1
Franklin D. Roosevelt SP - Dead Pine TC	62	C1
Franklin D. Roosevelt SP - Grindstone Gap TC	63	C1
Franklin D. Roosevelt SP - Jenkins Springs TC	64	C1
Franklin D. Roosevelt SP - Little Bridges TC	65	C1
Franklin D. Roosevelt SP - Old Sawmill TC	66	C1
Franklin D. Roosevelt SP - Sassafras Hill TC	67	C1

Name	ID	Map
Franklin D. Roosevelt SP - Sparks Creek TC	68	C1
Franklin D. Roosevelt SP - Whiskey Still TC	69	C1
General Coffee SP - Main CG	81	D3
George L Smith II SP	74	C3
George L Smith II SP - Primitive	75	C3
Georgia Veterans Memorial SP - Main CG	80	D2
Hamburg SP	76	C3
Hard Labor Creek SP - Horse Camp	37	B2
Hard Labor Creek SP - Main CG	38	B2
High Falls SP - Lakeside CG	71	C2
High Falls SP - River CG	72	C2
Indian Springs SP	73	C2
Jack Hill SP	82	D3
James H. "Sloppy" Floyd SP - Backcountry	29	B1
James H. "Sloppy" Floyd SP - Main CG	30	B1
Kolomoki Mounds SP - Main CG	79	D1
Laura S Walker SP - Main CG	91	E3
Little Ocmulgee SP	83	D3
Magnolia Springs SP - Main CG	77	C3
Mistletoe SP - Backcountry #1	43	B3
Mistletoe SP - Backcountry #2	44	B3
Mistletoe SP - Backcountry #3	45	B3
Mistletoe SP - Main CG	46	B3
Moccasin Creek SP	16	A2
Panola Mtn SP - Back-country	39	B2
Red Top Mountain SP - Main CG	31	B1
Reed Bingham SP	90	E2
Richard B Russell SP	47	B3
Seminole SP	87	E1
Seminole SP - Cummings Landing	88	E1
Seminole SP - Treehouse	89	E1
Skidaway Island SP	86	D4
Stephen C. Foster SP	92	E3
Sweetwater Creek SP	32	B1
Tallulah Gorge SP	17	A2
Tallulah Gorge SP - Backcountry #1	18	A2
Tallulah Gorge SP - Backcountry #2	19	A2
Tallulah Gorge SP - Backcountry #3	20	A2
Tugaloo SP - Main CG	21	A2
Tugaloo SP - Walk-in CG	22	A2
Unicoi SP - Big Brook Spur	23	A2
Unicoi SP - Hickory Hollow	24	A2
Unicoi SP - Laurel Ridge	25	A2
Unicoi SP - Little Brook Spur	26	A2
Unicoi SP - Squirrels Nests	27	A2
Victoria Bryant SP - Main CG	48	B3
Vogel SP - Main CG	28	A2
Watson Mill Bridge SP - Horse Camp	49	B3
Watson Mill Bridge SP - Main CG	50	B3

1 • A1 | Cloudland Canyon SP - Back-Country

Total sites: 13, No water, No toilets, Tents only: $8-10, Hike-in, Stay limit: 14 days, Open all year, Reservations accepted, Elev: 1860ft/567m, Tel: 706-657-4050, Nearest town: Rising Fawn. GPS: 34.820078, -85.475732

2 • A1 | Cloudland Canyon SP - East Rim

Total sites: 24, RV sites: 24, Elec sites: 24, Water at site, Flush toilet, Free showers, RV dump, Tent & RV camping: $32-38, Also cabins, Stay limit: 14 days, Open Mar-Nov, Max Length: 50ft,

Reservations accepted, Elev: 1782ft/543m, Tel: 706-657-4050, Nearest town: Rising Fawn. GPS: 34.833218, -85.481955

3 • A1 | Cloudland Canyon SP - Walk-in

Total sites: 30, No water, No toilets, Tents only: $20-25, Walk-to sites, Comfort station closed in winter, Stay limit: 14 days, Open all year, Reservations accepted, Elev: 1837ft/560m, Tel: 706-657-4050, Nearest town: Rising Fawn. GPS: 34.838518, -85.489386

4 • A1 | Cloudland Canyon SP - West Rim

Total sites: 48, RV sites: 48, Elec sites: 48, Water at site, Flush toilet, Free showers, RV dump, Tent & RV camping: $32-38, Also cabins, Stay limit: 14 days, Open all year, Max Length: 50ft, Reservations accepted, Elev: 1827ft/557m, Tel: 706-657-4050, Nearest town: Rising Fawn. GPS: 34.836477, -85.487736

5 • A1 | Fort Mountain SP - Backcountry #1

Total sites: 1, No water, Tents only: $10, Hike-in, Stay limit: 14 days, Reservations accepted, Elev: 2476ft/755m, Tel: 706-422-1932, Nearest town: Chatsworth. GPS: 34.763922, -84.698551

6 • A1 | Fort Mountain SP - Backcountry #2

Total sites: 1, No water, Tents only: $10, Hike-in, Stay limit: 14 days, Reservations accepted, Elev: 2564ft/782m, Tel: 706-422-1932, Nearest town: Chatsworth. GPS: 34.754396, -84.698225

7 • A1 | Fort Mountain SP - Backcountry #3

Total sites: 1, No water, Tents only: $10, Hike-in, Stay limit: 14 days, Reservations accepted, Elev: 2147ft/654m, Tel: 706-422-1932, Nearest town: Chatsworth. GPS: 34.759098, -84.713928

8 • A1 | Fort Mountain SP - Backcountry #4

Total sites: 1, No water, Tents only: $10, Hike-in, Stay limit: 14 days, Reservations accepted, Elev: 2206ft/672m, Tel: 706-422-1932, Nearest town: Chatsworth. GPS: 34.773013, -84.708159

9 • A1 | Fort Mountain SP - Main CG

Total sites: 80, RV sites: 70, Elec sites: 70, Water available, Flush toilet, Free showers, RV dump, Tents: $18/RVs: $34-38, Also walk-to sites/cabins, 10 walk-to sites, Stay limit: 14 days, Open all year, Max Length: 50ft, Reservations accepted, Elev: 2441ft/744m, Tel: 706-422-1932, Nearest town: Chatsworth. GPS: 34.759202, -84.706614

10 • A2 | Black Rock Mountain SP

Total sites: 44, RV sites: 44, Elec sites: 44, Water at site, Flush toilet, Free showers, RV dump, Tent & RV camping: $34-38, Also cabins, Open Mar-Dec, Reservations accepted, Elev: 3285ft/1001m, Tel: 706-746-2123, Nearest town: Mountain City. GPS: 34.906445, -83.405247

11 • A2 | Black Rock Mountain SP - Creek Ridge

Total sites: 1, Central water, Vault/pit toilet, Tents only: $20, Hike-in, Open Mar-Nov, Elev: 2471ft/753m, Tel: 706-746-2123, Nearest town: Mountain City. GPS: 34.919466, -83.413018

12 • A2 | Black Rock Mountain SP - Fern Cove

Total sites: 1, Central water, Vault/pit toilet, Tents only: $20, Hike-in, Open Mar-Nov, Elev: 2981ft/909m, Tel: 706-746-2123, Nearest town: Mountain City. GPS: 34.911827, -83.413067

13 • A2 | Black Rock Mountain SP - Hickory Cove

Total sites: 12, RV sites: 0, Central water, Vault/pit toilet, Tents only: $22, Walk-to sites, Open Mar-Nov, Reservations accepted, Elev: 2963ft/903m, Tel: 706-746-2123, Nearest town: Mountain City. GPS: 34.905541, -83.401612

14 • A2 | Black Rock Mountain SP - Laurel Ridge

Total sites: 1, Central water, Vault/pit toilet, Tents only: $20, Hike-in, Open Mar-Nov, Elev: 3073ft/937m, Tel: 706-746-2123, Nearest town: Mountain City. GPS: 34.929489, -83.402955

15 • A2 | Black Rock Mountain SP - Lookoff Mt

Total sites: 1, Central water, Vault/pit toilet, Tents only: $20, Hike-in, Open Mar-Nov, Elev: 3141ft/957m, Tel: 706-746-2123, Nearest town: Mountain City. GPS: 34.930256, -83.400882

16 • A2 | Moccasin Creek SP

Total sites: 54, RV sites: 54, Elec sites: 54, Water at site, Flush toilet, Free showers, RV dump, Tent & RV camping: $34-36, Stay limit: 14 days, Open all year, Max Length: 50ft, Reservations accepted, Elev: 2011ft/613m, Tel: 706-947-3194, Nearest town: Clayton. GPS: 34.844954, -83.587346

17 • A2 | Tallulah Gorge SP

Total sites: 50, RV sites: 50, Elec sites: 50, Water at site, Flush toilet, Free showers, RV dump, Tent & RV camping: $34-37, CG operated by GA Power, Stay limit: 14 days, Open all year, Reservations accepted, Elev: 1660ft/506m, Tel: 706-754-7979, Nearest town: Tallulah Falls. GPS: 34.742259, -83.396949

18 • A2 | Tallulah Gorge SP - Backcountry #1

Dispersed sites, No water, Hike-to shelter: $20, Stay limit: 14 days, Open all year, Reservations accepted, Elev: 1137ft/347m, Tel: 706-754-7979, Nearest town: Tallulah Falls. GPS: 34.730598, -83.358107

19 • A2 | Tallulah Gorge SP - Backcountry #2

Dispersed sites, No water, Hike-to shelter: $20, Stay limit: 14 days, Open all year, Reservations accepted, Elev: 1678ft/511m, Tel: 706-754-7979, Nearest town: Tallulah Falls. GPS: 34.740194, -83.383872

20 • A2 | Tallulah Gorge SP - Backcountry #3

Dispersed sites, No water, Hike-to shelter: $20, Stay limit: 14 days, Open all year, Reservations accepted, Elev: 1669ft/509m, Tel: 706-754-7979, Nearest town: Tallulah Falls. GPS: 34.738632, -83.384977

21 • A2 | Tugaloo SP - Main CG

Total sites: 105, RV sites: 105, Elec sites: 105, Water at site, Flush toilet, Free showers, RV dump, Tent & RV camping: $35-38, Also cabins, Stay limit: 14 days, Open all year, Max Length: 50ft, Reservations accepted, Elev: 745ft/227m, Tel: 706-356-4362, Nearest town: Lavonia. GPS: 34.499616, -83.059379

22 • A2 | Tugaloo SP - Walk-in CG

Dispersed sites, Central water, Tents only: $25, Walk-to sites, 6 yurts, Stay limit: 14 days, Open all year, Reservations accepted, Elev: 729ft/222m, Tel: 706-356-4362, Nearest town: Lavonia. GPS: 34.493228, -83.073823

23 • A2 | Unicoi SP - Big Brook Spur

Total sites: 13, RV sites: 13, Elec sites: 13, Water at site, Flush toilet, Free showers, RV dump, Tent & RV camping: $79, Also cabins, Full hookups sites, Stay limit: 14 days, Open all year, Reservations accepted, Elev: 1711ft/522m, Tel: Info: 706-878-2201/Res: 800-573-9659, Nearest town: Helen. GPS: 34.731374, -83.717795

24 • A2 | Unicoi SP - Hickory Hollow

Total sites: 33, Water at site, Flush toilet, Free showers, RV dump, Tents only: $25, Walk-to sites, Stay limit: 14 days, Open all year, Elev: 1673ft/510m, Tel: Info: 706-878-2201/Res: 800-573-9659, Nearest town: Helen. GPS: 34.728925, -83.718633

25 • A2 | Unicoi SP - Laurel Ridge

Total sites: 23, RV sites: 23, Elec sites: 23, Water at site, Flush toilet, Free showers, RV dump, Tent & RV camping: $64-69, Also cabins, Stay limit: 14 days, Open all year, Elev: 1745ft/532m, Tel: Info: 706-878-2201/Res: 800-573-9659, Nearest town: Helen. GPS: 34.730635, -83.719411

26 • A2 | Unicoi SP - Little Brook Spur

Total sites: 16, RV sites: 16, Elec sites: 16, Water at site, Flush toilet, Free showers, RV dump, Tent & RV camping: $64-69, Also cabins, Stay limit: 14 days, Open all year, Elev: 1736ft/529m, Tel: Info: 706-878-2201/Res: 800-573-9659, Nearest town: Helen. GPS: 34.727495, -83.716856

27 • A2 | Unicoi SP - Squirrels Nests

Total sites: 16, Central water, Flush toilet, Shelter: $15, Stay limit: 14 days, Open all year, Reservations accepted, Elev: 1666ft/508m, Tel: Info: 706-878-2201/Res: 800-573-9659, Nearest town: Helen. GPS: 34.729615, -83.722751

28 • A2 | Vogel SP - Main CG

Total sites: 103, RV sites: 60, Elec sites: 103, Water at site, Flush toilet, Free showers, RV dump, Tents: $30/RVs: $34-38, Also walk-to sites/cabins, 16 walk-to sites, Stay limit: 14 days, Open all year, Max Length: 40ft, Elev: 2342ft/714m, Tel: 706-745-2628, Nearest town: Blairsville. GPS: 34.761049, -83.927514

29 • B1 | James H. "Sloppy" Floyd SP - Backcountry

Total sites: 1, RV sites: 0, No water, Vault/pit toilet, Tents only: $15, Hike-in, Stay limit: 14 days, Open all year, Reservations accepted, Elev: 717ft/219m, Tel: 706-857-0826, Nearest town: Summerville. GPS: 34.434773, -85.337098

30 • B1 | James H. "Sloppy" Floyd SP - Main CG

Total sites: 25, RV sites: 25, Elec sites: 25, Flush toilet, Free showers, Tent & RV camping: $31-33, Also cabins, Stay limit: 14 days, Open all year, Max Length: 50ft, Reservations accepted, Elev: 787ft/240m, Tel: 706-857-0826, Nearest town: Summerville. GPS: 34.434627, -85.344431

31 • B1 | Red Top Mountain SP - Main CG

Total sites: 92, RV sites: 92, Elec sites: 92, Water at site, Flush toilet, Free showers, RV dump, Tents: $25-30/RVs: $35-40, Also cabins, Stay limit: 14 days, Open all year, Max Length: 40ft, Reservations accepted, Elev: 965ft/294m, Tel: 770-975-0055, Nearest town: Cartersville. GPS: 34.141025, -84.707168

32 • B1 | Sweetwater Creek SP

Total sites: 5, RV sites: 0, Central water, Flush toilet, No showers, No RV dump, Tents only: $27, Walk-to sites, Stay limit: 14 days, Reservations accepted, Elev: 958ft/292m, Tel: 770-732-5871, Nearest town: Lithia Springs. GPS: 33.761366, -84.642347

33 • B2 | Amicalola Falls SP

Total sites: 24, RV sites: 24, Elec sites: 24, Water at site, Flush toilet, Free showers, RV dump, Tent & RV camping: $47, Also cabins, 25% grade to CG, Open all year, Reservations accepted, Elev: 2641ft/805m, Tel: 706-265-4703, Nearest town: Dawsonville. GPS: 34.571241, -84.244407

34 • B2 | Don Carter SP - Main

Total sites: 44, RV sites: 44, Elec sites: 44, Water at site, Flush toilet, Free showers, RV dump, Tent & RV camping: $32-35, Also walk-to sites/cabins, 12 tent sites, Stay limit: 14 days, Open all year, Max Length: 100ft, Reservations accepted, Elev: 1160ft/354m, Tel: 678-450-7726, Nearest town: Gainesville. GPS: 34.385205, -83.741439

35 • B2 | Don Carter SP - Primitive

Total sites: 12, Central water, Vault/pit toilet, Tents only: $20, Walk-to sites, Stay limit: 14 days, Open all year, Reservations accepted, Elev: 1125ft/343m, Tel: 678-450-7726, Nearest town: Gainesville. GPS: 34.391528, -83.742116

36 • B2 | Fort Yargo SP

Total sites: 53, RV sites: 40, Elec sites: 40, Water available, Flush toilet, Free showers, RV dump, Tents: $25-26/RVs: $34-36, Also walk-to sites/cabins, 13 walk-to sites, Stay limit: 14 days, Open all year, Max Length: 50ft, Reservations accepted, Elev: 892ft/272m, Tel: 770-867-3489, Nearest town: Winder. GPS: 33.968642, -83.721343

37 • B2 | Hard Labor Creek SP - Horse Camp

Total sites: 11, RV sites: 11, Elec sites: 11, Water at site, Vault/pit toilet, Tent & RV camping: $35-38, Stay limit: 14 days, Open all year, Max Length: 45ft, Elev: 612ft/187m, Tel: 706-557-3001, Nearest town: Rutledge. GPS: 33.665119, -83.593417

38 • B2 | Hard Labor Creek SP - Main CG

Total sites: 48, RV sites: 48, Elec sites: 48, Water at site, Flush toilet, Free showers, RV dump, Tent & RV camping: $35-59, Also cabins, 12 Full hookups, Stay limit: 14 days, Open all year, Max Length: 45ft, Reservations accepted, Elev: 646ft/197m, Tel: 706-557-3001, Nearest town: Rutledge. GPS: 33.668377, -83.605088

39 • B2 | Panola Mtn SP - Back-country

Total sites: 5, No water, Tents only: $22, Hike-in, Open all year, Reservations accepted, Elev: 710ft/216m, Tel: 770-389-7801, Nearest town: Conyers. GPS: 33.637714, -84.152899

40 • B3 | A H Stephens Historic Park

Total sites: 21, RV sites: 21, Elec sites: 21, Water at site, Flush toilet, Free showers, RV dump, Tent & RV camping: $32, Also cabins, If RV is taller than 12' 10", check web site for directions, Stay limit: 14 days, Open all year, Max Length: 50ft, Reservations accepted, Elev: 615ft/187m, Tel: 706-456-2602, Nearest town: Crawfordville. GPS: 33.564721, -82.900646

41 • B3 | A H Stephens Historic Park - Horse Camp

Total sites: 18, RV sites: 18, Elec sites: 18, Water at site, Flush toilet, Tent & RV camping: $26, Also cabins, If RV is taller than 12' 10", check web site for directions. 18 equestrian sites, Stay limit: 14 days, Open all year, Max Length: 50ft, Reservations accepted, Elev: 560ft/171m, Tel: 706-456-2602, Nearest town: Crawfordville. GPS: 33.572948, -82.895756

42 • B3 | Elijah Clark SP

Total sites: 175, RV sites: 165, Elec sites: 165, Central water, Flush toilet, Free showers, RV dump, Tents: $20-22/RVs: $32-38, Also walk-to sites/cabins, 10 walk-to sites, Stay limit: 14 days, Open all year, Max Length: 50ft, Reservations accepted, Elev: 381ft/116m, Tel: 706-359-3458, Nearest town: Lincolnton. GPS: 33.855154, -82.407582

43 • B3 | Mistletoe SP - Backcountry #1

Dispersed sites, Tents only: $10, Hike-in, Stay limit: 14 days, Open all year, Reservations accepted, Elev: 428ft/130m, Tel: 706-541-0321, Nearest town: Appling. GPS: 33.637354, -82.362204

44 • B3 | Mistletoe SP - Backcountry #2

Dispersed sites, Tents only: $10, Hike-in, Stay limit: 14 days, Open all year, Reservations accepted, Elev: 390ft/119m, Tel: 706-541-0321, Nearest town: Appling. GPS: 33.641747, -82.361505

45 • B3 | Mistletoe SP - Backcountry #3

Dispersed sites, Tents only: $10, Hike-in, Stay limit: 14 days, Open all year, Reservations accepted, Elev: 424ft/129m, Tel: 706-541-0321, Nearest town: Appling. GPS: 33.642109, -82.365177

46 • B3 | Mistletoe SP - Main CG

Total sites: 96, RV sites: 92, Elec sites: 92, Water at site, Flush toilet, Free showers, RV dump, Tents: $15/RVs: $32-35, Also walk-to sites/cabins, 4 walk-to sites, Stay limit: 14 days, Open all year, Max Length: 55ft, Reservations accepted, Elev: 363ft/111m, Tel: 706-541-0321, Nearest town: Appling. GPS: 33.665766, -82.381986

47 • B3 | Richard B Russell SP

Total sites: 28, RV sites: 28, Elec sites: 28, Water available, Flush toilet, Free showers, RV dump, Tent & RV camping: $33-35, Also cabins, Stay limit: 14 days, Open all year, Max Length: 35ft, Reservations accepted, Elev: 564ft/172m, Tel: 706-213-2045, Nearest town: Elberton. GPS: 34.167378, -82.750201

48 • B3 | Victoria Bryant SP - Main CG

Total sites: 35, RV sites: 27, Elec sites: 27, Water at site, Flush toilet, Free showers, Tents: $28/RVs: $30-42, Tent sites have platforms, Stay limit: 14 days, Open all year, Max Length: 50ft, Reservations accepted, Elev: 742ft/226m, Tel: 706-245-6270, Nearest town: Royston. GPS: 34.297754, -83.164357

49 • B3 | Watson Mill Bridge SP - Horse Camp

Total sites: 11, RV sites: 11, Elec sites: 11, Water at site, Flush toilet, Free showers, RV dump, Tent & RV camping: $30-60, Stay limit: 14 days, Open all year, Max Length: 50ft, Reservations accepted, Elev: 600ft/183m, Tel: 706-245-6270, Nearest town: Comer. GPS: 34.029203, -83.073356

50 • B3 | Watson Mill Bridge SP - Main CG

Total sites: 21, RV sites: 21, Elec sites: 21, Water at site, Flush toilet, Free showers, RV dump, Tent & RV camping: $30-32, Also cabins, Stay limit: 14 days, Open Mar-Nov, Max Length: 50ft, Reservations accepted, Elev: 564ft/172m, Tel: 706-245-6270, Nearest town: Comer. GPS: 34.022307, -83.069646

51 • C1 | Chattahoochee Bend SP - Loop 1

Total sites: 24, RV sites: 24, Elec sites: 24, Water at site, Flush toilet, Free showers, RV dump, Tent & RV camping: $28, Open all year, Max Length: 40ft, Reservations accepted, Elev: 714ft/218m, Tel: 770-254-7271, Nearest town: Newnan. GPS: 33.428376, -85.005694

52 • C1 | Chattahoochee Bend SP - Loop 2

Total sites: 22, RV sites: 10, Elec sites: 10, Central water, Flush toilet, Free showers, RV dump, Tents: $20/RVs: $28, Also walk-to sites, 12, Open all year, Max Length: 15ft, Reservations accepted, Elev: 708ft/216m, Tel: 770-254-7271, Nearest town: Newnan. GPS: 33.427449, -85.008768

53 • C1 | Chattahoochee Bend SP - North Camp

Total sites: 7, No water, Vault/pit toilet, Tents only: $11, Hike-in/boat-in, 5 mi, Open all year, Reservations accepted, Elev: 687ft/209m, Tel: 770-254-7271, Nearest town: Newnan. GPS: 33.456519, -84.981934

54 • C1 | Chattahoochee Bend SP - Platform West

Total sites: 7, Tents only: $17, Walk-to sites, Open all year, Reservations accepted, Elev: 679ft/207m, Tel: 770-254-7271, Nearest town: Newnan. GPS: 33.427427, -85.013565

55 • C1 | Franklin D. Roosevelt SP

Total sites: 140, RV sites: 140, Elec sites: 140, Water at site, Flush toilet, Free showers, RV dump, Tent & RV camping: $30, Also cabins, Stay limit: 14 days, Open all year, Max Length: 85ft, Reservations accepted, Elev: 981ft/299m, Tel: 706-663-4858, Nearest town: Pine Mountain. GPS: 32.843782, -84.828457

56 • C1 | Franklin D. Roosevelt SP - Beech Bottom

Dispersed sites, No water, Vault/pit toilet, Tents only: $10, Hike-in, Stay limit: 14 days, Reservations accepted, Elev: 1029ft/314m, Tel: 706-663-4858, Nearest town: Pine Mountain. GPS: 32.859603, -84.777304

57 • C1 | Franklin D. Roosevelt SP - Bethel Creek TC

Dispersed sites, No water, Vault/pit toilet, Tents only: $10, Hike-in, Stay limit: 14 days, Reservations accepted, Elev: 1105ft/337m, Tel: 706-663-4858, Nearest town: Pine Mountain. GPS: 32.843409, -84.750854

58 • C1 | Franklin D. Roosevelt SP - Big Knot TC

Dispersed sites, No water, Vault/pit toilet, Tents only: $10, Hike-in, Stay limit: 14 days, Reservations accepted, Elev: 1068ft/326m, Tel: 706-663-4858, Nearest town: Pine Mountain. GPS: 32.856034, -84.793592

59 • C1 | Franklin D. Roosevelt SP - Broken Tree TC

Dispersed sites, No water, Vault/pit toilet, Tents only: $10, Hike-in, Location approximate, Stay limit: 14 days, Reservations accepted, Elev: 1069ft/326m, Tel: 706-663-4858, Nearest town: Pine Mountain. GPS: 32.840677, -84.798615

60 • C1 | Franklin D. Roosevelt SP - Brown Dog

Dispersed sites, No water, Vault/pit toilet, Tents only: $10, Hike-in, Location approximate, Stay limit: 14 days, Reservations accepted, Elev: 1196ft/365m, Tel: 706-663-4858, Nearest town: Pine Mountain. GPS: 32.854924, -84.738149

61 • C1 | Franklin D. Roosevelt SP - Bumblebee Ridge

Dispersed sites, No water, Vault/pit toilet, Tents only: $10, Hike-in, Stay limit: 14 days, Reservations accepted, Elev: 1210ft/369m, Tel: 706-663-4858, Nearest town: Pine Mountain. GPS: 32.867329, -84.702653

62 • C1 | Franklin D. Roosevelt SP - Dead Pine TC

Dispersed sites, No water, Vault/pit toilet, Tents only: $10, Hike-in, Stay limit: 14 days, Reservations accepted, Elev: 932ft/284m, Tel: 706-663-4858, Nearest town: Pine Mountain. GPS: 32.837711, -84.830008

63 • C1 | Franklin D. Roosevelt SP - Grindstone Gap TC

Dispersed sites, No water, Vault/pit toilet, Tents only: $10, Hike-in, Location approximate, Stay limit: 14 days, Reservations accepted, Elev: 1001ft/305m, Tel: 706-663-4858, Nearest town: Pine Mountain. GPS: 32.843584, -84.774402

64 • C1 | Franklin D. Roosevelt SP - Jenkins Springs TC

Dispersed sites, No water, Vault/pit toilet, Tents only: $10, Hike-in, Location approximate, Stay limit: 14 days, Reservations accepted, Elev: 1034ft/315m, Tel: 706-663-4858, Nearest town: Pine Mountain. GPS: 32.857797, -84.785936

65 • C1 | Franklin D. Roosevelt SP - Little Bridges TC

Dispersed sites, No water, Vault/pit toilet, Tents only: $10, Hike-in, Location approximate, Stay limit: 14 days, Reservations accepted, Elev: 935ft/285m, Tel: 706-663-4858, Nearest town: Pine Mountain. GPS: 32.829564, -84.838018

66 • C1 | Franklin D. Roosevelt SP - Old Sawmill TC

Dispersed sites, No water, Vault/pit toilet, Tents only: $10, Hike-in, Location approximate, Stay limit: 14 days, Reservations accepted, Elev: 1013ft/309m, Tel: 706-663-4858, Nearest town: Pine Mountain. GPS: 32.874269, -84.698303

67 • C1 | Franklin D. Roosevelt SP - Sassafras Hill TC

Dispersed sites, No water, Vault/pit toilet, Tents only: $10, Hike-in, Location approximate, Stay limit: 14 days, Reservations accepted, Elev: 1155ft/352m, Tel: 706-663-4858, Nearest town: Pine Mountain. GPS: 32.867964, -84.718274

68 • C1 | Franklin D. Roosevelt SP - Sparks Creek TC

Dispersed sites, No water, Vault/pit toilet, Tents only: $10, Hike-in, Location approximate, Stay limit: 14 days, Reservations accepted, Elev: 1057ft/322m, Tel: 706-663-4858, Nearest town: Pine Mountain. GPS: 32.857273, -84.729996

69 • C1 | Franklin D. Roosevelt SP - Whiskey Still TC

Dispersed sites, No water, Vault/pit toilet, Tents only: $10, Hike-in, Stay limit: 14 days, Reservations accepted, Elev: 1021ft/311m,

Tel: 706-663-4858, Nearest town: Pine Mountain. GPS: 32.845954, -84.765032

70 • C2 | Dames Ferry SP

Total sites: 37, RV sites: 37, Elec sites: 37, Central water, RV dump, Tent & RV camping: $35-38, Max Length: 28ft, Reservations accepted, Elev: 507ft/155m, Tel: 478-994-7945, Nearest town: Juliette. GPS: 33.042349, -83.757431

71 • C2 | High Falls SP - Lakeside CG

Total sites: 17, RV sites: 17, Elec sites: 17, Water at site, Flush toilet, Free showers, RV dump, Tent & RV camping: $35, 6 yurts, Stay limit: 14 days, Open all year, Max Length: 25ft, Reservations accepted, Elev: 666ft/203m, Tel: 478-993-3053, Nearest town: Jackson. GPS: 33.182302, -84.017719

72 • C2 | High Falls SP - River CG

Total sites: 89, RV sites: 89, Elec sites: 89, Water at site, Flush toilet, Free showers, RV dump, Tent & RV camping: $35-38, Stay limit: 14 days, Open all year, Max Length: 50ft, Reservations accepted, Elev: 495ft/151m, Tel: 478-993-3053, Nearest town: Jackson. GPS: 33.171329, -84.007709

73 • C2 | Indian Springs SP

Total sites: 60, RV sites: 60, Elec sites: 60, Water at site, Flush toilet, Free showers, RV dump, Tent & RV camping: $32, Also cabins, Stay limit: 14 days, Open all year, Max Length: 60ft, Reservations accepted, Elev: 588ft/179m, Tel: 770-504-2277, Nearest town: Jackson. GPS: 33.251409, -83.938576

74 • C3 | George L Smith II SP

Total sites: 25, RV sites: 25, Elec sites: 25, Water available, Flush toilet, Free showers, RV dump, Tent & RV camping: $33-36, Also cabins, Stay limit: 14 days, Open all year, Max Length: 40ft, Reservations accepted, Elev: 230ft/70m, Tel: 478-763-2759, Nearest town: Twin City. GPS: 32.550219, -82.124983

75 • C3 | George L Smith II SP - Primitive

Total sites: 5, Tents only: $8, Hike-in, Stay limit: 14 days, Open all year, Reservations accepted, Elev: 277ft/84m, Tel: 478-763-2759, Nearest town: Twin City. GPS: 32.562218, -82.120065

76 • C3 | Hamburg SP

Total sites: 30, RV sites: 30, Elec sites: 30, Water at site, Flush toilet, Free showers, RV dump, Tent & RV camping: $28-32, Stay limit: 14 days, Open all year, Max Length: 40ft, Reservations accepted, Elev: 364ft/111m, Tel: 706-456-2602, Nearest town: Mitchell. GPS: 33.208293, -82.789374

77 • C3 | Magnolia Springs SP - Main CG

Total sites: 29, RV sites: 26, Elec sites: 26, Water at site, Flush toilet, Free showers, RV dump, Tents: $20/RVs: $33-36, Also walk-to sites/cabins, Stay limit: 14 days, Open all year, Max Length: 40ft, Reservations accepted, Elev: 233ft/71m, Tel: 478-982-1660, Nearest town: Millen. GPS: 32.883163, -81.952088

78 • D1 | Florence Marina SP

Total sites: 43, RV sites: 43, Elec sites: 43, Water available, Flush toilet, Free showers, RV dump, Tent & RV camping: $32-34, Also cabins, Stay limit: 14 days, Open all year, Max Length: 150ft,

Reservations accepted, Elev: 246ft/75m, Tel: 229-838-6870, Nearest town: Omaha. GPS: 32.093976, -85.044108

79 • D1 | Kolomoki Mounds SP - Main CG

Total sites: 24, RV sites: 24, Elec sites: 24, Water at site, Flush toilet, Free showers, RV dump, Tent & RV camping: $26-30, Stay limit: 14 days, Open all year, Max Length: 79ft, Reservations accepted, Elev: 299ft/91m, Tel: 229-724-2150, Nearest town: Blakely. GPS: 31.469217, -84.931668

80 • D2 | Georgia Veterans Memorial SP - Main CG

Total sites: 77, RV sites: 77, Elec sites: 77, Water at site, Flush toilet, Free showers, RV dump, Tents: $25/RVs: $40, Also cabins, SAM Shortline RR excursion, military museum, Stay limit: 14 days, Open all year, Max Length: 50ft, Reservations accepted, Elev: 292ft/89m, Tel: 229-276-2371, Nearest town: Cordele. GPS: 31.951772, -83.910702

81 • D3 | General Coffee SP - Main CG

Total sites: 50, RV sites: 50, Elec sites: 50, Water available, Flush toilet, Free showers, RV dump, Tent & RV camping: $30-32, Also cabins, Stay limit: 14 days, Open all year, Max Length: 50ft, Reservations accepted, Elev: 199ft/61m, Tel: 912-384-7082, Nearest town: Douglas. GPS: 31.523609, -82.766993

82 • D3 | Jack Hill SP

Total sites: 29, RV sites: 28, Elec sites: 28, Water at site, Flush toilet, Free showers, RV dump, Tents: $22/RVs: $30-35, Also walk-to sites/cabins, 5 Full hookups sites, 1 tent site, Stay limit: 14 days, Open all year, Elev: 184ft/56m, Tel: 912-557-7744, Nearest town: Reidsville. GPS: 32.086314, -82.132967

83 • D3 | Little Ocmulgee SP

Total sites: 54, RV sites: 54, Elec sites: 54, Flush toilet, Free showers, RV dump, Tent & RV camping: $45-55, Also cabins, Stay limit: 14 days, Open all year, Reservations accepted, Elev: 197ft/60m, Tel: 229-868-7474, Nearest town: McRae. GPS: 32.091659, -82.893282

84 • D4 | Fort Mc Allister SP - Backcountry

Total sites: 2, No water, Vault/pit toilet, Tents only: $10, Hike-in, Stay limit: 14 days, Open all year, Reservations accepted, Elev: 6ft/2m, Tel: 912-727-2339, Nearest town: Savannah. GPS: 31.878832, -81.201765

85 • D4 | Fort McAllister SP

Total sites: 65, RV sites: 65, Elec sites: 65, Water available, Flush toilet, Free showers, RV dump, Tent & RV camping: $33-42, Also cabins, Stay limit: 14 days, Open all year, Max Length: 50ft, Reservations accepted, Elev: 66ft/20m, Tel: 912-727-2339, Nearest town: Savannah. GPS: 31.883190, -81.181050

86 • D4 | Skidaway Island SP

Total sites: 87, RV sites: 87, Elec sites: 87, Water at site, Flush toilet, Free showers, RV dump, Tent & RV camping: $45-53, 17 Full hookups sites, Stay limit: 14 days, Open all year, Max Length: 70ft, Reservations accepted, Elev: 46ft/14m, Tel: 912-598-2300, Nearest town: Savannah. GPS: 31.950661, -81.050501

87 • E1 | Seminole SP

Total sites: 50, RV sites: 50, Elec sites: 50, Water at site, Flush toilet, Free showers, RV dump, Tent & RV camping: $32-38, Also cabins, Stay limit: 14 days, Open all year, Max Length: 40ft, Reservations accepted, Elev: 105ft/32m, Tel: 229-861-3137, Nearest town: Donalsonville. GPS: 30.801825, -84.876748

88 • E1 | Seminole SP - Cummings Landing

Total sites: 3, RV sites: 0, Vault/pit toilet, Tents only: $20, Stay limit: 14 days, Open all year, Reservations accepted, Elev: 82ft/25m, Tel: 229-861-3137, Nearest town: Donalsonville. GPS: 30.801409, -84.882549

89 • E1 | Seminole SP - Treehouse

Total sites: 1, No water, Vault/pit toilet, Shelter: $25, Sleeps 15, Stay limit: 14 days, Open all year, Reservations accepted, Elev: 100ft/30m, Tel: 229-861-3137, Nearest town: Donalsonville. GPS: 30.800459, -84.869396

90 • E2 | Reed Bingham SP

Total sites: 46, RV sites: 46, Elec sites: 46, Water at site, Flush toilet, Free showers, RV dump, Tent & RV camping: $30-38, 19 Full hookups sites, Stay limit: 14 days, Open all year, Max Length: 50ft, Reservations accepted, Elev: 223ft/68m, Tel: 229-896-3551, Nearest town: Adel. GPS: 31.165886, -83.538451

91 • E3 | Laura S Walker SP - Main CG

Total sites: 44, RV sites: 44, Elec sites: 44, Water at site, Flush toilet, Free showers, RV dump, Tent & RV camping: $32-36, Stay limit: 14 days, Open all year, Max Length: 40ft, Reservations accepted, Elev: 144ft/44m, Tel: 912-287-4900, Nearest town: Waycross. GPS: 31.142636, -82.214478

92 • E3 | Stephen C. Foster SP

Total sites: 64, RV sites: 64, Elec sites: 64, Water at site, Flush toilet, Free showers, RV dump, Tent & RV camping: $35-37, Also cabins, Stay limit: 14 days, Open all year, Max Length: 50ft, Reservations accepted, Elev: 167ft/51m, Tel: 912-637-5274, Nearest town: Fargo. GPS: 30.821218, -82.364778

93 • E4 | Crooked River SP

Total sites: 62, RV sites: 62, Elec sites: 62, Water at site, Flush toilet, Free showers, RV dump, Tent & RV camping: $34-42, Also cabins, Stay limit: 14 days, Open all year, Max Length: 90ft, Reservations accepted, Elev: 43ft/13m, Tel: 912-882-5256, Nearest town: St. Marys. GPS: 30.842981, -81.551962

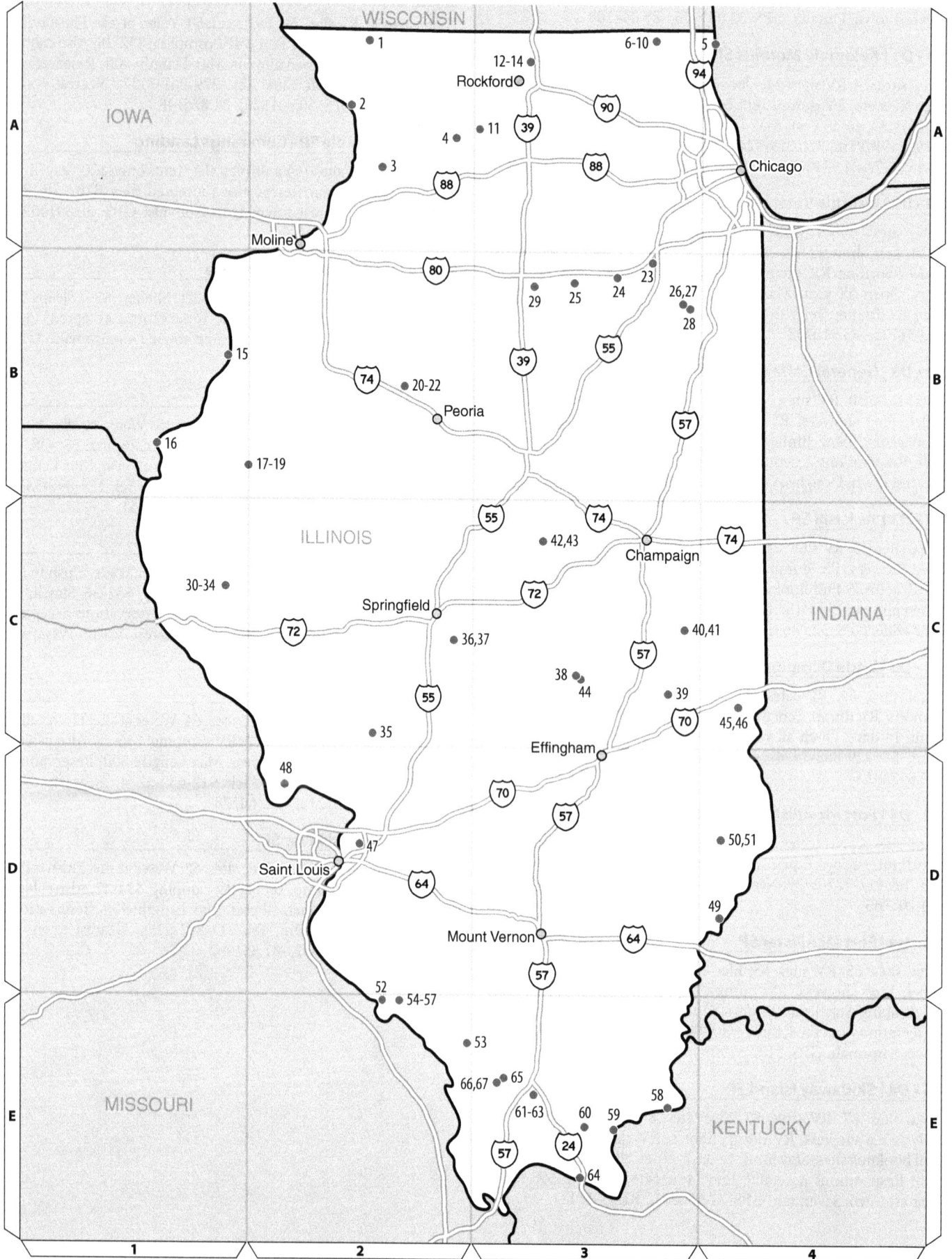

Illinois

WISCONSIN

1

6-10

5

94

12-14

Rockford

IOWA

2

90

A

11

39

4

88

3

Chicago

88

88

80

Moline

23

26,27

80

29 25 24

28

15

74

55

20-22

39

B

Peoria

57

16

17-19

ILLINOIS

55

74

74

42,43

Champaign

30-34

72

INDIANA

Springfield

72

C

72

36,37

40,41

57

38

44

39

35

70

45,46

55

Effingham

48

70

50,51

70

57

47

49

Saint Louis

64

D

Mount Vernon

64

57

52

54-57

53

66,67 65

58

61-63 60 59

MISSOURI

57

24

KENTUCKY

64

E

Map	ID	Map	ID
A2	1-4	C3	38-44
A3	5-14	C4	45-46
B1	15-16	D2	47-48
B2	17-22	D4	49-51
B3	23-29	E2	52-57
C1	30-34	E3	58-67
C2	35-37		

Alphabetical List of Camping Areas

1 • A2 | Apple River Canyon SP - Canyon Ridge

Total sites: 49, RV sites: 49, No toilets, RV dump, Tent & RV camping: $8, Youth group site: $60, Stay limit: 14 days, Open all year, Max Length: 100ft, Reservations accepted, Elev: 873ft/266m, Tel: 815-745-3302, Nearest town: Apple River. GPS: 42.449119, -90.054105

2 • A2 | Mississippi Palisades SP

Total sites: 241, RV sites: 241, Elec sites: 110, Flush toilet, Free showers, RV dump, Tent & RV camping: $18-30, Stay limit: 14 days, Open all year, Max Length: 40ft, Reservations accepted, Elev: 627ft/191m, Tel: 815-273-2731, Nearest town: Savanna. GPS: 42.143726, -90.162798

3 • A2 | Morrison Rockwood SP

Total sites: 92, RV sites: 92, Elec sites: 92, Central water, Flush toilet, Free showers, RV dump, Tent & RV camping: $20-30, Stay limit: 14 days, Open all year, Max Length: 40ft, Reservations accepted, Elev: 774ft/236m, Tel: 815-772-4708, Nearest town: Morrison. GPS: 41.854066, -89.963054

4 • A2 | White Pines Forest SP

Total sites: 106, RV sites: 3, Elec sites: 3, Central water, Flush toilet, Free showers, RV dump, Tents: $10/RVs: $10-30, Stay limit: 14 days, Open all year, Reservations accepted, Elev: 810ft/247m, Tel: 815-946-3717, Nearest town: Mt. Morris. GPS: 41.993493, -89.474923   .

5 • A3 | Adeline Jay Geo-Karis Illinois Beach SP

Total sites: 241, RV sites: 241, Elec sites: 241, Central water, Flush toilet, Free showers, RV dump, Tent & RV camping: $25-35, Open Apr-Dec, Max Length: 62ft, Reservations accepted, Elev: 600ft/183m, Tel: 847-662-4811, Nearest town: Zion. GPS: 42.436869, -87.806779

6 • A3 | Chain O'Lakes SP - Fox Den

Total sites: 45, RV sites: 45, Elec sites: 45, Central water, Flush toilet, Free showers, RV dump, Tent & RV camping: $25-35, Stay limit: 14 days, Open Jan-Oct, Max Length: 40ft, Reservations accepted, Elev: 764ft/233m, Tel: 847-587-5512, Nearest town: Spring Grove. GPS: 42.444414, -88.186042

7 • A3 | Chain O'Lakes SP - Honeysuckle Hollow

Total sites: 106, RV sites: 106, Elec sites: 106, Central water, Flush toilet, Free showers, RV dump, Tent & RV camping: $25-35, Stay limit: 14 days, Open Jan-Oct, Max Length: 40ft, Reservations accepted, Elev: 768ft/234m, Tel: 847-587-5512, Nearest town: Spring Grove. GPS: 42.450486, -88.188048

8 • A3 | Chain O'Lakes SP - Mud Lake East

Total sites: 12, RV sites: 12, Central water, Flush toilet, Free showers, RV dump, Tent & RV camping: $12, Stay limit: 14 days, Open Jan-Oct, Max Length: 30ft, Reservations accepted, Elev: 777ft/237m, Tel: 847-587-5512, Nearest town: Spring Grove. GPS: 42.443583, -88.183207

9 • A3 | Chain O'Lakes SP - Prairie View

Total sites: 39, RV sites: 39, Central water, Flush toilet, Free showers, RV dump, Tent & RV camping: $12, Stay limit: 14 days, Open Jan-Oct, Max Length: 35ft, Reservations accepted, Elev: 755ft/230m, Tel: 847-587-5512, Nearest town: Spring Grove. GPS: 42.443101, -88.188889

10 • A3 | Chain O'Lakes SP - Turner Lake South

Total sites: 36, RV sites: 36, Central water, Flush toilet, Free showers, RV dump, Tent & RV camping: $12, Stay limit: 14 days, Open Jan-Oct, Max Length: 35ft, Reservations accepted, Elev: 753ft/230m, Tel: 847-587-5512, Nearest town: Spring Grove. GPS: 42.445074, -88.189434

11 • A3 | Lowden Memorial SP

Total sites: 126, RV sites: 118, Elec sites: 80, Central water, Flush toilet, Free showers, RV dump, Tents: $10/RVs: $20-30, Also cabins, Stay limit: 14 days, Open all year, Max Length: 40ft, Reservations accepted, Elev: 853ft/260m, Tel: 815-732-6828, Nearest town: Oregon. GPS: 42.034093, -89.327434

12 • A3 | Rock Cut SP - Hickory Hills

Total sites: 58, RV sites: 0, Central water, Flush toilet, Free showers, RV dump, Tents only: $20, No water Nov-Apr, Stay limit: 14 days, Open all year, Reservations accepted, Elev: 869ft/265m, Tel: 815-885-3311, Nearest town: Loves Park. GPS: 42.351223, -88.982475

13 • A3 | Rock Cut SP - Horse Camp

Total sites: 10, RV sites: 10, Flush toilet, Free showers, RV dump, Tent & RV camping: $10, No water Nov-Apr, Stay limit: 14 days, Open all year, Reservations not accepted, Elev: 863ft/263m, Tel: 815-885-3311, Nearest town: Loves Park. GPS: 42.357036, -88.997598

14 • A3 | Rock Cut SP - Plum Grove/White Oak/Prairie View/Staghorn

Total sites: 208, RV sites: 208, Elec sites: 208, Central water, Flush toilet, Free showers, RV dump, Tent & RV camping: $25, No water Nov-Apr, Stay limit: 14 days, Open all year, Max Length: 40ft, Reservations accepted, Elev: 892ft/272m, Tel: 815-885-3311, Nearest town: Loves Park. GPS: 42.355502, -88.983549

15 • B1 | Delabar SP

Total sites: 56, RV sites: 56, Elec sites: 56, Central water, No toilets, No showers, RV dump, Tent & RV camping: $20-30, Group site available, Open all year, Reservations not accepted, Elev: 584ft/178m, Tel: 309-374-2496, Nearest town: Oquawka. GPS: 40.963505, -90.940126

16 • B1 | Nauvoo SP

Total sites: 105, RV sites: 105, Elec sites: 35, Flush toilet, Free showers, RV dump, Tents: $18/RVs: $20-30, Stay limit: 14 days, Open all year, Max Length: 68ft, Reservations accepted, Elev: 640ft/195m, Tel: 217-453-2512, Nearest town: Nauvoo. GPS: 40.543981, -91.380159

17 • B2 | Argyle Lake SP - Big Oaks

Total sites: 42, RV sites: 42, Elec sites: 24, Central water, Flush toilet, Free showers, No RV dump, Tent & RV camping: $8-18, Open all year, Max Length: 42ft, Reservations accepted, Elev: 712ft/217m, Tel: 309-776-3422, Nearest town: Colchester. GPS: 40.452397, -90.782531

18 • B2 | Argyle Lake SP - Twin Oaks

Total sites: 31, RV sites: 0, Central water, Flush toilet, Free showers, No RV dump, Tents only: $8, Open all year, Reservations not accepted, Elev: 709ft/216m, Tel: 309-776-3422, Nearest town: Colchester. GPS: 40.457926, -90.789031

19 • B2 | Argyle Lake SP - Twisted Oaks

Total sites: 86, RV sites: 86, Elec sites: 86, Central water, Flush toilet, Free showers, RV dump, Tent & RV camping: $20-25, Open all year, Max Length: 42ft, Reservations accepted, Elev: 709ft/216m, Tel: 309-776-3422, Nearest town: Colchester. GPS: 40.453547, -90.798553

20 • B2 | Jubilee College SP - Coyote Cove/Possum Bend

Total sites: 57, RV sites: 57, Elec sites: 57, Central water, Flush toilet, Free showers, RV dump, Tents: $20/RVs: $20-30, No water Nov-Apr: $20, Stay limit: 14 days, Open all year, Max Length: 40ft, Reservations accepted, Elev: 669ft/204m, Tel: 309-446-3758, Nearest town: Brimfield. GPS: 40.822127, -89.810779

21 • B2 | Jubilee College SP - Horse Camp

Total sites: 13, RV sites: 13, Central water, Vault/pit toilet, No showers, No RV dump, Tent & RV camping: $12, Stay limit: 14 days, Open all year, Reservations not accepted, Elev: 663ft/202m, Tel: 309-446-3758, Nearest town: Brimfield. GPS: 40.842113, -89.804685

22 • B2 | Jubilee College SP - Woodchuck Ridge

Total sites: 46, RV sites: 46, Elec sites: 46, Central water, Flush toilet, Free showers, RV dump, Tent & RV camping: $20-30, Stay limit: 14 days, Open Apr-Nov, Max Length: 40ft, Reservations accepted, Elev: 659ft/201m, Tel: 309-446-3758, Nearest town: Brimfield. GPS: 40.826439, -89.817604

23 • B3 | Channahon SP

Dispersed sites, Central water, Vault/pit toilet, No showers, No RV dump, Tents only: $6, Walk-to sites, Elev: 515ft/157m, Tel: 815-467-4271, Nearest town: Channahon. GPS: 41.421892, -88.226963

24 • B3 | Gebhard Woods SP

Total sites: 4, RV sites: 0, Central water, Vault/pit toilet, No showers, No RV dump, Tents only: $6, Walk-to sites, Reservations not accepted, Elev: 499ft/152m, Nearest town: Morris. GPS: 41.356818, -88.438358

25 • B3 | Illini SP

Total sites: 75, RV sites: 75, Elec sites: 75, Central water, Flush toilet, Free showers, RV dump, Tents: $10/RVs: $20-30, Open all year, Max Length: 48ft, Reservations accepted, Elev: 532ft/162m, Tel: 815-795-2448, Nearest town: Marseilles. GPS: 41.321503, -88.718633

26 • B3 | Kankakee River SP - Chippewa CG

Total sites: 150, RV sites: 98, Elec sites: 98, Central water, Vault/pit toilet, No showers, RV dump, Tents: $8/RVs: $18, Stay limit: 14 days, Generator hours: 0700-2200, Open all year, Reservations accepted, Elev: 623ft/190m, Tel: 815-933-1383, Nearest town: Bourbonnais. GPS: 41.213126, -88.023861

27 • B3 | Kankakee River SP - Horse Camp

Total sites: 12, RV sites: 12, Central water, Vault/pit toilet, No showers, No RV dump, Tent & RV camping: $18, Stay limit: 14 days, Generator hours: 0700-2200, Open Apr-Oct, Reservations accepted, Elev: 587ft/179m, Tel: 815-933-1383, Nearest town: Bourbonnais. GPS: 41.203243, -88.007699

28 • B3 | Kankakee River SP - Potowatomi CG

Total sites: 110, RV sites: 110, Elec sites: 110, Central water, Flush toilet, Free showers, RV dump, Tent & RV camping: $20-30, Also cabins, Stay limit: 14 days, Generator hours: 0700-2200, Open Apr-Oct, Max Length: 41ft, Reservations accepted, Elev: 636ft/194m, Tel: 815-933-1383, Nearest town: Bourbonnais. GPS: 41.195465, -87.968103

29 • B3 | Starved Rock SP

Total sites: 129, RV sites: 129, Elec sites: 129, Central water, Flush toilet, Free showers, RV dump, Tent & RV camping: $25-35, Also cabins, Stay limit: 14 days, Open all year, Max Length: 45ft, Reservations accepted, Elev: 656ft/200m, Tel: 815-667-4726, Nearest town: Utica. GPS: 41.306773, -88.975146

30 • C1 | Siloam Springs SP - Equestrian

Total sites: 16, RV sites: 16, Elec sites: 8, Central water, No RV dump, Tents: $10/RVs: $20, Stay limit: 14 days, Open all year, Max Length: 45ft, Reservations accepted, Elev: 729ft/222m, Tel: 217-894-6205, Nearest town: Clayton. GPS: 39.901082, -90.923096

31 • C1 | Siloam Springs SP - Hickory Hill

Total sites: 32, RV sites: 32, Elec sites: 32, Central water, Flush toilet, Free showers, RV dump, Tent & RV camping: $20-30, Stay limit: 14 days, Open all year, Max Length: 45ft, Elev: 686ft/209m, Tel: 217-894-6205, Nearest town: Clayton. GPS: 39.886970, -90.942730

32 • C1 | Siloam Springs SP - Oak Ridge

Total sites: 20, RV sites: 20, Elec sites: 9, Central water, Flush toilet, Free showers, RV dump, Tents: $10/RVs: $20-30, Stay limit: 14 days, Open all year, Max Length: 48ft, Elev: 656ft/200m, Tel: 217-894-6205, Nearest town: Clayton. GPS: 39.883758, -90.936889

33 • C1 | Siloam Springs SP - Pine Grove

Total sites: 18, RV sites: 18, Elec sites: 18, Central water, Flush toilet, Free showers, RV dump, Tent & RV camping: $20-30, Stay limit: 14 days, Open all year, Max Length: 36ft, Elev: 660ft/201m, Tel: 217-894-6205, Nearest town: Clayton. GPS: 39.886825, -90.937133

34 • C1 | Siloam Springs SP - Whispering Pines

Total sites: 53, RV sites: 49, Elec sites: 49, Central water, Flush toilet, Free showers, RV dump, Tents: $20/RVs: $20-30, Stay limit: 14 days, Open all year, Max Length: 40ft, Elev: 712ft/217m, Tel: 217-894-6205, Nearest town: Clayton. GPS: 39.888657, -90.935408

35 • C2 | Beaver Dam SP

Total sites: 84, RV sites: 84, Elec sites: 40, Central water, Flush toilet, Free showers, RV dump, Tents: $20/RVs: $20-30, Open all year, Max Length: 53ft, Reservations accepted, Elev: 607ft/185m, Tel: 217-854-8020, Nearest town: Plainview. GPS: 39.215685, -89.976802

36 • C2 | Sangchris Lake SP - Deer Run

Total sites: 130, RV sites: 125, Elec sites: 80, Central water, Flush toilet, Free showers, RV dump, Tents: $8-12/RVs: $20-30, 5 equestrian sites, Stay limit: 14 days, Open Mar-Dec, Max Length: 55ft, Elev: 594ft/181m, Tel: 217-498-9208, Nearest town: Rochester. GPS: 39.653734, -89.469828

37 • C2 | Sangchris Lake SP - Hickory Point

Total sites: 65, RV sites: 55, Elec sites: 55, Flush toilet, Free showers, RV dump, Tents: $8/RVs: $20-30, Stay limit: 14 days, Open Mar-Dec, Max Length: 55ft, Elev: 594ft/181m, Tel: 217-498-9208, Nearest town: Rochester. GPS: 39.643311, -89.460693

38 • C3 | Eagle Creek SP

Total sites: 148, RV sites: 148, Elec sites: 75, Water at site, Flush toilet, Free showers, RV dump, Tents: $6-10/RVs: $20-30, Stay limit: 14 days, Open all year, Max Length: 45ft, Reservations accepted, Elev: 669ft/204m, Tel: 217-756-8260, Nearest town: Findlay. GPS: 39.499272, -88.709506

39 • C3 | Fox Ridge SP

Total sites: 42, RV sites: 42, Elec sites: 42, Central water, Flush toilet, Free showers, RV dump, Tent & RV camping: $20-30, Showers closed Nov-Apr, Stay limit: 14 days, Open all year, Max Length: 40ft, Elev: 725ft/221m, Tel: 217-345-6416, Nearest town: Charleston. GPS: 39.401611, -88.143311

40 • C3 | Walnut Point SP - Fox Squirrel

Total sites: 22, RV sites: 14, Elec sites: 14, Central water, Flush toilet, Free showers, RV dump, Tents: $8/RVs: $20-30, Stay limit: 14 days, Max Length: 40ft, Reservations accepted, Elev: 666ft/203m, Tel: 217-346-3336, Nearest town: Oakland. GPS: 39.698457, -88.039049

41 • C3 | Walnut Point SP - Gray Squirrel

Total sites: 32, RV sites: 20, Elec sites: 20, Central water, Flush toilet, Free showers, RV dump, Tents: $8/RVs: $20-30, Stay limit: 14 days, Max Length: 40ft, Reservations accepted, Elev:

673ft/205m, Tel: 217-346-3336, Nearest town: Oakland. GPS: 39.701422, -88.036044

42 • C3 | Weldon Springs SP - Backpack

Total sites: 6, No water, Vault/pit toilet, Tents only: $8, Walk-to sites, Stay limit: 14 days, Open all year, Reservations accepted, Elev: 725ft/221m, Tel: 217-935-2644, Nearest town: Clinton. GPS: 40.118701, -88.916031

43 • C3 | Weldon Springs SP - Main

Total sites: 75, RV sites: 75, Elec sites: 66, Central water, Flush toilet, Free showers, RV dump, Tents: $8/RVs: $20-30, Stay limit: 14 days, Open all year, Max Length: 63ft, Reservations accepted, Elev: 735ft/224m, Tel: 217-935-2644, Nearest town: Clinton. GPS: 40.121134, -88.926234

44 • C3 | Wolf Creek SP

Total sites: 382, RV sites: 304, Elec sites: 304, Central water, Flush toilet, Free showers, RV dump, Tents: $8/RVs: $20-30, Stay limit: 14 days, Open all year, Max Length: 42ft, Reservations accepted, Elev: 666ft/203m, Tel: 217-459-2831, Nearest town: Windsor. GPS: 39.478002, -88.684118

45 • C4 | Lincoln Trail SP - Lakeside

Total sites: 100, RV sites: 72, Elec sites: 72, Central water, Flush toilet, Free showers, RV dump, Tents: $8/RVs: $20-30, Bathhouse closed Nov-Apr, Stay limit: 14 days, Open all year, Max Length: 35ft, Reservations accepted, Elev: 627ft/191m, Tel: 217-826-2222, Nearest town: Marshall. GPS: 39.340137, -87.715194

46 • C4 | Lincoln Trail SP - Plainview

Total sites: 105, RV sites: 105, Elec sites: 105, Central water, Flush toilet, Free showers, RV dump, Tents: $8/RVs: $20-30, Bathhouse closed Nov-Apr, Stay limit: 14 days, Open all year, Max Length: 40ft, Reservations accepted, Elev: 630ft/192m, Tel: 217-826-2222, Nearest town: Marshall. GPS: 39.338159, -87.709942

47 • D2 | Horseshoe Lake SP

Total sites: 26, RV sites: 26, Central water, No showers, RV dump, Tent & RV camping: $8, Stay limit: 7 days, Open May-Sep, Reservations not accepted, Elev: 430ft/131m, Tel: 618-931-0270, Nearest town: East St. Louis. GPS: 38.698730, -90.066162

48 • D2 | Pere Marquette SP

Total sites: 80, RV sites: 80, Elec sites: 80, Central water, Flush toilet, Free showers, RV dump, Tent & RV camping: $20-30, Also cabins, Stay limit: 14 days, Open all year, Max Length: 60ft, Reservations accepted, Elev: 508ft/155m, Tel: 618-786-3323, Nearest town: Grafton. GPS: 38.969724, -90.537993

49 • D4 | Beall Woods SP

Total sites: 16, RV sites: 16, No toilets, RV dump, Tent & RV camping: $8, Open all year, Reservations not accepted, Elev: 423ft/129m, Tel: 618-298-2442, Nearest town: Mount Carmel. GPS: 38.350995, -87.835759

50 • D4 | Red Hills SP - Family

Total sites: 103, RV sites: 103, Elec sites: 103, Central water, Flush toilet, Free showers, RV dump, Tent & RV camping: $20-30, Stay limit: 14 days, Open all year, Max Length: 50ft, Reservations accepted, Elev: 545ft/166m, Tel: 618-936-2469, Nearest town: Sumner. GPS: 38.724521, -87.834255

51 • D4 | Red Hills SP - Horse Camp

Total sites: 12, RV sites: 12, Vault/pit toilet, Tent & RV camping: $8, Stay limit: 14 days, Open all year, Elev: 512ft/156m, Tel: 618-936-2469, Nearest town: Sumner. GPS: 38.717621, -87.840863

52 • E2 | Fort Kaskaskia SHS

Total sites: 32, RV sites: 32, Elec sites: 32, Central water, Vault/pit toilet, No showers, RV dump, Tents: $8/RVs: $18, Stay limit: 14 days, Open all year, Elev: 554ft/169m, Tel: 618-859-3741, Nearest town: Ellis Grove. GPS: 37.972464, -89.910347

53 • E2 | Lake Murphysboro SP

Total sites: 74, RV sites: 74, Elec sites: 54, Central water, Flush toilet, Free showers, RV dump, Tents: $10/RVs: $20-30, Stay limit: 14 days, Open all year, Max Length: 45ft, Reservations accepted, Elev: 440ft/134m, Tel: 618-684-2867, Nearest town: Murphysboro. GPS: 37.777670, -89.385660

54 • E2 | Randolph County SP - Horse Camp

Total sites: 8, RV sites: 8, Central water, Vault/pit toilet, Tent & RV camping: $20, Stalls, Stay limit: 14 days, Open all year, Max Length: 20ft, Reservations accepted, Elev: 508ft/155m, Tel: 618-826-2706, Nearest town: Chester. GPS: 37.969646, -89.806703

55 • E2 | Randolph County SP - Oak Ridge

Total sites: 40, RV sites: 40, Central water, Vault/pit toilet, Tent & RV camping: $8, Stay limit: 14 days, Open all year, Reservations not accepted, Elev: 515ft/157m, Tel: 618-826-2706, Nearest town: Chester. GPS: 37.973421, -89.803393

56 • E2 | Randolph County SP - Pine Ridge

Total sites: 50, RV sites: 50, Elec sites: 40, Central water, Flush toilet, RV dump, Tent & RV camping: $18, Stay limit: 14 days, Open all year, Max Length: 40ft, Reservations accepted, Elev: 515ft/157m, Tel: 618-826-2706, Nearest town: Chester. GPS: 37.968999, -89.800955

57 • E2 | Randolph County SP - Rolling Hills

Total sites: 40, RV sites: 40, Central water, Vault/pit toilet, Tent & RV camping: $8, Stay limit: 14 days, Open all year, Reservations not accepted, Elev: 512ft/156m, Tel: 618-826-2706, Nearest town: Chester. GPS: 37.982993, -89.802231

58 • E3 | Cave-In-Rock SP

Total sites: 59, RV sites: 34, Elec sites: 34, Central water, Flush toilet, Free showers, RV dump, Tents: $10/RVs: $20-30, Max Length: 60ft, Reservations accepted, Elev: 436ft/133m, Tel: 618-289-4325, Nearest town: Cave-in-Rock. GPS: 37.468750, -88.155762

59 • E3 | Dixon SP - Rauchfuss Hill

Total sites: 15, RV sites: 0, Tents only: $12, Reservations not accepted, Elev: 562ft/171m, Nearest town: Golconda. GPS: 37.375207, -88.484722

60 • E3 | Dixon Springs SP

Total sites: 20, RV sites: 12, Elec sites: 12, Central water, RV dump, Tents: $6/RVs: $18, Open Apr-Dec, Max Length: 40ft,

Reservations accepted, Elev: 503ft/153m, Tel: 618-949-3394, Nearest town: Golconda. GPS: 37.383222, -88.665974

61 • E3 | Ferne Clyffe SP - Deer Ridge

Total sites: 59, RV sites: 59, Elec sites: 59, Central water, Flush toilet, Free showers, RV dump, Tents: $20/RVs: $20-30, Stay limit: 14 days, Open all year, Max Length: 55ft, Reservations accepted, Elev: 722ft/220m, Tel: 618-995-2411, Nearest town: Goreville. GPS: 37.537856, -88.976929

62 • E3 | Ferne Clyffe SP - Horse Camp

Total sites: 6, RV sites: 6, Flush toilet, Free showers, RV dump, Tent & RV camping: $8, Call ahead to have gate unlocked, Stay limit: 14 days, Open all year, Reservations not accepted, Elev: 620ft/189m, Tel: 618-995-2411, Nearest town: Goreville. GPS: 37.529566, -88.984341

63 • E3 | Ferne Clyffe SP - Turkey Ridge

Total sites: 20, RV sites: 0, Central water, Flush toilet, No showers, RV dump, Tents only: $8, Walk-to sites, Stay limit: 14 days, Open all year, Reservations not accepted, Elev: 584ft/178m, Tel: 618-995-2411, Nearest town: Goreville. GPS: 37.532293, -88.982357

64 • E3 | Fort Massac SP

Total sites: 57, RV sites: 50, Elec sites: 50, Central water, Flush toilet, Free showers, RV dump, Tents: $6/RVs: $20-30, Stay limit: 14 days, Open all year, Max Length: 57ft, Reservations accepted, Elev: 344ft/105m, Tel: 618-524-4712, Nearest town: Metropolis. GPS: 37.146702, -88.708252

65 • E3 | Giant City SP - Family CG

Total sites: 99, RV sites: 85, Elec sites: 85, Flush toilet, Free showers, RV dump, Tents: $8/RVs: $20-30, Walk-to sites, Stay limit: 14 days, Open all year, Max Length: 40ft, Elev: 669ft/204m, Tel: 618-457-4836, Nearest town: Makanda. GPS: 37.605463, -89.167904

66 • E3 | Giant City SP - Horse Camp

Total sites: 25, RV sites: 25, Elec sites: 25, Flush toilet, Free showers, RV dump, Tents: $20/RVs: $20-30, Stay limit: 14 days, Open May-Oct, Max Length: 40ft, Elev: 607ft/185m, Tel: 618-457-4836, Nearest town: Makanda. GPS: 37.590121, -89.193904

67 • E3 | Giant City SP - Red Cedar TC

Dispersed sites, No water, Vault/pit toilet, Tents only: $6, Hike-in, 6 mi, Stay limit: 14 days, Elev: 545ft/166m, Tel: 618-457-4836, Nearest town: Makanda. GPS: 37.598915, -89.206881

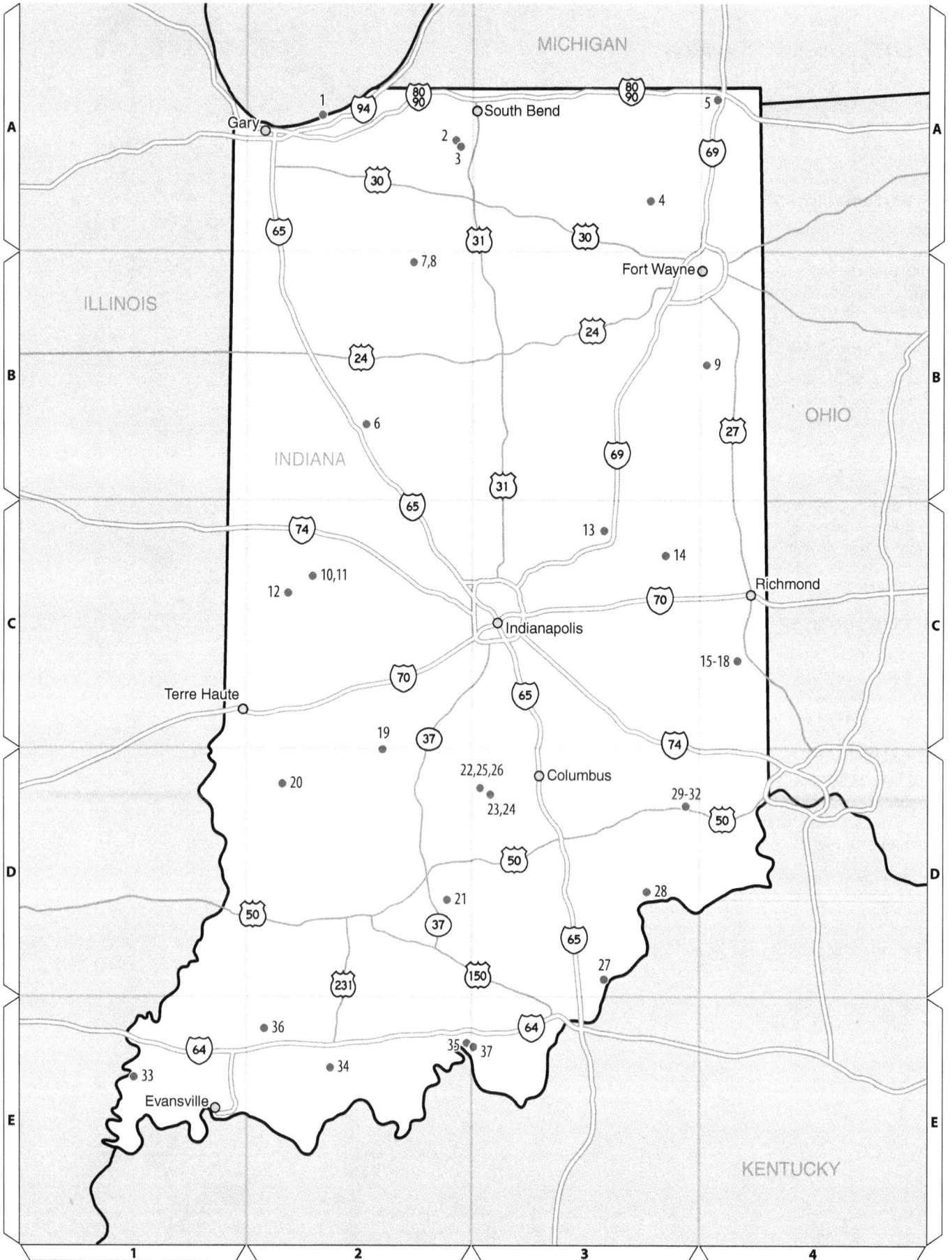

Indiana

MICHIGAN

Gary

South Bend

Fort Wayne

ILLINOIS

INDIANA

OHIO

Richmond

Indianapolis

Terre Haute

Columbus

Evansville

KENTUCKY

Map	ID	Map	ID
A2	1-3	C4	15-18
A3	4	D2	19-21
A4	5	D3	22-32
B2	6-8	E1	33
B4	9	E2	34-36
C2	10-12	E3	37
C3	13-14		

Alphabetical List of Camping Areas

Name	ID	Map
Brown County SP - Buffalo Ridge	22	D3
Brown County SP - Horseman's Electric CG	23	D3
Brown County SP - Horseman's Primitive CG	24	D3
Brown County SP - Raccoon Ridge	25	D3
Brown County SP - Taylor Ridge	26	D3
Chain O'Lakes SP	4	A3
Charlestown SP	27	D3
Clifty Falls SP	28	D3
Harmonie SP	33	E1
Indiana Dunes SP	1	A2
Lincoln SP	34	E2
McCormick's Creek SP	19	D2
Mounds SP	13	C3
O'Bannon Woods SP - Family	35	E2
O'Bannon Woods SP - Horse Camp	37	E3
Ouabache SP	9	B4
Patoka SP	36	E2
Pokagon SP	5	A4
Potato Creek SP - Family CG	2	A2
Potato Creek SP - Horse Camp	3	A2
Prophetstown SP	6	B2
Shades SP	10	C2
Shades SP - Backpack Camp	11	C2
Shakamak SP	20	D2
Spring Mill SP	21	D2
Summit Lake SP	14	C3
Tippecanoe River SP - Family CG	7	B2
Tippecanoe River SP - Horse Camp	8	B2
Turkey Run SP	12	C2
Versailles SP - Campground A	29	D3
Versailles SP - Campground B	30	D3
Versailles SP - Campground C	31	D3
Versailles SP - Horsemens Camp	32	D3
Whitewater Memorial SP - CG A	15	C4
Whitewater Memorial SP - CG B	16	C4
Whitewater Memorial SP - CG C	17	C4
Whitewater Memorial SP - Horseman's Camp	18	C4

1 • A2 | Indiana Dunes SP

Total sites: 140, RV sites: 140, Elec sites: 140, Central water, Flush toilet, Free showers, RV dump, Tent & RV camping: $23-33, One-time entrance fee of $9 ($7 IN residents), Open all year, Max Length: 55ft, Reservations accepted, Elev: 640ft/195m, Tel: 219-926-1952, Nearest town: Chesterton. GPS: 41.658693, -87.054934

2 • A2 | Potato Creek SP - Family CG

Total sites: 287, RV sites: 287, Elec sites: 287, Central water, Flush toilet, Free showers, RV dump, Tent & RV camping: $23-33, One-time entrance fee of $9 ($7 IN residents), Open all year, Max Length: 60ft, Reservations accepted, Elev: 781ft/238m, Tel: 574-656-8186, Nearest town: North Liberty. GPS: 41.559533, -86.365216

3 • A2 | Potato Creek SP - Horse Camp

Total sites: 70, RV sites: 70, Elec sites: 70, Central water, Flush toilet, Free showers, RV dump, Tent & RV camping: $23-33, One-time entrance fee of $9 ($7 IN residents), Open all year, Reservations accepted, Elev: 814ft/248m, Tel: 574-656-8186, Nearest town: North Liberty. GPS: 41.546134, -86.344487

4 • A3 | Chain O'Lakes SP

Total sites: 413, RV sites: 380, Elec sites: 331, Central water, Flush toilet, Free showers, RV dump, Tents: $12/RVs: $16-33, One-time entrance fee of $9 ($7 IN residents), Max Length: 65ft, Reservations accepted, Elev: 1007ft/307m, Tel: 847-587-5512, Nearest town: Albion. GPS: 41.330209, -85.371232

5 • A4 | Pokagon SP

Total sites: 273, RV sites: 273, Elec sites: 200, Central water, Flush toilet, Free showers, RV dump, Tents: $16-22/RVs: $23-33, One-time entrance fee of $9 ($7 IN residents), Open all year, Max Length: 60ft, Reservations accepted, Elev: 1027ft/313m, Tel: 260-833-2012, Nearest town: Angola. GPS: 41.710379, -85.027168

6 • B2 | Prophetstown SP

Total sites: 110, RV sites: 110, Elec sites: 110, Water at site, Flush toilet, Free showers, RV dump, Tent & RV camping: $23-44, 55 Full hookups, One-time entrance fee of $9 ($7 IN residents), Open all year, Max Length: 98ft, Reservations accepted, Elev: 558ft/170m, Tel: 765-567-4919, Nearest town: Battle Ground. GPS: 40.509027, -86.820949

7 • B2 | Tippecanoe River SP - Family CG

Total sites: 112, RV sites: 112, Elec sites: 112, Flush toilet, Free showers, RV dump, Tent & RV camping: $23-33, One-time entrance fee of $9 ($7 IN residents), Open all year, Max Length: 45ft, Reservations accepted, Elev: 742ft/226m, Tel: 574-946-3213, Nearest town: Winamac. GPS: 41.114989, -86.581419

8 • B2 | Tippecanoe River SP - Horse Camp

Total sites: 56, RV sites: 56, Flush toilet, Free showers, RV dump, Tent & RV camping: $13, One-time entrance fee of $9 ($7 IN residents), Open all year, Max Length: 65ft, Reservations accepted, Elev: 728ft/222m, Tel: 574-946-3213, Nearest town: Winamac. GPS: 41.103408, -86.579398

9 • B4 | Ouabache SP

Total sites: 124, RV sites: 124, Elec sites: 124, Central water, Flush toilet, Free showers, RV dump, Tent & RV camping: $23-33, One-time entrance fee of $9 ($7 IN residents), Open all year, Max Length: 45ft, Reservations accepted, Elev: 873ft/266m, Tel: 260-824-0926, Nearest town: Bluffton. GPS: 40.718989, -85.097725

10 • C2 | Shades SP

Total sites: 105, RV sites: 105, Central water, Flush toilet, Free showers, RV dump, Tent & RV camping: $16-22, One-time entrance fee of $9 ($7 IN residents), Open Apr-Oct, Max Length: 52ft, Reservations accepted, Elev: 771ft/235m, Tel: 765-435-2810, Nearest town: Waveland. GPS: 39.937385, -87.087045

11 • C2 | Shades SP - Backpack Camp

Total sites: 7, Central water, Vault/pit toilet, Tents only: $13, Hike-in, 2.5 mi, One-time entrance fee of $9 ($7 IN residents), Open Apr-Oct, Reservations not accepted, Elev: 671ft/205m, Tel: 765-435-2810, Nearest town: Waveland. GPS: 39.945954, -87.096749

12 • C2 | Turkey Run SP

Total sites: 213, RV sites: 213, Elec sites: 213, Central water, Flush toilet, Free showers, RV dump, Tent & RV camping: $23-33, One-time entrance fee of $9 ($7 IN residents), Max Length: 68ft, Reservations accepted, Elev: 682ft/208m, Tel: 765-597-2635, Nearest town: Marshall. GPS: 39.879063, -87.214313

13 • C3 | Mounds SP

Total sites: 75, RV sites: 75, Elec sites: 75, Central water, Flush toilet, Free showers, RV dump, Tent & RV camping: $23-33, One-time entrance fee of $9 ($7 IN residents), Open all year, Max Length: 80ft, Reservations accepted, Elev: 906ft/276m, Tel: 765-642-6627, Nearest town: Anderson. GPS: 40.106587, -85.616056

14 • C3 | Summit Lake SP

Total sites: 120, RV sites: 120, Elec sites: 120, Water at site, Flush toilet, Free showers, RV dump, Tent & RV camping: $23-33, One-time entrance fee of $9 ($7 IN residents), Open all year, Max Length: 100ft, Reservations accepted, Elev: 1089ft/332m, Tel: 765-766-5873, Nearest town: New Castle. GPS: 40.014395, -85.316646

15 • C4 | Whitewater Memorial SP - CG A

Total sites: 74, RV sites: 74, Elec sites: 74, Central water, Flush toilet, Free showers, RV dump, Tent & RV camping: $23-33, One-time entrance fee of $9 ($7 IN residents), Open all year, Max Length: 100ft, Reservations accepted, Elev: 911ft/278m, Tel: 765-458-5565, Nearest town: Liberty. GPS: 39.615815, -84.961631

16 • C4 | Whitewater Memorial SP - CG B

Total sites: 123, RV sites: 123, Elec sites: 82, Central water, Flush toilet, Free showers, RV dump, Tents: $16-22/RVs: $23-33, One-time entrance fee of $9 ($7 IN residents), Open all year, Max Length: 100ft, Reservations accepted, Elev: 927ft/283m, Tel: 765-458-5565, Nearest town: Liberty. GPS: 39.618264, -84.957137

17 • C4 | Whitewater Memorial SP - CG C

Total sites: 66, RV sites: 66, Elec sites: 66, Central water, Flush toilet, Free showers, RV dump, Tent & RV camping: $23-33, One-time entrance fee of $9 ($7 IN residents), Open all year, Max Length: 100ft, Reservations accepted, Elev: 921ft/281m, Tel: 765-458-5565, Nearest town: Liberty. GPS: 39.621085, -84.956134

18 • C4 | Whitewater Memorial SP - Horseman's Camp

Total sites: 37, RV sites: 37, Central water, Vault/pit toilet, No showers, No RV dump, Tent & RV camping: $13, One-time entrance fee of $9 ($7 IN residents), Open all year, Max Length: 75ft, Reservations accepted, Elev: 896ft/273m, Tel: 765-458-5565, Nearest town: Liberty. GPS: 39.624309, -84.955235

19 • D2 | McCormick's Creek SP

Total sites: 221, RV sites: 189, Elec sites: 189, Central water, Flush toilet, Free showers, RV dump, Tents: $12/RVs: $23-33, One-time entrance fee of $9 ($7 IN residents), Max Length: 40ft, Reservations accepted, Elev: 738ft/225m, Tel: 812-829-2235, Nearest town: Spencer. GPS: 39.298327, -86.725678

20 • D2 | Shakamak SP

Total sites: 122, RV sites: 122, Elec sites: 122, Water at site, Flush toilet, Free showers, RV dump, Tents: $23-33/RVs: $23-44, 8 Full hookups, One-time entrance fee of $9 ($7 IN residents), Open all year, Max Length: 117ft, Reservations accepted, Elev: 597ft/182m, Tel: 812-665-2158, Nearest town: Jasonville. GPS: 39.165039, -87.231934

21 • D2 | Spring Mill SP

Total sites: 223, RV sites: 223, Elec sites: 187, Central water, Flush toilet, Free showers, RV dump, Tents: $12/RVs: $23-33, One-time entrance fee of $9 ($7 IN residents), Open all year, Max Length: 109ft, Reservations accepted, Elev: 617ft/188m, Tel: 812-849-4129, Nearest town: Mitchell. GPS: 38.736579, -86.403767

22 • D3 | Brown County SP - Buffalo Ridge

Total sites: 111, RV sites: 111, Elec sites: 111, Central water, Flush toilet, Free showers, RV dump, Tent & RV camping: $16-22, RVs must use West Gate, One-time entrance fee of $9 ($7 IN residents), Open all year, Max Length: 50ft, Reservations accepted, Elev: 1034ft/315m, Tel: 812-988-6406, Nearest town: Nashville. GPS: 39.155302, -86.232512

23 • D3 | Brown County SP - Horseman's Electric CG

Total sites: 118, RV sites: 118, Elec sites: 118, Central water, Flush toilet, Free showers, No RV dump, Tent & RV camping: $26-36, MUST enter off SR 135, One-time entrance fee of $9 ($7 IN residents), Open all year, Max Length: 64ft, Reservations accepted, Elev: 627ft/191m, Tel: 812-988-6406, Nearest town: Nashville. GPS: 39.132169, -86.199643

24 • D3 | Brown County SP - Horseman's Primitive CG

Total sites: 86, RV sites: 86, Central water, Vault/pit toilet, No showers, No RV dump, Tent & RV camping: $19-25, MUST enter off SR 135, One-time entrance fee of $9 ($7 IN residents), Open all year, Max Length: 55ft, Reservations accepted, Elev: 659ft/201m, Tel: 812-988-6406, Nearest town: Nashville. GPS: 39.126387, -86.193221

25 • D3 | Brown County SP - Raccoon Ridge

Total sites: 49, RV sites: 49, Elec sites: 29, Flush toilet, Free showers, RV dump, Tents: $16-22/RVs: $23-33, RVs must use West Gate, One-time entrance fee of $9 ($7 IN residents), Open all year, Max Length: 35ft, Reservations accepted, Elev: 948ft/289m, Tel: 812-988-6406, Nearest town: Nashville. GPS: 39.149729, -86.234049

26 • D3 | Brown County SP - Taylor Ridge

Total sites: 260, RV sites: 260, Elec sites: 260, Flush toilet, Free showers, RV dump, Tent & RV camping: $23-33, RVs must use West Gate, One-time entrance fee of $9 ($7 IN residents), Open all year, Max Length: 60ft, Reservations accepted, Elev: 1020ft/311m, Tel: 812-988-6406, Nearest town: Nashville. GPS: 39.145168, -86.249406

27 • D3 | Charlestown SP

Total sites: 192, RV sites: 192, Elec sites: 192, Water at site, Flush toilet, Free showers, RV dump, Tents: $23-33/RVs: $23-44, Full hookups sites, One-time entrance fee of $9 ($7 IN residents), Open all year, Max Length: 45ft, Reservations accepted, Elev: 636ft/194m, Tel: 812-256-5600, Nearest town: Charlestown. GPS: 38.433627, -85.635191

28 • D3 | Clifty Falls SP

Total sites: 169, RV sites: 169, Elec sites: 106, Central water, Vault/pit toilet, No showers, RV dump, Tents: $16-22/RVs: $23-33, One-time entrance fee of $9 ($7 IN residents), Open all year, Max Length: 90ft, Reservations accepted, Elev: 853ft/260m, Tel: 812-273-8885, Nearest town: Madison. GPS: 38.758901, -85.421645

29 • D3 | Versailles SP - Campground A

Total sites: 96, RV sites: 96, Elec sites: 96, Central water, Flush toilet, Free showers, RV dump, Tent & RV camping: $23-33, One-time entrance fee of $9 ($7 IN residents), Open all year, Max Length: 72ft, Reservations accepted, Elev: 991ft/302m, Tel: 812-689-6424, Nearest town: Versailles. GPS: 39.078372, -85.229091

30 • D3 | Versailles SP - Campground B

Total sites: 84, RV sites: 84, Elec sites: 84, Central water, Flush toilet, Free showers, RV dump, Tent & RV camping: $23-33, One-time entrance fee of $9 ($7 IN residents), Open all year, Max Length: 72ft, Reservations accepted, Elev: 988ft/301m, Tel: 812-689-6424, Nearest town: Versailles. GPS: 39.077111, -85.222725

31 • D3 | Versailles SP - Campground C

Total sites: 45, RV sites: 45, Elec sites: 45, Central water, Flush toilet, Free showers, RV dump, Tent & RV camping: $23-33, One-time entrance fee of $9 ($7 IN residents), Open all year, Max Length: 100ft, Reservations accepted, Elev: 994ft/303m, Tel: 812-689-6424, Nearest town: Versailles. GPS: 39.075365, -85.220696

32 • D3 | Versailles SP - Horsemens Camp

Total sites: 9, RV sites: 9, Elec sites: 9, Tent & RV camping: $26-36, One-time entrance fee of $9 ($7 IN residents), Open all year, Max Length: 78ft, Elev: 976ft/297m, Tel: 812-689-6424, Nearest town: Versailles. GPS: 39.073347, -85.213503

33 • E1 | Harmonie SP

Total sites: 200, RV sites: 200, Elec sites: 200, Central water, Flush toilet, Free showers, RV dump, Tent & RV camping: $23-33, One-time entrance fee of $9 ($7 IN residents), Open all year, Max Length: 65ft, Reservations accepted, Elev: 466ft/142m, Tel: 812-682-4821, Nearest town: New Harmony. GPS: 38.064884, -87.950672

34 • E2 | Lincoln SP

Total sites: 269, RV sites: 238, Elec sites: 150, Central water, Flush toilet, Free showers, RV dump, Tents: $12/RVs: $16-33, Also cabins, One-time entrance fee of $9 ($7 IN residents), Max Length: 40ft, Reservations accepted, Elev: 515ft/157m, Tel: 812-937-4710, Nearest town: Lincoln City. GPS: 38.105965, -86.992274

35 • E2 | O'Bannon Woods SP - Family

Total sites: 306, RV sites: 281, Elec sites: 281, Central water, Flush toilet, Free showers, RV dump, Tents: $12/RVs: $23-33, One-time entrance fee of $9 ($7 IN residents), Max Length: 74ft, Reservations accepted, Elev: 814ft/248m, Tel: 812-738-8232, Nearest town: Corydon. GPS: 38.192524, -86.294765

36 • E2 | Patoka SP

Total sites: 495, RV sites: 450, Elec sites: 450, Water at site, Flush toilet, Free showers, RV dump, Tents: $12/RVs: $23-33, One-time entrance fee of $9 ($7 IN residents), Max Length: 65ft, Reservations accepted, Elev: 624ft/190m, Tel: 812-685-2464, Nearest town: Oakland City. GPS: 38.255560, -87.312500

37 • E3 | O'Bannon Woods SP - Horse Camp

Total sites: 47, RV sites: 47, Central water, Flush toilet, Free showers, RV dump, Tent & RV camping: $19-25, One-time entrance fee of $9 ($7 IN residents), Open all year, Max Length: 50ft, Reservations accepted, Elev: 554ft/169m, Tel: 812-738-8232, Nearest town: Corydon. GPS: 38.184611, -86.282317

Iowa

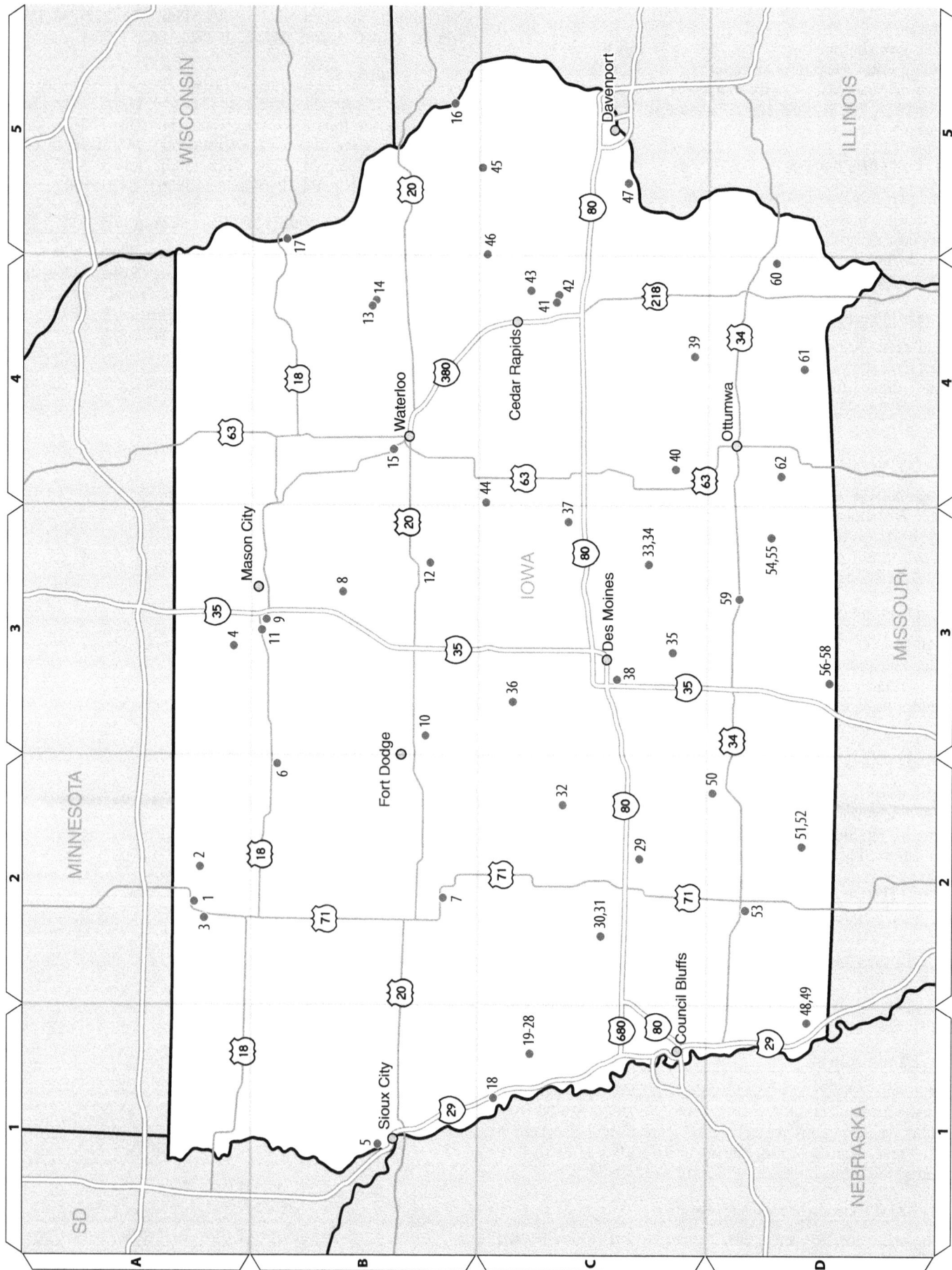

Map	ID	Map	ID
A2	1-3	C2	29-32
A3	4	C3	33-38
B1	5	C4	39-44
B2	6-7	C5	45-47
B3	8-12	D1	48-49
B4	13-15	D2	50-53
B5	16-17	D3	54-59
C1	18-28	D4	60-62

Alphabetical List of Camping Areas

1 • A2 | Elinor Bedell SP

Total sites: 8, RV sites: 8, Elec sites: 8, Water at site, Flush toilet, Free showers, RV dump, Tent & RV camping: $18-26, 8 Full hookups, Open all year, Max Length: 70ft, Reservations accepted, Elev: 1457ft/444m, Tel: 712-337-3211, Nearest town: Spirit Lake. GPS: 43.411909, -95.067645

2 • A2 | Fort Defiance SP

Total sites: 16, RV sites: 16, Elec sites: 8, Central water, Vault/pit toilet, No showers, No RV dump, Tents: $6-10/RVs: $12-16, Open Apr-Oct, Reservations not accepted, Elev: 1457ft/444m, Tel: 712-337-3211, Nearest town: Estherville. GPS: 43.391108, -94.869275

3 • A2 | Gull Point SP

Total sites: 104, RV sites: 104, Elec sites: 52, Central water, Flush toilet, Free showers, RV dump, Tents: $6-10/RVs: $12-16, Restrooms closed off-season, Open all year, Max Length: 45ft, Reservations accepted, Elev: 1414ft/431m, Tel: 712-337-3211, Nearest town: Milford. GPS: 43.370908, -95.166769

4 • A3 | Pilot Knob SP

Total sites: 61, RV sites: 61, Elec sites: 51, Central water, Flush toilet, Free showers, RV dump, Tents: $6-10/RVs: $12-22, Youth group site: $15, 1 Full hookups, Open all year, Reservations accepted, Elev: 1342ft/409m, Tel: 641-581-4835, Nearest town: Forest City. GPS: 43.254023, -93.558178

5 • B1 | Stone SP

Total sites: 30, RV sites: 16, Elec sites: 10, Central water, Flush toilet, Free showers, No RV dump, Tents: $12/RVs: $18, Large RVs not recommended, Open all year, Max Length: 42ft, Reservations accepted, Elev: 1302ft/397m, Tel: 712-255-4698, Nearest town: Sioux City. GPS: 42.559209, -96.466062

6 • B2 | Ambrose A. Call SP

Total sites: 16, RV sites: 16, Elec sites: 13, Central water, Vault/pit toilet, No showers, Tents: $6-10/RVs: $12-16, Open May-Sep, Reservations not accepted, Elev: 1214ft/370m, Tel: 641-581-4835, Nearest town: Algona. GPS: 43.052703, -94.248094

7 • B2 | Black Hawk SP

Total sites: 128, RV sites: 128, Elec sites: 89, Central water, Flush toilet, Free showers, RV dump, Tents: $6-12/RVs: $6-24, Open all year, Max Length: 90ft, Reservations accepted, Elev: 1211ft/369m, Tel: 712-657-8712, Nearest town: Lake View. GPS: 42.292567, -95.017855

8 • B3 | Beeds Lake SP

Total sites: 100, RV sites: 100, Elec sites: 69, Central water, Flush toilet, Free showers, RV dump, Tents: $6-10/RVs: $12-22, Max Length: 80ft, Reservations accepted, Elev: 1142ft/348m, Tel: 641-456-2047, Nearest town: Hampton. GPS: 42.768237, -93.236144

9 • B3 | Clear Lake SP

Total sites: 176, RV sites: 168, Elec sites: 168, Water at site, Flush toilet, Free showers, RV dump, Tents: $6-14/RVs: $12-26, 8 Full hookups, Open all year, Max Length: 109ft, Reservations accepted, Elev: 1234ft/376m, Tel: 641-357-4212, Nearest town: Clear Lake. GPS: 43.109737, -93.396301

10 • B3 | Dolliver Memorial SP

Total sites: 22, RV sites: 22, Elec sites: 22, Central water, Flush toilet, Free showers, RV dump, Tents: $6-16/RVs: $12-16, Open all year, Max Length: 66ft, Reservations accepted, Elev: 942ft/287m, Tel: 515-359-2539, Nearest town: Otho. GPS: 42.391549, -94.079498

11 • B3 | McIntosh Woods SP

Total sites: 49, RV sites: 49, Elec sites: 45, Central water, Flush toilet, Free showers, RV dump, Tents: $6-12/RVs: $12-18, Open all year, Max Length: 82ft, Reservations accepted, Elev: 1263ft/385m, Tel: 641-829-3847, Nearest town: Ventura. GPS: 43.125467, -93.457669

12 • B3 | Pine Lake SP

Total sites: 75, RV sites: 67, Elec sites: 67, Water at site, Flush toilet, Free showers, RV dump, Tents: $6-12/RVs: $12-24, Also cabins, 3 Full hookups, Youth group site: $20, Max Length: 105ft, Reservations accepted, Elev: 1040ft/317m, Tel: 641-858-5832, Nearest town: Eldora. GPS: 42.376197, -93.068309

13 • B4 | Backbone SP - Six Pine CG

Total sites: 27, RV sites: 27, Water available, Vault/pit toilet, No showers, No RV dump, Tents: $6-14/RVs: $6-26, Open all year, Reservations accepted, Elev: 1119ft/341m, Tel: 563-924-2000, Nearest town: Strawberry Point. GPS: 42.612374, -91.567478

14 • B4 | Backbone SP - South Lake CG

Total sites: 98, RV sites: 98, Water available, Flush toilet, Free showers, RV dump, Tents: $6-14/RVs: $6-26, Also cabins, Open all year, Reservations accepted, Elev: 1106ft/337m, Tel: 563-924-2000, Nearest town: Strawberry Point. GPS: 42.602385, -91.541880

15 • B4 | George Wyth SP

Total sites: 69, RV sites: 60, Elec sites: 47, Central water, Flush toilet, Free showers, RV dump, Tents: $6-12/RVs: $6-18, Open all year, Max Length: 60ft, Reservations accepted, Elev: 882ft/269m, Tel: 319-232-5505, Nearest town: Cedar Falls. GPS: 42.532437, -92.405056

16 • B5 | Bellevue SP - Dyas Unit

Total sites: 44, RV sites: 44, Elec sites: 31, Central water, Flush toilet, Free showers, RV dump, Tents: $6-12/RVs: $12-24, Also walk-to sites, Max Length: 50ft, Reservations accepted, Elev: 863ft/263m, Tel: 563-872-4019, Nearest town: Bellevue. GPS: 42.225372, -90.406917

17 • B5 | Pikes Peak SP

Total sites: 67, RV sites: 65, Elec sites: 50, Water at site, Flush toilet, Free showers, RV dump, Tents: $6-14/RVs: $12-26, 2 youth group sites: $20, I Full hookups, Open all year, Max Length: 65ft, Reservations accepted, Elev: 1132ft/345m, Tel: 563-873-2341, Nearest town: McGregor. GPS: 42.994866, -91.166102

18 • C1 | Lewis and Clark SP

Total sites: 77, RV sites: 77, Elec sites: 77, Water at site, Flush toilet, Free showers, RV dump, Tents: $12-20/RVs: $12-26, 13 Full hookups, Youth group site: $15, Open all year, Max Length: 65ft, Reservations accepted, Elev: 1040ft/317m, Tel: 712-423-2829, Nearest town: Onawa. GPS: 42.046976, -96.162282

19 • C1 | Preparation Canyon SP - TC 1

Dispersed sites, No water, Tents only: $9, Hike-in, Reservations not accepted, Elev: 1106ft/337m, Tel: 712-456-2924, Nearest town: Pisgah. GPS: 41.889455, -95.899365

20 • C1 | Preparation Canyon SP - TC 10

Dispersed sites, No water, Tents only: $9, Hike-in, Reservations not accepted, Elev: 1232ft/376m, Tel: 712-456-2924, Nearest town: Pisgah. GPS: 41.893808, -95.915312

21 • C1 | Preparation Canyon SP - TC 2

Dispersed sites, No water, Tents only: $9, Hike-in, Reservations not accepted, Elev: 1109ft/338m, Tel: 712-456-2924, Nearest town: Pisgah. GPS: 41.890792, -95.899301

22 • C1 | Preparation Canyon SP - TC 3

Dispersed sites, No water, Tents only: $9, Hike-in, Reservations not accepted, Elev: 1197ft/365m, Tel: 712-456-2924, Nearest town: Pisgah. GPS: 41.894657, -95.897564

23 • C1 | Preparation Canyon SP - TC 4

Dispersed sites, No water, Tents only: $9, Hike-in, Reservations not accepted, Elev: 1140ft/347m, Tel: 712-456-2924, Nearest town: Pisgah. GPS: 41.895716, -95.899523

24 • C1 | Preparation Canyon SP - TC 5

Dispersed sites, No water, Tents only: $9, Hike-in, Reservations not accepted, Elev: 1129ft/344m, Tel: 712-456-2924, Nearest town: Pisgah. GPS: 41.893909, -95.900759

25 • C1 | Preparation Canyon SP - TC 6

Dispersed sites, No water, Tents only: $9, Hike-in, Reservations not accepted, Elev: 1107ft/337m, Tel: 712-456-2924, Nearest town: Pisgah. GPS: 41.893147, -95.899802

26 • C1 | Preparation Canyon SP - TC 7

Dispersed sites, No water, Tents only: $9, Hike-in, Reservations not accepted, Elev: 1114ft/340m, Tel: 712-456-2924, Nearest town: Pisgah. GPS: 41.891548, -95.900053

27 • C1 | Preparation Canyon SP - TC 8

Dispersed sites, No water, Tents only: $9, Hike-in, Reservations not accepted, Elev: 1164ft/355m, Tel: 712-456-2924, Nearest town: Pisgah. GPS: 41.890442, -95.903291

28 • C1 | Preparation Canyon SP - TC 9

Dispersed sites, No water, Tents only: $9, Hike-in, Reservations not accepted, Elev: 1203ft/367m, Tel: 712-456-2924, Nearest town: Pisgah. GPS: 41.893369, -95.914832

29 • C2 | Lake Anita SP

Total sites: 152, RV sites: 152, Elec sites: 92, Water at site, Flush toilet, Free showers, RV dump, Tents: $6-14/RVs: $12-26, 40 Full hookups, Youth group site: $15, Max Length: 70ft, Reservations accepted, Elev: 1326ft/404m, Tel: 712-762-3564, Nearest town: Anita. GPS: 41.430706, -94.773055

30 • C2 | Prairie Rose SP - East

Total sites: 61, RV sites: 61, Elec sites: 61, Water at site, Flush toilet, Free showers, RV dump, Tents: $12-20/RVs: $12-26, 8 Full hookups, Max Length: 60ft, Reservations accepted, Elev: 1257ft/383m, Tel: 712-773-2701, Nearest town: Harlan. GPS: 41.599829, -95.218224

31 • C2 | Prairie Rose SP - West

Total sites: 34, RV sites: 34, Elec sites: 16, Central water, Flush toilet, Free showers, RV dump, Tents: $6-14/RVs: $12-20, Youth group site: $20, Max Length: 67ft, Reservations accepted, Elev: 1295ft/395m, Tel: 712-773-2701, Nearest town: Harlan. GPS: 41.599056, -95.224324

32 • C2 | Springbrook SP

Total sites: 116, RV sites: 91, Elec sites: 73, Central water, Flush toilet, Free showers, RV dump, Tents: $6-12/RVs: $12-18, Also cabins, Reservations accepted, Elev: 1079ft/329m, Tel: 641-747-3591, Nearest town: Guthrie Center. GPS: 41.773883, -94.467248

33 • C3 | Elk Rock SP - Equestrian

Total sites: 57, RV sites: 57, Elec sites: 42, Central water, Flush toilet, Free showers, RV dump, Tent & RV camping: $10-20, Open all year, Max Length: 75ft, Reservations accepted, Elev: 827ft/252m, Tel: 641-842-6008, Nearest town: Knoxville. GPS: 41.400276, -93.084294

34 • C3 | Elk Rock SP - Family

Total sites: 30, RV sites: 30, Elec sites: 21, Central water, Flush toilet, Free showers, RV dump, Tents: $6-12/RVs: $6-18, Open all year, Max Length: 80ft, Reservations accepted, Elev: 814ft/248m, Tel: 641-842-6008, Nearest town: Knoxville. GPS: 41.402324, -93.092221

35 • C3 | Lake Ahquabi SP

Total sites: 104, RV sites: 104, Elec sites: 75, Central water, Flush toilet, Free showers, RV dump, Tents: $6-14/RVs: $12-20, Also group sites & cabins, Youth group site: $25, Max Length: 60ft, Reservations accepted, Elev: 922ft/281m, Tel: 515-961-7101, Nearest town: Indianola. GPS: 41.295817, -93.591792

36 • C3 | Ledges SP

Total sites: 94, RV sites: 82, Elec sites: 69, Central water, Flush toilet, Free showers, RV dump, Tents: $6-14/RVs: $12-26, 16 Full hookups, Open all year, Max Length: 138ft, Reservations accepted, Elev: 1056ft/322m, Tel: 515-432-1852, Nearest town: Boone. GPS: 41.996308, -93.874518

37 • C3 | Rock Creek SP

Total sites: 171, RV sites: 102, Elec sites: 102, Central water, Flush toilet, Free showers, RV dump, Tents: $6-14/RVs: $12-20, 2 youth group sites: $20, Open all year, Max Length: 50ft, Reservations accepted, Elev: 919ft/280m, Tel: 641-236-3722, Nearest town: Kellogg. GPS: 41.756888, -92.837203

38 • C3 | Walnut Woods SP

Total sites: 21, RV sites: 21, Elec sites: 21, Water at site, Flush toilet, No showers, RV dump, Tents: $12-20/RVs: $12-26, 8 Full hookups, Youth group site: $25, Open all year, Max Length: 69ft, Reservations accepted, Elev: 873ft/266m, Tel: 515-285-4502, Nearest town: West Des Moines. GPS: 41.542219, -93.740216

39 • C4 | Lake Darling SP

Total sites: 80, RV sites: 80, Elec sites: 80, Water at site, Flush toilet, Free showers, RV dump, Tents: $6-14/RVs: $12-26, Also cabins, 15 Full hookups, Max Length: 140ft, Reservations accepted, Elev: 709ft/216m, Tel: 319-694-2323, Nearest town: Brighton. GPS: 41.188898, -91.898894

40 • C4 | Lake Keomah SP

Total sites: 65, RV sites: 51, Elec sites: 51, Central water, Flush toilet, Free showers, RV dump, Tents: $6-10/RVs: $12-16, Open all year, Max Length: 39ft, Reservations accepted, Elev: 824ft/251m, Tel: 641-673-6975, Nearest town: Oskaloosa. GPS: 41.284204, -92.541351

41 • C4 | Lake Macbride SP - North

Total sites: 43, RV sites: 43, Elec sites: 43, Water at site, Flush toilet, Free showers, RV dump, Tent & RV camping: $12-26, 10 Full hookups, Open May-Oct, Reservations accepted, Elev: 833ft/254m, Tel: 319-624-2200, Nearest town: Solon. GPS: 41.798713, -91.573198

42 • C4 | Lake Macbride SP - South

Total sites: 56, RV sites: 56, Central water, Vault/pit toilet, No showers, No RV dump, Tent & RV camping: $6-12, Open all year, Elev: 787ft/240m, Tel: 319-624-2200, Nearest town: Solon. GPS: 41.794087, -91.535603

43 • C4 | Palisades Kepler SP

Total sites: 44, RV sites: 41, Elec sites: 31, Water at site, Flush toilet, Free showers, RV dump, Tents: $6-20/RVs: $12-26, Youth group site: $20, 1 Full hookups, Open all year, Reservations accepted, Elev: 889ft/271m, Tel: 319-895-6039, Nearest town: Mount Vernon. GPS: 41.909151, -91.508686

44 • C4 | Union Grove SP

Total sites: 25, RV sites: 25, Elec sites: 11, Water at site, Vault/pit toilet, No showers, No RV dump, Tents: $6-12/RVs: $18-24, 9 Full hookups, Max Length: 40ft, Reservations accepted, Elev: 1020ft/311m, Tel: 641-473-2556, Nearest town: Gladbrook. GPS: 42.124742, -92.724774

45 • C5 | Maquoketa Caves SP

Total sites: 30, RV sites: 24, Elec sites: 24, Central water, Flush toilet, Free showers, RV dump, Tents: $6-14/RVs: $12-20, Also walk-to & group sites, 6 walk-to sites, 2 youth group sites: $25, Open all year, Max Length: 68ft, Reservations accepted, Elev: 932ft/284m, Tel: 563-652-5833, Nearest town: Maquoketa. GPS: 42.119432, -90.779016

46 • C5 | Wapsipinicon SP

Total sites: 26, RV sites: 20, Elec sites: 13, Central water, Flush toilet, Free showers, RV dump, Tents: $6-10/RVs: $12-22, 1 Full hookups, Open all year, Max Length: 60ft, Reservations accepted, Elev: 906ft/276m, Tel: 319-462-2761, Nearest town: Anamosa. GPS: 42.096321, -91.287753

47 • C5 | Wildcat Den SP

Total sites: 20, RV sites: 20, Central water, Vault/pit toilet, No showers, No RV dump, Tent & RV camping: $6-10, Youth group site: $25, Open all year, Max Length: 98ft, Reservations accepted, Elev: 755ft/230m, Tel: 563-263-4337, Nearest town: Muscatine,. GPS: 41.468717, -90.885635

48 • D1 | Waubonsie SP - Equestrian CG

Total sites: 36, RV sites: 36, Central water, Vault/pit toilet, No showers, No RV dump, Tent & RV camping: $10-13, Open all year, Max Length: 79ft, Reservations accepted, Elev: 1207ft/368m, Tel: 712-382-2786, Nearest town: Hamburg. GPS: 40.683626, -95.679438

49 • D1 | Waubonsie SP - Main CG

Total sites: 42, RV sites: 34, Elec sites: 25, Central water, Flush toilet, Free showers, RV dump, Tents: $6-12/RVs: $12-18, Also cabins, Open all year, Max Length: 75ft, Reservations accepted, Elev: 1191ft/363m, Tel: 712-382-2786, Nearest town: Hamburg. GPS: 40.673122, -95.687891

50 • D2 | Green Valley SP

Total sites: 80, RV sites: 63, Elec sites: 63, Water at site, Flush toilet, Free showers, RV dump, Tents: $6-14/RVs: $12-26, Also group sites & cabins, 15 Full hookups, Yough group site: $20, Open all year, Max Length: 97ft, Reservations accepted, Elev: 1299ft/396m, Tel: 641-782-5131, Nearest town: Creston. GPS: 41.114502, -94.383057

51 • D2 | Lake of Three Fires SP - Equestrian

Total sites: 25, RV sites: 25, Elec sites: 8, Central water, Flush toilet, Free showers, RV dump, Tents: $10-16/RVs: $16-22, Max Length: 68ft, Reservations accepted, Elev: 1212ft/369m, Tel: 712-523-2700, Nearest town: Bedford. GPS: 40.715704, -94.683644

52 • D2 | Lake of Three Fires SP - Main

Total sites: 96, RV sites: 96, Elec sites: 60, Central water, Flush toilet, Free showers, RV dump, Tents: $6-12/RVs: $12-18, Max Length: 126ft, Reservations accepted, Elev: 1217ft/371m, Tel: 712-523-2700, Nearest town: Bedford. GPS: 40.715348, -94.685633

53 • D2 | Viking Lake SP

Total sites: 120, RV sites: 120, Elec sites: 90, Water at site, Flush toilet, Free showers, RV dump, Tents: $6-14/RVs: $12-26, 22 Full hookups, Youth group site: $20, Max Length: 79ft, Reservations

accepted, Elev: 1158ft/353m, Tel: 712-829-2235, Nearest town: Stanton. GPS: 40.963989, -95.043795

54 • D3 | Honey Creek SP - North

Total sites: 91, RV sites: 91, Elec sites: 49, Water at site, Flush toilet, Free showers, RV dump, Tents: $6-10/RVs: $12-22, Also cabins, 28 Full hookups, Open all year, Max Length: 90ft, Reservations accepted, Elev: 985ft/300m, Tel: 641-724-3739, Nearest town: Moravia. GPS: 40.861294, -92.934337

55 • D3 | Honey Creek SP - South

Total sites: 57, RV sites: 57, Elec sites: 54, Water at site, Flush toilet, Free showers, RV dump, Tents: $6-10/RVs: $12-16, Open all year, Max Length: 35ft, Reservations accepted, Elev: 977ft/298m, Tel: 641-724-3739, Nearest town: Moravia. GPS: 40.858435, -92.933894

56 • D3 | Nine Eagles SP - Equestrian

Total sites: 7, RV sites: 7, Central water, Flush toilet, No showers, RV dump, Tent & RV camping: $10-14, Open all year, Max Length: 72ft, Reservations accepted, Elev: 1091ft/333m, Tel: 641-442-2855, Nearest town: Davis City. GPS: 40.603996, -93.754284

57 • D3 | Nine Eagles SP - Modern

Total sites: 28, RV sites: 28, Elec sites: 28, Central water, Flush toilet, Free showers, RV dump, Tent & RV camping: $12-16, Youth group site: $15, Open all year, Max Length: 100ft, Reservations accepted, Elev: 1086ft/331m, Tel: 641-442-2855, Nearest town: Davis City. GPS: 40.595498, -93.755041

58 • D3 | Nine Eagles SP - Primitive

Total sites: 27, RV sites: 27, Central water, Flush toilet, Free showers, RV dump, Tent & RV camping: $6-10, Open all year, Max Length: 30ft, Reservations accepted, Elev: 1053ft/321m, Tel: 641-442-2855, Nearest town: Davis City. GPS: 40.595906, -93.762805

59 • D3 | Red Haw SP

Total sites: 76, RV sites: 59, Elec sites: 64, Central water, Flush toilet, Free showers, RV dump, Tents: $6-10/RVs: $12-16, Open all year, Max Length: 60ft, Reservations accepted, Elev: 1020ft/311m, Tel: 641-774-5632, Nearest town: Chariton. GPS: 40.997787, -93.280087

60 • D4 | Geode SP

Total sites: 90, RV sites: 66, Elec sites: 66, Central water, Flush toilet, Free showers, RV dump, Tents: $6-12/RVs: $12-24, 14 Full hookups, Open all year, Reservations accepted, Elev: 709ft/216m, Tel: 319-392-4601, Nearest town: Danville. GPS: 40.824022, -91.382565

61 • D4 | Lacey-Keosauqua SP

Total sites: 64, RV sites: 64, Elec sites: 51, Water at site, Flush toilet, Free showers, RV dump, Tents: $6-12/RVs: $12-24, Also cabins, 13 Full hookups, Max Length: 134ft, Reservations accepted, Elev: 751ft/229m, Tel: 319-293-3502, Nearest town: Keosauqua. GPS: 40.708479, -91.979838

62 • D4 | Lake Wapello SP

Total sites: 72, RV sites: 49, Elec sites: 49, Water at site, Flush toilet, Free showers, RV dump, Tents: $6-12/RVs: $12-24, Also cabins, 15 Full hookups, Reservations accepted, Elev: 833ft/254m, Tel: 641-722-3371, Nearest town: Drakesville. GPS: 40.817800, -92.588708

Kentucky

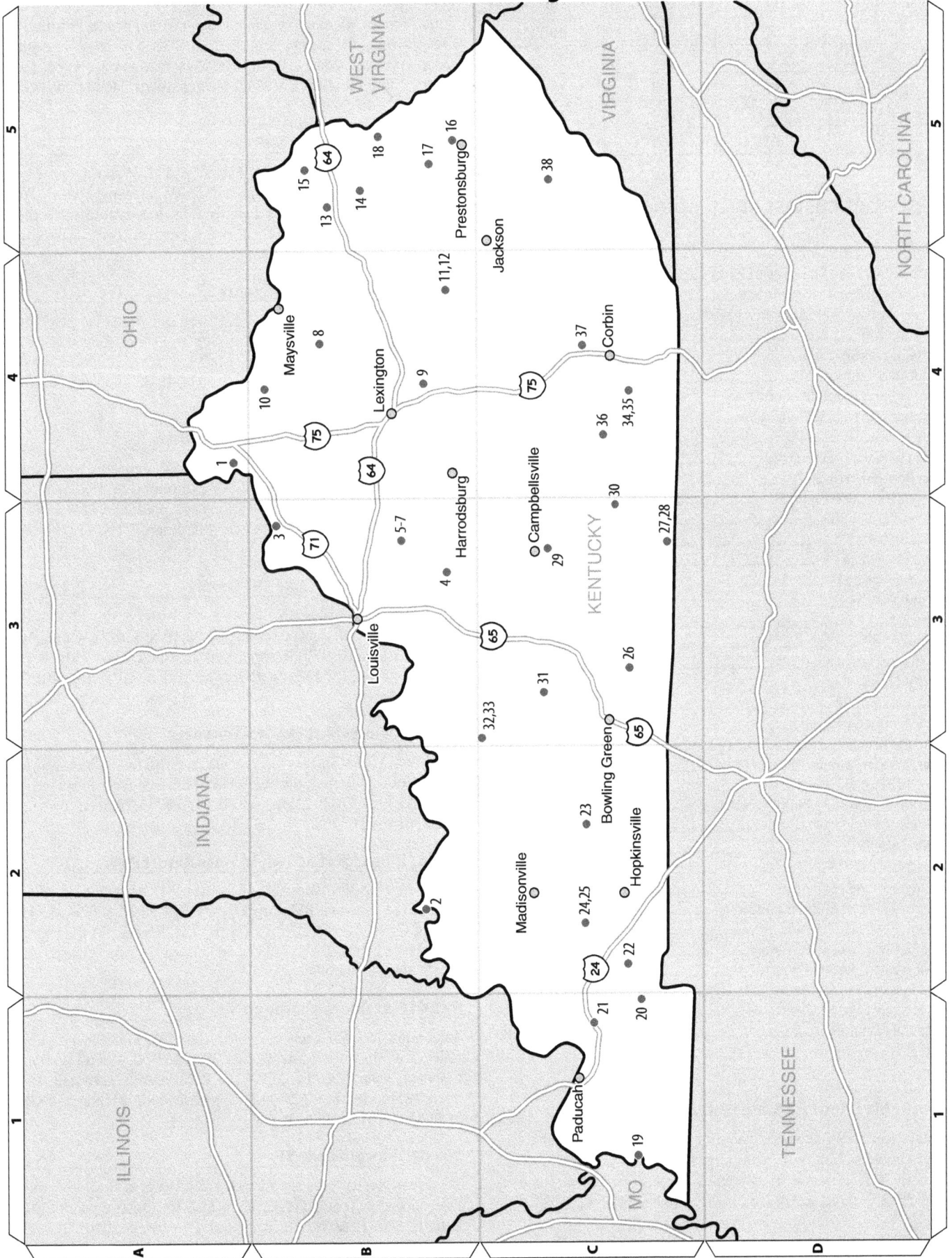

Map	ID	Map	ID
A4	1	C1	19-21
B2	2	C2	22-25
B3	3-7	C3	26-33
B4	8-12	C4	34-37
B5	13-18	C5	38

Alphabetical List of Camping Areas

1 • A4 | Big Bone Lick State Historic Site

Total sites: 62, RV sites: 62, Elec sites: 62, Water at site, Flush toilet, Free showers, Tent & RV camping: $25-35, Open Mar-Nov, Max Length: 47ft, Reservations accepted, Elev: 636ft/194m, Tel: 859-384-3522, Nearest town: Union. GPS: 38.882244, -84.745335

2 • B2 | John J. Audubon SP

Total sites: 87, RV sites: 70, Elec sites: 66, Water at site, Flush toilet, Free showers, RV dump, Tents: $16-20/RVs: $19-29, Also cabins, Open Apr-Nov, Max Length: 63ft, Reservations accepted, Elev: 476ft/145m, Tel: 270-826-2247, Nearest town: Henderson. GPS: 37.879681, -87.563533

3 • B3 | General Butler SRP

Total sites: 111, RV sites: 111, Elec sites: 111, Water at site, Flush toilet, Free showers, RV dump, Tent & RV camping: $32-47, Also cabins, Open all year, Max Length: 60ft, Reservations accepted, Elev: 508ft/155m, Tel: 502-732-4384, Nearest town: Carrollton. GPS: 38.670042, -85.150589

4 • B3 | My Old Kentucky Home SP

Total sites: 39, RV sites: 39, Elec sites: 39, Water at site, Flush toilet, Free showers, RV dump, Tents: $16-20/RVs: $24-37, 5 Full hookups, Open Apr-Oct, Max Length: 55ft, Reservations accepted, Elev: 679ft/207m, Tel: 502-348-3502, Nearest town: Bardstown. GPS: 37.798645, -85.457674

5 • B3 | Taylorsville Lake SP - Equestrian

Total sites: 10, RV sites: 10, Elec sites: 10, Water at site, Flush toilet, Free showers, RV dump, Tent & RV camping: $28-35, Open Apr-Dec, Max Length: 88ft, Reservations accepted, Elev: 746ft/227m, Tel: 502-477-8713, Nearest town: Mt. Eden. GPS: 38.032616, -85.257519

6 • B3 | Taylorsville Lake SP - Family

Total sites: 45, RV sites: 45, Elec sites: 45, Water at site, Flush toilet, Free showers, RV dump, Tents: $22-32/RVs: $26-32, Open Apr-Dec, Max Length: 67ft, Reservations accepted, Elev: 750ft/229m, Tel: 502-477-8713, Nearest town: Mt. Eden. GPS: 38.030125, -85.259588

7 • B3 | Taylorsville Lake SP - Tent Area

Total sites: 15, RV sites: 0, Central water, Flush toilet, Free showers, No RV dump, Tents only: $19-24, Open Apr-Dec, Reservations accepted, Elev: 741ft/226m, Tel: 502-477-8713, Nearest town: Mt. Eden. GPS: 38.032756, -85.255596

8 • B4 | Blue Licks Battlefield State Resort Park

Total sites: 51, RV sites: 51, Elec sites: 51, Water at site, Flush toilet, Free showers, RV dump, Tents: $15-25/RVs: $20-35, Also cabins, Open Apr-Oct, Max Length: 51ft, Reservations accepted, Elev: 689ft/210m, Tel: 859-289-5507, Nearest town: Carlisle. GPS: 38.427809, -83.993594

9 • B4 | Fort Boonesborough SP

Total sites: 167, RV sites: 167, Elec sites: 167, Water at site, Flush toilet, Free showers, Tents: $17-21/RVs: $31-40, 18 Full hookups, Open all year, Max Length: 81ft, Reservations accepted, Elev: 607ft/185m, Tel: 859-527-3131, Nearest town: Richmond. GPS: 37.900391, -84.267090

10 • B4 | Kincaid Lake SP

Total sites: 84, RV sites: 84, Elec sites: 84, Water at site, Flush toilet, Free showers, Tents: $19-26/RVs: $22-30, Open Apr-Oct, Max Length: 67ft, Reservations accepted, Elev: 666ft/203m, Tel: 859-654-3531, Nearest town: Falmouth. GPS: 38.721581, -84.277475

11 • B4 | Natural Bridge SRP - Middle Fork

Total sites: 46, RV sites: 46, Elec sites: 35, Water at site, Flush toilet, Free showers, RV dump, Tents: $18-24/RVs: $29-37, Also cabins, Open Mar-Nov, Max Length: 58ft, Reservations accepted, Elev: 909ft/277m, Tel: 606-663-2214, Nearest town: Slade. GPS: 37.767562, -83.675188

12 • B4 | Natural Bridge SRP - Whittleton

Total sites: 37, RV sites: 37, Elec sites: 18, Water at site, Flush toilet, Free showers, RV dump, Tents: $17-22/RVs: $26-30, Also cabins, Open Mar-Nov, Max Length: 40ft, Reservations accepted, Elev: 830ft/253m, Tel: 606-663-2214, Nearest town: Slade. GPS: 37.780368, -83.673804

13 • B5 | Carter Caves SP

Total sites: 129, RV sites: 98, Elec sites: 98, Water at site, Flush toilet, Free showers, RV dump, Tents: $18-25/RVs: $20-35, Also cabins, 8 Full hookups equestrian sites ($35-$42) open all year, Open Mar-Nov, Max Length: 64ft, Reservations accepted, Elev: 1030ft/314m, Tel: 606-286-4411, Nearest town: Olive Hill. GPS: 38.374708, -83.127536

14 • B5 | Grayson Lake SP

Total sites: 71, RV sites: 71, Elec sites: 71, Water at site, Flush toilet, Free showers, RV dump, Tent & RV camping: $25-32, Open Apr-Oct, Max Length: 112ft, Reservations accepted, Elev: 735ft/224m, Tel: 606-474-9727, Nearest town: Olive Hill. GPS: 38.200299, -83.026132

15 • B5 | Greenbo Lake SRP

Total sites: 101, RV sites: 57, Elec sites: 57, Water at site, Flush toilet, Free showers, RV dump, Tents: $18-22/RVs: $30-43, Also cabins, 22 Full hookups, 9 equestrian sites, Open Mar-Oct, Max Length: 100ft, Reservations accepted, Elev: 797ft/243m, Tel: 606-473-7324, Nearest town: Greenup. GPS: 38.484781, -82.892119

16 • B5 | Jenny Wiley SRP

Total sites: 121, RV sites: 121, Elec sites: 121, Water at site, Flush toilet, Free showers, RV dump, Tent & RV camping: $23-37, Also cabins, Open Apr-Oct, Max Length: 95ft, Reservations accepted, Elev: 718ft/219m, Tel: 606-889-1790, Nearest town: Prestonsburg. GPS: 37.712778, -82.742657

17 • B5 | Paintsville Lake SP

Total sites: 42, RV sites: 42, Elec sites: 32, Water at site, Flush toilet, Free showers, RV dump, Tents: $19-23/RVs: $30-34, Open all year, Max Length: 48ft, Reservations accepted, Elev: 784ft/239m, Tel: 606-297-8486, Nearest town: Staffordsville. GPS: 37.843724, -82.878368

18 • B5 | Yatesville Lake SP

Total sites: 47, RV sites: 27, Elec sites: 27, Water at site, Flush toilet, Free showers, RV dump, Tents: $18-22/RVs: $24-30, Also walk-to and boat-in sites, Open Mar-Oct, Max Length: 35ft, Reservations accepted, Elev: 722ft/220m, Tel: 606-673-1492, Nearest town: Louisa. GPS: 38.097180, -82.683220

19 • C1 | Columbus-Belmont SP

Total sites: 38, RV sites: 38, Elec sites: 38, Water at site, Flush toilet, Free showers, RV dump, Tent & RV camping: $22-40, No water at sites in winter, Open all year, Max Length: 53ft, Reservations accepted, Elev: 463ft/141m, Tel: 270-677-2327, Nearest town: Columbus. GPS: 36.761879, -89.107425

20 • C1 | Kenlake SRP

Total sites: 90, RV sites: 90, Elec sites: 90, Water at site, Flush toilet, Free showers, RV dump, Tents: $15-20/RVs: $19-30, Also cabins, Open Apr-Oct, Max Length: 39ft, Reservations accepted, Elev: 463ft/141m, Tel: 270-474-2211, Nearest town: Hardin. GPS: 36.772633, -88.136723

21 • C1 | Kentucky Dam Village SRP

Total sites: 219, RV sites: 219, Elec sites: 219, Water at site, Flush toilet, Free showers, RV dump, Tents: $16-21/RVs: $22-29, Also cabins, Open Apr-Oct, Max Length: 81ft, Reservations accepted, Elev: 368ft/112m, Tel: 270-362-4271, Nearest town: Gilbertsville. GPS: 37.014956, -88.282529

22 • C2 | Lake Barkley SRP

Total sites: 78, RV sites: 78, Elec sites: 78, Water at site, Flush toilet, Free showers, RV dump, Tents: $14-18/RVs: $17-26, Also cabins, Open Apr-Oct, Max Length: 71ft, Reservations accepted, Elev: 548ft/167m, Tel: 270-924-1131, Nearest town: Cadiz. GPS: 36.848018, -87.913198

23 • C2 | Lake Malone SP

Total sites: 25, RV sites: 24, Elec sites: 24, Water at site, Flush toilet, Free showers, RV dump, Tents: $17-21/RVs: $22-27, Open all year, Max Length: 69ft, Reservations accepted, Elev: 568ft/173m, Tel: 270-657-2111, Nearest town: Dunmor. GPS: 37.074906, -87.039834

24 • C2 | Pennyrile Forest SRP - Family

Total sites: 36, RV sites: 36, Elec sites: 36, Water at site, Flush toilet, Free showers, RV dump, Tent & RV camping: $20-30, Also cabins, Open Apr-Oct, Max Length: 60ft, Reservations accepted, Elev: 623ft/190m, Tel: 270-797-3421, Nearest town: Dawson Springs. GPS: 37.071588, -87.655907

25 • C2 | Pennyrile Forest SRP - Horse Camp

Total sites: 8, RV sites: 8, Elec sites: 8, Water at site, Flush toilet, Free showers, RV dump, Tent & RV camping: $35-45, Also cabins, Open Apr-Oct, Max Length: 40ft, Reservations accepted, Elev: 642ft/196m, Tel: 270-797-3421, Nearest town: Dawson Springs. GPS: 37.069049, -87.655217

26 • C3 | Barren River Lake State Resort Park

Total sites: 101, RV sites: 99, Elec sites: 99, Water at site, Flush toilet, Free showers, RV dump, Tent & RV camping: $20-40, Also cabins, Open May-Oct, Max Length: 119ft, Reservations accepted, Elev: 656ft/200m, Tel: 270-646-2151, Nearest town: Lucas. GPS: 36.852124, -86.063468

27 • C3 | Dale Hollow SP

Total sites: 121, RV sites: 121, Elec sites: 121, Water at site, Flush toilet, Free showers, RV dump, Tent & RV camping: $25-45, Also cabins, 32 Full hookups in loops B-C-G-H, Open Apr-Oct, Max Length: 41ft, Reservations accepted, Elev: 920ft/280m, Tel: 270-433-7431, Nearest town: Burkesville. GPS: 36.653326, -85.283299

28 • C3 | Dale Hollow SP - Equestrian

Total sites: 24, RV sites: 24, Elec sites: 24, Water at site, Flush toilet, Free showers, RV dump, Tent & RV camping: $30-45, Also cabins, 8 Full hookups in Loop Q, Open Apr-Oct, Max Length: 41ft, Reservations accepted, Elev: 939ft/286m, Tel: 270-433-7431, Nearest town: Burkesville. GPS: 36.656387, -85.283442

29 • C3 | Green River Lake SP

Total sites: 229, RV sites: 157, Elec sites: 157, Water at site, Flush toilet, Free showers, RV dump, Tents: $18-24/RVs: $26-36, Open Mar-Dec, Max Length: 49ft, Reservations accepted, Elev: 666ft/203m, Tel: 270-465-8255, Nearest town: Campbellsville. GPS: 37.275419, -85.317306

30 • C3 | Lake Cumberland SRP

Total sites: 129, RV sites: 129, Elec sites: 129, Water at site, Flush toilet, Free showers, RV dump, Tents: $15-22/RVs: $22-28, Also cabins, Open Apr-Oct, Max Length: 55ft, Reservations accepted, Elev: 912ft/278m, Tel: 270-343-3111, Nearest town: Jamestown. GPS: 36.922115, -85.049632

31 • C3 | Nolin Lake SP

Total sites: 92, RV sites: 32, Elec sites: 32, Water at site, Flush toilet, Free showers, RV dump, Tents: $16-20/RVs: $22-32, Open Apr-Oct, Max Length: 99ft, Reservations accepted, Elev: 548ft/167m, Tel: 270-286-4240, Nearest town: Mammoth Cave. GPS: 37.293855, -86.214013

32 • C3 | Rough River Dam SRP - Fly-in

Dispersed sites, Central water, Flush toilet, Free showers, Tents only: $10, Open all year, Reservations accepted, Elev: 574ft/175m, Tel: 270-257-2311, Nearest town: Falls Of Rough. GPS: 37.612677, -86.505397

33 • C3 | Rough River Lake SRP - Family

Total sites: 85, RV sites: 34, Elec sites: 34, Water at site, Flush toilet, Free showers, RV dump, Tents: $12-25/RVs: $20-25, Open Apr-Oct, Reservations accepted, Elev: 453ft/138m, Tel: 270-257-2311, Nearest town: Falls Of Rough. GPS: 37.621913, -86.506394

34 • C4 | Cumberland Falls SRP - Clifty

Total sites: 10, RV sites: 0, Elec sites: 8, Central water, Flush toilet, Free showers, No RV dump, Tents only: $25-31, Open Mar-Nov, Max Length: 20ft, Reservations accepted, Elev: 1085ft/331m, Tel: 606-528-4121, Nearest town: Corbin. GPS: 36.841503, -84.339321

35 • C4 | Cumberland Falls SRP - Ridgeline

Total sites: 39, RV sites: 29, Elec sites: 34, Water at site, Flush toilet, Free showers, RV dump, Tents: $22-34/RVs: $27-34, Also cabins, Open Mar-Nov, Reservations accepted, Elev: 1161ft/354m, Tel: 606-528-4121, Nearest town: Corbin. GPS: 36.840941, -84.328613

36 • C4 | General Burnside Island SP

Total sites: 94, RV sites: 94, Elec sites: 94, Water at site, Flush toilet, Free showers, RV dump, Tents: $20-22/RVs: $24-30, Open Apr-Oct, Max Length: 98ft, Reservations accepted, Elev: 758ft/231m, Tel: 606-561-4104, Nearest town: Burnside. GPS: 36.980624, -84.601896

37 • C4 | Levi Jackson Wilderness Road SP

Total sites: 136, RV sites: 136, Elec sites: 136, Water at site, Flush toilet, Free showers, RV dump, Tents: $20-24/RVs: $26-40, 22 Full hookups, Open all year, Max Length: 82ft, Reservations accepted, Elev: 1211ft/369m, Tel: 606-330-2130, Nearest town: London. GPS: 37.079695, -84.046461

38 • C5 | Carr Creek SP

Total sites: 62, RV sites: 62, Elec sites: 62, Water at site, Flush toilet, Free showers, RV dump, Tent & RV camping: $22-27, Open all year, Max Length: 60ft, Reservations accepted, Elev: 1076ft/328m, Tel: 606-642-4050, Nearest town: Sassafras. GPS: 37.232863, -83.002251

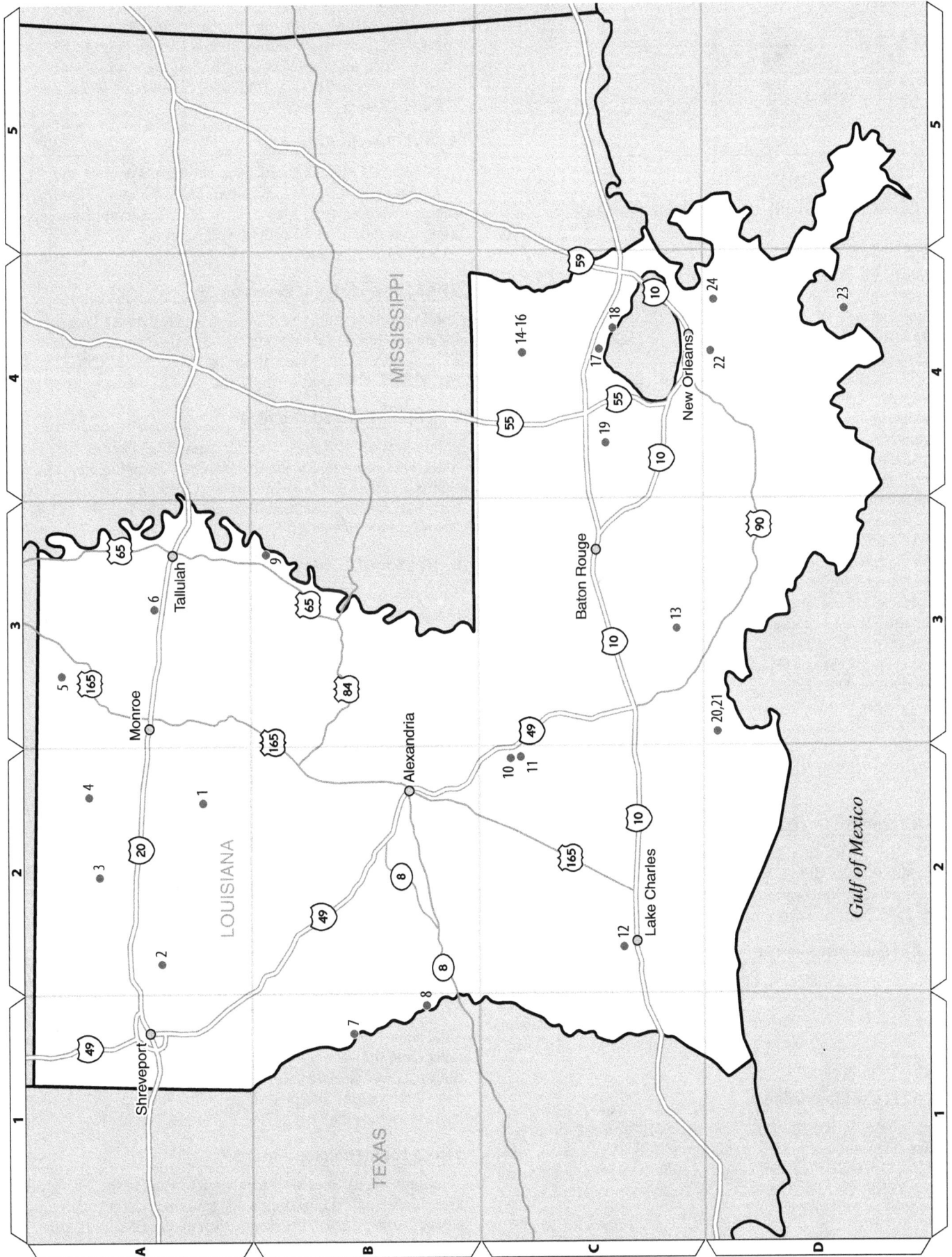

Louisiana

MISSISSIPPI

TEXAS

LOUISIANA

Gulf of Mexico

Shreveport

Monroe

Tallulah

Alexandria

Lake Charles

Baton Rouge

New Orleans

Map	ID	Map	ID
A2	1-4	C3	13
A3	5-6	C4	14-19
B1	7-8	D3	20-21
B3	9	D4	22-24
C2	10-12		

Alphabetical List of Camping Areas

1 • A2 | Jimmie Davis SP

Total sites: 73, RV sites: 73, Elec sites: 73, Water at site, Flush toilet, Free showers, RV dump, Tent & RV camping: $20-33, Also cabins, Open all year, Reservations accepted, Elev: 256ft/78m, Tel: 318-249-2595, Nearest town: Chatham. GPS: 32.253209, -92.519914

2 • A2 | Lake Bistineau SP

Total sites: 61, RV sites: 61, Elec sites: 61, Water at site, Free showers, RV dump, Tents: $20-23/RVs: $20-33, Open all year, Max Length: 62ft, Reservations accepted, Elev: 164ft/50m, Tel: 318-745-3503, Nearest town: Doyline. GPS: 32.440001, -93.379831

3 • A2 | Lake Claiborne SP

Total sites: 89, RV sites: 89, Elec sites: 87, Water at site, Flush toilet, Free showers, RV dump, Tents: $18/RVs: $20-33, Also cabins, Open all year, Max Length: 120ft, Reservations accepted, Elev: 236ft/72m, Tel: 318-927-2976, Nearest town: Homer. GPS: 32.730583, -92.919293

4 • A2 | Lake D'Arbonne SP

Total sites: 58, RV sites: 58, Elec sites: 58, Water at site, Flush toilet, Free showers, RV dump, Tent & RV camping: $20-33, Also cabins, Open all year, Max Length: 63ft, Reservations accepted, Elev: 184ft/56m, Tel: 318-368-2086, Nearest town: Farmerville. GPS: 32.777465, -92.488573

5 • A3 | Chemin-A-Haut SP

Total sites: 27, RV sites: 26, Elec sites: 26, Water at site, Flush toilet, Free showers, RV dump, Tent & RV camping: $25-33, Also cabins, Open all year, Max Length: 50ft, Reservations accepted, Elev: 164ft/50m, Tel: 318-283-0812, Nearest town: Bastrop. GPS: 32.908693, -91.845946

6 • A3 | Poverty Point Reservoir SP

Total sites: 54, RV sites: 54, Elec sites: 54, Flush toilet, Free showers, RV dump, Tent & RV camping: $20-33, Also cabins, Open all year, Max Length: 170ft, Reservations accepted, Elev: 105ft/32m, Tel: 318-878-7536, Nearest town: Delhi. GPS: 32.482805, -91.491392

7 • B1 | North Toledo Bend SP

Total sites: 63, RV sites: 63, Elec sites: 63, Water at site, Flush toilet, Free showers, RV dump, Tent & RV camping: $20-33, Also cabins, Lower weekday/winter rates, Open all year, Max Length: 45ft, Reservations accepted, Elev: 203ft/62m, Tel: 318-645-4715, Nearest town: Zwolle. GPS: 31.547101, -93.735605

8 • B1 | South Toledo Bend SP

Total sites: 60, RV sites: 55, Elec sites: 55, Water at site, Flush toilet, Free showers, RV dump, Tents: $18/RVs: $20-33, Also cabins, Open all year, Max Length: 110ft, Reservations accepted, Elev: 230ft/70m, Tel: 337-286-9075, Nearest town: Anacoco. GPS: 31.208502, -93.581508

9 • B3 | Lake Bruin SP

Total sites: 48, RV sites: 48, Elec sites: 48, Water at site, Flush toilet, Free showers, RV dump, Tent & RV camping: $20-33, Open all year, Max Length: 84ft, Reservations accepted, Elev: 105ft/32m, Tel: 318-766-3530, Nearest town: St. Joseph. GPS: 31.960449, -91.201172

10 • C2 | Chicot SP - North Loop

Total sites: 100, RV sites: 100, Elec sites: 100, Central water, Flush toilet, Free showers, No RV dump, Tent & RV camping: $20-28, Group site: $50, Lower weekday/winter rates, Open all year, Max Length: 85ft, Reservations accepted, Elev: 108ft/33m, Tel: 337-363-2403, Nearest town: Ville Platte. GPS: 30.834631, -92.281117

11 • C2 | Chicot SP - South Loop

Total sites: 108, RV sites: 108, Elec sites: 108, Water at site, Flush toilet, Free showers, RV dump, Tent & RV camping: $20-28, Also cabins, Lower weekday/winter rates, Open all year, Max Length: 64ft, Reservations accepted, Elev: 95ft/29m, Tel: 337-363-2403, Nearest town: Ville Platte. GPS: 30.788552, -92.274459

12 • C2 | Sam Houston Jones SP

Total sites: 81, RV sites: 62, Elec sites: 81, Water at site, Flush toilet, Free showers, RV dump, Tent & RV camping: $20-33, Also cabins, 5 backcountry sites: $9/person, Open all year, Max Length: 75ft,

Reservations accepted, Elev: 52ft/16m, Tel: 337-855-2665, Nearest town: Lake Charles. GPS: 30.294547, -93.258501

13 • C3 | Lake Fausse Pointe SP

Total sites: 62, RV sites: 55, Elec sites: 55, Water at site, Flush toilet, Free showers, RV dump, Tents: $20-23/RVs: $20-33, Also cabins, 7 backcountry/5 canoe sites, Open all year, Max Length: 90ft, Reservations accepted, Elev: 20ft/6m, Tel: 337-229-4764, Nearest town: Martinville. GPS: 30.060785, -91.606772

14 • C4 | Bogue Chitto SP - Bottomland

Total sites: 35, RV sites: 35, Elec sites: 35, Water at site, Flush toilet, Free showers, RV dump, Tent & RV camping: $25-33, Also cabins, Open all year, Max Length: 92ft, Elev: 131ft/40m, Tel: 985-839-5707, Nearest town: Franklinton. GPS: 30.772522, -90.147447

15 • C4 | Bogue Chitto SP - Equestrian

Total sites: 28, RV sites: 28, Elec sites: 28, Central water, Vault/pit toilet, No showers, No RV dump, Tent & RV camping: $14, Also cabins, Open all year, Max Length: 55ft, Reservations accepted, Elev: 208ft/63m, Tel: 985-839-5707, Nearest town: Franklinton. GPS: 30.770574, -90.161329

16 • C4 | Bogue Chitto SP - Upland

Total sites: 46, RV sites: 46, Elec sites: 46, Water at site, Flush toilet, Free showers, RV dump, Tent & RV camping: $25-33, Also cabins, Open all year, Max Length: 92ft, Elev: 223ft/68m, Tel: 985-839-5707, Nearest town: Franklinton. GPS: 30.765112, -90.155318

17 • C4 | Fairview Riverside SP

Total sites: 101, RV sites: 101, Elec sites: 81, Water at site, Flush toilet, Free showers, RV dump, Tents: $18/RVs: $20-33, Open all year, Max Length: 58ft, Reservations accepted, Elev: 20ft/6m, Tel: 985-845-3318, Nearest town: Madisonville. GPS: 30.409281, -90.140592

18 • C4 | Fontainebleau SP

Total sites: 163, RV sites: 163, Elec sites: 126, Water at site, Flush toilet, Free showers, RV dump, Tents: $18/RVs: $20-33, Also cabins, 5 Full hookups, Open all year, Max Length: 155ft, Reservations accepted, Elev: 52ft/16m, Tel: 985-624-4443, Nearest town: Mandeville. GPS: 30.339901, -90.038269

19 • C4 | Tickfaw SP

Total sites: 50, RV sites: 50, Elec sites: 30, Water at site, Flush toilet, Free showers, RV dump, Tents: $18/RVs: $20-28, Also cabins, Open all year, Max Length: 81ft, Reservations accepted, Elev: 43ft/13m, Tel: 225-294-5020, Nearest town: Springfield. GPS: 30.382462, -90.637112

20 • D3 | Palmetto Island SP

Total sites: 96, RV sites: 96, Elec sites: 96, Water at site, Flush toilet, Free showers, RV dump, Tent & RV camping: $20-33, Also walk-to/group sites & cabins, Group site: $35, Open all year, Max Length: 75ft, Reservations accepted, Elev: 49ft/15m, Tel: 337-893-3930, Nearest town: Abbeville. GPS: 29.858354, -92.146252

21 • D3 | Palmetto Island SP Walk-in

Total sites: 4, RV sites: 0, No water, Vault/pit toilet, Tents only: $9, Walk-to sites, $9/person, Elev: 5ft/2m, Tel: 337-893-3930, Nearest town: Abbeville. GPS: 29.860401, -92.139399

22 • D4 | Bayou Segnette SP

Total sites: 98, RV sites: 98, Elec sites: 98, Water at site, Flush toilet, Free showers, RV dump, Tent & RV camping: $25-33, Lower weekday/winter rates, Open all year, Max Length: 50ft, Reservations accepted, Elev: 16ft/5m, Tel: 504-736-7140, Nearest town: Westwego. GPS: 29.887974, -90.163787

23 • D4 | Grand Isle SP

Total sites: 63, RV sites: 49, Elec sites: 49, Water at site, Flush toilet, Free showers, RV dump, Tents: $18/RVs: $25-33, 14 beach tent sites, Open all year, Max Length: 80ft, Reservations accepted, Elev: 13ft/4m, Tel: 985-787-2559, Nearest town: Grand Isle. GPS: 29.256619, -89.954838

24 • D4 | St. Bernard SP

Total sites: 51, RV sites: 51, Elec sites: 51, Water at site, Flush toilet, Free showers, RV dump, Tent & RV camping: $20-28, Open all year, Max Length: 63ft, Reservations accepted, Elev: 36ft/11m, Tel: 504-682-2101, Nearest town: Braithwaite. GPS: 29.862152, -89.899523

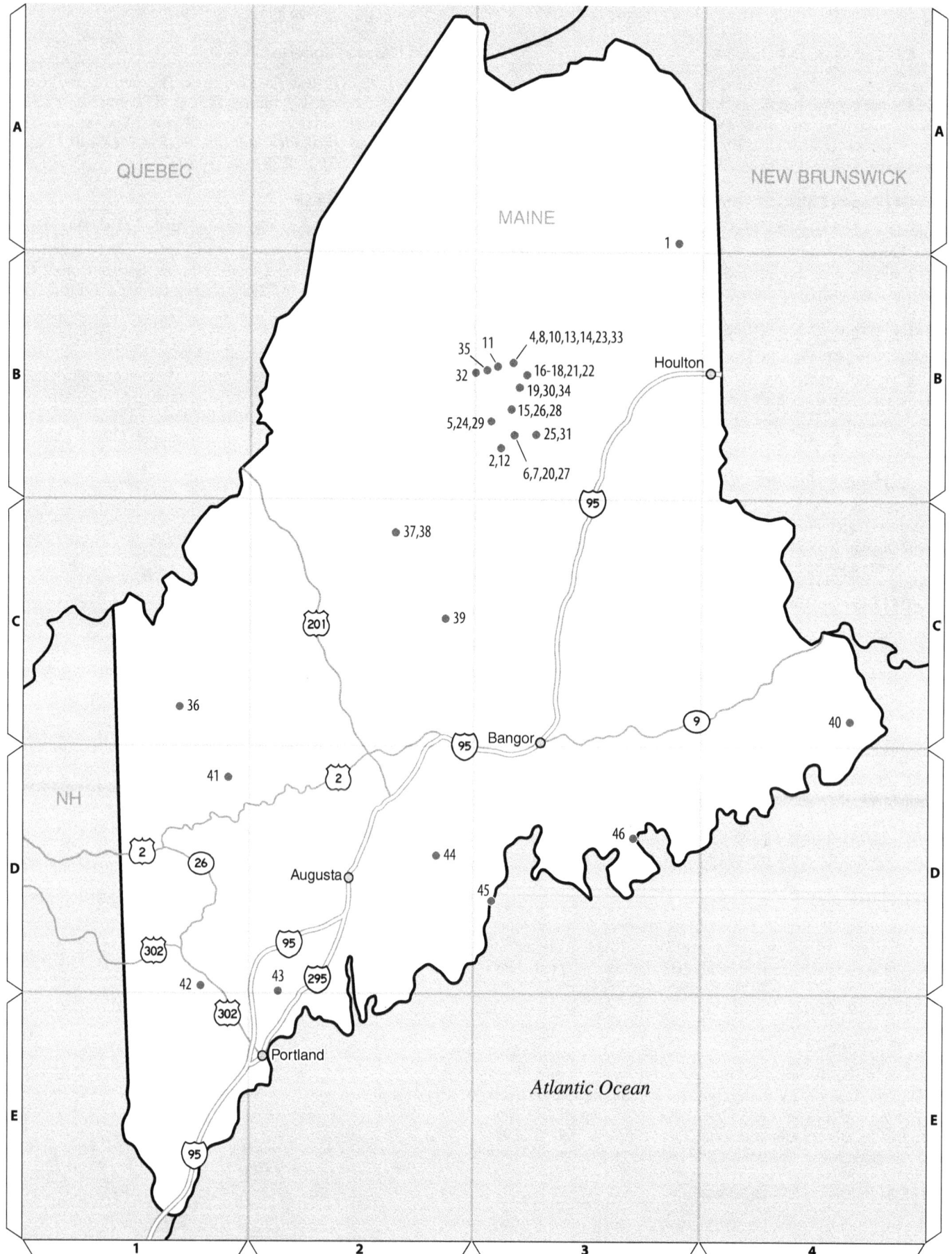

Maine

QUEBEC

NEW BRUNSWICK

MAINE

1 •

4,8,10,13,14,23,33

35   11
• • •   16-18,21,22
32 • •
         19,30,34
         •
         15,26,28
         •
5,24,29 •
         • 25,31
         •

2,12
    6,7,20,27

Houlton ◯

95

• 37,38

201   • 39

• 36

9

40 •

95   Bangor ◯

41 •

2

NH

2

26

46 •

• 44

Augusta ◯

45 •

95

302

43
42 •   •   295

302

◯ Portland

Atlantic Ocean

95

Map	ID	Map	ID
A3	1	C4	40
B3	2-35	D1	41-42
C1	36	D2	43-44
C2	37-39	D3	45-46

Alphabetical List of Camping Areas

1 • A3 | Aroostook SP

Total sites: 30, RV sites: 30, Elec sites: 5, Water at site, Flush toilet, Free showers, No RV dump, Tents: $25/RVs: $25-35, $15-$25 for ME residents, Open all year, Max Length: 35+ft, Reservations accepted, Elev: 614ft/187m, Tel: 207-768-8341, Nearest town: Presque Isle. GPS: 46.609462, -68.003991

2 • B3 | Baxter SP - Abol

Total sites: 21, RV sites: 0, No water, Vault/pit toilet, Tents only: $32, $14 entrance fee, Class B or smaller RVs only, Open May-Oct, Reservations accepted, Elev: 1339ft/408m, Tel: 207-723-5140, Nearest town: Millinockett. GPS: 45.873762, -68.963968

3 • B3 | Baxter SP - Billfish Pond

Dispersed sites, No water, Vault/pit toilet, Tents only: $21, Hike-in, Reservations accepted, Elev: 932ft/284m, Tel: 207-723-5140, Nearest town: Millinockett. GPS: 46.139295, -68.828533

4 • B3 | Baxter SP - Boody Brook

Dispersed sites, No water, Vault/pit toilet, Tents only: $21, Hike-in/boat-in, Reservations accepted, Elev: 655ft/200m, Tel: 207-723-5140, Nearest town: Millinockett. GPS: 46.178929, -68.862247

5 • B3 | Baxter SP - Center Pond

Dispersed sites, No water, Vault/pit toilet, Hike-to shelter: $21, Reservations accepted, Elev: 1710ft/521m, Nearest town: Millinockett. GPS: 46.001248, -69.013778

6 • B3 | Baxter SP - Chimney Pond

Total sites: 8, RV sites: 0, No water, Vault/pit toilet, Hike-to shelter: $32, 3.3 miles, Also open Dec-Mar, Open Jun-Oct, Reservations accepted, Elev: 2936ft/895m, Tel: 207-723-5140, Nearest town: Millinockett. GPS: 45.915512, -68.911366

7 • B3 | Baxter SP - Davis Pond

Dispersed sites, No water, Vault/pit toilet, Hike-to shelter: $21, No fires, Reservations accepted, Elev: 2918ft/889m, Nearest town: Millinockett. GPS: 45.943111, -68.939269

8 • B3 | Baxter SP - First Lake

Dispersed sites, No water, Vault/pit toilet, Tents only: Fee unk, Hike-in/boat-in, Reservations accepted, Elev: 659ft/201m, Tel: 207-723-5140, Nearest town: Millinockett. GPS: 46.163515, -68.805981

9 • B3 | Baxter SP - Fowler Pond Lower Outlet

Dispersed sites, No water, Vault/pit toilet, Tents only: Fee unk, Hike-in, Reservations accepted, Elev: 876ft/267m, Tel: 207-723-5140, Nearest town: Millinockett. GPS: 46.135249, -68.866828

10 • B3 | Baxter SP - Frost Pond

Dispersed sites, No water, Vault/pit toilet, Hike-to shelter: $21, Reservations accepted, Elev: 891ft/272m, Nearest town: Millinockett. GPS: 46.173578, -68.913305

11 • B3 | Baxter SP - Hudson Pond

Dispersed sites, No water, Vault/pit toilet, Hike-to shelter: $21, Reservations accepted, Elev: 965ft/294m, Nearest town: Millinockett. GPS: 46.170916, -68.995039

12 • B3 | Baxter SP - Katahdin Stream

Total sites: 21, RV sites: 0, No water, No toilets, Tents only: $32, $14 entrance fee, Class B or smaller RVs only, Open May-Oct, Reservations accepted, Elev: 1112ft/339m, Tel: 207-723-5140, Nearest town: Millinockett. GPS: 45.887135, -68.999373

13 • B3 | Baxter SP - KP Dam

Dispersed sites, No water, Vault/pit toilet, No showers, No RV dump, Tents only: $21, Hike-in/boat-in, Reservations accepted, Elev: 692ft/211m, Tel: 207-723-5140, Nearest town: Millinockett. GPS: 46.155525, -68.872991

14 • B3 | Baxter SP - Little East

Total sites: 8, No water, Vault/pit toilet, Tents only: $21, Reservations accepted, Elev: 687ft/209m, Nearest town: Millinockett. GPS: 46.204383, -68.918343

15 • B3 | Baxter SP - Little Wassataquoik Lake

Dispersed sites, No water, Vault/pit toilet, Tents only: $21, Hike-in, Reservations accepted, Elev: 1622ft/494m, Tel: 207-723-5140, Nearest town: Millinockett. GPS: 46.028157, -68.964035

16 • B3 | Baxter SP - Long Pond Outlet

Dispersed sites, No water, Vault/pit toilet, Tents only: $21, Hike-in, Reservations accepted, Elev: 911ft/278m, Tel: 207-723-5140, Nearest town: Millinockett. GPS: 46.136131, -68.844368

17 • B3 | Baxter SP - Long Pond Pines

Dispersed sites, No water, Vault/pit toilet, Tents only: $21, Hike-in, Reservations accepted, Elev: 916ft/279m, Tel: 207-723-5140, Nearest town: Millinockett. GPS: 46.138121, -68.839069

18 • B3 | Baxter SP - Lower Fowler Pond

Dispersed sites, No water, Vault/pit toilet, Tents only: $21, Hike-in, Reservations accepted, Elev: 881ft/269m, Tel: 207-723-5140, Nearest town: Millinockett. GPS: 46.133225, -68.859051

19 • B3 | Baxter SP - Lower South Branch Pond

Dispersed sites, No water, Vault/pit toilet, Hike-to shelter: $21, Reservations accepted, Elev: 1023ft/312m, Tel: 207-723-5140, Nearest town: Millinockett. GPS: 46.101416, -68.898938

20 • B3 | Baxter SP - Martin Ponds Shelter

Dispersed sites, No water, Vault/pit toilet, Hike-to shelter: $21, Reservations accepted, Elev: 1247ft/380m, Tel: 207-723-5140, Nearest town: Millinockett. GPS: 45.919115, -68.827269

21 • B3 | Baxter SP - Middle Fowler Pond North

Dispersed sites, No water, Vault/pit toilet, Tents only: $21, Hike-in, Reservations accepted, Elev: 1001ft/305m, Tel: 207-723-5140, Nearest town: Millinockett. GPS: 46.125752, -68.848953

22 • B3 | Baxter SP - Middle Fowler Pond South

Dispersed sites, No water, Vault/pit toilet, Tents only: $21, Hike-in, Reservations accepted, Elev: 996ft/304m, Tel: 207-723-5140, Nearest town: Millinockett. GPS: 46.119457, -68.843116

23 • B3 | Baxter SP - N.W. Cove

Total sites: 1, No water, Vault/pit toilet, Tents only: $21, Reservations accepted, Elev: 685ft/209m, Nearest town: Millinockett. GPS: 46.197892, -68.916735

24 • B3 | Baxter SP - Nesowadnehunk Field

Total sites: 20, RV sites: 0, No water, No toilets, Tents only: $32, 11 lean-to's, Bunkhouse, $14 entrance fee, Open May-Oct, Reservations accepted, Elev: 1308ft/399m, Tel: 207-723-5140, Nearest town: Millinockett. GPS: 45.976817, -69.074665

25 • B3 | Baxter SP - North Katahdin Lake Shelter

Dispersed sites, No water, Vault/pit toilet, Hike-to shelter: $21, Reservations accepted, Elev: 1060ft/323m, Tel: 207-723-5140, Nearest town: Millinockett. GPS: 45.934844, -68.800004

26 • B3 | Baxter SP - Pogy Pond

Dispersed sites, No water, Vault/pit toilet, Tents only: $21, Hike-in, Reservations accepted, Elev: 1144ft/349m, Tel: 207-723-5140, Nearest town: Millinockett. GPS: 46.031236, -68.890322

27 • B3 | Baxter SP - Roaring Brook

Total sites: 19, RV sites: 0, No water, Vault/pit toilet, Tents only: $32, $14 entrance fee, Class B or smaller RVs only, Open May-Oct, Reservations accepted, Elev: 1483ft/452m, Tel: 207-723-5140, Nearest town: Millinockett. GPS: 45.919125, -68.857159

28 • B3 | Baxter SP - Russell Pond

Total sites: 8, RV sites: 0, No water, Vault/pit toilet, Hike-to shelter: $21, 7.2 miles, Also open Dec-Mar, Open May-Oct, Reservations accepted, Elev: 1364ft/416m, Tel: 207-723-5140, Nearest town: Millinockett. GPS: 45.995049, -68.908744

29 • B3 | Baxter SP - Slide Dam

Dispersed sites, No water, Vault/pit toilet, Tents only: $21, Walk-to sites, Reservations accepted, Elev: 1195ft/364m, Nearest town: Millinockett. GPS: 45.939253, -69.041374

30 • B3 | Baxter SP - South Branch Pond

Total sites: 32, RV sites: 0, No water, No toilets, Tents only: $32, Also cabins, $14 entrance fee, Class B or smaller RVs only, Open May-Oct, Reservations accepted, Elev: 1024ft/312m, Tel: 207-723-5140, Nearest town: Millinockett. GPS: 46.108189, -68.901131

31 • B3 | Baxter SP - South Katahdin Lake Shelter

Dispersed sites, No water, Vault/pit toilet, Hike-to shelter: $21, Reservations accepted, Elev: 1035ft/315m, Tel: 207-723-5140, Nearest town: Millinockett. GPS: 45.915105, -68.793677

32 • B3 | Baxter SP - Telos Cut

Dispersed sites, No water, Vault/pit toilet, Tents only: $21, Reservations accepted, Elev: 894ft/272m, Tel: 207-723-5140, Nearest town: Millinockett. GPS: 46.152226, -69.115071

33 • B3 | Baxter SP - Trout Brook Farm

Total sites: 14, RV sites: 0, No water, No toilets, Tents only: $32, $14 entrance fee, Class B or smaller RVs only, Open May-Oct, Reservations accepted, Elev: 679ft/207m, Tel: 207-723-5140, Nearest town: Millinockett. GPS: 46.166832, -68.851128

34 • B3 | Baxter SP - Upper South Branch Pond

Dispersed sites, No water, Vault/pit toilet, Hike-to shelter: $21,

Reservations accepted, Elev: 999ft/304m, Tel: 207-723-5140, Nearest town: Millinockett. GPS: 46.086383, -68.897433

35 • B3 | Baxter SP - Webster Lake Outlet

Total sites: 12, RV sites: 0, No water, Vault/pit toilet, Tents only: $21, Hike-in, Reservations accepted, Elev: 907ft/276m, Tel: 207-723-5140, Nearest town: Millinockett. GPS: 46.158397, -69.054505

36 • C1 | Rangeley Lake SP

Total sites: 50, RV sites: 50, Water at site, Flush toilet, Free showers, RV dump, Tent & RV camping: $30-40, $20-$30 for ME residents, Open May-Sep, Max Length: 35ft, Reservations accepted, Elev: 1542ft/470m, Tel: 207-864-3858, Nearest town: Rangeley. GPS: 44.939071, -70.721248

37 • C2 | Lily Bay SP - Dunn Point

Total sites: 44, RV sites: 32, Central water, Flush toilet, Free showers, RV dump, Tent & RV camping: $30, $20 for ME residents, Open May-Oct, Max Length: 30ft, Reservations accepted, Elev: 1047ft/319m, Tel: 207-695-2700, Nearest town: Greenville. GPS: 45.578886, -69.550923

38 • C2 | Lily Bay SP - Rowell Cove

Total sites: 44, RV sites: 34, Central water, Flush toilet, Free showers, RV dump, Tent & RV camping: $30, $20 for ME residents, Open May-Oct, Max Length: 35ft, Reservations accepted, Elev: 1066ft/325m, Tel: 207-695-2700, Nearest town: Greenville. GPS: 45.572399, -69.563131

39 • C2 | Peaks-Kenny SP

Total sites: 56, RV sites: 55, Elec sites: 6, Water at site, Flush toilet, Free showers, RV dump, Tent & RV camping: $30-40, $20-$30 for ME residents, Open May-Sep, Max Length: 35+ft, Reservations accepted, Elev: 426ft/130m, Tel: 207-564-2003, Nearest town: Dover-Foxcroft. GPS: 45.259415, -69.290266

40 • C4 | Cobscook Bay SP

Total sites: 125, RV sites: 70, Central water, Flush toilet, Free showers, RV dump, Tent & RV camping: $30, $20 for ME residents, Open May-Oct, Max Length: 35+ft, Reservations accepted, Elev: 76ft/23m, Tel: 207-726-4412, Nearest town: Edmunds Twp. GPS: 44.853760, -67.152832

41 • D1 | Mount Blue SP

Total sites: 136, RV sites: 136, Elec sites: 12, Water at site, Flush toilet, Free showers, RV dump, Tent & RV camping: $30-40, $20-$30 for ME residents, Open all year, Max Length: 35+ft, Reservations accepted, Elev: 745ft/227m, Tel: 207-585-2347, Nearest town: Weld. GPS: 44.679171, -70.450651

42 • D1 | Sebago Lake SP

Total sites: 250, RV sites: 232, Elec sites: 100, Water at site, Flush toilet, Free showers, RV dump, Tents: $35/RVs: $35-45, $25-$35 for ME residents, Open May-Oct, Max Length: 35+ft, Reservations accepted, Elev: 351ft/107m, Tel: 207-693-6613, Nearest town: Casco. GPS: 43.916558, -70.593399

43 • D2 | Bradbury Mountain SP

Total sites: 35, RV sites: 35, Central water, Flush toilet, Free showers, No RV dump, Tent & RV camping: $25, $15 for ME residents, Open all year, Max Length: 35ft, Reservations accepted, Elev: 292ft/89m, Tel: 207-688-4712, Nearest town: Pownal. GPS: 43.900898, -70.177137

44 • D2 | Lake St George SP

Total sites: 38, RV sites: 38, Central water, Flush toilet, Free showers, RV dump, Tent & RV camping: $30, $20 for ME residents, Max Length: 35+ft, Reservations accepted, Elev: 515ft/157m, Tel: 207-589-425, Nearest town: Liberty. GPS: 44.397036, -69.347483

45 • D3 | Camden Hills SP

Total sites: 107, RV sites: 107, Elec sites: 43, Central water, Flush toilet, Free showers, RV dump, Tents: $35/RVs: $35-45, $25-$35 for ME residents, Max Length: 35+ft, Reservations accepted, Elev: 230ft/70m, Tel: 207-236-3109, Nearest town: Camden. GPS: 44.231033, -69.049337

46 • D3 | Lamoine SP

Total sites: 62, RV sites: 62, Central water, Flush toilet, Free showers, RV dump, Tent & RV camping: $30, $20 for ME residents, Open May-Oct, Max Length: 35+ft, Reservations accepted, Elev: 69ft/21m, Tel: 207-667-4778, Nearest town: Trenton. GPS: 44.453280, -68.299210

Maryland

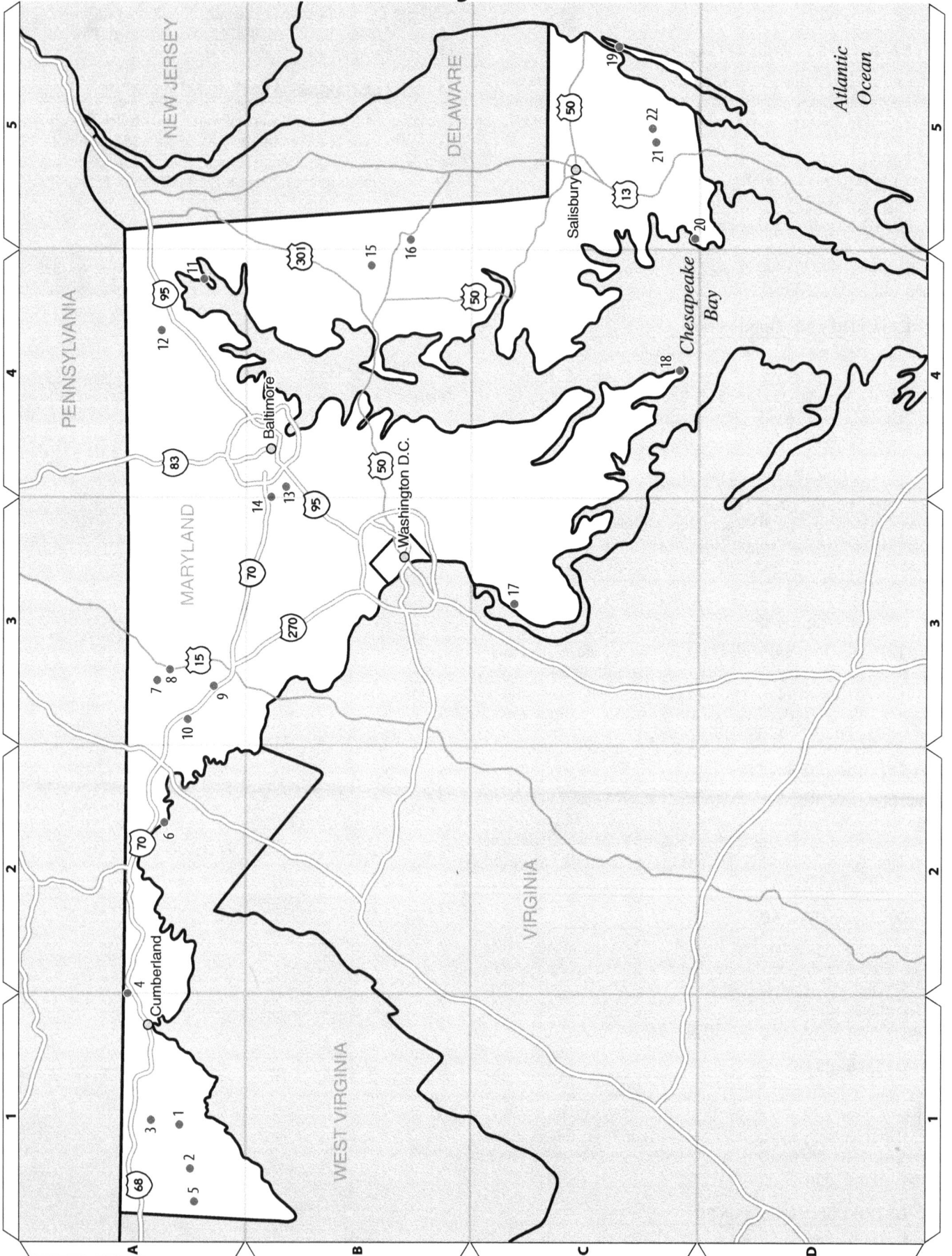

Map	ID	Map	ID
A1	1-5	B5	16
A2	6	C3	17
A3	7-10	C4	18
A4	11-12	C5	19-22
B4	13-15		

Alphabetical List of Camping Areas

Name	ID	Map
Assateague SP	19	C5
Big Run SP	1	A1
Cunningham Falls SP - Houck Area	7	A3
Cunningham Falls SP - Manor Area	8	A3
Deep Creek Lake SP	2	A1
Elk Neck SP	11	A4
Fort Frederick SP	6	A2
Gambrill SP	9	A3
Greenbrier SP	10	A3
Janes Island SP	20	C5
Martinak SP	16	B5
New Germany SP	3	A1
Patapsco SP - Hilton	13	B4
Patapsco SP - Hollofield	14	B4
Pocomoke SP - Milburn Landing	21	C5
Pocomoke SP - Shad Landing	22	C5
Point Lookout SP	18	C4
Rocky Gap SP	4	A1
Smallwood SP	17	C3
Susquehanna SP	12	A4
Swallow Falls SP	5	A1
Tuckahoe SP	15	B4

1 • A1 | Big Run SP

Total sites: 29, RV sites: 29, No water, Vault/pit toilet, Tent & RV camping: $10, Group site: $55, Open all year, Reservations not accepted, Elev: 1503ft/458m, Tel: 301-895-5453, Nearest town: Grantsville. GPS: 39.544059, -79.138659

2 • A1 | Deep Creek Lake SP

Total sites: 112, RV sites: 112, Elec sites: 26, Water available, Flush toilet, Free showers, RV dump, Tents: $22/RVs: $28, Also cabins, Open Apr-Dec, Reservations accepted, Elev: 2641ft/805m, Tel: 301-387-5563, Nearest town: Swanton. GPS: 39.514201, -79.300503

3 • A1 | New Germany SP

Total sites: 48, RV sites: 48, Central water, Flush toilet, Free showers, RV dump, Tents: $19/RVs: $28, Also cabins, Limited winter services, Open all year, Reservations accepted, Elev: 2546ft/776m, Tel: 301-895-5453, Nearest town: Grantsville. GPS: 39.634034, -79.119202

4 • A1 | Rocky Gap SP

Total sites: 278, RV sites: 278, Elec sites: 30, Water available, Flush toilet, Free showers, RV dump, Tents: $22/RVs: $28, Also group sites & cabins, Group site: $222, Limited services Nov-Apr, Open all year, Reservations accepted, Elev: 1211ft/369m, Tel: 301-722-1480, Nearest town: Flintstone. GPS: 39.711182, -78.647461

5 • A1 | Swallow Falls SP

Total sites: 65, RV sites: 65, Water at site, Flush toilet, Free showers, No RV dump, Tents: $22/RVs: $28-33, Also group sites & cabins, Some Full hookups sites, Youth group site: Free with the required MD Park Service youth group pass, Open Apr-Nov, Reservations accepted, Elev: 2434ft/742m, Nearest town: Oakland. GPS: 39.498874, -79.422102

6 • A2 | Fort Frederick SP

Total sites: 29, RV sites: 29, Central water, No toilets, No showers, No RV dump, Tent & RV camping: $15, No tents Nov-Apr, Open May-Nov, Reservations accepted, Elev: 443ft/135m, Tel: 301-842-2155, Nearest town: Frederick. GPS: 39.606468, -78.005763

7 • A3 | Cunningham Falls SP - Houck Area

Total sites: 140, RV sites: 140, Elec sites: 33, Central water, Flush toilet, Free showers, RV dump, Tents: $22/RVs: $28, Also cabins, Open Apr-Oct, Reservations accepted, Elev: 1545ft/471m, Tel: 301-271-7574, Nearest town: Thurmont. GPS: 39.627286, -77.475522

8 • A3 | Cunningham Falls SP - Manor Area

Total sites: 31, RV sites: 31, Elec sites: 8, Central water, Flush toilet, Free showers, Tents: $22/RVs: $28, Bathhouse closed in winter, Open Apr-Dec, Reservations accepted, Elev: 653ft/199m, Tel: 301-271-7574, Nearest town: Thurmont. GPS: 39.591064, -77.436035

9 • A3 | Gambrill SP

Total sites: 34, RV sites: 34, Elec sites: 7, Central water, Flush toilet, Free showers, RV dump, Tents: $19/RVs: $25, Also cabins, Open Apr-Oct, Reservations accepted, Elev: 1161ft/354m, Tel: 301-271-7574, Nearest town: Frederick. GPS: 39.457379, -77.493761

10 • A3 | Greenbrier SP

Total sites: 165, RV sites: 165, Elec sites: 40, Central water, Flush toilet, Free showers, RV dump, Tents: $22/RVs: $28, Open Apr-Oct, Reservations accepted, Elev: 886ft/270m, Tel: 301-791-4767, Nearest town: Boonsboro. GPS: 39.533483, -77.620271

11 • A4 | Elk Neck SP

Total sites: 259, RV sites: 259, Elec sites: 60, Water at site, Flush toilet, Free showers, RV dump, Tents: $22/RVs: $28-37, Also cabins, 28 Full hookups, Generator hours: 0700-2200, Open Apr-Nov, Reservations accepted, Elev: 128ft/39m, Tel: 410-287-5333, Nearest town: North East. GPS: 39.478259, -75.977564

12 • A4 | Susquehanna SP

Total sites: 69, RV sites: 69, Elec sites: 6, Flush toilet, Free showers, Tents: $22/RVs: $28, Also cabins, Open Apr-Oct, Elev: 259ft/79m, Nearest town: Havre de Grace. GPS: 39.612259, -76.164984

13 • B4 | Patapsco SP - Hilton

Total sites: 12, RV sites: 0, Water available, Flush toilet, Free showers, No RV dump, Tents only: $19, Open Apr-Oct, Elev:

410ft/125m, Tel: 410-461-5005, Nearest town: Catonsville. GPS: 39.245724, -76.745397

14 • B4 | Patapsco SP - Hollofield

Total sites: 73, RV sites: 73, Elec sites: 30, Water available, Flush toilet, Free showers, RV dump, Tents: $19/RVs: $22, RVs over 11'1" in height must enter via the Route 40 East Entrance, Open Apr-Oct, Reservations accepted, Elev: 433ft/132m, Tel: 410-461-5005, Nearest town: Ellicott City. GPS: 39.286829, -76.788719

15 • B4 | Tuckahoe SP

Total sites: 54, RV sites: 54, Elec sites: 33, Central water, Flush toilet, Free showers, RV dump, Tents: $22/RVs: $28, Also group sites & cabins, Youth group site: Free with the required MD Park Service youth group pass, Open Mar-Oct, Reservations accepted, Elev: 59ft/18m, Tel: 410-820-1668, Nearest town: Queen Anne. GPS: 38.984629, -75.931583

16 • B5 | Martinak SP

Total sites: 63, RV sites: 63, Elec sites: 30, Central water, Flush toilet, Free showers, RV dump, Tents: $19/RVs: $25, Also cabins, Open Mar-Oct, Elev: 46ft/14m, Tel: 410) 820-1668, Nearest town: Denton. GPS: 38.865234, -75.836670

17 • C3 | Smallwood SP

Total sites: 15, RV sites: 15, Elec sites: 15, Water available, Flush toilet, Free showers, RV dump, Tent & RV camping: $28, Also group sites & cabins, Youth group site: Free with the required MD Park Service youth group pass, Open Apr-Oct, Elev: 72ft/22m, Tel: 301-743-7613, Nearest town: Marbury. GPS: 38.555042, -77.187616

18 • C4 | Point Lookout SP

Total sites: 143, RV sites: 143, Elec sites: 59, Water at site, Flush toilet, Free showers, RV dump, Tents: $22/RVs: $34-39, Also cabins, Some Full hookups, Open all year, Reservations accepted, Elev: 8ft/2m, Tel: 301-872-5688, Nearest town: Scotland. GPS: 38.062500, -76.331299

19 • C5 | Assateague SP

Total sites: 342, RV sites: 342, Elec sites: 35, No water, Vault/pit toilet, Tents: $28/RVs: $39, Generator hours: 0700-2200, Open Apr-Oct, Reservations accepted, Elev: 8ft/2m, Tel: 410-641-2918, Nearest town: Ocean City. GPS: 38.228114, -75.142058

20 • C5 | Janes Island SP

Total sites: 104, RV sites: 104, Elec sites: 49, Central water, Flush toilet, Free showers, RV dump, Tents: $22/RVs: $28, Also group sites & cabins, 4 sites open all year, Youth group site: Free, Open Apr-Nov, Elev: 59ft/18m, Tel: 410-968-1565, Nearest town: Crisfield. GPS: 38.011166, -75.847056

21 • C5 | Pocomoke SP - Milburn Landing

Total sites: 28, RV sites: 28, Elec sites: 13, Central water, No toilets, No showers, RV dump, Tents: $19/RVs: $25, Also group sites & cabins, Open Apr-Dec, Elev: 89ft/27m, Tel: 410) 632-2566, Nearest town: Pocomoke City. GPS: 38.125219, -75.490034

22 • C5 | Pocomoke SP - Shad Landing

Total sites: 175, RV sites: 175, Elec sites: 60, Central water, Flush toilet, Free showers, RV dump, Tents: $22/RVs: $28, Also cabins, Youth group site: Free with the required MD Park Service youth group pass, Open all year, Elev: 52ft/16m, Tel: 410) 632-2566, Nearest town: Snow Hill. GPS: 38.135498, -75.442139

Massachusetts

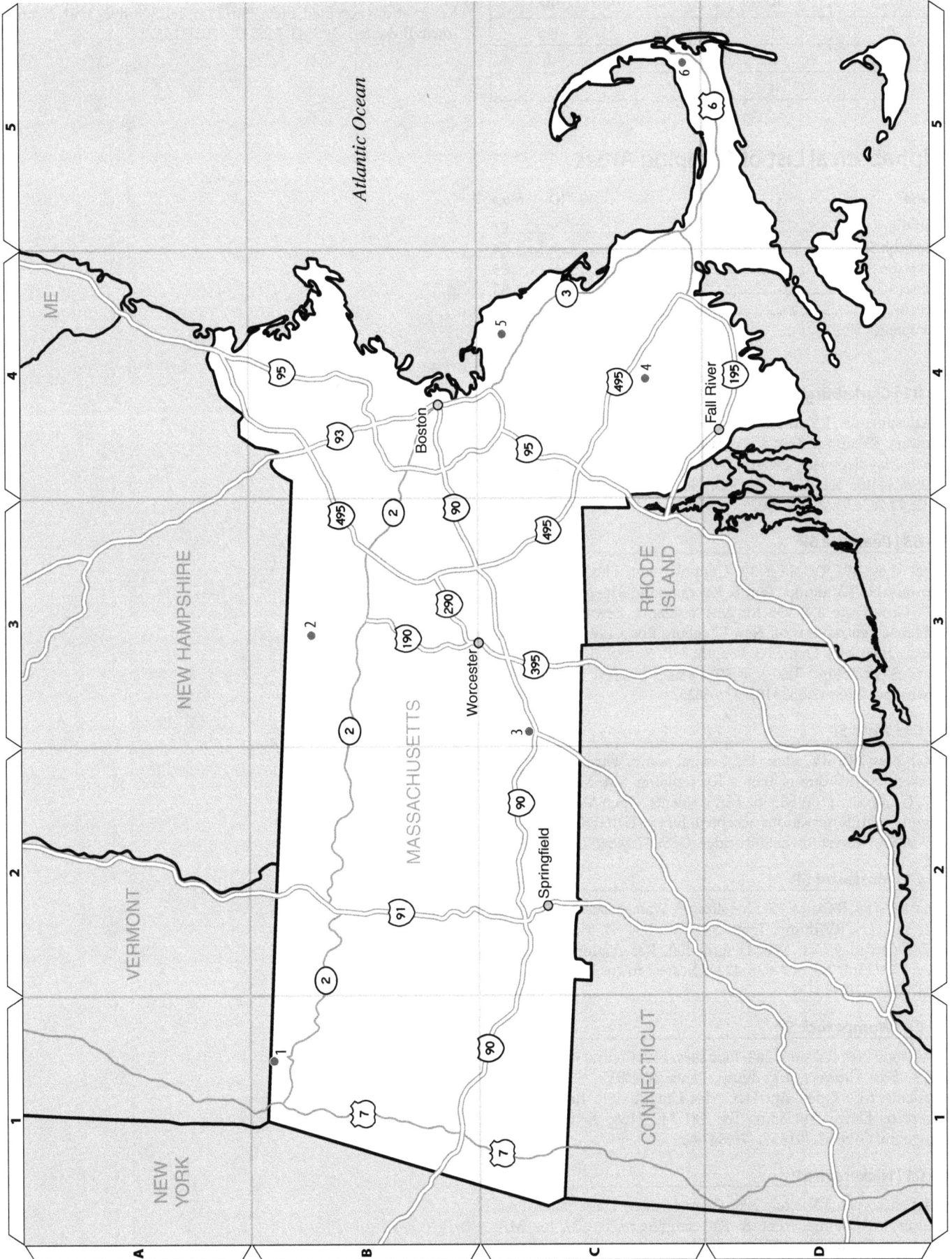

Atlantic Ocean

ME

NEW HAMPSHIRE

VERMONT

NEW YORK

MASSACHUSETTS

RHODE ISLAND

CONNECTICUT

Boston

Worcester

Springfield

Fall River

95

93

495

2

90

95

495

290

190

395

91

90

2

2

2

7

7

90

7

3

5

4

6

9

195

1

3

3

Map	ID	Map	ID
B1	1	C4	4-5
B3	2	C5	6
C3	3		

for out-of-state campers, Open May-Oct, Max Length: 35ft, Reservations accepted, Elev: 79ft/24m, Tel: 508-896-3491, Nearest town: Brewster. GPS: 41.766533, -70.031537

Alphabetical List of Camping Areas

1 • B1 | Clarksburg SP

Total sites: 45, RV sites: 45, Central water, Flush toilet, Free showers, RV dump, Tent & RV camping: $54, MA residents: $17, Open May-Sep, Max Length: 54ft, Reservations accepted, Elev: 1129ft/344m, Tel: 413-664-8345, Nearest town: North Adams. GPS: 42.733833, -73.077802

2 • B3 | Pearl Hill SP

Total sites: 49, RV sites: 35, Central water, Flush toilet, Free showers, No RV dump, Tent & RV camping: $54, MA residents: $17, Group site $50/$35 for MA residents, Beware your GPS guidance - entrance is off New Fitchburg Road, not Vinton Pond Road, Open May-Oct, Max Length: 35ft, Reservations accepted, Elev: 551ft/168m, Tel: 978-597 8802, Nearest town: West Townsend. GPS: 42.653319, -71.766253

3 • C3 | Wells SP

Total sites: 60, RV sites: 45, Central water, Flush toilet, Free showers, No RV dump, Tent & RV camping: $54, MA residents: $17, Group site $100/$35 for MA residents, Open May-Oct, Max Length: 30ft, Reservations accepted, Elev: 617ft/188m, Tel: 508-347-9257, Nearest town: Sturbridge. GPS: 42.146467, -72.061657

4 • C4 | Massasoit SP

Total sites: 84, RV sites: 77, Elec sites: 48, Water at site, Flush toilet, Free showers, RV dump, Tents: $54/RVs: $54-64, MA residents: $17, Open May-Oct, Max Length: 40ft, Reservations accepted, Elev: 77ft/23m, Tel: 508-828-4231, Nearest town: Taunton. GPS: 41.870349, -70.985158

5 • C4 | Wompatuck SP

Total sites: 262, RV sites: 262, Elec sites: 140, Central water, Flush toilet, Free showers, RV dump, Tents: $54/RVs: $54-60, MA residents: $17, Open Apr-Oct, Max Length: 40ft, Reservations accepted, Elev: 174ft/53m, Tel: 781-749-7160, Nearest town: Hingham. GPS: 42.201457, -70.847982

6 • C5 | Nickerson SP

Total sites: 391, RV sites: 206, Central water, Flush toilet, Free showers, RV dump, Tent & RV camping: $70, $22 for MA residents, Group site $50/$35 for MA residents, $5 surcharge

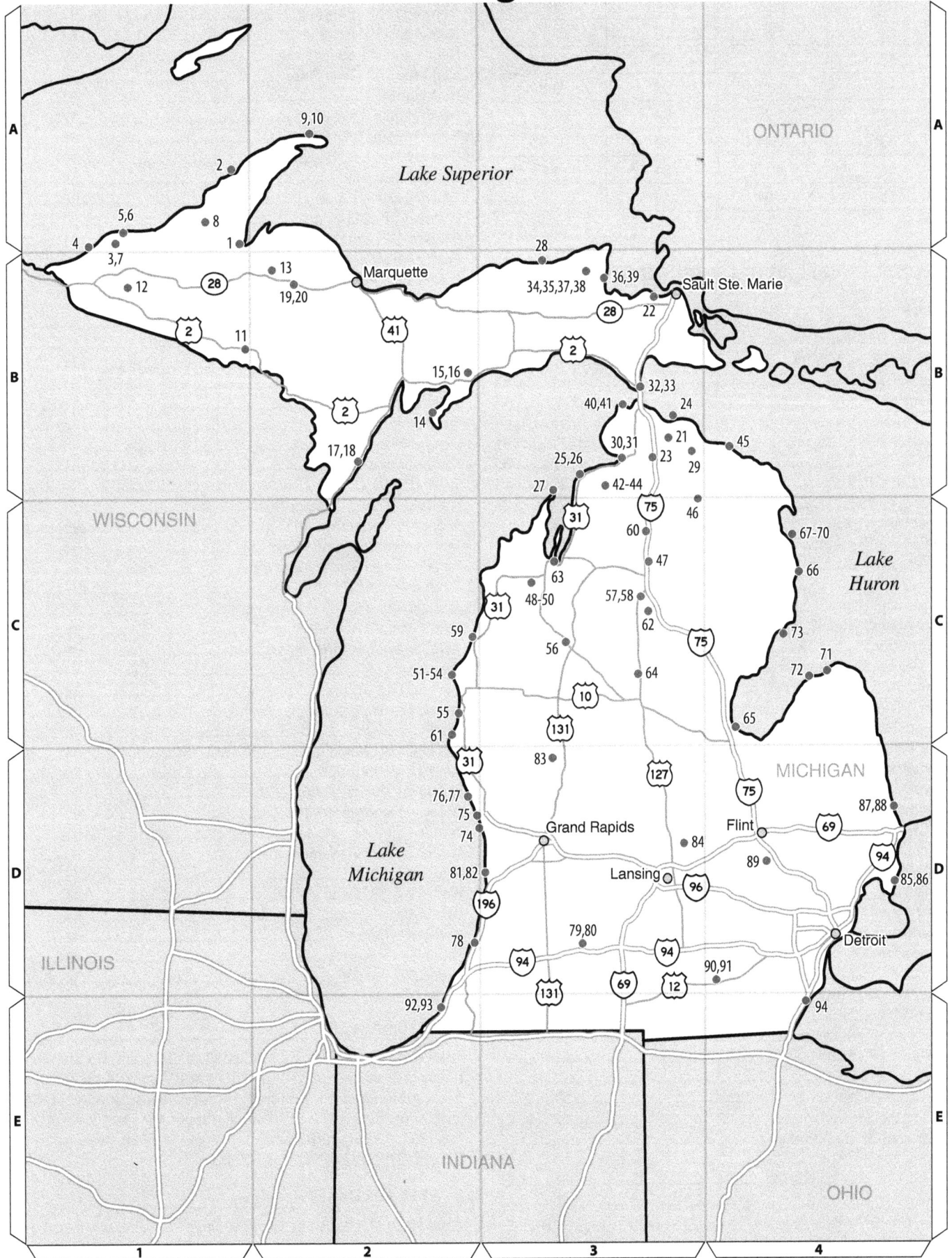

Michigan

Lake Superior

ONTARIO

Lake Huron

WISCONSIN

Lake Michigan

MICHIGAN

ILLINOIS

INDIANA

OHIO

Marquette

Sault Ste. Marie

Grand Rapids

Flint

Lansing

Detroit

Map	ID	Map	ID
A1	1-8	C4	65-73
A2	9-10	D2	74-78
B1	11-12	D3	79-84
B2	13-20	D4	85-91
B3	21-44	E2	92-93
B4	45	E4	94
C3	46-64		

Alphabetical List of Camping Areas

Name	ID	Map
Algonac SP - Wagon Wheel	85	D4
Algonac SP -River Front	86	D4
Aloha SP	21	B3
Baraga SP	1	A1
Bay City SP	65	C4
Bewabic SP	11	B1
Brimley SP	22	B3
Burt Lake SP	23	B3
Cheboygan SP	24	B3
Clear Lake SP	46	C3
Craig Lake SP	13	B2
F J McLain SP	2	A1
Fayette Historic SP	14	B2
Fishermans Island SP - North CG	25	B3
Fishermans Island SP - South CG	26	B3
Fort Custer SP	79	D3
Fort Custer SP - Equestrian	80	D3
Fort Wilkins SP - East	9	A2
Fort Wilkins SP - West	10	A2
Grand Haven SP	74	D2
Harrisville SP	66	C4
Hartwick Pines SP	47	C3
Hoeft SP	45	B4
Hoffmaster SP	75	D2
Holland SP - Beach CG	81	D3
Holland SP - Lake Macatawa CG	82	D3
Indian Lake SP - South CG	15	B2
Indian Lake SP - West CG	16	B2
Interlochen SP - Duck Lake North	48	C3
Interlochen SP - Duck Lake South	49	C3
Interlochen SP - Green Lake	50	C3
J.W. Wells SP - Modern	17	B2
J.W. Wells SP - Rustic	18	B2
Lake Gogebic SP	12	B1
Lakeport SP - North	87	D4
Lakeport SP - South	88	D4
Leelanau SP	27	B3
Ludington SP - Beechwood	51	C3
Ludington SP - Cedar	52	C3
Ludington SP - Jack Pine	53	C3
Ludington SP - Pines	54	C3
Mears SP	55	C3
Mitchell SP	56	C3
Muskallonge Lake SP	28	B3
Muskegon SP - Lake Michighan	76	D2

Name	ID	Map
Muskegon SP - South Channel	77	D2
Negwegon SP - Blue Bell	67	C4
Negwegon SP - Pewabic	68	C4
Negwegon SP - South Point	69	C4
Negwegon SP - Twin Pines	70	C4
Newaygo SP	83	D3
North Higgins Lake SP - East	57	C3
North Higgins Lake SP - West	58	C3
Onaway SP	29	B3
Orchard Beach SP	59	C3
Otsego Lake SP	60	C3
Petoskey SP - Dunes	30	B3
Petoskey SP - Tannery Creek	31	B3
Porcupine Mountains SP - Lost Creek	3	A1
Porcupine Mountains SP - Presque Isle	4	A1
Porcupine Mountains SP - Union Bay	5	A1
Porcupine Mountains SP - Union River Outpost	6	A1
Porcupine Mountains SP - White Pine Extension	7	A1
Port Crescent SP	71	C4
Seven Lakes SP - Sand Lake	89	D4
Silver Lake SP	61	C3
Sleeper SP	72	C4
Sleepy Hollow SP	84	D3
South Higgins Lake SP	62	C3
Sterling SP	94	E4
Straits SP - Lower (waterfront)	32	B3
Straits SP - Upper (inland)	33	B3
Tahquamenon Falls SP - Clark Lake TC	34	B3
Tahquamenon Falls SP - Hemlock	35	B3
Tahquamenon Falls SP - Pines	36	B3
Tahquamenon Falls SP - Portage	37	B3
Tahquamenon Falls SP - River TC	38	B3
Tahquamenon Falls SP - Rivermouth	39	B3
Tawas Point SP	73	C4
Traverse City SP	63	C3
Twin Lakes SP	8	A1
Van Buren SP	78	D2
Van Riper SP - Modern	19	B2
Van Riper SP - Rustic	20	B2
W J Hayes SP - Sites 2-96	90	D4
W J Hayes SP - Sites 97-185	91	D4
Warren Dunes SP - Modern	92	E2
Warren Dunes SP - Semi-modern	93	E2
Wilderness SP	40	B3
Wilderness SP - Nebo Shelter	41	B3
Wilson SP	64	C3
Young SP - Oak	42	B3
Young SP - Spruce	43	B3
Young SP - Terrace	44	B3

1 • A1 | Baraga SP

Total sites: 126, RV sites: 126, Elec sites: 116, Central water, Flush toilet, Free showers, RV dump, Tent & RV camping: $24-43, MI Recreation Passport required -non-residents: $9/day or $34/annual/residents: $12-$17/annual, Open Apr-Dec, Reservations accepted, Elev: 620ft/189m, Tel: 906-353-6558, Nearest town: Baraga. GPS: 46.761562, -88.500572

2 • A1 | F J McLain SP

Total sites: 98, RV sites: 98, Elec sites: 98, Central water, Flush toilet, Free showers, RV dump, Tent & RV camping: $27-42, Also cabins, $22 off-season, MI Recreation Passport required -non-residents: $9/day or $34/annual/residents: $12-$17/annual, Open May-Oct, Reservations accepted, Elev: 617ft/188m, Tel: 906-482-0278, Nearest town: Hancock. GPS: 47.237780, -88.609830

3 • A1 | Porcupine Mountains SP - Lost Creek

Total sites: 3, RV sites: 3, No water, Vault/pit toilet, Tent & RV camping: $20, MI Recreation Passport required -non-residents: $9/day or $34/annual/residents: $12-$17/annual, Open May-Nov, Reservations not accepted, Elev: 1125ft/343m, Tel: 906-885-5275, Nearest town: Ontonagon. GPS: 46.754165, -89.678506

4 • A1 | Porcupine Mountains SP - Presque Isle

Total sites: 50, RV sites: 50, Central water, Vault/pit toilet, No showers, No RV dump, Tent & RV camping: $20, MI Recreation Passport required -non-residents: $9/day or $34/annual/residents: $12-$17/annual, Open May-Nov, Reservations accepted, Elev: 692ft/211m, Tel: 906-885-5275, Nearest town: Bessemer. GPS: 46.706576, -89.978756

5 • A1 | Porcupine Mountains SP - Union Bay

Total sites: 100, RV sites: 100, Elec sites: 100, Central water, Flush toilet, Free showers, No RV dump, Tent & RV camping: $25-38, MI Recreation Passport required -non-residents: $9/day or $34/annual/residents: $12-$17/annual, Open May-Nov, Reservations accepted, Elev: 620ft/189m, Tel: 906-885-5275, Nearest town: Ontonagon. GPS: 46.821874, -89.639912

6 • A1 | Porcupine Mountains SP - Union River Outpost

Total sites: 3, No water, Vault/pit toilet, Tents only: $17, Walk-to sites, MI Recreation Passport required -non-residents: $9/day or $34/annual/residents: $12-$17/annual, Open Apr-Nov, Reservations not accepted, Elev: 778ft/237m, Tel: 906-885-5277, Nearest town: Ontonagon. GPS: 46.797969, -89.623044

7 • A1 | Porcupine Mountains SP - White Pine Extension

Dispersed sites, Vault/pit toilet, Tent & RV camping: $20, MI Recreation Passport required -non-residents: $9/day or $34/annual/residents: $12-$17/annual, Open May-Nov, Reservations not accepted, Elev: 1224ft/373m, Tel: 906-885-5276, Nearest town: Ontonagon. GPS: 46.742712, -89.727117

8 • A1 | Twin Lakes SP

Total sites: 62, RV sites: 62, Elec sites: 62, Central water, Flush toilet, Free showers, RV dump, Tent & RV camping: $22-34, MI Recreation Passport required -non-residents: $9/day or $34/annual/residents: $12-$17/annual, Open May-Oct, Reservations accepted, Elev: 1217ft/371m, Tel: 906-288-3321, Nearest town: Toivola. GPS: 46.889784, -88.857938

9 • A2 | Fort Wilkins SP - East

Total sites: 81, RV sites: 81, Elec sites: 81, Central water, Flush toilet, Free showers, RV dump, Tent & RV camping: $25-37, Also cabins, MI Recreation Passport required -non-residents: $9/day or $34/annual/residents: $12-$17/annual, Open May-Oct, Reservations accepted, Elev: 626ft/191m, Tel: 906-289-4215, Nearest town: Copper Harbor. GPS: 47.466185, -87.859719

10 • A2 | Fort Wilkins SP - West

Total sites: 79, RV sites: 79, Elec sites: 79, Central water, Flush

toilet, Free showers, RV dump, Tent & RV camping: $25-37, Also cabins, MI Recreation Passport required -non-residents: $9/day or $34/annual/residents: $12-$17/annual, Open May-Oct, Reservations accepted, Elev: 628ft/191m, Tel: 906-289-4215, Nearest town: Copper Harbor. GPS: 47.466456, -87.870766

11 • B1 | Bewabic SP

Total sites: 137, RV sites: 137, Elec sites: 137, Central water, Flush toilet, Free showers, RV dump, Tent & RV camping: $20-29, MI Recreation Passport required -non-residents: $9/day or $34/annual/residents: $12-$17/annual, Open May-Oct, Reservations accepted, Elev: 1519ft/463m, Tel: 906-875-3324, Nearest town: Crystal Falls. GPS: 46.089740, -88.435120

12 • B1 | Lake Gogebic SP

Total sites: 165, RV sites: 165, Elec sites: 105, Water at site, Flush toilet, Free showers, RV dump, Tents: $20-25/RVs: $20-33, Group site: $17, Some Full hookups sites, MI Recreation Passport required -non-residents: $9/day or $34/annual/residents: $12-$17/annual, Open Apr-Nov, Reservations accepted, Elev: 1289ft/393m, Tel: 906-842-3341, Nearest town: Marenisco. GPS: 46.457230, -89.568830

13 • B2 | Craig Lake SP

Total sites: 17, RV sites: 0, Vault/pit toilet, Tents only: $20, High-clearance vehicle recommended, MI Recreation Passport required -non-residents: $9/day or $34/annual/residents: $12-$17/annual, Open Apr-Oct, Reservations accepted, Elev: 1739ft/530m, Tel: 906-339-4461, Nearest town: Three Lakes. GPS: 46.599449, -88.189811

14 • B2 | Fayette Historic SP

Total sites: 61, RV sites: 61, Elec sites: 61, Central water, Vault/pit toilet, No showers, No RV dump, Tent & RV camping: $25-37, MI Recreation Passport required -non-residents: $9/day or $34/annual/residents: $12-$17/annual, Open May-Dec, Reservations accepted, Elev: 620ft/189m, Tel: 906-644-2603, Nearest town: Garden. GPS: 45.711763, -86.668146

15 • B2 | Indian Lake SP - South CG

Total sites: 145, RV sites: 145, Elec sites: 145, Central water, Flush toilet, Free showers, RV dump, Tents: $20/RVs: $22-34, Also cabins, $20-$24 off-season, MI Recreation Passport required -non-residents: $9/day or $34/annual/residents: $12-$17/annual, Open Apr-Nov, Reservations accepted, Elev: 607ft/185m, Tel: 906-341-2355, Nearest town: Manistique. GPS: 45.944852, -86.330439

16 • B2 | Indian Lake SP - West CG

Total sites: 72, RV sites: 72, Elec sites: 72, Central water, Vault/pit toilet, No showers, No RV dump, Tent & RV camping: $20-23, $17 off-season, MI Recreation Passport required -non-residents: $9/day or $34/annual/residents: $12-$17/annual, Open Jun-Sep, Reservations accepted, Elev: 673ft/205m, Tel: 906-341-2355, Nearest town: Manistique. GPS: 45.971156, -86.360903

17 • B2 | J.W. Wells SP - Modern

Total sites: 150, RV sites: 150, Elec sites: 150, Central water, Flush toilet, Free showers, RV dump, Tent & RV camping: $20-31, Also cabins, $17-$24 off-season, MI Recreation Passport required -

non-residents: $9/day or $34/annual/residents: $12-$17/annual, Open Apr-Oct, Reservations accepted, Elev: 597ft/182m, Tel: 906-863-9747, Nearest town: Cedar River. GPS: 45.389670, -87.365260

18 • B2 | J.W. Wells SP - Rustic

Total sites: 3, RV sites: 3, No water, Vault/pit toilet, Tent & RV camping: $20, $17 off-season, MI Recreation Passport required -non-residents: $9/day or $34/annual/residents: $12-$17/annual, Open Apr-Oct, Reservations accepted, Elev: 597ft/182m, Tel: 906-863-9747, Nearest town: Cedar River. GPS: 45.399671, -87.361258

19 • B2 | Van Riper SP - Modern

Total sites: 147, RV sites: 147, Elec sites: 147, Central water, Flush toilet, Free showers, RV dump, Tent & RV camping: $22-34, MI Recreation Passport required -non-residents: $9/day or $34/annual/residents: $12-$17/annual, Open Apr-Oct, Reservations accepted, Elev: 1598ft/487m, Tel: 906-339-4461, Nearest town: Champion. GPS: 46.520320, -87.987950

20 • B2 | Van Riper SP - Rustic

Total sites: 40, RV sites: 40, Central water, Vault/pit toilet, Tent & RV camping: $20, MI Recreation Passport required -non-residents: $9/day or $34/annual/residents: $12-$17/annual, Open May-Oct, Reservations accepted, Elev: 1580ft/482m, Tel: 906-339-4461, Nearest town: Champion. GPS: 46.519004, -87.992639

21 • B3 | Aloha SP

Total sites: 285, RV sites: 285, Elec sites: 285, Central water, Flush toilet, Free showers, RV dump, Tent & RV camping: $35-42, MI Recreation Passport required -non-residents: $9/day or $34/annual/residents: $12-$17/annual, Open Apr-Oct, Reservations accepted, Elev: 594ft/181m, Tel: 231-625-2522, Nearest town: Cheboygan. GPS: 45.518030, -84.463980

22 • B3 | Brimley SP

Total sites: 237, RV sites: 237, Elec sites: 237, Central water, Flush toilet, Free showers, RV dump, Tent & RV camping: $22-34, Also group sites & cabins, Group site: $17, MI Recreation Passport required -non-residents: $9/day or $34/annual/residents: $12-$17/annual, Open May-Oct, Reservations accepted, Elev: 610ft/186m, Tel: 906-248-3422, Nearest town: Brimley. GPS: 46.415410, -84.557080

23 • B3 | Burt Lake SP

Total sites: 308, RV sites: 308, Elec sites: 308, Central water, Flush toilet, Free showers, RV dump, Tent & RV camping: $24-42, Group site: $17, MI Recreation Passport required -non-residents: $9/day or $34/annual/residents: $12-$17/annual, Open Apr-Nov, Reservations accepted, Elev: 610ft/186m, Tel: 231-238-9392, Nearest town: Indian River. GPS: 45.400743, -84.628565

24 • B3 | Cheboygan SP

Total sites: 76, RV sites: 76, Elec sites: 76, Central water, Flush toilet, Free showers, RV dump, Tent & RV camping: $22-30, Also cabins, MI Recreation Passport required -non-residents: $9/day or $34/annual/residents: $12-$17/annual, Open May-Nov, Reservations accepted, Elev: 584ft/178m, Tel: 231-627-2811, Nearest town: Cheboygan. GPS: 45.658080, -84.418080

25 • B3 | Fishermans Island SP - North CG

Total sites: 35, RV sites: 35, Central water, Vault/pit toilet, No showers, No RV dump, Tent & RV camping: $20, MI Recreation Passport required -non-residents: $9/day or $34/annual/residents: $12-$17/annual, Open Apr-Nov, Reservations accepted, Elev: 600ft/183m, Tel: 231-547-6641, Nearest town: Charlevoix. GPS: 45.307419, -85.310344

26 • B3 | Fishermans Island SP - South CG

Total sites: 45, RV sites: 45, Central water, Vault/pit toilet, No showers, No RV dump, Tent & RV camping: $20, MI Recreation Passport required -non-residents: $9/day or $34/annual/residents: $12-$17/annual, Open Apr-Nov, Reservations accepted, Elev: 600ft/183m, Tel: 231-547-6641, Nearest town: Charlevoix. GPS: 45.304365, -85.314449

27 • B3 | Leelanau SP

Total sites: 52, RV sites: 52, Central water, Vault/pit toilet, No showers, No RV dump, Tent & RV camping: $20, MI Recreation Passport required -non-residents: $9/day or $34/annual/residents: $12-$17/annual, Open Apr-Nov, Reservations accepted, Elev: 564ft/172m, Tel: 231-386-5422, Nearest town: Northport. GPS: 45.210479, -85.546231

28 • B3 | Muskallonge Lake SP

Total sites: 159, RV sites: 159, Elec sites: 159, Central water, Flush toilet, Free showers, RV dump, Tent & RV camping: $25-37, MI Recreation Passport required -non-residents: $9/day or $34/annual/residents: $12-$17/annual, Open Apr-Oct, Reservations accepted, Elev: 636ft/194m, Tel: 906-658-3338, Nearest town: Newberry. GPS: 46.675450, -85.629150

29 • B3 | Onaway SP

Total sites: 82, RV sites: 82, Elec sites: 82, Central water, Flush toilet, Free showers, RV dump, Tent & RV camping: $22-27, Also cabins, MI Recreation Passport required -non-residents: $9/day or $34/annual/residents: $12-$17/annual, Open Apr-Nov, Reservations accepted, Elev: 597ft/182m, Tel: 989-733-8279, Nearest town: Onaway. GPS: 45.435505, -84.232379

30 • B3 | Petoskey SP - Dunes

Total sites: 80, RV sites: 80, Elec sites: 80, Central water, Flush toilet, Free showers, RV dump, Tent & RV camping: $38-41, MI Recreation Passport required -non-residents: $9/day or $34/annual/residents: $12-$17/annual, Open May-Oct, Reservations accepted, Elev: 620ft/189m, Tel: 231-347-2311, Nearest town: Petoskey. GPS: 45.404071, -84.909772

31 • B3 | Petoskey SP - Tannery Creek

Total sites: 98, RV sites: 98, Elec sites: 98, Central water, Flush toilet, Free showers, RV dump, Tent & RV camping: $33-37, Also cabins, MI Recreation Passport required -non-residents: $9/day or $34/annual/residents: $12-$17/annual, Open May-Oct, Reservations accepted, Elev: 610ft/186m, Tel: 231-347-2311, Nearest town: Petoskey. GPS: 45.394247, -84.913413

32 • B3 | Straits SP - Lower (waterfront)

Total sites: 129, RV sites: 129, Elec sites: 120, Central water, Flush toilet, Free showers, RV dump, Tent & RV camping: $22, Also cabins, MI Recreation Passport required -non-residents: $9/day or $34/annual/residents: $12-$17/annual, No generators, Open all year, Reservations accepted, Elev: 623ft/190m, Tel: 906-643-8620, Nearest town: St Ignace. GPS: 45.849404, -84.718058

33 • B3 | Straits SP - Upper (inland)

Total sites: 149, RV sites: 149, Elec sites: 149, Water at site, Flush toilet, Free showers, RV dump, Tents: $27-42/RVs: $27-50, Also cabins, Some Full hookups, MI Recreation Passport required - non-residents: $9/day or $34/annual/residents: $12-$17/annual, Open all year, Reservations accepted, Elev: 679ft/207m, Tel: 906-643-8620, Nearest town: St Ignace. GPS: 45.854124, -84.721911

34 • B3 | Tahquamenon Falls SP - Clark Lake TC

Dispersed sites, No water, Vault/pit toilet, Tents only: $20, Hike-in, MI Recreation Passport required -non-residents: $9/day or $34/annual/residents: $12-$17/annual, Open all year, Elev: 759ft/231m, Tel: 906-492-3415, Nearest town: Paradise. GPS: 46.616828, -85.237737

35 • B3 | Tahquamenon Falls SP - Hemlock

Total sites: 88, RV sites: 88, Elec sites: 88, Central water, Flush toilet, Pay showers, RV dump, Tent & RV camping: $27-42, MI Recreation Passport required -non-residents: $9/day or $34/annual/residents: $12-$17/annual, Open all year, Reservations accepted, Elev: 732ft/223m, Tel: 906-492-3415, Nearest town: Paradise. GPS: 46.609171, -85.208847

36 • B3 | Tahquamenon Falls SP - Pines

Total sites: 36, RV sites: 36, Central water, Flush toilet, Free showers, RV dump, Tents: $20-28/RVs: $25-28, MI Recreation Passport required -non-residents: $9/day or $34/annual/residents: $12-$17/annual, Open Apr-Nov, Max Length: 30ft, Reservations accepted, Elev: 642ft/196m, Tel: 906-492-3415, Nearest town: Paradise. GPS: 46.554804, -85.039335

37 • B3 | Tahquamenon Falls SP - Portage

Total sites: 81, RV sites: 81, Elec sites: 81, Central water, Flush toilet, Pay showers, RV dump, Tent & RV camping: $35-42, MI Recreation Passport required -non-residents: $9/day or $34/annual/residents: $12-$17/annual, Open May-Oct, Reservations accepted, Elev: 634ft/193m, Tel: 906-492-3415, Nearest town: Paradise. GPS: 46.603076, -85.197908

38 • B3 | Tahquamenon Falls SP - River TC

Dispersed sites, No water, Vault/pit toilet, Tents only: $20, Hike-in, MI Recreation Passport required -non-residents: $9/day or $34/annual/residents: $12-$17/annual, Open all year, Elev: 680ft/207m, Tel: 906-492-3415, Nearest town: Paradise. GPS: 46.572723, -85.181056

39 • B3 | Tahquamenon Falls SP - Rivermouth

Total sites: 72, RV sites: 72, Elec sites: 72, Central water, Flush toilet, Free showers, RV dump, Tent & RV camping: $27-42, Group site: $17, MI Recreation Passport required -non-residents: $9/day or $34/annual/residents: $12-$17/annual, Open Apr-Oct, Reservations accepted, Elev: 607ft/185m, Tel: 906-492-3415, Nearest town: Paradise. GPS: 46.558754, -85.036208

40 • B3 | Wilderness SP

Total sites: 280, RV sites: 280, Elec sites: 270, Central water, Flush toilet, Free showers, RV dump, Tent & RV camping: $30-53, 18 Full hookups, MI Recreation Passport required -non-residents: $9/day or $34/annual/residents: $12-$17/annual, Open May-Nov, Reservations accepted, Elev: 587ft/179m, Tel: 231-436-5381, Nearest town: Carp Lake. GPS: 45.746227, -84.900196

41 • B3 | Wilderness SP - Nebo Shelter

Dispersed sites, No water, Vault/pit toilet, Hike-to shelter: $20, MI Recreation Passport required -non-residents: $9/day or $34/annual/residents: $12-$17/annual, Open all year, Reservations accepted, Elev: 630ft/192m, Tel: 231-436-5381, Nearest town: Carp Lake. GPS: 45.723664, -84.873174

42 • B3 | Young SP - Oak

Total sites: 51, RV sites: 51, Elec sites: 51, Central water, Flush toilet, Free showers, RV dump, Tent & RV camping: $38-45, MI Recreation Passport required -non-residents: $9/day or $34/annual/residents: $12-$17/annual, Open May-Oct, Reservations accepted, Elev: 591ft/180m, Tel: 231-582-7523, Nearest town: Boyne City. GPS: 45.235051, -85.060805

43 • B3 | Young SP - Spruce

Total sites: 148, RV sites: 148, Elec sites: 148, Central water, Flush toilet, Free showers, RV dump, Tent & RV camping: $38-45, Also cabins, MI Recreation Passport required -non-residents: $9/day or $34/annual/residents: $12-$17/annual, Open May-Oct, Reservations accepted, Elev: 607ft/185m, Tel: 231-582-7523, Nearest town: Boyne City. GPS: 45.237710, -85.056390

44 • B3 | Young SP - Terrace

Total sites: 38, RV sites: 38, Elec sites: 38, Central water, Flush toilet, Free showers, RV dump, Tent & RV camping: $38-45, MI Recreation Passport required -non-residents: $9/day or $34/annual/residents: $12-$17/annual, Open May-Oct, Reservations accepted, Elev: 591ft/180m, Tel: 231-582-7523, Nearest town: Boyne City. GPS: 45.233866, -85.058701

45 • B4 | Hoeft SP

Total sites: 144, RV sites: 144, Elec sites: 144, Water at site, Flush toilet, Free showers, RV dump, Tent & RV camping: $22-34, Also cabins, Some Full hookups sites, MI Recreation Passport required -non-residents: $9/day or $34/annual/residents: $12-$17/annual, Open Apr-Oct, Reservations accepted, Elev: 574ft/175m, Tel: 989-734-2543, Nearest town: Rogers City. GPS: 45.467943, -83.886236

46 • C3 | Clear Lake SP

Total sites: 200, RV sites: 200, Elec sites: 200, Central water, Flush toilet, Free showers, RV dump, Tent & RV camping: $22-34, Also group sites & cabins, Group site: $17, MI Recreation Passport required -non-residents: $9/day or $34/annual/residents: $12-$17/annual, Open all year, Reservations accepted, Elev: 879ft/268m, Tel: 989-785-4388, Nearest town: Atlanta. GPS: 45.132274, -84.184152

47 • C3 | Hartwick Pines SP

Total sites: 100, RV sites: 100, Elec sites: 100, Water at site, Flush toilet, Free showers, RV dump, Tent & RV camping: $27-46, Also cabins, Some Full hookups sites, Bike camp: $20, MI Recreation Passport required -non-residents: $9/day or $34/annual/residents:

$12-$17/annual, Open Apr-Oct, Reservations accepted, Elev: 1191ft/363m, Tel: 989-348-7068, Nearest town: Grayling. GPS: 44.738640, -84.684650

48 • C3 | Interlochen SP - Duck Lake North

Total sites: 204, RV sites: 204, Elec sites: 204, Central water, Flush toilet, Free showers, RV dump, Tent & RV camping: $27-34, MI Recreation Passport required -non-residents: $9/day or $34/annual/residents: $12-$17/annual, Open May-Oct, Reservations accepted, Elev: 862ft/263m, Tel: 231-276-9511, Nearest town: Interlochen. GPS: 44.631372, -85.762654

49 • C3 | Interlochen SP - Duck Lake South

Total sites: 208, RV sites: 208, Elec sites: 208, Central water, Flush toilet, Free showers, RV dump, Tent & RV camping: $27-34, MI Recreation Passport required -non-residents: $9/day or $34/annual/residents: $12-$17/annual, Open May-Sep, Reservations accepted, Elev: 853ft/260m, Tel: 231-276-9511, Nearest town: Interlochen. GPS: 44.625594, -85.759157

50 • C3 | Interlochen SP - Green Lake

Total sites: 61, RV sites: 61, Central water, Vault/pit toilet, No showers, No RV dump, Tent & RV camping: $20, MI Recreation Passport required -non-residents: $9/day or $34/annual/residents: $12-$17/annual, Open May-Oct, Reservations accepted, Elev: 876ft/267m, Tel: 231-276-9511, Nearest town: Interlochen. GPS: 44.622515, -85.762356

51 • C3 | Ludington SP - Beechwood

Total sites: 147, RV sites: 147, Elec sites: 147, Central water, Flush toilet, Free showers, RV dump, Tent & RV camping: $30-45, Also cabins, MI Recreation Passport required -non-residents: $9/day or $34/annual/residents: $12-$17/annual, Open Apr-Nov, Reservations accepted, Elev: 617ft/188m, Tel: 231-843-2423, Nearest town: Ludington. GPS: 44.037411, -86.494839

52 • C3 | Ludington SP - Cedar

Total sites: 106, RV sites: 106, Elec sites: 106, Central water, Flush toilet, Free showers, RV dump, Tents: $20/RVs: $30-41, Also cabins, MI Recreation Passport required -non-residents: $9/day or $34/annual/residents: $12-$17/annual, Open all year, Reservations accepted, Elev: 617ft/188m, Tel: 231-843-2423, Nearest town: Ludington. GPS: 44.036406, -86.501888

53 • C3 | Ludington SP - Jack Pine

Total sites: 10, RV sites: 0, Central water, Vault/pit toilet, Tents only: $20, Hike-in, MI Recreation Passport required -non-residents: $9/day or $34/annual/residents: $12-$17/annual, Open all year, Reservations accepted, Elev: 585ft/178m, Nearest town: Ludington. GPS: 44.044497, -86.511737

54 • C3 | Ludington SP - Pines

Total sites: 97, RV sites: 97, Elec sites: 97, Central water, Flush toilet, Free showers, RV dump, Tent & RV camping: $30-45, Also cabins, MI Recreation Passport required -non-residents: $9/day or $34/annual/residents: $12-$17/annual, Open May-Oct, Reservations accepted, Elev: 607ft/185m, Tel: 231-843-2423, Nearest town: Ludington. GPS: 44.035338, -86.506521

55 • C3 | Mears SP

Total sites: 175, RV sites: 175, Elec sites: 175, Central water, Flush toilet, Free showers, RV dump, Tent & RV camping: $38-41, Also cabins, MI Recreation Passport required -non-residents: $9/day or $34/annual/residents: $12-$17/annual, Open Apr-Oct, Reservations accepted, Elev: 600ft/183m, Tel: 231-869-2051, Nearest town: Pentwater. GPS: 43.783681, -86.438011

56 • C3 | Mitchell SP

Total sites: 221, RV sites: 221, Elec sites: 221, Central water, Flush toilet, Free showers, RV dump, Tent & RV camping: $38-45, Also cabins, MI Recreation Passport required -non-residents: $9/day or $34/annual/residents: $12-$17/annual, Open all year, Reservations accepted, Elev: 1306ft/398m, Tel: 231-775-7911, Nearest town: Cadillac. GPS: 44.238290, -85.452310

57 • C3 | North Higgins Lake SP - East

Total sites: 82, RV sites: 82, Elec sites: 82, Central water, Flush toilet, Free showers, RV dump, Tent & RV camping: $35-42, Also cabins, MI Recreation Passport required -non-residents: $9/day or $34/annual/residents: $12-$17/annual, Open May-Sep, Reservations accepted, Elev: 1177ft/359m, Tel: 989-821-6125, Nearest town: Roscommon. GPS: 44.514126, -84.753785

58 • C3 | North Higgins Lake SP - West

Total sites: 93, RV sites: 93, Elec sites: 93, Central water, Flush toilet, Free showers, RV dump, Tent & RV camping: $27-42, Also cabins, MI Recreation Passport required -non-residents: $9/day or $34/annual/residents: $12-$17/annual, Open all year, Reservations accepted, Elev: 1175ft/358m, Tel: 989-821-6125, Nearest town: Roscommon. GPS: 44.513527, -84.764451

59 • C3 | Orchard Beach SP

Total sites: 166, RV sites: 166, Elec sites: 166, Central water, Flush toilet, Free showers, RV dump, Tent & RV camping: $24-50, Also cabins, $22-$26 off-season, MI Recreation Passport required -non-residents: $9/day or $34/annual/residents: $12-$17/annual, Open Apr-Nov, Reservations accepted, Elev: 656ft/200m, Tel: 231-723-7422, Nearest town: Manistee. GPS: 44.281610, -86.314910

60 • C3 | Otsego Lake SP

Total sites: 155, RV sites: 155, Elec sites: 155, Central water, Flush toilet, Free showers, RV dump, Tent & RV camping: $27-38, Also cabins, MI Recreation Passport required - non-residents: $9/day or $33/annual, Open Apr-Oct, Reservations accepted, Elev: 1316ft/401m, Tel: 989-732-5485, Nearest town: Gaylord. GPS: 44.930230, -84.689820

61 • C3 | Silver Lake SP

Total sites: 200, RV sites: 200, Elec sites: 200, Central water, Flush toilet, Free showers, RV dump, Tent & RV camping: $30-41, MI Recreation Passport required -non-residents: $9/day or $34/annual/residents: $12-$17/annual, Open Apr-Oct, Reservations accepted, Elev: 614ft/187m, Tel: 231-873-3083, Nearest town: Mears. GPS: 43.661617, -86.495538

62 • C3 | South Higgins Lake SP

Total sites: 400, RV sites: 400, Elec sites: 400, Water at site, Flush toilet, Free showers, RV dump, Tent & RV camping: $34-53, Also cabins, Some Full hookups sites, MI Recreation Passport required

-non-residents: $9/day or $34/annual/residents: $12-$17/annual, Open May-Nov, Reservations accepted, Elev: 1165ft/355m, Tel: 989-821-6374, Nearest town: Roscommon. GPS: 44.424867, -84.684496

63 • C3 | Traverse City SP

Total sites: 343, RV sites: 343, Elec sites: 343, Central water, Flush toilet, Free showers, RV dump, Tent & RV camping: $38-45, Also cabins, MI Recreation Passport required -non-residents: $9/day or $34/annual/residents: $12-$17/annual, Open Apr-Nov, Reservations accepted, Elev: 607ft/185m, Tel: 231-922-5270, Nearest town: Traverse City. GPS: 44.746196, -85.551101

64 • C3 | Wilson SP

Total sites: 160, RV sites: 160, Elec sites: 160, Central water, Flush toilet, Free showers, RV dump, Tent & RV camping: $24-27, Also group sites & cabins, Group site:$17, MI Recreation Passport required -non-residents: $9/day or $34/annual/residents: $12-$17/annual, Open May-Nov, Reservations accepted, Elev: 1165ft/355m, Tel: 989-539-3021, Nearest town: Harrison. GPS: 44.029010, -84.804990

65 • C4 | Bay City SP

Total sites: 193, RV sites: 193, Elec sites: 193, Central water, Flush toilet, Free showers, RV dump, Tent & RV camping: $22-34, Group site: $20, MI Recreation Passport required -non-residents: $9/day or $34/annual/residents: $12-$17/annual, Open all year, Elev: 594ft/181m, Tel: 989-684-3020, Nearest town: Bay City. GPS: 43.665193, -83.904003

66 • C4 | Harrisville SP

Total sites: 195, RV sites: 195, Elec sites: 195, Central water, Flush toilet, Free showers, No RV dump, Tent & RV camping: $30-37, Also cabins, MI Recreation Passport required -non-residents: $9/day or $34/annual/residents: $12-$17/annual, Open Apr-Oct, Reservations accepted, Elev: 610ft/186m, Tel: 989-724-5126, Nearest town: Harrisville. GPS: 44.649270, -83.294180

67 • C4 | Negwegon SP - Blue Bell

Total sites: 1, No water, Vault/pit toilet, Tents only: $20, Hike-in/boat-in, MI Recreation Passport required -non-residents: $9/day or $34/annual/residents: $12-$17/annual, Open Apr-Nov, Reservations accepted, Elev: 582ft/177m, Nearest town: Harrisville. GPS: 44.867117, -83.316656

68 • C4 | Negwegon SP - Pewabic

Total sites: 1, No water, Vault/pit toilet, Tents only: $20, Hike-in/boat-in, MI Recreation Passport required -non-residents: $9/day or $34/annual/residents: $12-$17/annual, Open Apr-Nov, Reservations accepted, Elev: 583ft/178m, Nearest town: Harrisville. GPS: 44.873692, -83.319523

69 • C4 | Negwegon SP - South Point

Total sites: 1, No water, Vault/pit toilet, Tents only: $20, Hike-in/boat-in, MI Recreation Passport required -non-residents: $9/day or $34/annual/residents: $12-$17/annual, Open Apr-Nov, Reservations accepted, Elev: 582ft/177m, Nearest town: Harrisville. GPS: 44.881152, -83.315932

70 • C4 | Negwegon SP - Twin Pines

Total sites: 1, No water, Vault/pit toilet, Tents only: $20, Hike-in/boat-in, MI Recreation Passport required -non-residents: $9/day or $34/annual/residents: $12-$17/annual, Open Apr-Nov, Reservations accepted, Elev: 583ft/178m, Nearest town: Harrisville. GPS: 44.871463, -83.319114

71 • C4 | Port Crescent SP

Total sites: 137, RV sites: 137, Elec sites: 137, Water at site, Flush toilet, Free showers, RV dump, Tent & RV camping: $38-41, Also cabins, Some Full hookups sites, MI Recreation Passport required -non-residents: $9/day or $34/annual/residents: $12-$17/annual, Open Apr-Oct, Reservations accepted, Elev: 610ft/186m, Tel: 989-738-8663, Nearest town: Port Austin. GPS: 44.007717, -83.052334

72 • C4 | Sleeper SP

Total sites: 226, RV sites: 226, Elec sites: 226, Central water, Flush toilet, Free showers, RV dump, Tent & RV camping: $22-37, Also cabins, MI Recreation Passport required -non-residents: $9/day or $34/annual/residents: $12-$17/annual, Open Apr-Nov, Reservations accepted, Elev: 617ft/188m, Tel: 989-856-4411, Nearest town: Caseville. GPS: 43.979651, -83.210241

73 • C4 | Tawas Point SP

Total sites: 193, RV sites: 193, Elec sites: 193, Central water, Flush toilet, Free showers, RV dump, Tent & RV camping: $38-41, Also cabins, MI Recreation Passport required -non-residents: $9/day or $34/annual/residents: $12-$17/annual, Open Apr-Nov, Reservations accepted, Elev: 584ft/178m, Tel: 989-362-5041, Nearest town: East Tawas. GPS: 44.258430, -83.443110

74 • D2 | Grand Haven SP

Total sites: 174, RV sites: 174, Elec sites: 174, Central water, Flush toilet, Free showers, RV dump, Tent & RV camping: $38-45, Also cabins, MI Recreation Passport required -non-residents: $9/day or $34/annual/residents: $12-$17/annual, Open May-Oct, Reservations accepted, Elev: 614ft/187m, Tel: 616-847-1309, Nearest town: Grand Haven. GPS: 43.056621, -86.246659

75 • D2 | Hoffmaster SP

Total sites: 293, RV sites: 293, Elec sites: 293, Central water, Flush toilet, Free showers, RV dump, Tent & RV camping: $38-45, MI Recreation Passport required -non-residents: $9/day or $34/annual/residents: $12-$17/annual, Open Apr-Oct, Reservations accepted, Elev: 646ft/197m, Tel: 231-798-3711, Nearest town: Muskegon. GPS: 43.138139, -86.272478

76 • D2 | Muskegon SP - Lake Michighan

Total sites: 105, RV sites: 105, Elec sites: 105, Central water, Flush toilet, Free showers, RV dump, Tent & RV camping: $30-45, Also cabins, MI Recreation Passport required -non-residents: $9/day or $34/annual/residents: $12-$17/annual, Open all year, Reservations accepted, Elev: 650ft/198m, Tel: 231-744-3480, Nearest town: North Muskegon. GPS: 43.261545, -86.356866

77 • D2 | Muskegon SP - South Channel

Total sites: 139, RV sites: 139, Elec sites: 139, Central water, Flush toilet, Free showers, RV dump, Tent & RV camping: $38-45, MI Recreation Passport required -non-residents: $9/day or $34/

annual/residents: $12-$17/annual, Open Apr-Oct, Reservations accepted, Elev: 591ft/180m, Tel: 231-744-3480, Nearest town: North Muskegon. GPS: 43.234754, -86.329492

78 • D2 | Van Buren SP

Total sites: 220, RV sites: 220, Elec sites: 220, Central water, Flush toilet, Free showers, RV dump, Tent & RV camping: $35-42, MI Recreation Passport required -non-residents: $9/day or $34/annual/residents: $12-$17/annual, Open Apr-Oct, Reservations accepted, Elev: 630ft/192m, Tel: 269-637-2788, Nearest town: South Haven. GPS: 42.330445, -86.303926

79 • D3 | Fort Custer SP

Total sites: 219, RV sites: 219, Elec sites: 219, Central water, Flush toilet, Free showers, RV dump, Tent & RV camping: $22-34, Also group sites & cabins, Group site: $17-$20, MI Recreation Passport required -non-residents: $9/day or $34/annual/residents: $12-$17/annual, Open all year, Reservations accepted, Elev: 824ft/251m, Tel: 269-731-4200, Nearest town: Augusta. GPS: 42.318990, -85.348950

80 • D3 | Fort Custer SP - Equestrian

Total sites: 7, RV sites: 7, Central water, Vault/pit toilet, No showers, No RV dump, Tent & RV camping: $20, MI Recreation Passport required -non-residents: $9/day or $33/annual, Open all year, Reservations accepted, Elev: 828ft/252m, Tel: 269-731-4200, Nearest town: Augusta. GPS: 42.315339, -85.342572

81 • D3 | Holland SP - Beach CG

Total sites: 98, RV sites: 98, Elec sites: 98, Water at site, Flush toilet, Free showers, Tent & RV camping: $38-53, Also cabins, Some Full hookups, MI Recreation Passport required -non-residents: $9/day or $34/annual/residents: $12-$17/annual, Open May-Sep, Reservations accepted, Elev: 607ft/185m, Tel: 800-447-2757, Nearest town: Holland. GPS: 42.775311, -86.207137

82 • D3 | Holland SP - Lake Macatawa CG

Total sites: 211, RV sites: 211, Elec sites: 211, Central water, Flush toilet, Free showers, RV dump, Tent & RV camping: $38-45, MI Recreation Passport required -non-residents: $9/day or $34/annual/residents: $12-$17/annual, Open Apr-Oct, Reservations accepted, Elev: 600ft/183m, Tel: 800-447-2757, Nearest town: Holland. GPS: 42.779350, -86.199250

83 • D3 | Newaygo SP

Total sites: 99, RV sites: 99, Central water, Vault/pit toilet, No showers, No RV dump, Tent & RV camping: $20, MI Recreation Passport required -non-residents: $9/day or $34/annual/residents: $12-$17/annual, Open May-Oct, Reservations accepted, Elev: 856ft/261m, Tel: 231-856-4452, Nearest town: Newaygo. GPS: 43.503449, -85.587187

84 • D3 | Sleepy Hollow SP

Total sites: 181, RV sites: 181, Elec sites: 181, Central water, Flush toilet, Free showers, RV dump, Tents: $20-34/RVs: $27-34, MI Recreation Passport required -non-residents: $9/day or $34/annual/residents: $12-$17/annual, Open Apr-Oct, Reservations accepted, Elev: 824ft/251m, Tel: 517-651-6217, Nearest town: Laingsburg. GPS: 42.942846, -84.402848

85 • D4 | Algonac SP - Wagon Wheel

Total sites: 76, RV sites: 76, Elec sites: 76, Flush toilet, Free showers, RV dump, Tent & RV camping: $24-27, Group site: $17, MI Recreation Passport required -non-residents: $9/day or $34/annual/residents: $12-$17/annual, Open May-Oct, Reservations accepted, Elev: 600ft/183m, Tel: 810-765-5605, Nearest town: Marine City. GPS: 42.656673, -82.523154

86 • D4 | Algonac SP -River Front

Total sites: 220, RV sites: 220, Elec sites: 220, Central water, Flush toilet, Free showers, RV dump, Tent & RV camping: $22-37, MI Recreation Passport required -non-residents: $9/day or $34/annual/residents: $12-$17/annual, Open all year, Reservations accepted, Elev: 591ft/180m, Tel: 810-765-5605, Nearest town: Marine City. GPS: 42.653352, -82.515691

87 • D4 | Lakeport SP - North

Total sites: 94, RV sites: 94, Elec sites: 94, Central water, Flush toilet, Free showers, RV dump, Tent & RV camping: $35-42, Also cabins, MI Recreation Passport required -non-residents: $9/day or $34/annual/residents: $12-$17/annual, Open Apr-Oct, Reservations accepted, Elev: 600ft/183m, Tel: 810-327-6224, Nearest town: Lakeport. GPS: 43.130819, -82.494834

88 • D4 | Lakeport SP - South

Total sites: 56, RV sites: 56, Elec sites: 56, Central water, Flush toilet, Free showers, RV dump, Tent & RV camping: $35-42, Also group sites & cabins, Group site: $20, MI Recreation Passport required -non-residents: $9/day or $34/annual/residents: $12-$17/annual, Open Apr-Oct, Reservations accepted, Elev: 633ft/193m, Tel: 810-327-6224, Nearest town: Lakeport. GPS: 43.124778, -82.496101

89 • D4 | Seven Lakes SP - Sand Lake

Total sites: 70, RV sites: 70, Elec sites: 70, Central water, Flush toilet, Free showers, Tent & RV camping: $22-30, MI Recreation Passport required -non-residents: $9/day or $34/annual/residents: $12-$17/annual, Open May-Nov, Reservations accepted, Elev: 938ft/286m, Tel: 248-634-7271, Nearest town: Holly. GPS: 42.808210, -83.656760

90 • D4 | W J Hayes SP - Sites 2-96

Total sites: 95, RV sites: 95, Elec sites: 95, Water at site, Flush toilet, Free showers, RV dump, Tent & RV camping: $30-37, Also cabins, Full hookups sites, MI Recreation Passport required -non-residents: $9/day or $34/annual/residents: $12-$17/annual, Open Apr-Oct, Reservations accepted, Elev: 985ft/300m, Tel: 517-467-7401, Nearest town: Onsted. GPS: 42.066949, -84.131456

91 • D4 | W J Hayes SP - Sites 97-185

Total sites: 89, RV sites: 89, Elec sites: 89, Central water, Flush toilet, Free showers, RV dump, Tent & RV camping: $30-37, Also cabins, MI Recreation Passport required -non-residents: $9/day or $34/annual/residents: $12-$17/annual, Open Apr-Oct, Reservations accepted, Elev: 988ft/301m, Tel: 517-467-7401, Nearest town: Onsted. GPS: 42.066034, -84.126057

92 • E2 | Warren Dunes SP - Modern

Total sites: 184, RV sites: 184, Elec sites: 184, Central water, Flush toilet, Free showers, RV dump, Tent & RV camping: $38-53, Also cabins, Full hookups sites, MI Recreation Passport required -non-residents: $9/day or $34/annual/residents: $12-$17/annual, Open Apr-Oct, Reservations accepted, Elev: 636ft/194m, Tel: 269-426-4013, Nearest town: Sawyer. GPS: 41.910982, -86.587585

93 • E2 | Warren Dunes SP - Semi-modern

Total sites: 37, RV sites: 37, Central water, Flush toilet, Free showers, RV dump, Tent & RV camping: $30-33, Also cabins, MI Recreation Passport required -non-residents: $9/day or $34/annual/residents: $12-$17/annual, Open Apr-Oct, Reservations accepted, Elev: 662ft/202m, Tel: 269-426-4013, Nearest town: Sawyer. GPS: 41.915631, -86.583724

94 • E4 | Sterling SP

Total sites: 256, RV sites: 256, Elec sites: 256, Water at site, Flush toilet, Free showers, RV dump, Tents: $30-33/RVs: $30-45, Some Full hookups sites, MI Recreation Passport required -non-residents: $9/day or $34/annual/residents: $12-$17/annual, Open Apr-Oct, Reservations accepted, Elev: 581ft/177m, Tel: 734-289-2715, Nearest town: Monroe. GPS: 41.905405, -83.336206

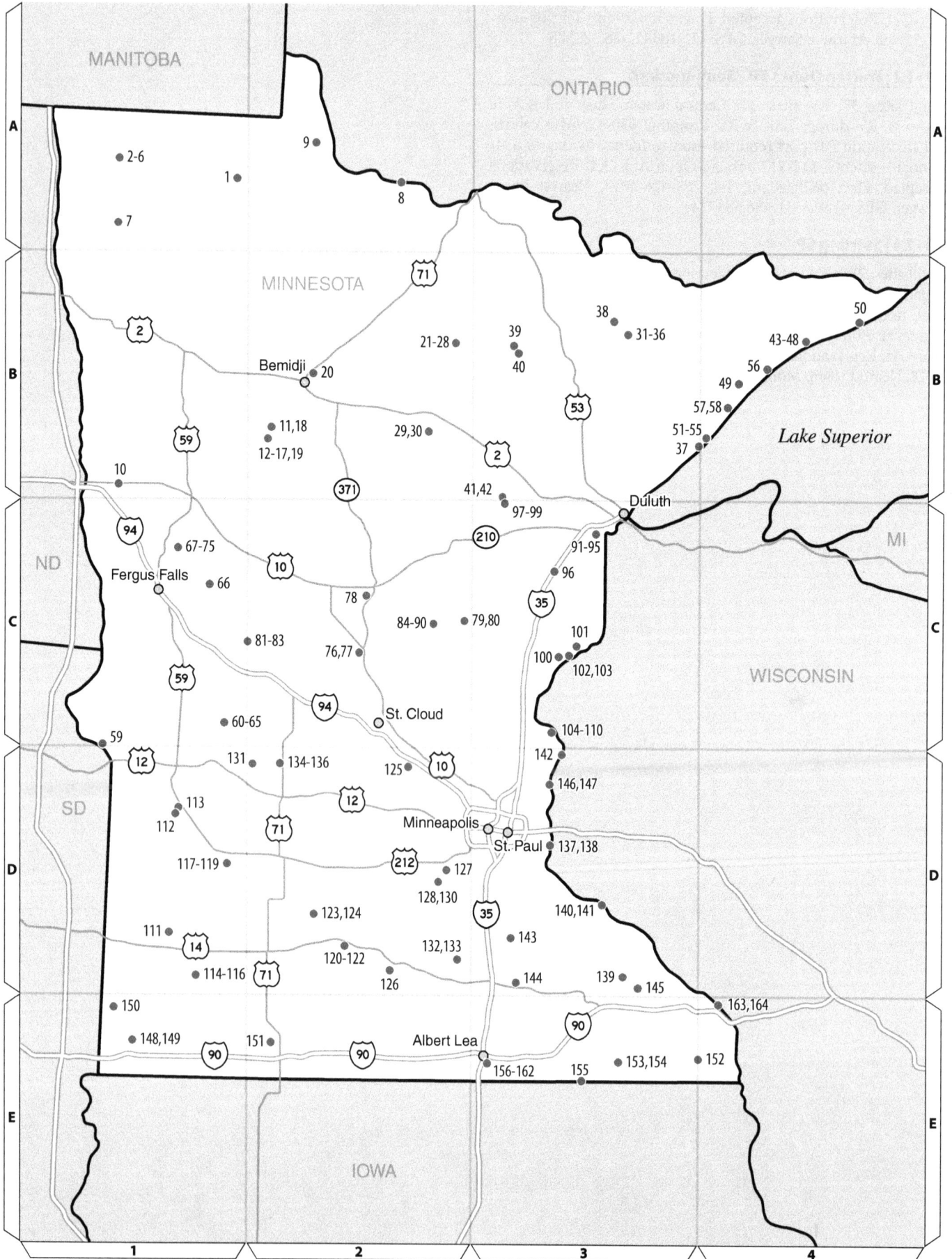

Minnesota

MANITOBA

ONTARIO

MINNESOTA

● 2-6

● 9

● 1

● 8

● 7

71

● 38

● 50

2

● 21-28

● 39

● 31-36

● 43-48

● 40

56

49 ●

Bemidji ● 20

53

57,58

● 11,18

51-55

● 12-17,19

59

● 29,30

2

37

Lake Superior

● 10

371

● 41,42

94

● 67-75

210

● 97-99

Duluth

10

MI

Fergus Falls

● 66

78

● 91-95

● 96

● 81-83

84-90 ●

● 79,80

35

101 ●

76,77

● 100

102,103

ND

59

WISCONSIN

94

St. Cloud

● 104-110

● 60-65

131 ●

● 134-136

125 ●

142 ●

10

146,147 ●

12

113 ●

112 ●

12

Minneapolis

71

St. Paul ● 137,138

SD

117-119 ●

212

● 127

● 140,141

128,130 ●

35

● 123,124

● 143

111 ●

14

132,133 ●

120-122

● 144

139 ●

● 145

● 114-116

71

126 ●

● 163,164

● 150

90

● 148,149

151 ●

Albert Lea

● 153,154

● 152

90

90

156-162

155 ●

IOWA

Map	ID	Map	ID
A1	1-7	C3	91-110
A2	8-9	D1	111-119
B1	10	D2	120-136
B2	11-30	D3	137-147
B3	31-42	E1	148-150
B4	43-58	E2	151
C1	59-75	E3	152-162
C2	76-90	E4	163-164

Alphabetical List of Camping Areas

Name	ID	Map
Afton SP - Back-Country	137	D3
Afton SP - River Site	138	D3
Bear Head Lake SP	31	B3
Bear Head Lake SP - Canoe/Trail Camp BP5	32	B3
Bear Head Lake SP - TC 1	33	B3
Bear Head Lake SP - TC 2	34	B3
Bear Head Lake SP - TC 3	35	B3
Bear Head Lake SP - TC 4	36	B3
Beaver Creek Valley SP	152	E3
Big Stone Lake SP	59	C1
Blue Mounds SP	148	E1
Blue Mounds SP - Cart-in	149	E1
Buffalo River SP	10	B1
Camden SP	111	D1
Carley SP	139	D3
Cascade River SP	43	B4
Cascade River SP - TC 1	44	B4
Cascade River SP - TC 2	45	B4
Cascade River SP - TC 3	46	B4
Cascade River SP - TC 4	47	B4
Cascade River SP - TC 5	48	B4
Charles A. Lindbergh SP	76	C2
Charles A. Lindbergh SP - Trail Camp	77	C2
Crow Wing SP - Main CG	78	C2
Father Hennepin SP - Lakeview	79	C2
Father Hennepin SP - Maple Grove	80	C2
Flandrau SP - Electric	120	D2
Flandrau SP - Non-Electric	121	D2
Flandrau SP - Rustic	122	D2
Forestville Mystery Cave SP - Family	153	E3
Forestville Mystery Cave SP - Horse Camp	154	E3
Fort Ridgely SP - Creekside/Rustic	123	D2
Fort Ridgely SP - Horse Camp	124	D2
Franz Jevne SP	8	A2
Frontenac SP	140	D3
Frontenac SP - Cart-in	141	D3
George H Crosby-Manitou SP	49	B4
Glacial Lakes SP - Baby Lake TC	60	C1
Glacial Lakes SP - Hill TC	61	C1
Glacial Lakes SP - Horse Camp	62	C1
Glacial Lakes SP - Kettle Lake TC	63	C1
Glacial Lakes SP - Main	64	C1
Glacial Lakes SP - Oak TC	65	C1
Glendalough SP - Cart-in	66	C1
Gooseberry Falls SP	37	B3
Great River Bluffs SP - Bicycle Camp	163	E4
Great River Bluffs SP - Main	164	E4
Hayes Lake SP	1	A1
Interstate SP	142	D3
Itasca SP - Bear Paw	11	B2
Itasca SP - Deer Park Lake TC B10	12	B2
Itasca SP - Deer Park Lake TC B11	13	B2
Itasca SP - Hernando Desoto Lake TC B03-B04	14	B2
Itasca SP - Iron Corner Lake TC B06	15	B2
Itasca SP - McKay Lake TC B05	16	B2
Itasca SP - Myrtle Lake TC B07-B09	17	B2
Itasca SP - Pine Ridge	18	B2
Itasca SP - Whipple Lake TC B01-B02	19	B2
Jay Cooke SP - Ash Ridge	91	C3
Jay Cooke SP - High Landing	92	C3
Jay Cooke SP - Lost Lake	93	C3
Jay Cooke SP - Main	94	C3
Jay Cooke SP - Silver Creek	95	C3
Judge CR Magney SP	50	B4
Kilen Woods SP	151	E2
Lac Qui Parle SP - Lower CG	112	D1
Lac Qui Parle SP - Upper CG	113	D1
Lake Bemidji SP	20	B2
Lake Bronson SP - Lakeside	2	A1
Lake Bronson SP - Old Ranch Riverview TC	3	A1
Lake Bronson SP - River Meadow TC	4	A1
Lake Bronson SP - River Sandhole TC	5	A1
Lake Bronson SP - Two Rivers	6	A1
Lake Carlos SP - Horse Camp	81	C2
Lake Carlos SP - Lower CG	82	C2
Lake Carlos SP - Upper CG	83	C2
Lake Louise SP	155	E3
Lake Maria SP	125	D2
Lake Shetek SP - Main CG	114	D1
Lake Shetek SP - Park Lake	115	D1
Lake Shetek SP - Prairie	116	D1
Lake Vermilion Soudan Underground Mine SP	38	B3
Maplewood SP - Beers Lake TC	67	C1
Maplewood SP - Cow Lake North TC	68	C1
Maplewood SP - Cow Lake South TC	69	C1
Maplewood SP - Grass Lake TC	70	C1
Maplewood SP - Hollow	71	C1
Maplewood SP - Horseriders	72	C1
Maplewood SP - Knoll	73	C1
Maplewood SP - Lake Lida	74	C1
Maplewood SP - Main	75	C1
McCarthy Beach SP - Beatrice Lake	39	B3
McCarthy Beach SP - Side Lake	40	B3
Mille Lacs Kathio SP - Black Bass Lake TC	84	C2
Mille Lacs Kathio SP - GR TC	85	C2
Mille Lacs Kathio SP - Horse Camp	86	C2
Mille Lacs Kathio SP - KT TC	87	C2
Mille Lacs Kathio SP - Ogechie	88	C2
Mille Lacs Kathio SP - Petega	89	C2
Mille Lacs Kathio SP - SM TC	90	C2
Minneopa SP	126	D2
Minnesotta Valley SP - Carver Rapids TC	127	D2
Minnesotta Valley SP - Horse Camp	128	D2
Minnesotta Valley SP - Paine Pond TC	129	D2
Minnesotta Valley SP - Quarry	130	D2
Monson Lake SP	131	D2

1 • A1 | Hayes Lake SP

Total sites: 37, RV sites: 35, Elec sites: 18, Central water, Flush toilet, Free showers, RV dump, Tents: $15/RVs: $23, Also walk-to sites/cabins, $7 daily entrance fee, Open May-Oct, Max Length: 40ft, Reservations accepted, Elev: 1184ft/361m, Tel: 218-425-7504, Nearest town: Roseau. GPS: 48.634047, -95.536456

2 • A1 | Lake Bronson SP - Lakeside

Total sites: 61, RV sites: 61, Elec sites: 54, Central water, Flush toilet, Free showers, RV dump, Tents: $19/RVs: $19-27, $7 daily entrance fee, Open all year, Max Length: 50ft, Reservations accepted, Elev: 991ft/302m, Tel: 218-754-2200, Nearest town: Lake Bronson. GPS: 48.724051, -96.626749

3 • A1 | Lake Bronson SP - Old Ranch Riverview TC

Total sites: 1, No water, No toilets, Tents only: $15, Hike-in, $7 daily entrance fee, Open all year, Elev: 997ft/304m, Tel: 218-754-2200, Nearest town: Lake Bronson. GPS: 48.735343, -96.585826

4 • A1 | Lake Bronson SP - River Meadow TC

Total sites: 1, No water, No toilets, Tents only: $15, Hike-in, $7 daily entrance fee, Open all year, Elev: 974ft/297m, Tel: 218-754-2200, Nearest town: Lake Bronson. GPS: 48.725282, -96.593555

5 • A1 | Lake Bronson SP - River Sandhole TC

Total sites: 1, No water, No toilets, Tents only: $15, Hike-in, $7 daily entrance fee, Open all year, Elev: 994ft/303m, Tel: 218-754-2200, Nearest town: Lake Bronson. GPS: 48.739763, -96.585883

6 • A1 | Lake Bronson SP - Two Rivers

Total sites: 97, RV sites: 97, Elec sites: 12, Central water, Flush toilet, Free showers, RV dump, Tents: $15/RVs: $23, $7 daily entrance fee, Open all year, Max Length: 50ft, Reservations accepted, Elev: 997ft/304m, Tel: 218-754-2200, Nearest town: Lake Bronson. GPS: 48.726184, -96.603134

7 • A1 | Old Mill SP

Total sites: 26, RV sites: 26, Elec sites: 10, Central water, Flush toilet, Free showers, No RV dump, Tents: $15/RVs: $15-23, $7 daily entrance fee, Open May-Oct, Max Length: 67ft, Reservations accepted, Elev: 971ft/296m, Tel: 218-437-8174, Nearest town: Argyle. GPS: 48.365719, -96.568546

8 • A2 | Franz Jevne SP

Total sites: 21, RV sites: 18, Elec sites: 1, Central water, Vault/pit toilet, No showers, No RV dump, Tents: $15/RVs: $15-23, Also walk-to sites, $7 daily entrance fee, Reservations accepted, Elev: 1070ft/326m, Tel: 218-783-6252, Nearest town: Birchdale. GPS: 48.641720, -94.059110

9 • A2 | Zippel Bay SP

Total sites: 57, RV sites: 57, Central water, Flush toilet, Free showers, RV dump, Tents: $24/RVs: $32, $7 daily entrance fee, Open Apr-Oct, Max Length: 50ft, Reservations accepted, Elev: 1089ft/332m, Tel: 218-783-6252, Nearest town: Williams. GPS: 48.858328, -94.836873

10 • B1 | Buffalo River SP

Total sites: 44, RV sites: 44, Elec sites: 35, Central water, Flush toilet, Free showers, RV dump, Tents: $23/RVs: $31, $7 daily entrance fee, Open all year, Max Length: 60ft, Reservations accepted, Elev: 981ft/299m, Tel: 218-498-2124, Nearest town: Glyndon. GPS: 46.864738, -96.470024

11 • B2 | Itasca SP - Bear Paw

Total sites: 81, RV sites: 81, Elec sites: 56, Central water, Flush toilet, Free showers, RV dump, Tents: $24/RVs: $32, Also cabins, $7 daily entrance fee, Open May-Oct, Reservations accepted, Elev: 1526ft/465m, Tel: 218-699-7251, Nearest town: Park Rapids. GPS: 47.218423, -95.190007

12 • B2 | Itasca SP - Deer Park Lake TC B10

Total sites: 1, No water, Vault/pit toilet, Tents only: $19, Hike-in, $7 daily entrance fee, Elev: 1583ft/482m, Tel: 218-699-7251, Nearest town: Park Rapids. GPS: 47.177031, -95.184067

13 • B2 | Itasca SP - Deer Park Lake TC B11

Total sites: 1, No water, Vault/pit toilet, Tents only: $19, Hike-in, $7 daily entrance fee, Elev: 1588ft/484m, Tel: 218-699-7251, Nearest town: Park Rapids. GPS: 47.180626, -95.180487

14 • B2 | Itasca SP - Hernando Desoto Lake TC B03-B04

Total sites: 2, No water, Vault/pit toilet, Tents only: $19, Hike-in, $7 daily entrance fee, Elev: 1580ft/482m, Tel: 218-699-7251, Nearest town: Park Rapids. GPS: 47.148935, -95.219958

15 • B2 | Itasca SP - Iron Corner Lake TC B06

Total sites: 1, No water, Vault/pit toilet, Tents only: $19, Hike-in, $7 daily entrance fee, Elev: 1604ft/489m, Tel: 218-699-7251, Nearest town: Park Rapids. GPS: 47.152164, -95.170748

16 • B2 | Itasca SP - McKay Lake TC B05

Total sites: 1, No water, Vault/pit toilet, Tents only: $19, Hike-in, $7 daily entrance fee, Elev: 1594ft/486m, Tel: 218-699-7251, Nearest town: Park Rapids. GPS: 47.163991, -95.194204

17 • B2 | Itasca SP - Myrtle Lake TC B07-B09

Total sites: 3, No water, Vault/pit toilet, Tents only: $19, Hike-in, $7 daily entrance fee, Elev: 1587ft/484m, Tel: 218-699-7251, Nearest town: Park Rapids. GPS: 47.173994, -95.180866

18 • B2 | Itasca SP - Pine Ridge

Total sites: 158, RV sites: 158, Elec sites: 112, Central water, Flush toilet, Free showers, No RV dump, Tents: $23/RVs: $31, RV Dump at Bear Paw CG, $7 daily entrance fee, Open all year, Reservations accepted, Elev: 1542ft/470m, Tel: 218-699-7251, Nearest town: Park Rapids. GPS: 47.234374, -95.191126

19 • B2 | Itasca SP - Whipple Lake TC B01-B02

Total sites: 2, No water, Vault/pit toilet, Tents only: $24, Hike-in, $7 daily entrance fee, Elev: 1577ft/481m, Tel: 218-699-7251, Nearest town: Park Rapids. GPS: 47.167198, -95.230892

20 • B2 | Lake Bemidji SP

Total sites: 95, RV sites: 95, Elec sites: 43, Central water, Flush toilet, Free showers, RV dump, Tents: $23/RVs: $31, Also cabins, $7 daily entrance fee, Open all year, Max Length: 50ft, Reservations accepted, Elev: 1381ft/421m, Tel: 218-308-2300, Nearest town: Bemidji. GPS: 47.537004, -94.826018

21 • B2 | Scenic SP - Chase Point

Total sites: 69, RV sites: 69, Elec sites: 21, Central water, Flush toilet, Free showers, RV dump, Tents: $24/RVs: $32, $7 daily entrance fee, Open all year, Max Length: 90ft, Reservations accepted, Elev: 1365ft/416m, Tel: 218-743-3362, Nearest town: Bigfork. GPS: 47.714581, -93.569233

22 • B2 | Scenic SP - Lodge CG

Total sites: 29, RV sites: 29, Central water, Flush toilet, Free showers, No RV dump, Tent & RV camping: $24, $7 daily entrance fee, Open all year, Max Length: 40ft, Reservations accepted, Elev: 1378ft/420m, Tel: 218-743-3362, Nearest town: Bigfork. GPS: 47.721808, -93.568843

23 • B2 | Scenic SP - Pine Lake 1 TC

Dispersed sites, No water, Vault/pit toilet, Tents only: $24, Hike-in, $7 daily entrance fee, Open all year, Reservations accepted, Elev: 1450ft/442m, Tel: 218-743-3362, Nearest town: Bigfork. GPS: 47.735973, -93.571616

24 • B2 | Scenic SP - Pine Lake 2 TC

Dispersed sites, No water, Vault/pit toilet, Tents only: $24, Hike-in, $7 daily entrance fee, Open all year, Reservations accepted, Elev: 1434ft/437m, Tel: 218-743-3362, Nearest town: Bigfork. GPS: 47.738374, -93.569568

25 • B2 | Scenic SP - Sandwick Lake TC 4

Dispersed sites, No water, Vault/pit toilet, Tents only: $24, Hike-in/boat-in, $7 daily entrance fee, Open all year, Reservations accepted, Elev: 1360ft/415m, Tel: 218-743-3362, Nearest town: Bigfork. GPS: 47.711428, -93.554552

26 • B2 | Scenic SP - Sandwick Lake TC 5

Dispersed sites, No water, Vault/pit toilet, Tents only: $24, Hike-in/boat-in, $7 daily entrance fee, Open all year, Reservations accepted, Elev: 1375ft/419m, Tel: 218-743-3362, Nearest town: Bigfork. GPS: 47.709663, -93.555141

27 • B2 | Scenic SP - Sandwick Lake TC 6

Dispersed sites, No water, Vault/pit toilet, Tents only: $24, Hike-in/boat-in, $7 daily entrance fee, Open all year, Reservations accepted, Elev: 1360ft/415m, Tel: 218-743-3362, Nearest town: Bigfork. GPS: 47.707756, -93.556647

28 • B2 | Scenic SP - Sandwick Lake TC 7

Dispersed sites, No water, Vault/pit toilet, Tents only: $24, Hike-in/boat-in, $7 daily entrance fee, Open all year, Reservations accepted, Elev: 1365ft/416m, Tel: 218-743-3362, Nearest town: Bigfork. GPS: 47.705068, -93.558357

29 • B2 | Schoolcraft SP

Total sites: 29, RV sites: 28, Central water, Vault/pit toilet, No showers, No RV dump, Tent & RV camping: $24, $7 daily entrance fee, Open May-Sep, Elev: 1319ft/402m, Tel: 218-743-3362, Nearest town: Calumet. GPS: 47.223362, -93.804033

30 • B2 | Schoolcraft SP - Canoe Camp

Dispersed sites, No water, Vault/pit toilet, Tents only: $24, Hike-in, $7 daily entrance fee, Open May-Sep, Elev: 1294ft/394m,

Tel: 218-743-3362, Nearest town: Calumet. GPS: 47.220357, -93.800629

31 • B3 | Bear Head Lake SP

Total sites: 73, RV sites: 73, Elec sites: 45, Central water, Flush toilet, Free showers, RV dump, Tents: $23/RVs: $31, Also cabins, $7 daily entrance fee, Open all year, Max Length: 60ft, Reservations accepted, Elev: 1529ft/466m, Tel: 218-365-7229, Nearest town: Ely. GPS: 47.792385, -92.085343

32 • B3 | Bear Head Lake SP - Canoe/Trail Camp BP5

Dispersed sites, No water, Tents only: $15, Hike-in/boat-in, Open all year, Reservations accepted, Elev: 1512ft/461m, Tel: 218-365-7229, Nearest town: Ely. GPS: 47.785096, -92.071254

33 • B3 | Bear Head Lake SP - TC 1

Dispersed sites, No water, Tents only: $15, Hike-in, Open all year, Reservations accepted, Elev: 1527ft/465m, Tel: 218-365-7229, Nearest town: Ely. GPS: 47.782925, -92.058767

34 • B3 | Bear Head Lake SP - TC 2

Dispersed sites, No water, Tents only: $15, Hike-in, Open all year, Reservations accepted, Elev: 1564ft/477m, Tel: 218-365-7229, Nearest town: Ely. GPS: 47.781538, -92.054354

35 • B3 | Bear Head Lake SP - TC 3

Dispersed sites, No water, Tents only: $15, Hike-in, Open all year, Reservations accepted, Elev: 1525ft/465m, Tel: 218-365-7229, Nearest town: Ely. GPS: 47.781561, -92.052205

36 • B3 | Bear Head Lake SP - TC 4

Dispersed sites, No water, Tents only: $15, Hike-in, Open all year, Reservations accepted, Elev: 1515ft/462m, Tel: 218-365-7229, Nearest town: Ely. GPS: 47.777476, -92.052824

37 • B3 | Gooseberry Falls SP

Total sites: 69, RV sites: 69, Central water, Flush toilet, Free showers, RV dump, Tent & RV camping: $23, $7 daily entrance fee, Open all year, Max Length: 40ft, Reservations accepted, Elev: 673ft/205m, Tel: 218-834-3855, Nearest town: Two Harbors. GPS: 47.139291, -91.461741

38 • B3 | Lake Vermilion Soudan Underground Mine SP

Total sites: 33, RV sites: 33, Elec sites: 33, Central water, Flush toilet, Free showers, RV dump, Tent & RV camping: $31, 3 group sites: $50-$250, $7 daily entrance fee, Open all year, Reservations accepted, Elev: 1448ft/441m, Tel: 218-300-7000, Nearest town: Soudan. GPS: 47.843724, -92.190049

39 • B3 | McCarthy Beach SP - Beatrice Lake

Total sites: 30, RV sites: 27, Central water, Vault/pit toilet, No showers, No RV dump, Tent & RV camping: $15, $7 daily entrance fee, Open Apr-Nov, Max Length: 40ft, Reservations accepted, Elev: 1404ft/428m, Tel: 218-254-7979, Nearest town: Side Lake. GPS: 47.710907, -93.070182

40 • B3 | McCarthy Beach SP - Side Lake

Total sites: 59, RV sites: 59, Elec sites: 20, Central water, Flush toilet, Free showers, RV dump, Tents: $23/RVs: $23-31, $7 daily entrance fee, Open Apr-Nov, Max Length: 40ft, Reservations

accepted, Elev: 1421ft/433m, Tel: 218-254-7979, Nearest town: Side Lake. GPS: 47.673535, -93.026326

41 • B3 | Savanna Portage SP - Condi TC

Dispersed sites, No water, Vault/pit toilet, Tents only: $24, Hike-in, $7 daily entrance fee, Open all year, Reservations accepted, Elev: 1366ft/416m, Tel: 218-426-3271, Nearest town: McGregor. GPS: 46.844991, -93.173152

42 • B3 | Savanna Portage SP - Wolf Lake TC

Dispersed sites, No water, Vault/pit toilet, Tents only: $24, Hike-in, $7 daily entrance fee, Open all year, Reservations accepted, Elev: 1297ft/395m, Tel: 218-426-3271, Nearest town: McGregor. GPS: 46.847147, -93.165496

43 • B4 | Cascade River SP

Total sites: 45, RV sites: 40, Elec sites: 20, Central water, Flush toilet, Free showers, RV dump, Tents: $23/RVs: $31, Walk-to sites, $7 daily entrance fee, Open all year, Max Length: 35ft, Reservations accepted, Elev: 699ft/213m, Tel: 218-387-3053, Nearest town: Lutsen. GPS: 47.709036, -90.518692

44 • B4 | Cascade River SP - TC 1

Dispersed sites, No water, Tents only: $15, Hike-in, Reservations accepted, Elev: 645ft/197m, Tel: 218-387-3053, Nearest town: Lutsen. GPS: 47.713602, -90.493759

45 • B4 | Cascade River SP - TC 2

Dispersed sites, No water, Tents only: $15, Hike-in, Reservations accepted, Elev: 1099ft/335m, Tel: 218-387-3053, Nearest town: Lutsen. GPS: 47.721109, -90.509282

46 • B4 | Cascade River SP - TC 3

Dispersed sites, No water, Tents only: $15, Hike-in, Reservations accepted, Elev: 983ft/300m, Tel: 218-387-3053, Nearest town: Lutsen. GPS: 47.720477, -90.518013

47 • B4 | Cascade River SP - TC 4

Dispersed sites, No water, Tents only: $15, Hike-in, Reservations accepted, Elev: 955ft/291m, Tel: 218-387-3053, Nearest town: Lutsen. GPS: 47.715468, -90.519455

48 • B4 | Cascade River SP - TC 5

Dispersed sites, No water, Tents only: $15, Hike-in, Reservations accepted, Elev: 1138ft/347m, Tel: 218-387-3053, Nearest town: Lutsen. GPS: 47.713317, -90.540386

49 • B4 | George H Crosby-Manitou SP

Dispersed sites, No water, Vault/pit toilet, Tents only: $19, Hike-in, .5 - 4.5 mile, $7 daily entrance fee, Open all year, Elev: 1499ft/457m, Tel: 218-226-6365, Nearest town: Silver Bay. GPS: 47.478934, -91.112102

50 • B4 | Judge CR Magney SP

Total sites: 27, RV sites: 27, Central water, Flush toilet, Free showers, No RV dump, Tent & RV camping: $23, $7 daily entrance fee, Open May-Sep, Max Length: 45ft, Reservations accepted, Elev: 636ft/194m, Tel: 218-387-3039, Nearest town: Grand Marais. GPS: 47.818465, -90.053479

51 • B4 | Split Rock Lighthouse SP

Total sites: 24, RV sites: 0, Central water, Flush toilet, Free showers, No RV dump, Tents only: $24, Walk-to sites, $7 daily entrance fee, Open all year, Elev: 650ft/198m, Tel: 218-226-6377, Nearest town: Two Harbors. GPS: 47.195411, -91.379769

52 • B4 | Split Rock Lighthouse SP - BP/K1 TC

Dispersed sites, No water, Tents only: $24, Hike-in/boat-in, Open all year, Elev: 611ft/186m, Tel: 218-226-6377, Nearest town: Two Harbors. GPS: 47.190173, -91.386783

53 • B4 | Split Rock Lighthouse SP - BP/K3 TC

Dispersed sites, No water, Tents only: $24, Hike-in/boat-in, Open all year, Elev: 621ft/189m, Tel: 218-226-6377, Nearest town: Two Harbors. GPS: 47.186054, -91.399544

54 • B4 | Split Rock Lighthouse SP - BP2 TC

Dispersed sites, No water, Tents only: $24, Hike-in, Open all year, Elev: 638ft/194m, Tel: 218-226-6377, Nearest town: Two Harbors. GPS: 47.187868, -91.390111

55 • B4 | Split Rock Lighthouse SP - BP4 TC

Dispersed sites, No water, Tents only: $24, Hike-in, Open all year, Elev: 642ft/196m, Tel: 218-226-6377, Nearest town: Two Harbors. GPS: 47.181544, -91.401328

56 • B4 | Temperance River SP

Total sites: 57, RV sites: 51, Elec sites: 18, Central water, Flush toilet, Free showers, No RV dump, Tents: $23/RVs: $23-31, $7 daily entrance fee, Open all year, Max Length: 60ft, Reservations accepted, Elev: 686ft/209m, Tel: 218-663-7476, Nearest town: Silver Bay. GPS: 47.555026, -90.872161

57 • B4 | Tettegouche SP - Baptism River

Total sites: 34, RV sites: 28, Elec sites: 20, Central water, Flush toilet, Free showers, No RV dump, Tents: $23/RVs: $23-31, Also walk-to sites, 6 walk-to sites, $7 daily entrance fee, Open all year, Max Length: 60ft, Reservations accepted, Elev: 928ft/283m, Tel: 218-226-6365, Nearest town: Silver Bay. GPS: 47.345814, -91.209665

58 • B4 | Tettegouche SP - Lake Superior Cart-in

Total sites: 14, RV sites: 0, No water, Vault/pit toilet, Tents only: $23, Walk-to sites, $7 daily entrance fee, Open all year, Max Length: 60ft, Elev: 659ft/201m, Tel: 218-226-6365, Nearest town: Silver Bay. GPS: 47.335202, -91.200045

59 • C1 | Big Stone Lake SP

Total sites: 37, RV sites: 10, Elec sites: 10, Central water, Flush toilet, Free showers, RV dump, Tents: $19/RVs: $27, $7 daily entrance fee, Open Apr-Oct, Max Length: 48ft, Reservations accepted, Elev: 997ft/304m, Tel: 320-839-3663, Nearest town: Ortonville. GPS: 45.387076, -96.537062

60 • C1 | Glacial Lakes SP - Baby Lake TC

Dispersed sites, Tents only: $15, Hike-in, $7 daily entrance fee, Open Apr-Oct, Reservations accepted, Elev: 1265ft/386m, Tel: 320-239-2860, Nearest town: Starbuck. GPS: 45.530137, -95.496162

61 • C1 | Glacial Lakes SP - Hill TC

Dispersed sites, Tents only: $15, Hike-in, $7 daily entrance fee, Open Apr-Oct, Reservations accepted, Elev: 1262ft/385m, Tel: 320-239-2860, Nearest town: Starbuck. GPS: 45.532826, -95.522778

62 • C1 | Glacial Lakes SP - Horse Camp

Total sites: 8, RV sites: 8, Central water, Flush toilet, Free showers, RV dump, Tents: $21/RVs: $29, $7 daily entrance fee, Open Apr-Oct, Reservations accepted, Elev: 1302ft/397m, Tel: 320-239-2860, Nearest town: Starbuck. GPS: 45.534685, -95.521025

63 • C1 | Glacial Lakes SP - Kettle Lake TC

Dispersed sites, Tents only: $15, Hike-in, $7 daily entrance fee, Open Apr-Oct, Reservations accepted, Elev: 1232ft/376m, Tel: 320-239-2860, Nearest town: Starbuck. GPS: 45.526768, -95.500078

64 • C1 | Glacial Lakes SP - Main

Total sites: 41, RV sites: 37, Elec sites: 14, Central water, Flush toilet, Free showers, RV dump, Tents: $21/RVs: $29, Also cabins, $7 daily entrance fee, Open Apr-Oct, Max Length: 45ft, Reservations accepted, Elev: 1174ft/358m, Tel: 320-239-2860, Nearest town: Starbuck. GPS: 45.543792, -95.523082

65 • C1 | Glacial Lakes SP - Oak TC

Dispersed sites, Tents only: $15, Hike-in, $7 daily entrance fee, Open Apr-Oct, Reservations accepted, Elev: 1274ft/388m, Tel: 320-239-2860, Nearest town: Starbuck. GPS: 45.537945, -95.506215

66 • C1 | Glendalough SP - Cart-in

Total sites: 26, RV sites: 0, Central water, Flush toilet, Free showers, No RV dump, Tents only: $21, Walk-to sites, $7 daily entrance fee, Reservations accepted, Elev: 1348ft/411m, Tel: 218-864-0110, Nearest town: Battle Lake. GPS: 46.327753, -95.668412

67 • C1 | Maplewood SP - Beers Lake TC

Dispersed sites, No water, Vault/pit toilet, Tents only: $15, Hike-in, $7 daily entrance fee, Open all year, Reservations accepted, Elev: 1426ft/435m, Tel: 218-863-8383, Nearest town: Pelican Rapids. GPS: 46.510962, -95.936492

68 • C1 | Maplewood SP - Cow Lake North TC

Dispersed sites, No water, Vault/pit toilet, Tents only: $15, Hike-in, $7 daily entrance fee, Open all year, Reservations accepted, Elev: 1456ft/444m, Tel: 218-863-8383, Nearest town: Pelican Rapids. GPS: 46.508459, -95.951627

69 • C1 | Maplewood SP - Cow Lake South TC

Dispersed sites, No water, Vault/pit toilet, Tents only: $15, Hike-in, $7 daily entrance fee, Open all year, Reservations accepted, Elev: 1475ft/450m, Tel: 218-863-8383, Nearest town: Pelican Rapids. GPS: 46.504856, -95.955505

70 • C1 | Maplewood SP - Grass Lake TC

Dispersed sites, No water, Vault/pit toilet, Tents only: $15, Hike-in, $7 daily entrance fee, Open all year, Reservations accepted, Elev: 1477ft/450m, Tel: 218-863-8383, Nearest town: Pelican Rapids. GPS: 46.510053, -95.954271

71 • C1 | Maplewood SP - Hollow

Total sites: 13, RV sites: 13, No water, Vault/pit toilet, Tent & RV camping: $23, $7 daily entrance fee, Open all year, Max Length: 50ft, Reservations accepted, Elev: 1414ft/431m, Tel: 218-863-8383, Nearest town: Pelican Rapids. GPS: 46.528526, -95.945529

72 • C1 | Maplewood SP - Horseriders

Total sites: 24, RV sites: 24, Central water, Vault/pit toilet, No showers, No RV dump, Tent & RV camping: $23, $7 daily entrance fee, Open all year, Max Length: 50ft, Reservations accepted, Elev: 1434ft/437m, Tel: 218-863-8383, Nearest town: Pelican Rapids. GPS: 46.535167, -95.938183

73 • C1 | Maplewood SP - Knoll

Total sites: 14, RV sites: 14, No water, Vault/pit toilet, Tent & RV camping: $23, $7 daily entrance fee, Open all year, Max Length: 50ft, Reservations accepted, Elev: 1362ft/415m, Tel: 218-863-8383, Nearest town: Pelican Rapids. GPS: 46.523106, -95.948467

74 • C1 | Maplewood SP - Lake Lida

Total sites: 12, RV sites: 12, Central water, Vault/pit toilet, No showers, No RV dump, Tent & RV camping: $23, $7 daily entrance fee, Open all year, Max Length: 50ft, Reservations accepted, Elev: 1378ft/420m, Tel: 218-863-8383, Nearest town: Pelican Rapids. GPS: 46.535028, -95.977233

75 • C1 | Maplewood SP - Main

Total sites: 32, RV sites: 32, Elec sites: 32, Central water, Flush toilet, Free showers, RV dump, Tents: $23/RVs: $31, $7 daily entrance fee, Open all year, Max Length: 50ft, Reservations accepted, Elev: 1408ft/429m, Tel: 218-863-8383, Nearest town: Pelican Rapids. GPS: 46.524622, -95.941145

76 • C2 | Charles A. Lindbergh SP

Total sites: 40, RV sites: 38, Elec sites: 15, Central water, Flush toilet, Free showers, RV dump, Tents: $21/RVs: $29, Also walk-to sites, $7 daily entrance fee, Open Apr-Dec, Max Length: 50ft, Reservations accepted, Elev: 1122ft/342m, Tel: 320-616-2525, Nearest town: Little Falls. GPS: 45.962763, -94.392131

77 • C2 | Charles A. Lindbergh SP - Trail Camp

Dispersed sites, Tents only: $15, Hike-in/boat-in, $7 daily entrance fee, Open Apr-Dec, Reservations accepted, Elev: 1125ft/343m, Tel: 320-616-2525, Nearest town: Little Falls. GPS: 45.955512, -94.391405

78 • C2 | Crow Wing SP - Main CG

Total sites: 59, RV sites: 59, Elec sites: 12, Central water, Flush toilet, Free showers, RV dump, Tents: $21/RVs: $29, $7 daily entrance fee, Open Apr-Dec, Max Length: 45ft, Reservations accepted, Elev: 1171ft/357m, Tel: 218-825-3075, Nearest town: Brainerd. GPS: 46.279829, -94.328431

79 • C2 | Father Hennepin SP - Lakeview

Total sites: 62, RV sites: 62, Elec sites: 41, Central water, Flush toilet, Free showers, RV dump, Tents: $23/RVs: $31, $7 daily entrance fee, Open May-Oct, Max Length: 60ft, Elev: 1257ft/383m, Tel: 320-676-8763, Nearest town: Isle. GPS: 46.147853, -93.485856

80 • C2 | Father Hennepin SP - Maple Grove

Total sites: 41, RV sites: 41, Elec sites: 10, Central water, Flush toilet, Free showers, RV dump, Tents: $24/RVs: $32, $7 daily entrance fee, Open Apr-Oct, Max Length: 60ft, Reservations accepted, Elev: 1276ft/389m, Tel: 320-676-8763, Nearest town: Isle. GPS: 46.147043, -93.490606

81 • C2 | Lake Carlos SP - Horse Camp

Total sites: 7, RV sites: 7, Central water, Vault/pit toilet, No showers, No RV dump, Tent & RV camping: $23, $7 daily entrance fee, Open all year, Reservations accepted, Elev: 1411ft/430m, Tel: 320-852-7200, Nearest town: Carlos. GPS: 46.004703, -95.341163

82 • C2 | Lake Carlos SP - Lower CG

Total sites: 74, RV sites: 74, Elec sites: 59, Central water, Flush toilet, Free showers, RV dump, Tents: $23/RVs: $31, $7 daily entrance fee, Open all year, Max Length: 50ft, Reservations accepted, Elev: 1371ft/418m, Tel: 320-852-7200, Nearest town: Carlos. GPS: 45.997773, -95.337194

83 • C2 | Lake Carlos SP - Upper CG

Total sites: 51, RV sites: 51, Elec sites: 22, Central water, Flush toilet, Free showers, RV dump, Tents: $23/RVs: $31, Also cabins, $7 daily entrance fee, Open all year, Max Length: 50ft, Reservations accepted, Elev: 1430ft/436m, Tel: 320-852-7200, Nearest town: Carlos. GPS: 46.002123, -95.337682

84 • C2 | Mille Lacs Kathio SP - Black Bass Lake TC

Dispersed sites, No water, No toilets, Tents only: $15, Hike-in, $7 daily entrance fee, Open all year, Elev: 1293ft/394m, Tel: 320-532-3523, Nearest town: Onamia. GPS: 46.125520, -93.703250

85 • C2 | Mille Lacs Kathio SP - GR TC

Dispersed sites, No water, No toilets, Tents only: $15, Hike-in, $7 daily entrance fee, Open all year, Elev: 1273ft/388m, Tel: 320-532-3523, Nearest town: Onamia. GPS: 46.139295, -93.733669

86 • C2 | Mille Lacs Kathio SP - Horse Camp

Total sites: 10, RV sites: 10, Central water, No toilets, No showers, No RV dump, Tent & RV camping: $24, $7 daily entrance fee, Open all year, Reservations accepted, Elev: 1319ft/402m, Tel: 320-532-3523, Nearest town: Onamia. GPS: 46.129175, -93.740359

87 • C2 | Mille Lacs Kathio SP - KT TC

Dispersed sites, No water, No toilets, Tents only: $15, Hike-in, $7 daily entrance fee, Open all year, Elev: 1329ft/405m, Tel: 320-532-3523, Nearest town: Onamia. GPS: 46.143247, -93.742458

88 • C2 | Mille Lacs Kathio SP - Ogechie

Total sites: 26, RV sites: 26, Central water, Vault/pit toilet, No showers, No RV dump, Tent & RV camping: $19, $7 daily entrance fee, Open all year, Max Length: 60ft, Elev: 1286ft/392m, Tel: 320-532-3523, Nearest town: Onamia. GPS: 46.144004, -93.771946

89 • C2 | Mille Lacs Kathio SP - Petega

Total sites: 38, RV sites: 38, Elec sites: 22, Central water, Flush toilet, Free showers, No RV dump, Tents: $23/RVs: $23-31, $7 daily entrance fee, Open all year, Max Length: 60ft, Reservations accepted, Elev: 1286ft/392m, Tel: 320-532-3523, Nearest town: Onamia. GPS: 46.127703, -93.767588

90 • C2 | Mille Lacs Kathio SP - SM TC

Dispersed sites, No water, No toilets, Tents only: $15, Hike-in, $7 daily entrance fee, Open all year, Elev: 1312ft/400m, Tel: 320-532-3523, Nearest town: Onamia. GPS: 46.144113, -93.753809

91 • C3 | Jay Cooke SP - Ash Ridge

Dispersed sites, No water, Vault/pit toilet, Tents only: $15, Hike-in, $7 daily entrance fee, Open all year, Elev: 705ft/215m, Tel: 218-384-4610, Nearest town: Carlton. GPS: 46.640996, -92.345562

92 • C3 | Jay Cooke SP - High Landing

Dispersed sites, No water, Vault/pit toilet, Tents only: $15, Hike-in, $7 daily entrance fee, Open all year, Elev: 705ft/215m, Tel: 218-384-4610, Nearest town: Carlton. GPS: 46.642965, -92.350618

93 • C3 | Jay Cooke SP - Lost Lake

Dispersed sites, No water, Vault/pit toilet, Tents only: $15, Hike-in, $7 daily entrance fee, Open all year, Elev: 728ft/222m, Tel: 218-384-4610, Nearest town: Carlton. GPS: 46.640875, -92.336651

94 • C3 | Jay Cooke SP - Main

Total sites: 86, RV sites: 79, Elec sites: 21, Central water, Flush toilet, Free showers, RV dump, Tents: $23/RVs: $31, Also cabins, $7 daily entrance fee, Open all year, Max Length: 60ft, Reservations accepted, Elev: 1014ft/309m, Tel: 218-384-4610, Nearest town: Carlton. GPS: 46.657135, -92.372133

95 • C3 | Jay Cooke SP - Silver Creek

Dispersed sites, No water, Vault/pit toilet, Tents only: $15, Hike-in, $7 daily entrance fee, Open all year, Elev: 771ft/235m, Tel: 218-384-4610, Nearest town: Carlton. GPS: 46.643352, -92.361557

96 • C3 | Moose Lake SP

Total sites: 35, RV sites: 33, Elec sites: 20, Central water, Flush toilet, Free showers, No RV dump, Tents: $24/RVs: $32, $7 daily entrance fee, Open Apr-Nov, Max Length: 60ft, Reservations accepted, Elev: 1132ft/345m, Tel: 218-485-5420, Nearest town: Moose Lake. GPS: 46.431024, -92.730886

97 • C3 | Savanna Portage SP

Total sites: 68, RV sites: 61, Elec sites: 18, Central water, Flush toilet, Free showers, RV dump, Tents: $24/RVs: $24-32, Also hike-in/boat-in sites, $7 daily entrance fee, Open all year, Max Length: 55ft, Reservations accepted, Elev: 1286ft/392m, Tel: 218-426-3271, Nearest town: McGregor. GPS: 46.827033, -93.150745

98 • C3 | Savanna Portage SP - Site G TC

Dispersed sites, No water, Vault/pit toilet, Tents only: $24, Hike-in, $7 daily entrance fee, Open all year, Reservations accepted, Elev: 1300ft/396m, Tel: 218-426-3271, Nearest town: McGregor. GPS: 46.832329, -93.159183

99 • C3 | Savanna Portage SP - Site K TC

Dispersed sites, No water, No toilets, Tents only: $24, Hike-in, $7 daily entrance fee, Open all year, Reservations accepted, Elev: 1307ft/398m, Tel: 218-426-3271, Nearest town: McGregor. GPS: 46.828588, -93.143748

100 • C3 | St Croix SP - Bear Creek Camp

Dispersed sites, No water, Vault/pit toilet, Tents only: $24, Hike-in, 5 mi, $7 daily entrance fee, Elev: 914ft/279m, Nearest town: Sandstone. GPS: 45.945844, -92.685468

101 • C3 | St Croix SP - Crooked Creek Camp

Dispersed sites, No water, Vault/pit toilet, Tents only: $24, Hike-in, 5 mi, $7 daily entrance fee, Elev: 960ft/293m, Nearest town: Sandstone. GPS: 46.005264, -92.527808

102 • C3 | St Croix SP - Horse Camp

Total sites: 25, RV sites: 25, Elec sites: 10, Central water, Flush toilet, Free showers, No RV dump, Tents: $24/RVs: $32, Also walk-to and boat-in sites, $7 daily entrance fee, Open all year, Reservations accepted, Elev: 928ft/283m, Tel: 320-384-6591, Nearest town: Hinckley. GPS: 45.959593, -92.605601

103 • C3 | St Croix SP - Main

Total sites: 227, RV sites: 211, Elec sites: 81, Central water, Flush toilet, Free showers, RV dump, Tents: $24/RVs: $32, Also walk-to and boat-in sites, $7 daily entrance fee, Open all year, Max Length: 71ft, Reservations accepted, Elev: 922ft/281m, Tel: 320-384-6591, Nearest town: Hinckley. GPS: 45.951227, -92.570632

104 • C3 | Wild River SP

Total sites: 105, RV sites: 94, Elec sites: 34, Central water, Flush toilet, Free showers, RV dump, Tents: $23/RVs: $23-31, Also hike-in/boat-in sites, $7 daily entrance fee, Open all year, Reservations accepted, Elev: 853ft/260m, Tel: 651-583-2125, Nearest town: Center City. GPS: 45.543036, -92.740422

105 • C3 | Wild River SP - Aspen Knob TC

Total sites: 9, Central water, Vault/pit toilet, Tents only: $24, Hike-in, Reservations accepted, Elev: 942ft/287m, Tel: 651-583-2125, Nearest town: Center City. GPS: 45.516604, -92.752958

106 • C3 | Wild River SP - Breezy Valley TC

Total sites: 9, Central water, Vault/pit toilet, Tents only: $24, Hike-in, Reservations accepted, Elev: 914ft/279m, Tel: 651-583-2125, Nearest town: Center City. GPS: 45.512522, -92.753729

107 • C3 | Wild River SP - Dry Creek Hollow TC

Total sites: 9, Central water, Vault/pit toilet, Tents only: $24, Hike-in, Reservations accepted, Elev: 862ft/263m, Tel: 651-583-2125, Nearest town: Center City. GPS: 45.513838, -92.750123

108 • C3 | Wild River SP - Horse Camp

Total sites: 20, RV sites: 20, Elec sites: 15, Central water, Flush toilet, No RV dump, Tents: $24/RVs: $32, Also hike-in/boat-in sites, $7 daily entrance fee, Open all year, Reservations accepted, Elev: 866ft/264m, Tel: 651-583-2125, Nearest town: Center City. GPS: 45.527374, -92.747233

109 • C3 | Wild River SP - Meadow Vista TC

Total sites: 9, Central water, Vault/pit toilet, Tents only: $24, Hike-in, Reservations accepted, Elev: 880ft/268m, Tel: 651-583-2125, Nearest town: Center City. GPS: 45.514085, -92.744295

110 • C3 | Wild River SP - Pine Ridge TC

Total sites: 9, Central water, Vault/pit toilet, Tents only: $24, Hike-in, Reservations accepted, Elev: 943ft/287m, Tel: 651-583-2125, Nearest town: Center City. GPS: 45.511917, -92.747406

111 • D1 | Camden SP

Total sites: 80, RV sites: 80, Elec sites: 29, Central water, Flush toilet, Free showers, RV dump, Tents: $21/RVs: $29, $7 daily entrance fee, Open Apr-Oct, Max Length: 60ft, Reservations accepted, Elev: 1496ft/456m, Tel: 507-865-4530, Nearest town: Lynd. GPS: 44.346624, -95.922031

112 • D1 | Lac Qui Parle SP - Lower CG

Total sites: 24, RV sites: 24, Elec sites: 8, Central water, Flush toilet, Free showers, RV dump, Tents: $19/RVs: $27, $7 daily entrance fee, Open all year, Max Length: 50ft, Reservations accepted, Elev: 955ft/291m, Tel: 320-734-4450, Nearest town: Watson. GPS: 45.021274, -95.887857

113 • D1 | Lac Qui Parle SP - Upper CG

Total sites: 46, RV sites: 43, Elec sites: 39, Central water, Flush toilet, Free showers, RV dump, Tents: $19/RVs: $27, $7 daily entrance fee, Open all year, Max Length: 60ft, Reservations accepted, Elev: 1020ft/311m, Tel: 320-734-4450, Nearest town: Watson. GPS: 45.045317, -95.880494

114 • D1 | Lake Shetek SP - Main CG

Total sites: 70, RV sites: 70, Elec sites: 64, Central water, Flush toilet, Free showers, RV dump, Tents: $23/RVs: $23-31, $7 daily entrance fee, Open all year, Max Length: 70ft, Reservations accepted, Elev: 1522ft/464m, Tel: 507-763-3256, Nearest town: Currie. GPS: 44.103990, -95.697880

115 • D1 | Lake Shetek SP - Park Lake

Total sites: 1, RV sites: 0, Central water, Vault/pit toilet, No showers, No RV dump, Tents only: $15, Walk-to sites, Walk-in group site, $7 daily entrance fee, Open all year, Reservations accepted, Elev: 1493ft/455m, Tel: 507-763-3256, Nearest town: Currie. GPS: 44.107996, -95.685337

116 • D1 | Lake Shetek SP - Prairie

Total sites: 12, RV sites: 0, Central water, Vault/pit toilet, No showers, No RV dump, Tents only: $19, Walk-to sites, $7 daily entrance fee, Open all year, Max Length: 70ft, Reservations accepted, Elev: 1521ft/464m, Tel: 507-763-3256, Nearest town: Currie. GPS: 44.106562, -95.697279

117 • D1 | Upper Sioux Agency SP - Horse Camp

Total sites: 40, RV sites: 20, Elec sites: 5, Central water, Vault/pit toilet, No showers, No RV dump, Tent & RV camping: $23, Also walk-to sites, $7 daily entrance fee, Open May-Oct, Elev: 925ft/282m, Tel: 320-564-4777, Nearest town: Granite Falls. GPS: 44.732936, -95.466459

118 • D1 | Upper Sioux Agency SP - Riverside

Total sites: 6, RV sites: 6, No water, Vault/pit toilet, Tent & RV camping: $19, Also walk-to sites, $7 daily entrance fee, Open May-Oct, Reservations accepted, Elev: 876ft/267m, Tel: 320-564-4777, Nearest town: Granite Falls. GPS: 44.740264, -95.456376

119 • D1 | Upper Sioux Agency SP - Yello+E20164w Medicine River

Total sites: 31, RV sites: 26, Elec sites: 14, Central water, Flush toilet, Free showers, No RV dump, Tents: $23/RVs: $31, Also walk-to sites, 3 walk-to sites, $7 daily entrance fee, Open May-Oct, Reservations accepted, Elev: 879ft/268m, Tel: 320-564-4777, Nearest town: Granite Falls. GPS: 44.730587, -95.434433

120 • D2 | Flandrau SP - Electric

Total sites: 34, RV sites: 34, Elec sites: 34, Central water, Flush toilet, Free showers, RV dump, Tent & RV camping: $31, $7 daily entrance fee, Open all year, Max Length: 66ft, Reservations accepted, Elev: 853ft/260m, Tel: 507-233-9800, Nearest town: New Ulm. GPS: 44.294446, -94.468774

121 • D2 | Flandrau SP - Non-Electric

Total sites: 17, RV sites: 17, Central water, Flush toilet, Free showers, RV dump, Tent & RV camping: $23, Max Length: 66ft, Reservations accepted, Elev: 833ft/254m, Tel: 507-233-9800, Nearest town: New Ulm. GPS: 44.294848, -94.470602

122 • D2 | Flandrau SP - Rustic

Total sites: 36, RV sites: 36, Central water, Flush toilet, Free showers, RV dump, Tent & RV camping: $19, $7 daily entrance fee, Reservations accepted, Elev: 827ft/252m, Tel: 507-233-9800, Nearest town: New Ulm. GPS: 44.297151, -94.476383

123 • D2 | Fort Ridgely SP - Creekside/Rustic

Total sites: 31, RV sites: 31, Elec sites: 15, Central water, Flush toilet, Free showers, RV dump, Tents: $15-19/RVs: $27, $7 daily entrance fee, Open Apr-Oct, Max Length: 60ft, Reservations accepted, Elev: 892ft/272m, Tel: 507-426-7840, Nearest town: Fairfax. GPS: 44.453979, -94.726161

124 • D2 | Fort Ridgely SP - Horse Camp

Total sites: 25, RV sites: 25, Elec sites: 15, Central water, Flush toilet, Free showers, RV dump, Tents: $19/RVs: $27, $7 daily entrance fee, Open Apr-Oct, Max Length: 60ft, Reservations accepted, Elev: 948ft/289m, Tel: 507-426-7840, Nearest town: Fairfax. GPS: 44.471735, -94.732631

125 • D2 | Lake Maria SP

Total sites: 17, RV sites: 0, No water, No toilets, Tents only: $19, Hike-in, $7 daily entrance fee, Open all year, Reservations accepted, Elev: 984ft/300m, Tel: 763-878-2325, Nearest town: Monticello. GPS: 45.319616, -93.949871

126 • D2 | Minneopa SP

Total sites: 61, RV sites: 61, Elec sites: 6, Central water, Flush toilet, Free showers, RV dump, Tents: $21/RVs: $21-29, $7 daily entrance fee, Open all year, Max Length: 60ft, Reservations accepted, Elev: 856ft/261m, Tel: 507-389-5464, Nearest town: Mankato. GPS: 44.159199, -94.087646

127 • D2 | Minnesotta Valley SP - Carver Rapids TC

Total sites: 1, RV sites: 0, No water, No toilets, Tents only: $23, Hike-in/boat-in, $7 daily entrance fee, Open Apr-Oct, Elev: 725ft/221m, Tel: 952-492-6400, Nearest town: Jordan. GPS: 44.723427, -93.624395

128 • D2 | Minnesotta Valley SP - Horse Camp

Total sites: 6, RV sites: 6, Central water, Vault/pit toilet, No showers, No RV dump, Tent & RV camping: $23, $7 daily entrance fee, Open Apr-Nov, Reservations accepted, Elev: 728ft/222m, Tel: 952-492-6400, Nearest town: Jordan. GPS: 44.650842, -93.716835

129 • D2 | Minnesotta Valley SP - Paine Pond TC

Total sites: 1, RV sites: 0, No water, No toilets, Tents only: $23, Hike-in/boat-in, $7 daily entrance fee, Open Apr-Oct, Elev: 696ft/212m, Tel: 952-492-6400, Nearest town: Jordan. GPS: 44.676512, -93.689107

130 • D2 | Minnesotta Valley SP - Quarry

Total sites: 33, RV sites: 25, Central water, Vault/pit toilet, No showers, No RV dump, Tent & RV camping: $19, $7 daily entrance fee, Open Apr-Oct, Elev: 735ft/224m, Tel: 952-492-6400, Nearest town: Jordan. GPS: 44.656132, -93.713341

131 • D2 | Monson Lake SP

Total sites: 20, RV sites: 20, Elec sites: 6, Central water, Flush toilet, Free showers, No RV dump, Tents: $19/RVs: $19-27, $7 daily entrance fee, Open all year, Max Length: 70ft, Reservations accepted, Elev: 1260ft/384m, Tel: 320-366-3797, Nearest town: Sunburg. GPS: 45.320557, -95.274902

132 • D2 | Sakatah Lake SP - Main CG

Total sites: 67, RV sites: 62, Elec sites: 14, Central water, Flush toilet, Free showers, RV dump, Tents: $23/RVs: $23-31, Also cabins, 5 bike-in sites, $7 daily entrance fee, Open all year, Max Length: 55ft, Reservations accepted, Elev: 1083ft/330m, Tel: 507-362-4438, Nearest town: Waterville. GPS: 44.220479, -93.534332

133 • D2 | Sakatah Lake SP - Primitive #1

Dispersed sites, No water, Vault/pit toilet, Tents only: $15, Walk-to/boat-in sites, Bike-in, $7 daily entrance fee, Elev: 1050ft/320m, Tel: 507-362-4438, Nearest town: Waterville. GPS: 44.225269, -93.519555

134 • D2 | Sibley SP - Horse Camp

Total sites: 9, RV sites: 9, Central water, Flush toilet, Free showers, RV dump, Tent & RV camping: $24, $7 daily entrance fee, Open all year, Reservations accepted, Elev: 1266ft/386m, Tel: 320-354-2055, Nearest town: New London. GPS: 45.324215, -95.046358

135 • D2 | Sibley SP - Lakeview

Total sites: 74, RV sites: 74, Elec sites: 53, Central water, Flush toilet, Free showers, RV dump, Tents: $24/RVs: $32, $7 daily entrance fee, Open all year, Max Length: 70ft, Reservations accepted, Elev: 1237ft/377m, Tel: 320-354-2055, Nearest town: New London. GPS: 45.314879, -95.038579

136 • D2 | Sibley SP - Oak Ridge

Total sites: 58, RV sites: 58, Elec sites: 34, Central water, Flush toilet, Free showers, No RV dump, Tents: $24/RVs: $32, $7 daily entrance fee, Open all year, Max Length: 70ft, Reservations accepted, Elev: 1266ft/386m, Tel: 320-354-2055, Nearest town: New London. GPS: 45.318730, -95.028570

137 • D3 | Afton SP - Back-Country

Total sites: 27, RV sites: 0, Central water, Vault/pit toilet, Tents only: $19, Hike-in, 3/4 mile, $7 daily entrance fee, Reservations accepted, Elev: 948ft/289m, Tel: 651-436-5391, Nearest town: Afton. GPS: 44.866548, -92.777247

138 • D3 | Afton SP - River Site

Dispersed sites, Central water, Vault/pit toilet, Tents only: $19, Hike-in/boat-in, Reservations accepted, Elev: 702ft/214m, Tel: 651-436-5391, Nearest town: Afton. GPS: 44.864585, -92.772796

139 • D3 | Carley SP

Total sites: 20, RV sites: 20, Central water, Vault/pit toilet, No showers, No RV dump, Tent & RV camping: $15, $7 daily entrance fee, Open May-Sep, Max Length: 30ft, Reservations accepted, Elev: 1040ft/317m, Tel: 507-932-3007, Nearest town: Altura. GPS: 44.117666, -92.175927

140 • D3 | Frontenac SP

Total sites: 58, RV sites: 58, Elec sites: 19, Central water, Flush toilet, Free showers, RV dump, Tents: $23/RVs: $31, $7 daily entrance fee, Open all year, Max Length: 53ft, Reservations accepted, Elev: 1053ft/321m, Tel: 651-345-3401, Nearest town: Frontenac. GPS: 44.539026, -92.351058

141 • D3 | Frontenac SP - Cart-in

Total sites: 6, RV sites: 0, Vault/pit toilet, Tents only: $15, Walk-to sites, 1/3 mi, Reservations accepted, Elev: 1033ft/315m, Tel: 651-345-3401, Nearest town: Frontenac. GPS: 44.534401, -92.343126

142 • D3 | Interstate SP

Total sites: 37, RV sites: 37, Elec sites: 22, Central water, Flush toilet, Free showers, RV dump, Tents: $23/RVs: $31, $7 daily entrance fee, Open Apr-Oct, Reservations accepted, Elev: 718ft/219m, Tel: 651-465-5711, Nearest town: Taylors Falls. GPS: 45.394182, -92.666756

143 • D3 | Nerstrand-Big Woods SP

Total sites: 55, RV sites: 51, Elec sites: 27, Central water, Flush toilet, Free showers, RV dump, Tents: $15-23/RVs: $23-31, Also walk-to sites, $7 daily entrance fee, Open all year, Max Length: 60ft, Reservations accepted, Elev: 1207ft/368m, Tel: 507-333-4840, Nearest town: Nerstrand. GPS: 44.343828, -93.103222

144 • D3 | Rice Lake SP

Total sites: 54, RV sites: 40, Elec sites: 18, Central water, Flush toilet, Free showers, RV dump, Tents: $21/RVs: $21-29, Also walk-to and boat-in sites, $7 daily entrance fee, Open all year, Max Length: 55ft, Reservations accepted, Elev: 1260ft/384m, Tel: 507-455-5871, Nearest town: Owatonna. GPS: 44.089631, -93.058709

145 • D3 | Whitewater SP

Total sites: 154, RV sites: 148, Elec sites: 87, Central water, Flush toilet, Free showers, RV dump, Tents: $23/RVs: $23-31, Also walk-to sites, $7 daily entrance fee, Open all year, Max Length: 50ft, Reservations accepted, Elev: 820ft/250m, Tel: 507-932-3007, Nearest town: Altura. GPS: 44.060449, -92.045607

146 • D3 | William O'Brien SP - Riverway

Total sites: 60, RV sites: 60, Elec sites: 37, Central water, Flush toilet, Free showers, RV dump, Tents: $24/RVs: $32, $7 daily entrance fee, Open Apr-Oct, Max Length: 60ft, Reservations accepted, Elev: 715ft/218m, Tel: 651-433-0500, Nearest town: Marine on St. Croix. GPS: 45.220734, -92.756827

147 • D3 | William O'Brien SP - Savanna

Total sites: 65, RV sites: 65, Elec sites: 35, Central water, Flush toilet, Free showers, RV dump, Tents: $24/RVs: $32, $7 daily entrance fee, Open all year, Max Length: 60ft, Reservations accepted, Elev: 824ft/251m, Tel: 651-433-0500, Nearest town: Marine on St. Croix. GPS: 45.224994, -92.772975

148 • E1 | Blue Mounds SP

Total sites: 73, RV sites: 73, Elec sites: 40, Central water, Flush toilet, Free showers, RV dump, Tents: $21/RVs: $29, $7 daily entrance fee, Open all year, Max Length: 50ft, Reservations accepted, Elev: 1549ft/472m, Tel: 507-283-1307, Nearest town: Luverne. GPS: 43.720206, -96.191693

149 • E1 | Blue Mounds SP - Cart-in

Total sites: 14, RV sites: 0, Central water, Vault/pit toilet, Tents only: $19, Walk-to sites, Open all year, Reservations accepted, Elev: 1534ft/468m, Tel: 507-283-1307, Nearest town: Luverne. GPS: 43.716467, -96.187502

150 • E1 | Split Rock Creek SP

Total sites: 34, RV sites: 34, Elec sites: 21, Central water, Flush toilet, Free showers, RV dump, Tents: $24/RVs: $32, $7 daily entrance fee, Open May-Oct, Max Length: 52ft, Reservations accepted, Elev: 1634ft/498m, Tel: 507-348-7908, Nearest town: Jasper. GPS: 43.900827, -96.366152

151 • E2 | Kilen Woods SP

Total sites: 33, RV sites: 33, Elec sites: 11, Central water, Flush toilet, Free showers, No RV dump, Tents: $19/RVs: $27, $7 daily entrance fee, Open May-Oct, Reservations accepted, Elev: 1411ft/430m, Tel: 507-831-2900 x221, Nearest town: Lakefield. GPS: 43.728807, -95.065558

152 • E3 | Beaver Creek Valley SP

Total sites: 42, RV sites: 42, Elec sites: 16, Water available, Flush toilet, Free showers, RV dump, Tents: $19/RVs: $27, Also cabins, $7 daily entrance fee, Reservations accepted, Elev: 922ft/281m, Tel: 507-724-2107, Nearest town: Caledonia. GPS: 43.640926, -91.579188

153 • E3 | Forestville Mystery Cave SP - Family

Total sites: 73, RV sites: 73, Elec sites: 23, Central water, Flush toilet, Free showers, RV dump, Tents: $23/RVs: $31, $7 daily entrance fee, Open Apr-Nov, Max Length: 50ft, Reservations accepted, Elev: 1135ft/346m, Tel: 507-352-5111, Nearest town: Preston. GPS: 43.629712, -92.221579

154 • E3 | Forestville Mystery Cave SP - Horse Camp

Total sites: 55, RV sites: 55, Elec sites: 23, Central water, Flush toilet, Free showers, RV dump, Tents: $23/RVs: $31, $7 daily entrance fee, Open May-Oct, Max Length: 50ft, Reservations accepted, Elev: 1257ft/383m, Tel: 507-352-5111, Nearest town: Preston. GPS: 43.636844, -92.206871

155 • E3 | Lake Louise SP

Total sites: 26, RV sites: 20, Elec sites: 11, Central water, Flush toilet, Free showers, RV dump, Tents: $19/RVs: $19-27, 6 horse camp sites, $7 daily entrance fee, Open May-Sep, Max Length: 45ft, Reservations accepted, Elev: 1276ft/389m, Tel: 507-352-5111, Nearest town: LeRoy. GPS: 43.529165, -92.523575

156 • E3 | Myre Big Island SP - Big Island CG

Total sites: 31, RV sites: 31, Elec sites: 17, Central water, Flush toilet, Free showers, RV dump, Tents: $21/RVs: $21-29, Also cabins, $7 daily entrance fee, Open all year, Max Length: 60ft, Reservations accepted, Elev: 1260ft/384m, Tel: 507-379-3403, Nearest town: Albert Lea. GPS: 43.623418, -93.292456

157 • E3 | Myre Big Island SP - TC 1

Dispersed sites, No water, No toilets, Tents only: $15, Hike-in/boat-in, $7 daily entrance fee, Open all year, Elev: 1220ft/372m, Tel: 507-379-3403, Nearest town: Albert Lea. GPS: 43.633869, -93.295368

158 • E3 | Myre Big Island SP - TC 2

Dispersed sites, No water, No toilets, Tents only: $15, Hike-in/boat-in, $7 daily entrance fee, Open all year, Elev: 1216ft/371m, Tel: 507-379-3403, Nearest town: Albert Lea. GPS: 43.635182, -93.290752

159 • E3 | Myre Big Island SP - TC 3

Dispersed sites, No water, No toilets, Tents only: $15, Hike-in/boat-in, $7 daily entrance fee, Open all year, Elev: 1226ft/374m, Tel: 507-379-3403, Nearest town: Albert Lea. GPS: 43.640729, -93.285329

160 • E3 | Myre Big Island SP - TC 4

Dispersed sites, No water, No toilets, Tents only: $15, Hike-in/boat-in, $7 daily entrance fee, Open all year, Elev: 1218ft/371m, Tel: 507-379-3403, Nearest town: Albert Lea. GPS: 43.641857, -93.283859

161 • E3 | Myre Big Island SP - TC 5

Dispersed sites, No water, No toilets, Tents only: $15, Hike-in/boat-in, $7 daily entrance fee, Open all year, Elev: 1217ft/371m, Tel: 507-379-3403, Nearest town: Albert Lea. GPS: 43.643094, -93.283518

162 • E3 | Myre Big Island SP - White Fox CG

Total sites: 62, RV sites: 62, Elec sites: 15, Central water, Flush toilet, Free showers, RV dump, Tents: $21/RVs: $21-29, $7 daily entrance fee, Open all year, Max Length: 60ft, Reservations accepted, Elev: 1250ft/381m, Tel: 507-379-3403, Nearest town: Albert Lea. GPS: 43.634937, -93.301858

163 • E4 | Great River Bluffs SP - Bicycle Camp

Total sites: 5, RV sites: 0, No water, Vault/pit toilet, Tents only: $15, Walk-to sites, Bicycles only, Open all year, Elev: 669ft/204m, Tel: 507-643-6849, Nearest town: Winona. GPS: 43.948605, -91.388166

164 • E4 | Great River Bluffs SP - Main

Total sites: 31, RV sites: 31, Central water, Flush toilet, Free showers, No RV dump, Tent & RV camping: $19, $7 daily entrance fee, Open all year, Max Length: 60ft, Reservations accepted, Elev: 1260ft/384m, Tel: 507-643-6849, Nearest town: Winona. GPS: 43.939516, -91.384715

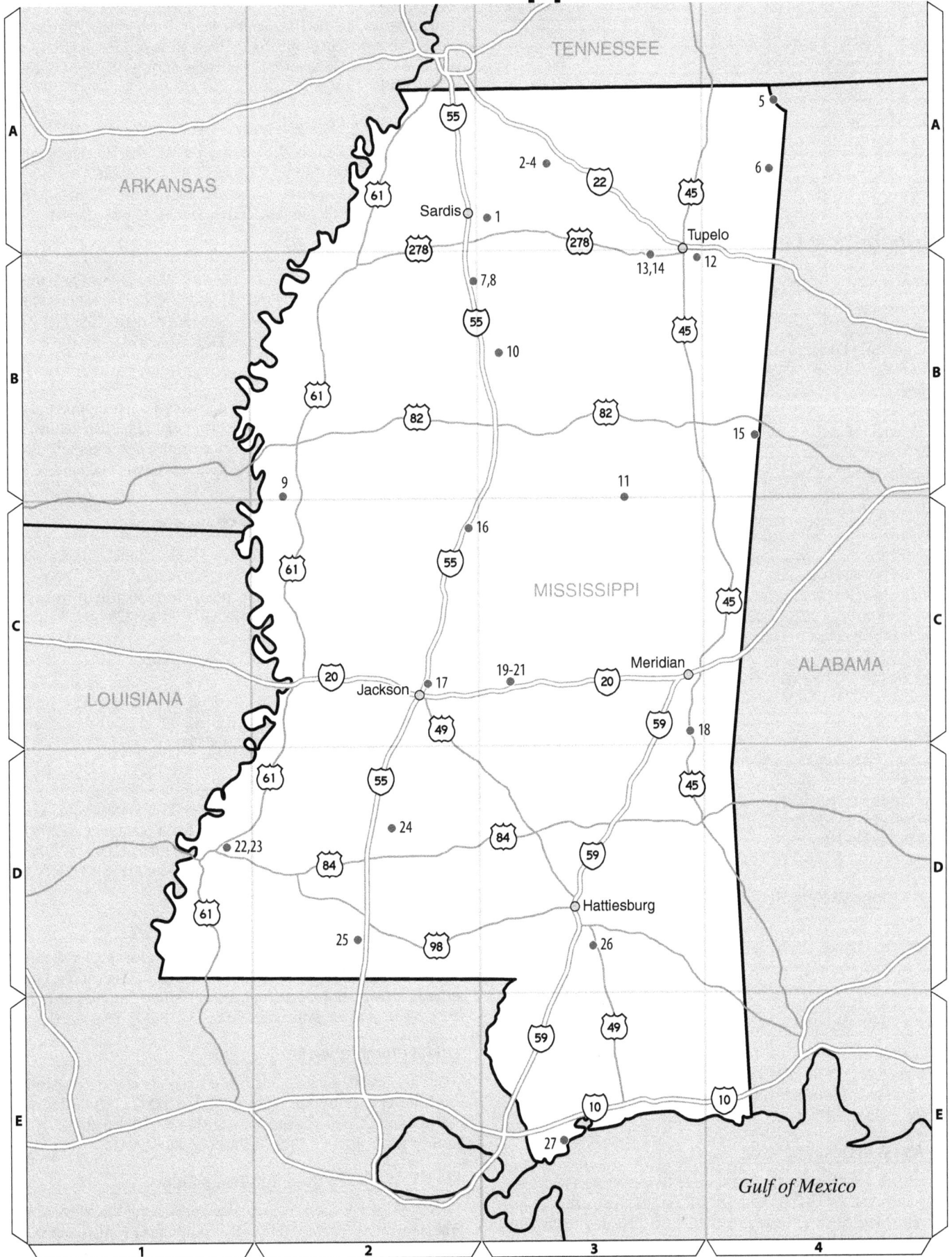

Mississippi

TENNESSEE

ARKANSAS

5

2-4

6

55

22

45

Sardis 1

Tupelo

278

278

13,14 12

7,8

55

45

10

61

82

82

61

15

9

11

16

MISSISSIPPI

55

45

61

20

Meridian

LOUISIANA

Jackson 17

19-21

20

ALABAMA

49

59

18

61

55

45

24

22,23

84

59

84

Hattiesburg

61

25

98

26

59

49

10

10

27

Gulf of Mexico

Map	ID	Map	ID
A3	1-4	C3	18-21
A4	5-6	D1	22-23
B2	7-9	D2	24-25
B3	10-14	D3	26
B4	15	E3	27
C2	16-17		

Alphabetical List of Camping Areas

1 • A3 | John W. Kyle SP

Total sites: 200, RV sites: 200, Elec sites: 200, Water at site, Flush toilet, Free showers, RV dump, Tent & RV camping: $22, Also cabins, Reservations accepted, Elev: 226ft/69m, Tel: 662-487-1345, Nearest town: Sardis. GPS: 34.410533, -89.807395

2 • A3 | Wall Doxey SP - New Back

Total sites: 49, RV sites: 49, Elec sites: 49, Water at site, Flush toilet, Free showers, RV dump, Tent & RV camping: $22, Also cabins, Open all year, Elev: 390ft/119m, Tel: 662-252-4231, Nearest town: Holly Springs. GPS: 34.657354, -89.462719

3 • A3 | Wall Doxey SP - Old Front

Total sites: 18, RV sites: 15, Elec sites: 15, Water at site, Flush toilet, Free showers, RV dump, Tents: $15/RVs: $22, Also cabins, Open all year, Elev: 426ft/130m, Tel: 662-252-4231, Nearest town: Holly Springs. GPS: 34.664408, -89.462438

4 • A3 | Wall Doxey SP - Primitive

Total sites: 14, RV sites: 0, Central water, Flush toilet, No showers, No RV dump, Tents only: $15, Open all year, Elev: 437ft/133m, Tel: 662-252-4231, Nearest town: Holly Springs. GPS: 34.661861, -89.463564

5 • A4 | J.P. Coleman SP

Total sites: 78, RV sites: 69, Elec sites: 69, Water at site, Flush toilet, Free showers, RV dump, Tents: $15/RVs: $24-28, Also cabins, Open all year, Reservations accepted, Elev: 476ft/145m, Tel: 662-423-6515, Nearest town: Iuka. GPS: 34.929242, -88.169304

6 • A4 | Tishomingo SP

Total sites: 79, RV sites: 62, Elec sites: 62, Water at site, Flush toilet, Free showers, RV dump, Tents: $15/RVs: $22, Also cabins, Open all year, Reservations accepted, Elev: 561ft/171m, Tel: 662-438-6914, Nearest town: Tishomingo. GPS: 34.620741, -88.196225

7 • B2 | George Payne Cossar SP - Jones Creek

Total sites: 41, RV sites: 41, Elec sites: 41, Flush toilet, Free showers, RV dump, Tent & RV camping: $24, Also cabins, 41 Full hookups, Open all year, Reservations not accepted, Elev: 335ft/102m, Tel: 662-623-7356, Nearest town: Oakland. GPS: 34.129353, -89.881966

8 • B2 | George Payne Cossar SP - Yocona Ridge

Total sites: 35, RV sites: 35, Elec sites: 35, Flush toilet, Free showers, RV dump, Tent & RV camping: $24, Also cabins, 35 Full hookups, Open all year, Reservations accepted, Elev: 291ft/89m, Tel: 662-623-7356, Nearest town: Oakland. GPS: 34.133329, -89.886058

9 • B2 | Leroy Percy SP

Total sites: 19, RV sites: 16, Elec sites: 16, Water at site, Flush toilet, Free showers, RV dump, Tents: $15/RVs: $22, Also cabins, Open all year, Elev: 131ft/40m, Tel: 662-827-5436, Nearest town: Hollandale. GPS: 33.166336, -90.936551

10 • B3 | Hugh White SP

Total sites: 163, RV sites: 163, Elec sites: 163, Water at site, Flush toilet, Free showers, RV dump, Tent & RV camping: $22, Also cabins, Open all year, Reservations accepted, Elev: 269ft/82m, Tel: 662-226-8963, Nearest town: Grenada. GPS: 33.806105, -89.739994

11 • B3 | Legion SP

Total sites: 27, RV sites: 15, Elec sites: 15, Water at site, Flush toilet, Free showers, RV dump, Tents: $15/RVs: $22, Also cabins, Open all year, Reservations accepted, Elev: 564ft/172m, Tel: 662-773-8323, Nearest town: Louisville. GPS: 33.153557, -89.044837

12 • B3 | Tombigbee SP

Total sites: 24, RV sites: 20, Elec sites: 20, Water at site, Flush toilet, Free showers, RV dump, Tents: $15/RVs: $22-24, Also cabins, 18 Full hookups, Open all year, Elev: 413ft/126m, Tel: 662-842-7669, Nearest town: Tupelo. GPS: 34.229606, -88.620051

13 • B3 | Trace SP - Deer Run/Eagle Ridge

Total sites: 76, RV sites: 76, Elec sites: 76, Water at site, Flush toilet, Free showers, RV dump, Tent & RV camping: $24, Also cabins, 76

Full hookups, Open all year, Elev: 413ft/126m, Tel: 662-489-2958, Nearest town: Belden. GPS: 34.251064, -88.895553

14 • B3 | Trace SP - Primitive

Total sites: 10, RV sites: 0, Water at site, Flush toilet, Free showers, No RV dump, Tents only: $15, Open all year, Elev: 410ft/125m, Tel: 662-489-2958, Nearest town: Belden. GPS: 34.256076, -88.889381

15 • B4 | Lake Lowndes SP

Total sites: 50, RV sites: 50, Elec sites: 50, Water at site, Flush toilet, Free showers, RV dump, Tents: $15/RVs: $24, Also cabins, Open all year, Reservations accepted, Elev: 305ft/93m, Tel: 662-328-2110, Nearest town: Columbus. GPS: 33.427276, -88.303927

16 • C2 | Holmes County SP

Total sites: 40, RV sites: 28, Elec sites: 28, Water at site, Flush toilet, Free showers, RV dump, Tents: $13/RVs: $18, Also cabins, Open all year, Elev: 410ft/125m, Tel: 662-653-3351, Nearest town: Durant. GPS: 33.026802, -89.918559

17 • C2 | Lefleur's Bluff SP

Total sites: 38, RV sites: 28, Elec sites: 28, Water at site, Flush toilet, Free showers, RV dump, Tents: $15/RVs: $22, Open all year, Reservations accepted, Elev: 289ft/88m, Tel: 601-987-3923, Nearest town: Jackson. GPS: 32.329008, -90.144589

18 • C3 | Clarkco SP

Total sites: 50, RV sites: 43, Elec sites: 43, Water at site, Flush toilet, Free showers, RV dump, Tents: $15/RVs: $24, Also cabins, 43 Full hookups, Open all year, Reservations accepted, Elev: 344ft/105m, Tel: 601-776-6651, Nearest town: Meridian. GPS: 32.102103, -88.696986

19 • C3 | Roosevelt SP - CCC CG

Total sites: 42, RV sites: 42, Elec sites: 42, Water at site, Flush toilet, Free showers, RV dump, No tents/RVs: $24-28, 42 Full hookups, Senior discount for non-premium sites, Open all year, Reservations accepted, Elev: 499ft/152m, Tel: 601-732-6316, Nearest town: Morton. GPS: 32.320613, -89.683442

20 • C3 | Roosevelt SP - R O Hannah CG

Total sites: 67, RV sites: 67, Elec sites: 67, Water at site, Flush toilet, Free showers, RV dump, Tent & RV camping: $22-24, Also cabins, 67 Full hookups, Open all year, Reservations accepted, Elev: 499ft/152m, Tel: 601-732-6316, Nearest town: Morton. GPS: 32.321372, -89.677481

21 • C3 | Roosevelt SP - Tent Camp

Total sites: 25, RV sites: 0, Central water, Flush toilet, No showers, No RV dump, Tents only: $15, Open all year, Reservations accepted, Elev: 455ft/139m, Tel: 601-732-6316, Nearest town: Morton. GPS: 32.324632, -89.677784

22 • D1 | Natchez SP - New CG

Total sites: 29, RV sites: 29, Elec sites: 29, Water at site, Flush toilet, Free showers, RV dump, Tents: $22/RVs: $22-24, Also cabins, 6 Full hookups, Open all year, Reservations accepted, Elev: 344ft/105m, Tel: 601-442-2658, Nearest town: Natchez. GPS: 31.596594, -91.216248

23 • D1 | Natchez SP - Old CG

Total sites: 25, RV sites: 21, Elec sites: 21, Water at site, Flush toilet, Free showers, RV dump, Tent & RV camping: $22, Open all year, Reservations accepted, Elev: 440ft/134m, Tel: 601-442-2658, Nearest town: Natchez. GPS: 31.603719, -91.233088

24 • D2 | Lake Lincoln SP

Total sites: 71, RV sites: 71, Elec sites: 71, Central water, Flush toilet, Free showers, RV dump, Tent & RV camping: $22-28, Also cabins, Senior discount for non-premium sites, Open all year, Reservations accepted, Elev: 387ft/118m, Tel: 601-643-9044, Nearest town: Wesson. GPS: 31.676028, -90.337524

25 • D2 | Percy Quin SP

Total sites: 122, RV sites: 100, Elec sites: 100, Water at site, Flush toilet, Free showers, RV dump, Tents: $15/RVs: $24-28, Also cabins, 100 Full hookups, Open all year, Reservations accepted, Elev: 407ft/124m, Tel: 601-684-3938, Nearest town: Mccomb. GPS: 31.178835, -90.522329

26 • D3 | Paul Johnson SP

Total sites: 150, RV sites: 125, Elec sites: 125, Water at site, Flush toilet, Free showers, RV dump, Tent & RV camping: $24, Also cabins, 125 Full hookups, Open all year, Reservations accepted, Elev: 253ft/77m, Tel: 601-582-7721, Nearest town: Hattiesburg. GPS: 31.142135, -89.245349

27 • E3 | Buccaneer SP

Total sites: 301, RV sites: 276, Elec sites: 276, Flush toilet, Free showers, RV dump, Tents: $15/RVs: $22-45, 206 Full hookups, Open all year, Reservations accepted, Elev: 26ft/8m, Tel: 228-467-3822, Nearest town: Waveland. GPS: 30.267287, -89.404754

Missouri

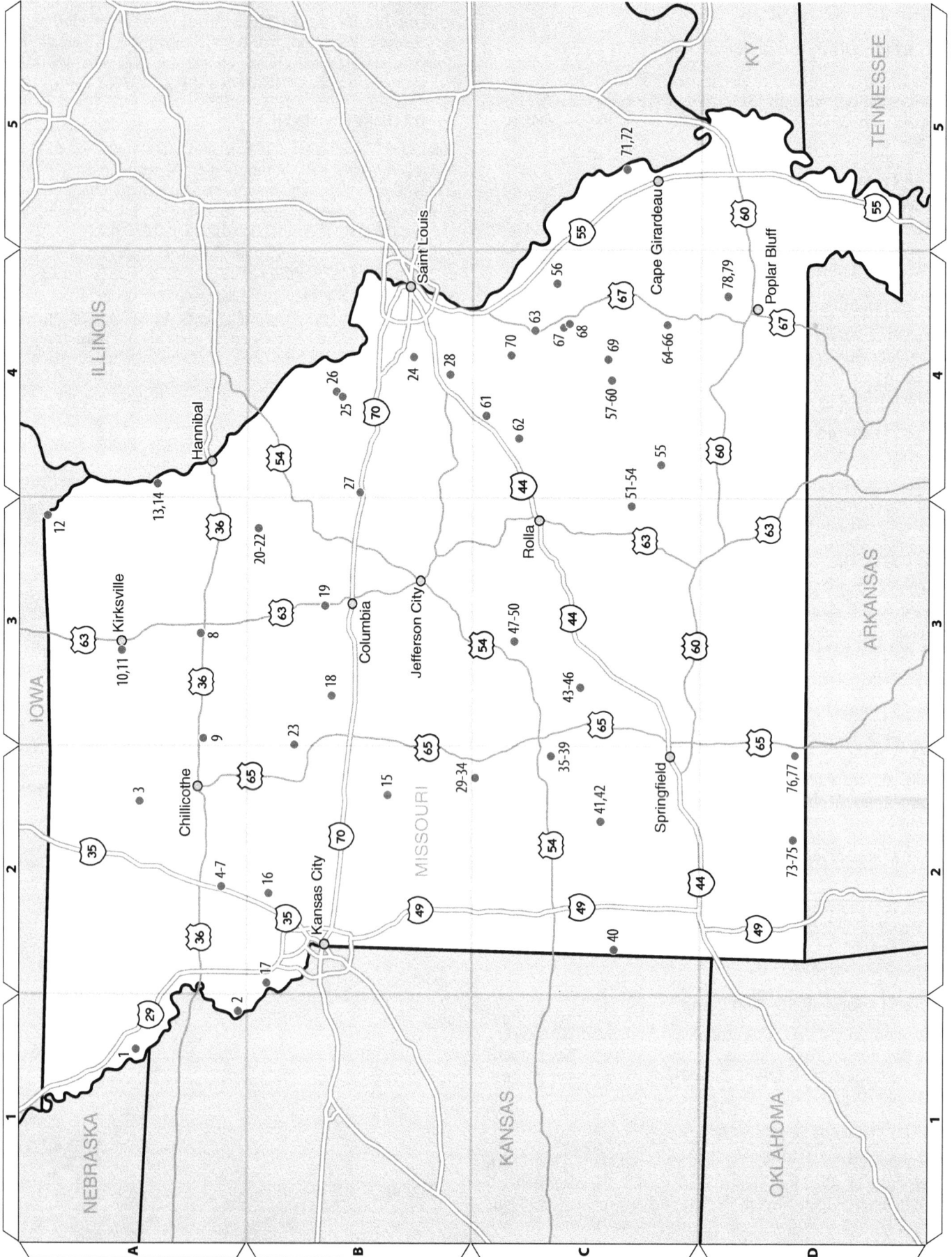

Map	ID	Map	ID
A1	1-2	C2	29-42
A2	3-7	C3	43-54
A3	8-11	C4	55-70
A4	12-14	C5	71-72
B2	15-17	D2	73-77
B3	18-23	D4	78-79
B4	24-28		

Alphabetical List of Camping Areas

1 • A1 | Big Lake SP

Total sites: 76, RV sites: 76, Elec sites: 59, Central water, Flush toilet, Free showers, RV dump, Tents: $13/RVs: $23-25, Lower rates Nov-Apr - no water, Open all year, Reservations accepted, Elev: 886ft/270m, Tel: 660-442-3770, Nearest town: Craig. GPS: 40.081884, -95.343563

2 • A1 | Lewis and Clark SP

Total sites: 70, RV sites: 70, Elec sites: 53, Flush toilet, Free showers, RV dump, Tents: $13/RVs: $23-25, No water Nov-Apr - lower rates, Open all year, Reservations accepted, Elev: 800ft/244m, Tel: 816-579-5564, Nearest town: Rushville. GPS: 39.539622, -95.053571

3 • A2 | Crowder SP

Total sites: 41, RV sites: 41, Elec sites: 29, Central water, Flush toilet, Free showers, RV dump, Tents: $13/RVs: $21-30, No water Nov and Mar-Apr - lower rates, Open Mar-Nov, Reservations accepted, Elev: 915ft/279m, Tel: 660-359-6473, Nearest town: Trenton. GPS: 40.089789, -93.671737

4 • A2 | Wallace SP - CG 1

Total sites: 33, RV sites: 29, Central water, Flush toilet, Free showers, RV dump, Tent & RV camping: $13, Also walk-to sites, 4 , No water 1 Nov-15 Apr - lower rates, Open all year, Reservations accepted, Elev: 1038ft/316m, Tel: 816-632-3745, Nearest town: Cameron. GPS: 39.655732, -94.211409

5 • A2 | Wallace SP - CG 2

Total sites: 22, RV sites: 22, Elec sites: 22, Central water, Flush toilet, Free showers, RV dump, Tent & RV camping: $23-25, No water 1 Nov-15 Apr - lower rates, Open all year, Reservations accepted, Elev: 1001ft/305m, Tel: 816-632-3745, Nearest town: Cameron. GPS: 39.654238, -94.211502

6 • A2 | Wallace SP - CG 3

Total sites: 5, RV sites: 5, Central water, Flush toilet, Free showers, RV dump, Tent & RV camping: $13, No water 1 Nov-15 Apr - lower rates, Open Apr-Oct, Reservations accepted, Elev: 981ft/299m, Tel: 816-632-3745, Nearest town: Cameron. GPS: 39.653097, -94.211355

7 • A2 | Wallace SP - CG 4

Total sites: 20, RV sites: 20, Elec sites: 20, Central water, Flush toilet, Free showers, RV dump, Tent & RV camping: $23-25, No water 1 Nov-15 Apr - lower rates, Open Apr-Oct, Reservations accepted, Elev: 990ft/302m, Tel: 816-632-3745, Nearest town: Cameron. GPS: 39.652047, -94.211508

8 • A3 | Long Branch SP

Total sites: 83, RV sites: 74, Elec sites: 63, Central water, Flush toilet, Free showers, RV dump, Tents: $14/RVs: $24-26, No water Nov-Apr - lower rates, Open all year, Reservations accepted, Elev: 824ft/251m, Tel: 660-773-5229, Nearest town: Macon. GPS: 39.770631, -92.521471

9 • A3 | Pershing SP

Total sites: 39, RV sites: 39, Elec sites: 26, Central water, Flush toilet, Free showers, RV dump, Tents: $13/RVs: $23, Open all year, Reservations accepted, Elev: 764ft/233m, Tel: 660-963-2299, Nearest town: Laclede. GPS: 39.758567, -93.214064

10 • A3 | Thousand Hills SP - CG 1

Total sites: 49, RV sites: 49, Elec sites: 35, Central water, Flush toilet, Free showers, RV dump, Tents: $13/RVs: $23-25, Also cabins, Open Apr-Oct, Reservations accepted, Elev: 925ft/282m, Tel: 660-665-6995, Nearest town: Kirksville. GPS: 40.194851, -92.642976

11 • A3 | Thousand Hills SP - CG 2

Total sites: 9, RV sites: 9, Elec sites: 9, Central water, Flush toilet, Free showers, RV dump, Tent & RV camping: $23-25, Also cabins, No water Nov-Apr - lower rates, Open all year, Reservations accepted, Elev: 863ft/263m, Tel: 660-665-6995, Nearest town: Kirksville. GPS: 40.189794, -92.643145

12 • A4 | Battle of Athens SHS

Total sites: 29, RV sites: 29, Elec sites: 15, Central water, Vault/pit toilet, No showers, RV dump, Tents: $13/RVs: $25, 1 mile to showers, Lower rates Nov - no water, Open Apr-Nov, Reservations not accepted, Elev: 702ft/214m, Tel: 660-877-3871, Nearest town: Athens. GPS: 40.588238, -91.712167

13 • A4 | Wakonda SP - Boulder Lake

Total sites: 82, RV sites: 82, Elec sites: 70, Central water, Flush toilet, Free showers, RV dump, Tents: $13/RVs: $25, No water 1 Nov-15 Apr - lower rates, Open all year, Reservations accepted, Elev: 472ft/144m, Tel: 573-655-2280, Nearest town: La Grange. GPS: 40.009106, -91.517717

14 • A4 | Wakonda SP - Wakonda Lake

Total sites: 9, RV sites: 9, Elec sites: 9, Water at site, No toilets, No showers, RV dump, Tent & RV camping: $30, 9 Full hookups, No water 1 Nov-15 Apr - lower rates, Open all year, Reservations accepted, Elev: 486ft/148m, Tel: 573-655-2280, Nearest town: La Grange. GPS: 39.997109, -91.519434

15 • B2 | Knob Noster SP

Total sites: 71, RV sites: 71, Elec sites: 37, Flush toilet, Free showers, RV dump, Tents: $13/RVs: $23, No water Nov-Mar - lower rates, Open all year, Reservations accepted, Elev: 784ft/239m, Tel: 660-563-2463, Nearest town: Knob Noster. GPS: 38.752930, -93.577881

16 • B2 | Watkins Mill SP

Total sites: 96, RV sites: 96, Elec sites: 74, Central water, Flush toilet, Free showers, RV dump, Tents: $13/RVs: $23-25, 5 family sites - $36-$40, No water Nov-Mar - lower rates, Open all year, Reservations accepted, Elev: 994ft/303m, Tel: 816-580-3387, Nearest town: Lawson. GPS: 39.390512, -94.257226

17 • B2 | Weston Bend SP

Total sites: 35, RV sites: 35, Elec sites: 32, Central water, Flush toilet, Free showers, RV dump, Tents: $13/RVs: $23-25, 2 family sites - $26-$46, No water 1 Nov-15 Apr - lower rates, Open all year, Elev: 922ft/281m, Tel: 816-640-5443, Nearest town: Weston. GPS: 39.395215, -94.871003

18 • B3 | Arrow Rock SHS

Total sites: 47, RV sites: 47, Elec sites: 35, Central water, Flush toilet, Free showers, RV dump, Tents: $13/RVs: $23-30, 1 Full hookups, Lower rates Nov-Mar - no water, Reservations accepted, Elev: 722ft/220m, Tel: 660-837-3330, Nearest town: Arrow Rock. GPS: 39.064172, -92.942106

19 • B3 | Finger Lakes SP

Total sites: 35, RV sites: 35, Elec sites: 16, Central water, Flush toilet, Free showers, RV dump, Tents: $13/RVs: $23-25, Lower rates Nov-Apr - no water, Open all year, Reservations accepted, Elev: 814ft/248m, Tel: 573-443-5315, Nearest town: Columbia. GPS: 39.104509, -92.316815

20 • B3 | Mark Twain SP - Badger

Total sites: 26, RV sites: 26, Elec sites: 26, Central water, Flush toilet, Free showers, RV dump, Tent & RV camping: $21-23, Also cabins, No water Nov-Mar - lower rates, Open all year, Reservations accepted, Elev: 670ft/204m, Tel: 573-565-3440, Nearest town: Florida. GPS: 39.465673, -91.800591

21 • B3 | Mark Twain SP - Coyote

Total sites: 31, RV sites: 31, Elec sites: 9, Central water, Flush toilet, Free showers, RV dump, Tents: $12-13/RVs: $21-23, Also cabins, No water Nov-Mar - lower rates, Open all year, Reservations accepted, Elev: 681ft/208m, Tel: 573-565-3440, Nearest town: Florida. GPS: 39.465494, -91.803693

22 • B3 | Mark Twain SP - Puma

Total sites: 37, RV sites: 37, Elec sites: 37, Central water, Flush toilet, Free showers, RV dump, Tent & RV camping: $22-28, Also cabins, 4 family sites $32-$40, No water Nov-Mar - lower rates, Open all year, Reservations accepted, Elev: 673ft/205m, Tel: 573-565-3440, Nearest town: Florida. GPS: 39.464908, -91.805796

23 • B3 | Van Meter SP

Total sites: 21, RV sites: 21, Elec sites: 12, Central water, Flush toilet, Free showers, No RV dump, Tents: $12-13/RVs: $21-25, No water Oct-Apr - lower rates, Open all year, Reservations accepted, Elev: 725ft/221m, Tel: 660-886-7537, Nearest town: Miami. GPS: 39.264159, -93.268527

24 • B4 | Babler Memorial SP

Total sites: 75, RV sites: 75, Elec sites: 43, Central water, Flush toilet, Free showers, RV dump, Tents: $13/RVs: $23-25, Lower rates Nov-Mar - no water, Open all year, Reservations accepted, Elev: 751ft/229m, Tel: 636-458-3813, Nearest town: Wildwood. GPS: 38.610232, -90.685897

25 • B4 | Cuivre River SP - Equestrian

Total sites: 14, RV sites: 14, Elec sites: 8, No water, Vault/pit toilet, Tents: $13/RVs: $23, Must have horse, No water Nov-Apr - lower rates, Open all year, Reservations accepted, Elev: 554ft/169m, Tel: 636-528-7247, Nearest town: Troy. GPS: 39.004097, -90.942964

26 • B4 | Cuivre River SP - Family CG

Total sites: 94, RV sites: 94, Elec sites: 47, Water at site, Flush toilet, Free showers, RV dump, Tents: $13/RVs: $23-30, 31 Full hookups, No water Nov-Apr - lower rates, Open all year, Reservations accepted, Elev: 679ft/207m, Tel: 636-528-7247, Nearest town: Troy. GPS: 39.030053, -90.912189

27 • B4 | Graham Cave SP

Total sites: 53, RV sites: 53, Elec sites: 18, Central water, Flush toilet, Free showers, RV dump, Tents: $12-13/RVs: $21-23, No water Nov-Mar - lower rates, Open all year, Elev: 758ft/231m, Tel: 573-564-3476, Nearest town: Montgomery City. GPS: 38.908858, -91.582113

28 • B4 | Robertsville SP

Total sites: 27, RV sites: 27, Elec sites: 15, Central water, Flush toilet, Free showers, RV dump, Tents: $12-13/RVs: $21-25, 1 family site - $26-$42, No water Nov-Mar - lower rates, 1 restroom open, Open Mar-Nov, Reservations accepted, Elev: 594ft/181m, Tel: 636-257-3788, Nearest town: Robertsville. GPS: 38.420765, -90.809917

29 • C2 | Harry S Truman SP - Bobcat Run CG

Total sites: 9, RV sites: 9, Elec sites: 9, Central water, No toilets, No showers, No RV dump, Tent & RV camping: $17-27, No water in March - lower rates, Open Mar-Oct, Reservations accepted, Elev: 863ft/263m, Tel: 660-438-7711, Nearest town: Warsaw. GPS: 38.283312, -93.453356

30 • C2 | Harry S Truman SP - Buck Ridge CG

Total sites: 63, RV sites: 63, Elec sites: 63, Central water, Flush toilet, Free showers, No RV dump, Tent & RV camping: $17-27, 7 family sites $38-$42, Open Apr-Oct, Reservations accepted, Elev: 800ft/244m, Tel: 660-438-7711, Nearest town: Warsaw. GPS: 38.287157, -93.452413

31 • C2 | Harry S Truman SP - Devils Backbone CG

Total sites: 20, RV sites: 20, Elec sites: 20, Central water, Flush toilet, Free showers, RV dump, Tent & RV camping: $17-27, 1 family site - $38, No water Nov-Mar - lower rates, Open all year, Reservations accepted, Elev: 837ft/255m, Tel: 660-438-7711, Nearest town: Warsaw. GPS: 38.280627, -93.449149

32 • C2 | Harry S Truman SP - Raccoon Ridge

Total sites: 29, RV sites: 29, Elec sites: 29, Central water, Flush toilet, Free showers, RV dump, Tent & RV camping: $17-27, 1 family site - $38, No water Nov and Mar - lower rates, Open Mar-Nov, Reservations accepted, Elev: 784ft/239m, Tel: 660-438-7711, Nearest town: Warsaw. GPS: 38.281166, -93.457447

33 • C2 | Harry S Truman SP - Thorny Ridge CG

Total sites: 40, RV sites: 40, Central water, Flush toilet, Free showers, No RV dump, Tent & RV camping: $10-15, 5 family sites $18-$20, No water in Mar - lower rates, Open Mar-Oct, Reservations accepted, Elev: 781ft/238m, Tel: 660-438-7711, Nearest town: Warsaw. GPS: 38.290575, -93.457982

34 • C2 | Harry S Truman SP - Wild Turkey Ridge CG

Total sites: 43, RV sites: 43, Central water, Flush toilet, Free showers, No RV dump, Tent & RV camping: $10-15, 1 family site - $18-$20, Open Apr-Oct, Reservations accepted, Elev: 778ft/237m, Tel: 660-438-7711, Nearest town: Warsaw. GPS: 38.289531, -93.453125

35 • C2 | Pomme de Terre SP - Hermitage

Total sites: 127, RV sites: 127, Elec sites: 100, Central water, Flush toilet, Free showers, RV dump, Tents: $10-13/RVs: $17-25, No water Nov and Mar - lower rates, Open Mar-Nov, Reservations accepted, Elev: 869ft/265m, Tel: 417-852-4291, Nearest town: Pittsburg. GPS: 37.884939, -93.304876

36 • C2 | Pomme de Terre SP - Pittsburg Loop 100

Total sites: 20, RV sites: 20, Elec sites: 20, Water at site, Flush toilet, Free showers, RV dump, Tent & RV camping: $21-27, No water Nov-Feb - lower rates, Open all year, Reservations accepted, Elev: 919ft/280m, Tel: 417-852-4291, Nearest town: Pittsburg. GPS: 37.873959, -93.320624

37 • C2 | Pomme de Terre SP - Pittsburg Loop 200

Total sites: 40, RV sites: 40, Elec sites: 40, Central water, Flush toilet, Free showers, RV dump, Tent & RV camping: $17-25, 1 family site - $34-$40, No water Nov-Mar - lower rates, Open all year, Reservations accepted, Elev: 935ft/285m, Tel: 417-852-4291, Nearest town: Pittsburg. GPS: 37.876279, -93.320553

38 • C2 | Pomme de Terre SP - Pittsburg Loop 300

Total sites: 35, RV sites: 35, Elec sites: 35, Water at site, Vault/pit toilet, No showers, No RV dump, Tent & RV camping: $17-25, 3 family sites - $34-$40, No water Nov-Mar - lower rates, Open all year, Reservations accepted, Elev: 923ft/281m, Tel: 417-852-4291, Nearest town: Pittsburg. GPS: 37.877039, -93.324939

39 • C2 | Pomme de Terre SP - Pittsburg Loop 400

Total sites: 23, RV sites: 23, Elec sites: 23, Water at site, Vault/pit toilet, No showers, No RV dump, Tent & RV camping: $17-25, 4 family site - $34-$40, No water Nov-Mar - lower rates, Open all year, Reservations accepted, Elev: 911ft/278m, Tel: 417-852-4291, Nearest town: Pittsburg. GPS: 37.875092, -93.324874

40 • C2 | Prairie SP - Backpack Camp

Dispersed sites, No water, Vault/pit toilet, Tents only: $13, Hike-in, Open all year, Reservations not accepted, Elev: 896ft/273m, Tel: 417-843-6711, Nearest town: Mindenmines. GPS: 37.526442, -94.577474

41 • C2 | Stockton SP - East

Total sites: 30, RV sites: 30, Elec sites: 30, Central water, Flush toilet, Free showers, RV dump, Tent & RV camping: $19-25, 4 family sites - $26, No water Nov-Mar - lower rates, Open all year, Reservations accepted, Elev: 924ft/282m, Tel: 417-276-4259, Nearest town: Dadeville. GPS: 37.606122, -93.737445

42 • C2 | Stockton SP - West

Total sites: 33, RV sites: 33, Elec sites: 23, Central water, Flush toilet, Free showers, RV dump, Tents: $13/RVs: $19-25, 5 family sites - $20-$38, No water Nov-Mar - lower rates, Open all year, Reservations accepted, Elev: 927ft/283m, Tel: 417-276-4259, Nearest town: Dadeville. GPS: 37.608708, -93.740203

43 • C3 | Bennett Spring SP - CG 1

Total sites: 48, RV sites: 48, Elec sites: 48, Water at site, Flush toilet, Free showers, RV dump, Tent & RV camping: $30, 48 Full hookups sites, No water in winter - lower rates, Open all year, Reservations accepted, Elev: 876ft/267m, Tel: 417-532-4338, Nearest town: Lebanon. GPS: 37.731531, -92.860048

44 • C3 | Bennett Spring SP - CG 2 and 3

Total sites: 40, RV sites: 40, Elec sites: 29, Central water, Flush toilet, Free showers, No RV dump, Tents: $13/RVs: $23, Open Apr-Oct, Reservations accepted, Elev: 978ft/298m, Tel: 417-532-4338, Nearest town: Lebanon. GPS: 37.727153, -92.860884

45 • C3 | Bennett Spring SP - CG 4

Total sites: 50, RV sites: 50, Elec sites: 50, Central water, Flush toilet, Free showers, No RV dump, Tent & RV camping: $23, Open Mar-Oct, Reservations accepted, Elev: 1096ft/334m, Tel: 417-532-4338, Nearest town: Lebanon. GPS: 37.725717, -92.864994

46 • C3 | Bennett Spring SP - CG 5

Total sites: 52, RV sites: 52, Elec sites: 50, Flush toilet, Free showers, RV dump, Tents: $13/RVs: $23, Open Mar-Oct, Reservations accepted, Elev: 1125ft/343m, Tel: 417-532-4338, Nearest town: Lebanon. GPS: 37.725041, -92.867602

47 • C3 | Lake of the Ozarks SP - Section 1

Total sites: 29, RV sites: 29, Elec sites: 27, Central water, Flush toilet, Free showers, RV dump, Tents: $13/RVs: $23-25, Also cabins, No water Nov-Mar - lower rates, Open all year, Reservations accepted, Elev: 808ft/246m, Tel: 573-348-2694, Nearest town: Kaiser. GPS: 38.075325, -92.570547

48 • C3 | Lake of the Ozarks SP - Section 2

Total sites: 16, RV sites: 16, Elec sites: 15, Central water, Vault/pit toilet, No showers, RV dump, Tents: $13/RVs: $23-25, Also cabins, No water Nov-Mar - lower rates, Open all year, Reservations accepted, Elev: 759ft/231m, Tel: 573-348-2694, Nearest town: Kaiser. GPS: 38.072793, -92.570618

49 • C3 | Lake of the Ozarks SP - Section 3

Total sites: 46, RV sites: 46, Elec sites: 46, Central water, Flush toilet, Free showers, RV dump, Tent & RV camping: $23-25, Also cabins, No water Nov-Mar - lower rates, Open all year, Reservations accepted, Elev: 753ft/230m, Tel: 573-348-2694, Nearest town: Kaiser. GPS: 38.071206, -92.572664

50 • C3 | Lake of the Ozarks SP - Section 4

Total sites: 83, RV sites: 83, Elec sites: 39, Central water, Flush toilet, Free showers, RV dump, Tents: $13/RVs: $23-25, Also cabins, No water Nov-Mar - lower rates, Open all year, Reservations accepted, Elev: 675ft/206m, Tel: 573-348-2694, Nearest town: Kaiser. GPS: 38.070434, -92.576169

51 • C3 | Montauk SP - Section 1

Total sites: 31, RV sites: 31, Central water, Flush toilet, Free showers, RV dump, Tent & RV camping: $13, Also cabins, No water Nov-Feb - lower rates, Open all year, Reservations accepted, Elev: 917ft/280m, Tel: 573-548-2201, Nearest town: Salem. GPS: 37.454385, -91.678755

52 • C3 | Montauk SP - Section 2

Total sites: 56, RV sites: 56, Elec sites: 56, Central water, Flush toilet, Free showers, RV dump, Tent & RV camping: $23-25, Also cabins, No water Nov-Feb - lower rates, Open all year, Reservations accepted, Elev: 919ft/280m, Tel: 573-548-2201, Nearest town: Salem. GPS: 37.454987, -91.675793

53 • C3 | Montauk SP - Section 3

Total sites: 39, RV sites: 39, Elec sites: 39, Central water, Flush toilet, Free showers, RV dump, Tent & RV camping: $23-25, Also cabins, No water Nov-Feb - lower rates, Open all year, Reservations accepted, Elev: 912ft/278m, Tel: 573-548-2201, Nearest town: Salem. GPS: 37.454062, -91.673402

54 • C3 | Montauk SP - Section 4

Total sites: 30, RV sites: 30, Elec sites: 30, Central water, Flush toilet, Free showers, RV dump, Tent & RV camping: $23-25, Also cabins, No water Nov-Feb - lower rates, Open all year, Reservations accepted, Elev: 915ft/279m, Tel: 573-548-2201, Nearest town: Salem. GPS: 37.452533, -91.672769

55 • C4 | Echo Bluff SP - Timbkutu

Total sites: 72, RV sites: 60, Elec sites: 60, Water at site, Flush toilet, Free showers, RV dump, Tents: $13-15/RVs: $22-37, Also walk-to sites/cabins, 43 Full hookups, Open all year, Reservations accepted, Elev: 775ft/236m, Tel: 573-751-5211, Nearest town: Salem. GPS: 37.304371, -91.410039

56 • C4 | Hawn SP

Total sites: 50, RV sites: 45, Elec sites: 26, Water available, Flush toilet, Free showers, RV dump, Tents: $13/RVs: $23-25, No water Nov-Mar - lower rates, Open all year, Reservations accepted, Elev:

604ft/184m, Tel: 573-883-3603, Nearest town: Ste. Genevieve. GPS: 37.833119, -90.226233

57 • C4 | Johnson's Shut-ins SP - Equestrian

Total sites: 9, RV sites: 9, Elec sites: 9, Water at site, Flush toilet, Free showers, RV dump, No tents/RVs: $27, No water Nov-Mar - lower rates, Open all year, Reservations accepted, Elev: 909ft/277m, Tel: 573-546-2450, Nearest town: Middlebrook. GPS: 37.560683, -90.854158

58 • C4 | Johnson's Shut-ins SP - Loop 2

Total sites: 20, RV sites: 20, Elec sites: 20, Water available, Flush toilet, Free showers, RV dump, Tent & RV camping: $30, Also cabins, 20 Full hookups, No water Nov-Mar - lower rates, Open all year, Reservations accepted, Elev: 917ft/280m, Tel: 573-546-2450, Nearest town: Middlebrook. GPS: 37.560891, -90.860159

59 • C4 | Johnson's Shut-ins SP - Loop 3

Total sites: 21, RV sites: 21, Elec sites: 21, Central water, Flush toilet, Free showers, RV dump, Tent & RV camping: $25, No water Nov-Mar - lower rates, Open all year, Reservations accepted, Elev: 920ft/280m, Tel: 573-546-2450, Nearest town: Middlebrook. GPS: 37.560727, -90.863677

60 • C4 | Johnson's Shut-ins SP - Loops 4 and 5

Total sites: 28, RV sites: 14, Central water, Flush toilet, Free showers, RV dump, Tent & RV camping: $13, Also walk-to sites, No water Nov-Mar - lower rates, Open all year, Reservations accepted, Elev: 930ft/283m, Tel: 573-546-2450, Nearest town: Middlebrook. GPS: 37.560565, -90.866844

61 • C4 | Meramec SP

Total sites: 209, RV sites: 209, Elec sites: 159, Water at site, Flush toilet, Free showers, RV dump, Tents: $13/RVs: $25-30, Open all year, Reservations not accepted, Elev: 607ft/185m, Tel: 573-468-6072, Nearest town: Sullivan. GPS: 38.226524, -91.082162

62 • C4 | Onondaga Cave SP

Total sites: 68, RV sites: 68, Elec sites: 48, Water at site, Flush toilet, Free showers, RV dump, Tents: $13/RVs: $27, No water Nov-Feb - lower rates, Open all year, Reservations accepted, Elev: 696ft/212m, Tel: 573-245-6576, Nearest town: Leasburg. GPS: 38.056375, -91.233002

63 • C4 | Saint Francois SP

Total sites: 108, RV sites: 108, Elec sites: 62, Central water, Flush toilet, Free showers, RV dump, Tents: $13/RVs: $23, 1 family site - $20, No water Nov-Mar - lower rates, Open all year, Reservations accepted, Elev: 686ft/209m, Tel: 573-358-2173, Nearest town: Bonne Terre. GPS: 37.955826, -90.533252

64 • C4 | Sam A. Baker SP - CG 1

Total sites: 109, RV sites: 109, Elec sites: 60, Central water, Flush toilet, Free showers, RV dump, Tents: $13/RVs: $23-25, 10 family sites - $26-$46No water Nov-Mar - lower rates, Open Apr-Oct, Reservations accepted, Elev: 417ft/127m, Tel: 573-856-4411, Nearest town: Patterson. GPS: 37.236574, -90.512755

65 • C4 | Sam A. Baker SP - CG 2

Total sites: 92, RV sites: 92, Elec sites: 69, Central water, Flush toilet,

Free showers, RV dump, Tents: $13/RVs: $23-25, 1 family site - $42, No water Nov-Mar - lower rates, Open all year, Reservations accepted, Elev: 423ft/129m, Tel: 573-856-4411, Nearest town: Patterson. GPS: 37.256737, -90.503162

66 • C4 | Sam A. Baker SP - Equestrian

Total sites: 21, RV sites: 21, Elec sites: 10, Central water, Vault/pit toilet, No showers, No RV dump, Tents: $13/RVs: $23-25, No water Nov-Mar - lower rates, Open Mar-Nov, Reservations accepted, Elev: 450ft/137m, Tel: 573-856-4411, Nearest town: Patterson. GPS: 37.266672, -90.498884

67 • C4 | St. Joe SP - CG 1 (ORVs)

Total sites: 75, RV sites: 75, Elec sites: 40, Central water, Flush toilet, Free showers, RV dump, Tents: $13/RVs: $23-25, 2 family sites - $26, No water Nov-Mar - lower rates, Open all year, Reservations accepted, Elev: 1017ft/310m, Tel: 573-431-1069, Nearest town: Park Hills. GPS: 37.810327, -90.514961

68 • C4 | St. Joe SP - CG 2 (Equestrian)

Total sites: 25, RV sites: 25, Elec sites: 13, Central water, Flush toilet, Free showers, RV dump, Tents: $13/RVs: $23-25, Open Apr-Oct, Reservations accepted, Elev: 925ft/282m, Tel: 573-431-1069, Nearest town: Park Hills. GPS: 37.778839, -90.486823

69 • C4 | Taum Sauk Mountain SP

Total sites: 12, RV sites: 0, Central water, Vault/pit toilet, No showers, No RV dump, Tents only: $13, Walk-to sites, Reservations not accepted, Elev: 1758ft/536m, Tel: 573-546-2450, Nearest town: Middlebrook. GPS: 37.570775, -90.725914

70 • C4 | Washington SP

Total sites: 51, RV sites: 51, Elec sites: 24, Central water, Flush toilet, Free showers, RV dump, Tents: $10-13/RVs: $21-23, Also cabins, 1 family site $30-$36, No water Nov-Mar - lower rates, Open all year, Reservations accepted, Elev: 879ft/268m, Tel: 636-586-5768, Nearest town: De Soto. GPS: 38.085906, -90.694534

71 • C5 | Trail of Tears SP - Lake Boutin

Total sites: 54, RV sites: 54, Central water, Flush toilet, Free showers, RV dump, Tent & RV camping: $13, Open May-Oct, Reservations accepted, Elev: 663ft/202m, Tel: 573-290-5268, Nearest town: Jackson. GPS: 37.453174, -89.482688

72 • C5 | Trail of Tears SP - Mississippi River

Total sites: 19, RV sites: 19, Elec sites: 19, Water at site, Flush toilet, Free showers, RV dump, Tents: $13/RVs: $23-28, No water Nov-Apr - lower rates, Near RR, Open all year, Reservations accepted, Elev: 338ft/103m, Tel: 573-290-5268, Nearest town: Jackson. GPS: 37.454434, -89.463276

73 • D2 | Roaring River SP - CG 1

Total sites: 70, RV sites: 70, Elec sites: 70, Water available, Flush toilet, Free showers, RV dump, Tent & RV camping: $24-26, 8 family sites - $42, No water Nov-Mar - lower rates, Open all year, Reservations accepted, Elev: 1129ft/344m, Tel: 417-847-2539, Nearest town: Cassville. GPS: 36.584658, -93.840367

74 • D2 | Roaring River SP - CG 2

Total sites: 39, RV sites: 39, Elec sites: 39, Central water, Flush toilet, Free showers, No RV dump, Tent & RV camping: $24-26, 2 family sites - $42, No water Nov-Mar - lower rates, Open Mar-Oct, Reservations accepted, Elev: 1037ft/316m, Tel: 417-847-2539, Nearest town: Cassville. GPS: 36.579822, -93.834226

75 • D2 | Roaring River SP - CG 3

Total sites: 62, RV sites: 62, Elec sites: 21, Central water, Flush toilet, Free showers, RV dump, Tents: $14/RVs: $23-27, 5 family sites - $26-$42, No water Nov-Mar - lower rates, Open Mar-Oct, Reservations accepted, Elev: 1106ft/337m, Tel: 417-847-2539, Nearest town: Cassville. GPS: 36.577994, -93.828918

76 • D2 | Table Rock SP - CG 1

Total sites: 75, RV sites: 75, Elec sites: 75, Water at site, Flush toilet, Free showers, RV dump, Tent & RV camping: $23-30, 20 Full hookups, 5 family sites - $46, No water Dec-Feb - lower rates, Open all year, Reservations accepted, Elev: 997ft/304m, Tel: 417-334-4704, Nearest town: Branson. GPS: 36.580649, -93.303215

77 • D2 | Table Rock SP - CG 2

Total sites: 85, RV sites: 85, Elec sites: 62, Water at site, Flush toilet, Free showers, RV dump, Tents: $13/RVs: $23-30, 21 Full hookups, No water Dec-Feb - lower rates, Open Mar-Nov, Max Length: 85ft, Reservations accepted, Elev: 978ft/298m, Tel: 417-334-4704, Nearest town: Branson. GPS: 36.577254, -93.301631

78 • D4 | Lake Wappapello SP - Asher Creek

Total sites: 28, RV sites: 28, Elec sites: 20, Water available, Flush toilet, Free showers, RV dump, Tents: $14/RVs: $20-22, Also cabins, Open Apr-Oct, Reservations accepted, Elev: 502ft/153m, Tel: 573-297-3232, Nearest town: Williamsville. GPS: 36.938036, -90.334196

79 • D4 | Lake Wappapello SP - Ridge

Total sites: 50, RV sites: 50, Elec sites: 50, Central water, Flush toilet, Free showers, RV dump, Tent & RV camping: $15-17, Also cabins, No water Nov-Mar - lower rates, Open all year, Reservations accepted, Elev: 476ft/145m, Tel: 573-297-3232, Nearest town: Williamsville. GPS: 36.935375, -90.330569

New Hampshire

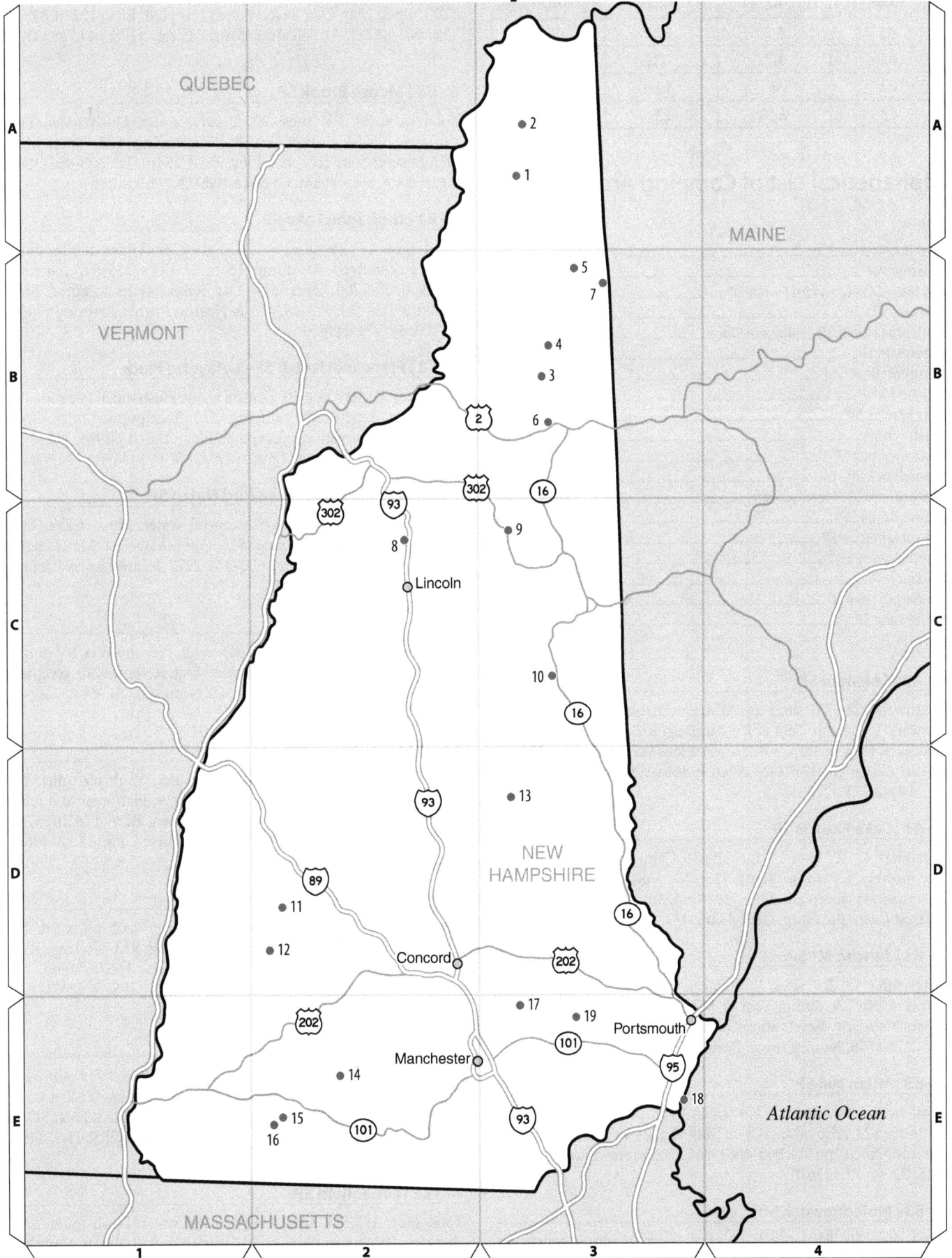

QUEBEC

MAINE

VERMONT

NEW HAMPSHIRE

MASSACHUSETTS

Atlantic Ocean

Lincoln

Concord

Manchester

Portsmouth

2
1
5
7
4
3
6
9
8
10
13
11
12
17
19
14
18
15
16

A B C D E

1 2 3 4

Map	ID	Map	ID
A3	1-2	D2	11-12
B3	3-7	D3	13
C2	8	E2	14-16
C3	9-10	E3	17-19

Alphabetical List of Camping Areas

1 • A3 | Coleman SP

Total sites: 24, RV sites: 24, Water available, Flush toilet, Pay showers, RV dump, Tent & RV camping: $25, Also cabins, Open May-Oct, Max Length: 40ft, Reservations accepted, Elev: 2244ft/684m, Tel: 603-237-5382, Nearest town: Stewartstown. GPS: 44.944092, -71.327881

2 • A3 | Lake Francis SP

Total sites: 42, RV sites: 17, Elec sites: 9, Central water, Flush toilet, Pay showers, RV dump, Tents: $25/RVs: $25-35, Open May-Oct, Reservations accepted, Elev: 1388ft/423m, Tel: 603-638-6707, Nearest town: Pittsburg. GPS: 45.059437, -71.301996

3 • B3 | Jericho Mt SP

Total sites: 13, RV sites: 9, Central water, Vault/pit toilet, No showers, No RV dump, Tent & RV camping: $25, Also cabins, Open May-Nov, Reservations accepted, Elev: 1377ft/420m, Tel: 603-752-4758, Nearest town: Berlin. GPS: 44.499856, -71.255191

4 • B3 | Milan Hill SP

Total sites: 6, RV sites: 3, No water, Vault/pit toilet, Tent & RV camping: $23, Also cabins, Open May-Oct, Reservations accepted, Elev: 1673ft/510m, Tel: 603-466-3860, Nearest town: Milan. GPS: 44.572220, -71.223610

5 • B3 | Mollidgewock SP

Total sites: 39, RV sites: 0, Central water, Vault/pit toilet, No showers, No RV dump, Tents only: $23, Generator hours: 0700-2200, Open May-Oct, Reservations accepted, Elev: 1224ft/373m, Tel: 603-482-3373, Nearest town: Errol. GPS: 44.738331, -71.143615

6 • B3 | Moose Brook SP

Total sites: 59, RV sites: 29, Central water, Flush toilet, Free showers, No RV dump, Tent & RV camping: $25, Open May-Oct, Reservations accepted, Elev: 965ft/294m, Tel: 603-466-3860, Nearest town: Gorham. GPS: 44.400932, -71.230124

7 • B3 | Umbagog Lake SP

Total sites: 27, RV sites: 27, Elec sites: 24, Water at site, Flush toilet, Pay showers, RV dump, Tents: $35/RVs: $35-50, Generator hours: 0700-2200, Open May-Oct, Reservations accepted, Elev: 1280ft/390m, Tel: 603-482-7795, Nearest town: Cambridge. GPS: 44.703613, -71.049805

8 • C2 | Franconia Notch SP - Lafayette Place

Total sites: 89, RV sites: 68, Central water, Flush toilet, Pay showers, RV dump, Tent & RV camping: $25, Tent/popups only, Open May-Oct, Reservations accepted, Elev: 1801ft/549m, Tel: 603-823-9513, Nearest town: Franconia. GPS: 44.143698, -71.684675

9 • C3 | Dry River CG - Crawford Notch SP

Total sites: 36, RV sites: 25, Central water, Flush toilet, Free showers, Tent & RV camping: $25, Open May-Oct, Max Length: 40ft, Elev: 1253ft/382m, Tel: 603-374-2272, Nearest town: Bartlett. GPS: 44.158287, -71.361315

10 • C3 | White Lake SP

Total sites: 166, RV sites: 156, Flush toilet, Free showers, RV dump, Tent & RV camping: $24, Open May-Oct, Reservations accepted, Elev: 495ft/151m, Tel: 603-323-7350, Nearest town: West Ossipee. GPS: 43.835845, -71.216103

11 • D2 | Mount Sunapee SP

Total sites: 10, RV sites: 0, Central water, Vault/pit toilet, No showers, No RV dump, Tents only: $23-29, Platforms and lean-to's, Open May-Oct, Reservations accepted, Elev: 1762ft/537m, Tel: 603-763-5561, Nearest town: Newbury. GPS: 43.327486, -72.066275

12 • D2 | Pillsbury SP

Total sites: 35, RV sites: 18, Central water, Vault/pit toilet, No showers, No RV dump, Tent & RV camping: $23, No large RVs, Open May-Oct, Reservations accepted, Elev: 1657ft/505m, Tel: 603-863-2860, Nearest town: Washington. GPS: 43.233176, -72.107979

13 • D3 | Ellacoya SP

Total sites: 37, RV sites: 37, Elec sites: 37, Flush toilet, Free showers, RV dump, No tents/RVs: $42-47, Full hookups sites, Must hook up to W/E/S, Open May-Oct, Reservations accepted, Elev: 512ft/156m, Tel: 603-293-7821, Nearest town: Gilford. GPS: 43.574463, -71.354980

14 • E2 | Greenfield SP

Total sites: 252, RV sites: 126, Central water, Flush toilet, Free showers, RV dump, Tent & RV camping: $25, Open May-Oct,

Reservations accepted, Elev: 892ft/272m, Tel: 603-547-3497, Nearest town: Greenfield. GPS: 42.954871, -71.885065

15 • E2 | Monadnock SP - Gilson Pond

Total sites: 40, RV sites: 35, Central water, Flush toilet, Free showers, No RV dump, Tents: $18-25/RVs: $18-35, No pets, Open May-Oct, Max Length: 30ft, Reservations accepted, Elev: 1260ft/384m, Tel: 603-532-2416, Nearest town: Jaffrey. GPS: 42.863747, -72.063193

16 • E2 | Monadnock SP - Headquarters

Total sites: 10, RV sites: 0, Central water, Flush toilet, Free showers, No RV dump, Tent & RV camping: $25, Open all year, Reservations accepted, Elev: 1417ft/432m, Tel: 603-532-8862, Nearest town: Jaffrey. GPS: 42.845912, -72.087939

17 • E3 | Bear Brook SP

Total sites: 101, RV sites: 36, Central water, Flush toilet, Free showers, RV dump, Tents: $18-40/RVs: $18-35, Also walk-to sites, Open May-Sep, Max Length: 38ft, Reservations accepted, Elev: 535ft/163m, Tel: 603-485-9869, Nearest town: Allenstown. GPS: 43.114528, -71.327465

18 • E3 | Hampton Beach SP

Total sites: 28, RV sites: 28, Elec sites: 28, Water at site, No toilets, No showers, RV dump, No tents/RVs: $50, 28 Full hookups, Open all year, Reservations accepted, Elev: 10ft/3m, Tel: 603-926-8990, Nearest town: Hampton. GPS: 42.897677, -70.813787

19 • E3 | Pawtuckaway SP

Total sites: 195, RV sites: 129, Central water, Flush toilet, Pay showers, No RV dump, Tents: $25/RVs: $25-30, No large RVs, No pets, Open May-Oct, Reservations accepted, Elev: 354ft/108m, Tel: 603-895-3031, Nearest town: Nottingham. GPS: 43.085495, -71.151821

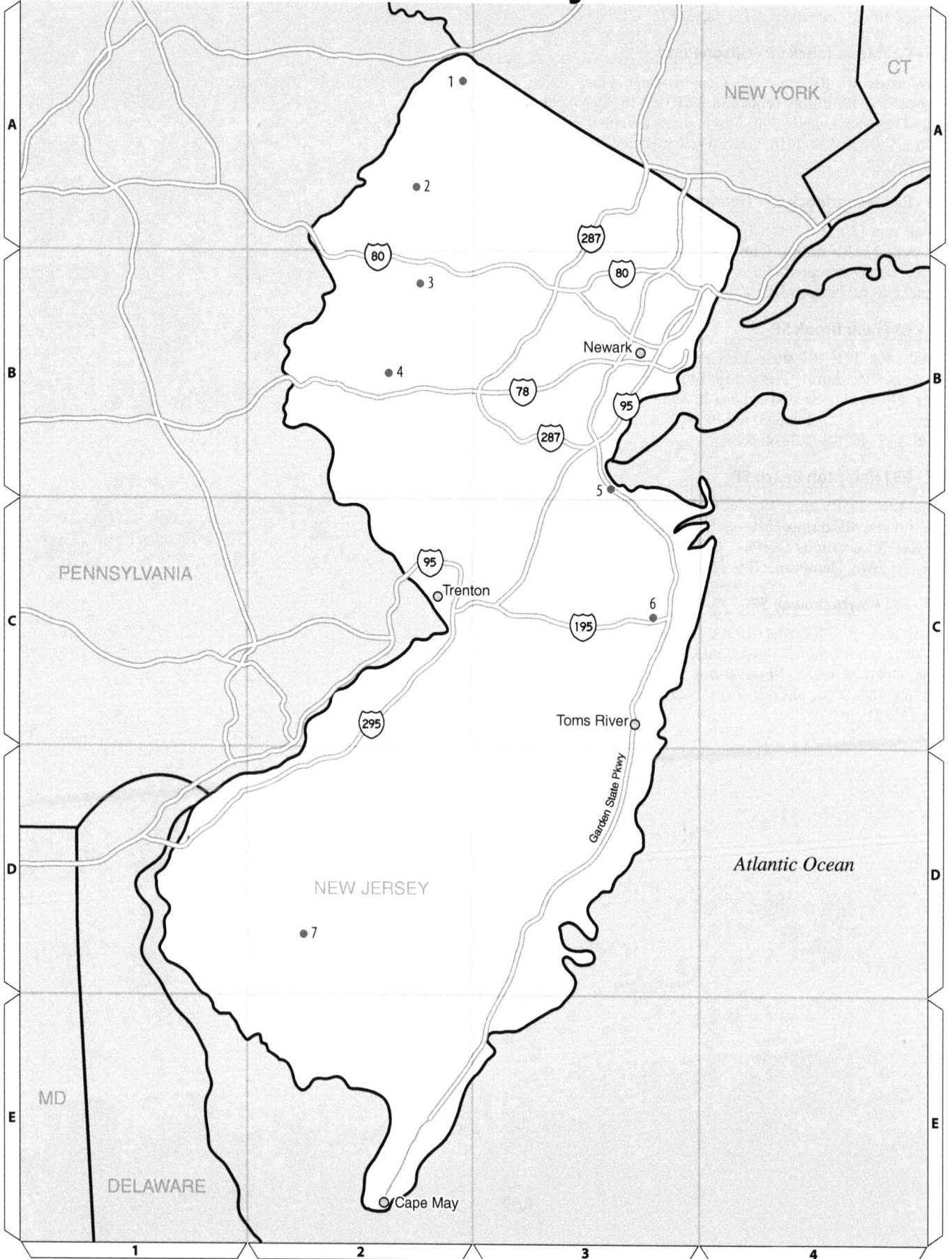

New Jersey

CT

NEW YORK

NEW JERSEY

PENNSYLVANIA

Newark

Trenton

Toms River

Cape May

MD

DELAWARE

Atlantic Ocean

Garden State Pkwy

1 2 3 4 5 6 7

Map	ID	Map	ID
A2	1-2	C3	6
B2	3-4	D2	7
B3	5		

Alphabetical List of Camping Areas

Name	ID	Map
Allaire SP	6	C3
Cheesequake SP	5	B3
High Point SP	1	A2
Parvin SP	7	D2
Stephens SP	3	B2
Swartswood SP	2	A2
Voorhees SP	4	B2

1 • A2 | High Point SP

Total sites: 50, RV sites: 0, Central water, Flush toilet, No showers, No RV dump, Tents only: $25, NJ residents: $20, 2 group sites: $50-$100, Open Apr-Oct, Reservations accepted, Elev: 1253ft/382m, Tel: 973-875-4800, Nearest town: Sussex. GPS: 41.295781, -74.688429

2 • A2 | Swartswood SP

Total sites: 65, RV sites: 65, Central water, Flush toilet, Free showers, RV dump, Tent & RV camping: $25, NJ residents: $20, 3 group sites: $40-$80, Open all year, Reservations accepted, Elev: 541ft/165m, Tel: 973-383-5230, Nearest town: Swartswood. GPS: 41.075928, -74.819580

3 • B2 | Stephens SP

Total sites: 40, RV sites: 40, Central water, No toilets, No showers, No RV dump, Tent & RV camping: $25, No large RVs, NJ residents: $20, Open Apr-Oct, Reservations accepted, Elev: 686ft/209m, Tel: 908-852-3790, Nearest town: Hackettstown. GPS: 40.872522, -74.806034

4 • B2 | Voorhees SP

Total sites: 47, RV sites: 7, Central water, Flush toilet, Free showers, RV dump, Tent & RV camping: $25, NJ residents: $20, 2 group sites: $60-$200, Astronomical observatory, Open Apr-Oct, Reservations accepted, Elev: 830ft/253m, Tel: 908-638-8572, Nearest town: Glen Gardner. GPS: 40.684104, -74.897606

5 • B3 | Cheesequake SP

Total sites: 53, RV sites: 53, Central water, Flush toilet, Free showers, RV dump, Tent & RV camping: $25, 11' height restriction, NJ residents: $20, Group sites: $50-$100, Open Apr-Oct, Reservations accepted, Elev: 0ft/0m, Tel: 732-566-2161, Nearest town: Matawan. GPS: 40.445557, -74.265625

6 • C3 | Allaire SP

Total sites: 45, RV sites: 45, Central water, Flush toilet, Free showers, RV dump, Tent & RV camping: $25, NJ residents: $20, 6 group sites: $50-$100, Open all year, Reservations accepted, Elev: 82ft/25m, Tel: 732-938-2371, Nearest town: Farmingdale. GPS: 40.166102, -74.144909

7 • D2 | Parvin SP

Total sites: 56, RV sites: 56, Central water, Flush toilet, Free showers, RV dump, Tent & RV camping: $25, Also group sites & cabins, NJ residents: $20, 4 group sites: $50-$100, Open Apr-Oct, Reservations accepted, Elev: 85ft/26m, Tel: 856-358-8616, Nearest town: Pittsgrove. GPS: 39.507658, -75.139318

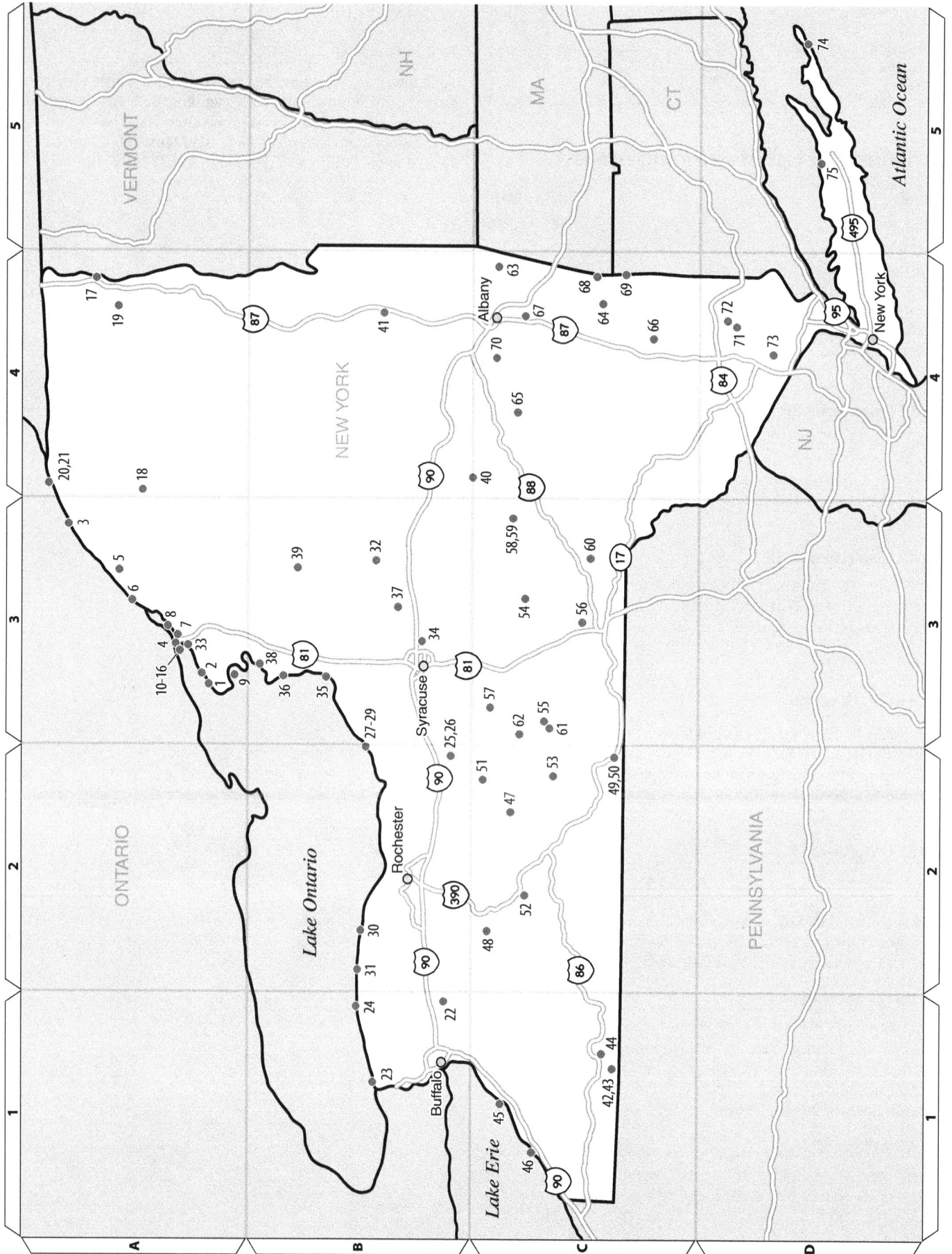

New York

VERMONT

NH

MA

CT

Atlantic Ocean

NEW YORK

NJ

PENNSYLVANIA

ONTARIO

Lake Ontario

Lake Erie

Albany

New York

Syracuse

Rochester

Buffalo

17
19
20,21
18
3
5
6
8
7
4
33
10-16
2
1
9
38
36
35
34
39
32
37
41
87
87
90
90
88
58,59
60
56
54
57
62
55
61
53
51
47
52
48
22
24
30
31
23
45
46
27-29
25,26
49,50
40
65
70
67
64
66
68
69
63
72
71
73
84
95
74
75
495
81
81
17
90
390
86
44
42,43

5
4
3
2
1

A
B
C
D

Map	ID	Map	ID
A3	1-16	C1	42-46
A4	17-21	C2	47-53
B1	22-24	C3	54-62
B2	25-31	C4	63-70
B3	32-39	D4	71-73
B4	40-41	D5	74-75

Alphabetical List of Camping Areas

1 • A3 | Burnham Point SP

Total sites: 47, RV sites: 47, Elec sites: 32, Central water, Flush toilet, Free showers, RV dump, Tents: $20/RVs: $34, Several surcharges, NY residents: $5 discount, Open May-Sep, Max Length: 40ft, Elev: 272ft/83m, Tel: 315-654-2522, Nearest town: Cape Vincent. GPS: 44.162354, -76.264160

2 • A3 | Cedar Point SP

Total sites: 165, RV sites: 165, Elec sites: 86, Central water, Flush toilet, Free showers, RV dump, Tent & RV camping: $23-39, Several surcharges, NY residents: $5 discount, Open May-Oct, Max Length: 40ft, Reservations accepted, Elev: 285ft/87m, Tel: 315-654-2522, Nearest town: Clayton. GPS: 44.203125, -76.195313

3 • A3 | Coles Creek SP

Total sites: 230, RV sites: 230, Elec sites: 150, Central water, Flush toilet, Free showers, RV dump, Tent & RV camping: $23-39, Several surcharges, NY residents: $5 discount, Open May-Sep, Max Length: 40ft, Elev: 249ft/76m, Tel: 315-388-5636, Nearest town: Waddington. GPS: 44.891609, -75.140332

4 • A3 | DeWolf Point SP

Total sites: 14, RV sites: 14, Central water, Flush toilet, Free showers, No RV dump, Tent & RV camping: $20-24, Also cabins, Several surcharges, NY residents: $5 discount, Open May-Sep, Max Length: 20ft, Reservations accepted, Elev: 299ft/91m, Tel: 315-482-2722, Nearest town: Fineview. GPS: 44.332485, -75.990875

5 • A3 | Eel Weir SP

Total sites: 34, RV sites: 34, Central water, Flush toilet, Free showers, No RV dump, Tent & RV camping: $20-28, Several surcharges, NY residents: $5 discount, Open May-Sep, Reservations accepted, Elev: 308ft/94m, Tel: 315-393-1138, Nearest town: Ogdensburg. GPS: 44.629913, -75.476432

6 • A3 | Jacques Cartier SP

Total sites: 89, RV sites: 89, Elec sites: 31, Central water, Flush toilet, Free showers, RV dump, Tent & RV camping: $20-36, Several surcharges, NY residents: $5 discount, Open May-Sep, Max Length: 50ft, Reservations accepted, Elev: 246ft/75m, Tel: 315-375-6371, Nearest town: Morristown. GPS: 44.562038, -75.686492

7 • A3 | Keewaydin SP

Total sites: 48, RV sites: 48, Central water, Flush toilet, Free showers, No RV dump, Tent & RV camping: $20-28, Several surcharges, NY residents: $5 discount, Open May-Sep, Max Length: 40ft, Reservations accepted, Elev: 279ft/85m, Tel: 315-482-3331, Nearest town: Alexandria Bay. GPS: 44.324996, -75.932882

8 • A3 | Kring Point SP

Total sites: 93, RV sites: 72, Elec sites: 26, Central water, Flush toilet, Free showers, RV dump, Tent & RV camping: $23-39, Several surcharges, NY residents: $5 discount, Open May-Oct, Max Length: 40ft, Reservations accepted, Elev: 249ft/76m, Tel: 315-482-2444, Nearest town: Redwood. GPS: 44.377197, -75.855469

9 • A3 | Long Point SP

Total sites: 80, RV sites: 80, Elec sites: 27, Central water, Flush toilet, Free showers, RV dump, Tent & RV camping: $20-34, Several surcharges, NY residents: $5 discount, Open May-Sep, Max Length: 50ft, Reservations accepted, Elev: 243ft/74m, Tel: 315-649-5258, Nearest town: Three Mile Bay. GPS: 44.028731, -76.216931

10 • A3 | Wellesley Island SP - Acorn

Total sites: 75, RV sites: 38, Central water, Flush toilet, Free showers, RV dump, Tent & RV camping: $23, Also cabins, Several surcharges, NY residents: $5 discount, Open May-Oct, Max Length: 40ft, Reservations accepted, Elev: 290ft/88m, Tel: 315-482-2722, Nearest town: Fineview. GPS: 44.325291, -76.050857

11 • A3 | Wellesley Island SP - Blue Jay

Total sites: 48, RV sites: 21, Central water, Flush toilet, Free showers, RV dump, Tent & RV camping: $23, Also cabins, Several surcharges, NY residents: $5 discount, Open May-Oct, Max Length: 30ft, Reservations accepted, Elev: 250ft/76m, Tel: 315-482-2722, Nearest town: Fineview. GPS: 44.329141, -76.046391

12 • A3 | Wellesley Island SP - Coyote

Total sites: 72, RV sites: 72, Elec sites: 72, Central water, Flush toilet, Free showers, RV dump, Tent & RV camping: $29, Also cabins, Several surcharges, NY residents: $5 discount, Open May-Oct, Max Length: 30ft, Reservations accepted, Elev: 257ft/78m, Tel: 315-482-2722, Nearest town: Fineview. GPS: 44.328305, -76.044594

13 • A3 | Wellesley Island SP - Deer

Total sites: 38, RV sites: 20, Central water, Flush toilet, Free showers, RV dump, Tent & RV camping: $23, Also cabins, Several surcharges, NY residents: $5 discount, Open May-Oct, Max Length: 20ft, Reservations accepted, Elev: 280ft/85m, Tel: 315-482-2722, Nearest town: Fineview. GPS: 44.331075, -76.039652

14 • A3 | Wellesley Island SP - Eagle

Total sites: 80, RV sites: 59, Central water, Flush toilet, Free showers, RV dump, Tent & RV camping: $29, Also cabins, Several surcharges, NY residents: $5 discount, Open May-Oct, Max Length: 30ft, Reservations accepted, Elev: 267ft/81m, Tel: 315-482-2722, Nearest town: Fineview. GPS: 44.332007, -76.028439

15 • A3 | Wellesley Island SP - Fox

Total sites: 57, RV sites: 57, Elec sites: 57, Water at site, Flush toilet, Free showers, RV dump, No tents/RVs: $37, 57 Full hookups, Several surcharges, NY residents: $5 discount, Open May-Oct, Max Length: 40ft, Reservations accepted, Elev: 265ft/81m, Tel: 315-482-2722, Nearest town: Fineview. GPS: 44.329321, -76.036527

16 • A3 | Wellesley Island SP - Heron

Total sites: 32, RV sites: 32, Elec sites: 32, Central water, Flush toilet, Free showers, RV dump, Tent & RV camping: $31, Also cabins, Several surcharges, NY residents: $5 discount, Open May-Oct, Max Length: 50ft, Reservations accepted, Elev: 279ft/85m, Tel: 315-482-2722, Nearest town: Fineview. GPS: 44.315247, -76.025148

17 • A4 | Cumberland Bay SP

Total sites: 133, RV sites: 133, Elec sites: 17, Central water, Flush toilet, Free showers, RV dump, Tents: $20/RVs: $34, Several surcharges, NY residents: $5 discount, Open May-Sep, Max Length: 50ft, Reservations accepted, Elev: 115ft/35m, Tel: 518-563-5240, Nearest town: Plattsburg. GPS: 44.724308, -73.422759

18 • A4 | Higley Flow SP

Total sites: 128, RV sites: 128, Elec sites: 59, Central water, Flush toilet, Free showers, RV dump, Tent & RV camping: $20-36, Several surcharges, NY residents: $5 discount, Open May-Sep, Max Length: 40ft, Reservations accepted, Elev: 945ft/288m, Tel: 315-262-2880, Nearest town: Colton. GPS: 44.503563, -74.912262

19 • A4 | Macomb Reservation SP

Total sites: 123, RV sites: 123, Elec sites: 31, Central water, Flush toilet, Free showers, RV dump, Tent & RV camping: $20-30, Several surcharges, NY residents: $5 discount, Open May-Sep, Max Length: 40ft, Reservations accepted, Elev: 653ft/199m, Tel: 518-643-9952, Nearest town: Schuyler Falls. GPS: 44.616486, -73.611536

20 • A4 | Robert Moses SP - Barnhart

Total sites: 55, RV sites: 55, Elec sites: 55, Central water, Flush toilet, Free showers, RV dump, Tent & RV camping: $23-39, Also cabins, Several surcharges, NY residents: $5 discount, Open May-Oct, Max Length: 50ft, Reservations accepted, Elev: 269ft/82m, Tel: 315-769-8663, Nearest town: Massena. GPS: 45.005702, -74.843634

21 • A4 | Robert Moses SP - Long Sault

Total sites: 145, RV sites: 145, Elec sites: 76, Central water, Flush toilet, Free showers, RV dump, Tent & RV camping: $23-39, Also cabins, Several surcharges, NY residents: $5 discount, Open May-Oct, Max Length: 50ft, Reservations accepted, Elev: 259ft/79m, Tel: 315-769-8663, Nearest town: Massena. GPS: 44.989261, -74.865509

22 • B1 | Darien Lakes SP

Total sites: 156, RV sites: 156, Elec sites: 136, Central water, Flush toilet, Free showers, RV dump, Tents: $23/RVs: $35, Several surcharges, NY residents: $5 discount, Open May-Oct, Max Length: 45ft, Reservations accepted, Elev: 922ft/281m, Tel: 585-547-9242, Nearest town: Darien Center. GPS: 42.908959, -78.427651

23 • B1 | Four Mile Creek SP

Total sites: 258, RV sites: 258, Elec sites: 142, Central water, Flush toilet, Free showers, RV dump, Tent & RV camping: $23-39, Several surcharges, NY residents: $5 discount, Open Apr-Oct, Reservations accepted, Elev: 279ft/85m, Tel: 716-745-3802, Nearest town: Youngstown. GPS: 43.274170, -78.995117

24 • B1 | Golden Hill SP

Total sites: 59, RV sites: 59, Elec sites: 34, Central water, Flush toilet, Free showers, RV dump, Tent & RV camping: $20-36, Several surcharges, NY residents: $5 discount, Open Apr-Oct, Max Length: 40ft, Reservations accepted, Elev: 243ft/74m, Tel: 716-795-3885, Nearest town: Barker. GPS: 43.374502, -78.488235

25 • B2 | Cayuga Lake SP - East Side

Total sites: 36, RV sites: 36, Elec sites: 36, Central water, Flush toilet, Free showers, RV dump, Tent & RV camping: $20-30, Also cabins, Several surcharges, NY residents: $5 discount, Open Apr-Oct, Max Length: 40ft, Reservations accepted, Elev: 489ft/149m, Tel: 315-568-5163, Nearest town: Seneca Falls. GPS: 42.897797, -76.753114

26 • B2 | Cayuga Lake SP - West Side

Total sites: 224, RV sites: 224, Central water, Flush toilet, Free showers, RV dump, Tent & RV camping: $20-30, Also cabins, Several surcharges, NY residents: $5 discount, Open Apr-Oct, Max Length: 40ft, Reservations accepted, Elev: 466ft/142m, Tel: 315-568-5163, Nearest town: Seneca Falls. GPS: 42.897537, -76.757731

27 • B2 | Fair Haven Beach SP - Bluff

Total sites: 43, RV sites: 43, Elec sites: 43, Central water, Flush toilet, Free showers, RV dump, Tent & RV camping: $33, Several surcharges, NY residents: $5 discount, Open Apr-Oct, Max Length: 35ft, Reservations accepted, Elev: 433ft/132m, Tel: 315-947-5205, Nearest town: Fair Haven. GPS: 43.346761, -76.688778

28 • B2 | Fair Haven Beach SP - Drumlin

Total sites: 127, RV sites: 127, Central water, Flush toilet, Free showers, RV dump, Tent & RV camping: $23, Several surcharges, NY residents: $5 discount, Open May-Oct, Max Length: 35ft, Reservations accepted, Elev: 285ft/87m, Tel: 315-947-5205, Nearest town: Fair Haven. GPS: 43.335559, -76.696481

29 • B2 | Fair Haven Beach SP - Lakeview

Total sites: 14, RV sites: 14, Elec sites: 2, Central water, Flush toilet, Free showers, RV dump, Tents: $23/RVs: $33, Several surcharges, NY residents: $5 discount, Open Apr-Oct, Max Length: 35ft, Reservations accepted, Elev: 349ft/106m, Tel: 315-947-5205, Nearest town: Fair Haven. GPS: 43.349092, -76.688301

30 • B2 | Hamlin Beach SP

Total sites: 264, RV sites: 264, Elec sites: 264, Central water, Flush toilet, Free showers, RV dump, Tent & RV camping: $29-35, No pets in loops D-F, Several surcharges, NY residents: $5 discount, Open May-Oct, Elev: 295ft/90m, Tel: 585-964-2462, Nearest town: Hamlin. GPS: 43.358788, -77.953214

31 • B2 | Lakeside Beach SP

Total sites: 274, RV sites: 274, Elec sites: 274, Central water, Flush toilet, Free showers, RV dump, Tent & RV camping: $20-32, Several surcharges, NY residents: $5 discount, Open May-Oct, Reservations accepted, Elev: 312ft/95m, Tel: 585-682-4888, Nearest town: Waterport. GPS: 43.367051, -78.229454

32 • B3 | Delta Lake SP

Total sites: 101, RV sites: 101, Elec sites: 101, Central water, Flush toilet, Free showers, RV dump, Tent & RV camping: $20-38, Several surcharges, NY residents: $5 discount, Open May-Oct, Reservations accepted, Elev: 594ft/181m, Tel: 315-337-4670, Nearest town: Rome. GPS: 43.293069, -75.420614

33 • B3 | Grass Point SP

Total sites: 72, RV sites: 72, Elec sites: 17, Central water, Flush toilet, Free showers, RV dump, Tent & RV camping: $20-36, Also cabins, Several surcharges, NY residents: $5 discount, Open May-Sep, Max Length: 40ft, Reservations accepted, Elev: 266ft/81m, Tel: 315-686-4472, Nearest town: Alexandria Bay. GPS: 44.281250, -75.999023

34 • B3 | Green Lakes SP

Total sites: 137, RV sites: 137, Elec sites: 23, Central water, Flush toilet, Free showers, RV dump, Tent & RV camping: $23-41, Also cabins, Several surcharges, NY residents: $5 discount, Open May-Oct, Max Length: 60ft, Reservations accepted, Elev: 600ft/183m, Tel: 315-637-6111, Nearest town: Fayetteville. GPS: 43.050696, -75.975262

35 • B3 | Selkirk Shores SP

Total sites: 143, RV sites: 143, Elec sites: 85, Central water, Flush toilet, Free showers, RV dump, Tent & RV camping: $20-24, Also cabins, Several surcharges, NY residents: $5 discount, Open May-Oct, Reservations accepted, Elev: 318ft/97m, Tel: 315-298-5737, Nearest town: Pulaski. GPS: 43.555584, -76.208689

36 • B3 | Southwick Beach SP

Total sites: 100, RV sites: 100, Elec sites: 38, Central water, Flush toilet, Free showers, RV dump, Tent & RV camping: $23-35, Several surcharges, NY residents: $5 discount, Open May-Oct, Max Length: 40ft, Reservations accepted, Elev: 266ft/81m, Tel: 315-846-5338, Nearest town: Henderson. GPS: 43.767043, -76.209874

37 • B3 | Verona Beach SP

Total sites: 45, RV sites: 45, Elec sites: 12, Central water, Flush toilet, Free showers, RV dump, Tent & RV camping: $23-35, Several surcharges, NY residents: $5 discount, Open May-Oct, Max Length: 50ft, Reservations accepted, Elev: 397ft/121m, Tel: 315-762-4463, Nearest town: Verona Beach. GPS: 43.179526, -75.731343

38 • B3 | Westcott Beach SP

Total sites: 154, RV sites: 154, Elec sites: 39, Central water, Flush toilet, Free showers, RV dump, Tent & RV camping: $23-33, Several surcharges, NY residents: $5 discount, Open May-Sep, Max Length: 40ft, Reservations accepted, Elev: 285ft/87m, Tel: 315-938-5083, Nearest town: Henderson. GPS: 43.902157, -76.124422

39 • B3 | Whetstone Gulf SP

Total sites: 56, RV sites: 56, Elec sites: 19, Central water, Flush toilet, Free showers, RV dump, Tent & RV camping: $20-32, Several surcharges, NY residents: $5 discount, Open May-Sep, Max Length: 40ft, Elev: 1326ft/404m, Tel: 315-376-6630, Nearest town: Lowville. GPS: 43.702504, -75.463993

40 • B4 | Glimmerglass SP

Total sites: 43, RV sites: 37, Elec sites: 37, Central water, Flush toilet, Free showers, RV dump, Tent & RV camping: $20-30, Several surcharges, NY residents: $5 discount, Open May-Oct, Max Length: 40ft, Reservations accepted, Elev: 1214ft/370m, Tel: 607-547-8662, Nearest town: Cooperstown. GPS: 42.787136, -74.864748

41 • B4 | Moreau Lake SP

Total sites: 144, RV sites: 144, Central water, Flush toilet, Free showers, RV dump, Tent & RV camping: $23-27, Several surcharges, NY residents: $5 discount, Open May-Oct, Max Length: 40ft, Reservations accepted, Elev: 446ft/136m, Tel: 518-793-0511, Nearest town: Gansevoort. GPS: 43.227801, -73.708609

42 • C1 | Allegany SP - Diehl Trail

Total sites: 24, RV sites: 24, Central water, Flush toilet, Free showers, RV dump, Tent & RV camping: $18-30, Several surcharges, Open Mar-Oct, Elev: 1498ft/457m, Tel: 716-354-9121, Nearest town: Salamanca. GPS: 42.012588, -78.823981

43 • C1 | Allegany SP - Quaker Area - Cain Hollow

Total sites: 158, RV sites: 158, Elec sites: 129, Central water, Flush toilet, Free showers, RV dump, Tent & RV camping: $18-30, Also cabins, Several surcharges, Open May-Oct, Elev: 1509ft/460m, Tel: 716-354-2182, Nearest town: Salamanca. GPS: 42.038990, -78.843833

44 • C1 | Allegany SP - Redhouse

Total sites: 121, RV sites: 121, Elec sites: 104, Central water, Flush toilet, Free showers, RV dump, Tent & RV camping: $18-30, Also cabins, Several surcharges, Open Mar-Oct, Elev: 1553ft/473m, Tel: 716-354-9121, Nearest town: Salamanca. GPS: 42.091433, -78.748498

45 • C1 | Evangola SP

Total sites: 77, RV sites: 77, Elec sites: 50, Central water, Flush toilet, Free showers, RV dump, Tents: $20/RVs: $32, Several surcharges, NY residents: $5 discount, Open Apr-Oct, Max Length: 40ft, Reservations accepted, Elev: 604ft/184m, Tel: 716-549-1802, Nearest town: Irving. GPS: 42.602858, -79.113453

46 • C1 | Lake Erie SP

Total sites: 99, RV sites: 99, Elec sites: 80, Flush toilet, Free showers, RV dump, Tent & RV camping: $20-32, Also cabins, Several surcharges, NY residents: $5 discount, Open May-Oct, Reservations accepted, Elev: 636ft/194m, Tel: 716-792-9214, Nearest town: Brocton. GPS: 42.422607, -79.432373

47 • C2 | Keuka Lake SP

Total sites: 150, RV sites: 150, Elec sites: 53, Central water, Flush toilet, Free showers, RV dump, Tent & RV camping: $23-35, Several surcharges, NY residents: $5 discount, Open May-Oct, Reservations accepted, Elev: 965ft/294m, Tel: 315-536-3666, Nearest town: Bluff Point. GPS: 42.582934, -77.125857

48 • C2 | Letchworth SP

Total sites: 258, RV sites: 258, Elec sites: 258, Central water, Flush toilet, Free showers, RV dump, Tent & RV camping: $29-31, Also cabins, Several surcharges, NY residents: $5 discount, Open May-Oct, Reservations accepted, Elev: 932ft/284m, Tel: 585-493-3600, Nearest town: Castile. GPS: 42.699059, -77.934504

49 • C2 | Newtown Battlefield SP - Main

Total sites: 6, RV sites: 6, Central water, Flush toilet, Free showers, RV dump, Tent & RV camping: $19-29, Several surcharges, NY residents: $5 discount, Open May-Oct, Max Length: 40ft, Reservations accepted, Elev: 1384ft/422m, Tel: 607-732-6067, Nearest town: Elmira. GPS: 42.047171, -76.733455

50 • C2 | Newtown Battlefield SP - North

Total sites: 10, RV sites: 10, Central water, Flush toilet, Free showers, RV dump, Tent & RV camping: $19-29, Several surcharges, NY residents: $5 discount, Open May-Oct, Max Length: 35ft, Reservations accepted, Elev: 1250ft/381m, Tel: 607-732-6067, Nearest town: Elmira. GPS: 42.056068, -76.742348

51 • C2 | Sampson SP

Total sites: 309, RV sites: 309, Elec sites: 245, Central water, Flush toilet, Free showers, RV dump, Tent & RV camping: $20-36, Several surcharges, NY residents: $5 discount, Open Apr-Nov, Max Length: 40ft, Reservations accepted, Elev: 551ft/168m, Tel: 315-585-6392, Nearest town: Romulus. GPS: 42.731695, -76.908409

52 • C2 | Stony Brook SP

Total sites: 113, RV sites: 98, Central water, Flush toilet, Free showers, RV dump, Tent & RV camping: $20, Several surcharges, NY residents: $5 discount, Open May-Oct, Reservations accepted, Elev: 1132ft/345m, Tel: 585-335-8111, Nearest town: Dansville. GPS: 42.509836, -77.688971

53 • C2 | Watkins Glen SP

Total sites: 293, RV sites: 293, Elec sites: 163, Central water, Flush toilet, Free showers, RV dump, Tent & RV camping: $23-35,

Several surcharges, NY residents: $5 discount, Open May-Oct, Max Length: 40ft, Reservations accepted, Elev: 991ft/302m, Tel: 607-535-4511, Nearest town: Watkins Glen. GPS: 42.369194, -76.881069

54 • C3 | Bowman Lake SP

Total sites: 168, RV sites: 168, Central water, Flush toilet, Free showers, RV dump, Tent & RV camping: $20-24, NY residents: $15-$19, Several surcharges, Open May-Oct, Max Length: 50ft, Reservations accepted, Elev: 1742ft/531m, Tel: 607-334-2718, Nearest town: Oxford. GPS: 42.520020, -75.680664

55 • C3 | Buttermilk Falls SP

Total sites: 60, RV sites: 60, Central water, Flush toilet, Free showers, No RV dump, Tent & RV camping: $24, Several surcharges, NY residents: $5 discount, Open May-Oct, Elev: 682ft/208m, Tel: 607-273-3440, Nearest town: Ithaca. GPS: 42.419478, -76.514395

56 • C3 | Chenango Valley SP

Total sites: 185, RV sites: 185, Elec sites: 53, Central water, Flush toilet, Free showers, RV dump, Tent & RV camping: $20-32, Also cabins, NY residents: $5 discount, Open May-Oct, Max Length: 50ft, Reservations accepted, Elev: 978ft/298m, Tel: 607-648-5251, Nearest town: Chenango Forks. GPS: 42.217653, -75.837153

57 • C3 | Fillmore Glen SP

Total sites: 57, RV sites: 57, Elec sites: 10, Central water, Flush toilet, Free showers, RV dump, Tent & RV camping: $20-32, Also cabins, Several surcharges, NY residents: $5 discount, Open May-Oct, Max Length: 50ft, Elev: 797ft/243m, Tel: 315-497-0130, Nearest town: Moravia. GPS: 42.700892, -76.416794

58 • C3 | Gilbert Lake SP - Deer Run

Total sites: 145, RV sites: 145, Elec sites: 29, Central water, Flush toilet, Free showers, RV dump, Tent & RV camping: $20-32, Several surcharges, NY residents: $5 discount, Open May-Oct, Max Length: 50ft, Reservations accepted, Elev: 1755ft/535m, Tel: 607-432-2114, Nearest town: Laurens. GPS: 42.580334, -75.135693

59 • C3 | Gilbert Lake SP - Hilltop

Total sites: 76, RV sites: 76, Elec sites: 17, Central water, Flush toilet, Free showers, RV dump, Tents: $20/RVs: $32, Several surcharges, NY residents: $5 discount, Open May-Oct, Max Length: 50ft, Reservations accepted, Elev: 1535ft/468m, Tel: 607-432-2114, Nearest town: Laurens. GPS: 42.577217, -75.126325

60 • C3 | Oquaga Creek SP

Total sites: 95, RV sites: 95, Central water, Flush toilet, Free showers, RV dump, Tent & RV camping: $19-24, Also cabins, Several surcharges, NY residents: $5 discount, Open May-Oct, Max Length: 50ft, Reservations accepted, Elev: 1683ft/513m, Tel: 607-467-4160, Nearest town: Bainbridge. GPS: 42.186443, -75.418879

61 • C3 | Robert H. Treman SP

Total sites: 72, RV sites: 64, Elec sites: 11, Central water, Flush toilet, Free showers, RV dump, Tent & RV camping: $23-33, Also cabins, Several surcharges, NY residents: $5 discount, Open Apr-Nov, Max Length: 50ft, Reservations accepted, Elev: 476ft/ 145m, Tel: 607-273-3440, Nearest town: Ithaca. GPS: 42.396407, -76.555251

62 • C3 | Taughannock Falls SP

Total sites: 78, RV sites: 36, Elec sites: 16, Central water, Flush toilet, Free showers, RV dump, Tent & RV camping: $23-33, Also cabins, Several surcharges, NY residents: $5 discount, Open Apr-Oct, Reservations accepted, Elev: 450ft/137m, Tel: 607-387-6739, Nearest town: Trumansburg. GPS: 42.546072, -76.604505

63 • C4 | Cherry Plain SP

Total sites: 30, RV sites: 10, Central water, Flush toilet, Free showers, No RV dump, Tent & RV camping: $17-24, Several surcharges, NY residents: $5 discount, Open Apr-Oct, Max Length: 15ft, Elev: 1460ft/445m, Tel: 518-733-5400, Nearest town: Cherry Plain. GPS: 42.621494, -73.410413

64 • C4 | Lake Taghkanic SP

Total sites: 55, RV sites: 55, RV dump, Tent & RV camping: $20-27, Also cabins, Several surcharges, NY residents: $5 discount, Open May-Oct, Max Length: 20ft, Reservations accepted, Elev: 797ft/243m, Tel: 518-851-3631, Nearest town: Ancram. GPS: 42.095025, -73.705404

65 • C4 | Max V Shaul SP

Total sites: 30, RV sites: 30, Central water, Flush toilet, Free showers, No RV dump, Tent & RV camping: $20-24, Several surcharges, NY residents: $5 discount, Open May-Sep, Max Length: 34ft, Reservations accepted, Elev: 800ft/244m, Tel: 518-827-4711, Nearest town: Fultonham. GPS: 42.547363, -74.411133

66 • C4 | Mills-Norrie SP

Total sites: 45, RV sites: 45, Central water, Flush toilet, Free showers, RV dump, Tent & RV camping: $20-24, Also cabins, Several surcharges, NY residents: $5 discount, Open May-Oct, Max Length: 40ft, Reservations accepted, Elev: 82ft/25m, Tel: 845-889-4646, Nearest town: Staatsburg. GPS: 41.840493, -73.939082

67 • C4 | Schodack Island SP

Total sites: 66, RV sites: 66, Elec sites: 43, Water at site, Flush toilet, Free showers, RV dump, Tent & RV camping: $20-32, Several surcharges, NY residents: $5 discount, Open Apr-Dec, Max Length: 50ft, Reservations accepted, Elev: 25ft/8m, Tel: 518-732-0187, Nearest town: Castleton-on-Hudson. GPS: 42.501349, -73.772423

68 • C4 | Taconic SP - Copake Falls

Total sites: 106, RV sites: 36, Central water, Flush toilet, Free showers, Tent & RV camping: $20-27, Several surcharges, NY residents: $5 discount, Open all year, Max Length: 30ft, Reservations accepted, Elev: 853ft/260m, Tel: 518-329-3993, Nearest town: Copake Falls. GPS: 42.123133, -73.514195

69 • C4 | Taconic SP - Rudd Pond

Total sites: 41, RV sites: 0, Central water, Flush toilet, Free showers, Tents only: $20-27, Several surcharges, NY residents: $5 discount, Max Length: 20ft, Reservations accepted, Elev: 945ft/288m, Tel: 518-789-3059, Nearest town: Millerton. GPS: 41.978649, -73.503678

70 • C4 | Thatcher SP - Thompson's Lake

Total sites: 140, RV sites: 140, Central water, Flush toilet, Free showers, RV dump, Tent & RV camping: $20-24, Several surcharges, NY residents: $5 discount, Open May-Oct, Max Length: 40ft, Reservations accepted, Elev: 1345ft/410m, Tel: 518-872-1674, Nearest town: East Berne. GPS: 42.653398, -74.045543

71 • D4 | Clarence Fahnestock SP - AT Trail Crossing

Dispersed sites, Central water, No toilets, Tents only: $24, NY residents: $5 discount, Open Apr-Dec, Elev: 902ft/275m, Tel: 845-225-7207, Nearest town: Carmel. GPS: 41.421012, -73.868465

72 • D4 | Clarence Fahnestock SP - Pelton Pond

Total sites: 72, RV sites: 38, Central water, Flush toilet, Free showers, No RV dump, Tent & RV camping: $24, Several surcharges, NY residents: $5 discount, Open Apr-Dec, Max Length: 30ft, Reservations accepted, Elev: 1063ft/324m, Tel: 845-225-7207, Nearest town: Carmel. GPS: 41.462526, -73.828975

73 • D4 | Harriman SP - Beaver Pond

Total sites: 137, Central water, Flush toilet, Free showers, RV dump, Tent & RV camping: $20-27, NY residents: $5 discount, Open Apr-Oct, Max Length: 38ft, Reservations accepted, Elev: 1073ft/327m, Tel: 845-786-2701, Nearest town: Stony Point. GPS: 41.232307, -74.068224

74 • D5 | Hither Hills SP

Total sites: 168, RV sites: 168, Central water, Flush toilet, Free showers, RV dump, Tent & RV camping: $70, NY residents: $35, Several surcharges, Open Apr-Nov, Max Length: 30ft, Reservations accepted, Elev: 33ft/10m, Tel: 631-668-2554, Nearest town: Montauk. GPS: 41.008521, -72.010688

75 • D5 | Wildwood SP

Total sites: 314, RV sites: 314, Elec sites: 74, Central water, Flush toilet, Free showers, RV dump, Tent & RV camping: $23-39, Several surcharges, NY residents: $5 discount, Open Apr-Oct, Max Length: 50ft, Reservations accepted, Elev: 125ft/38m, Tel: 631-929-4314, Nearest town: Wading River. GPS: 40.961194, -72.803928

North Carolina

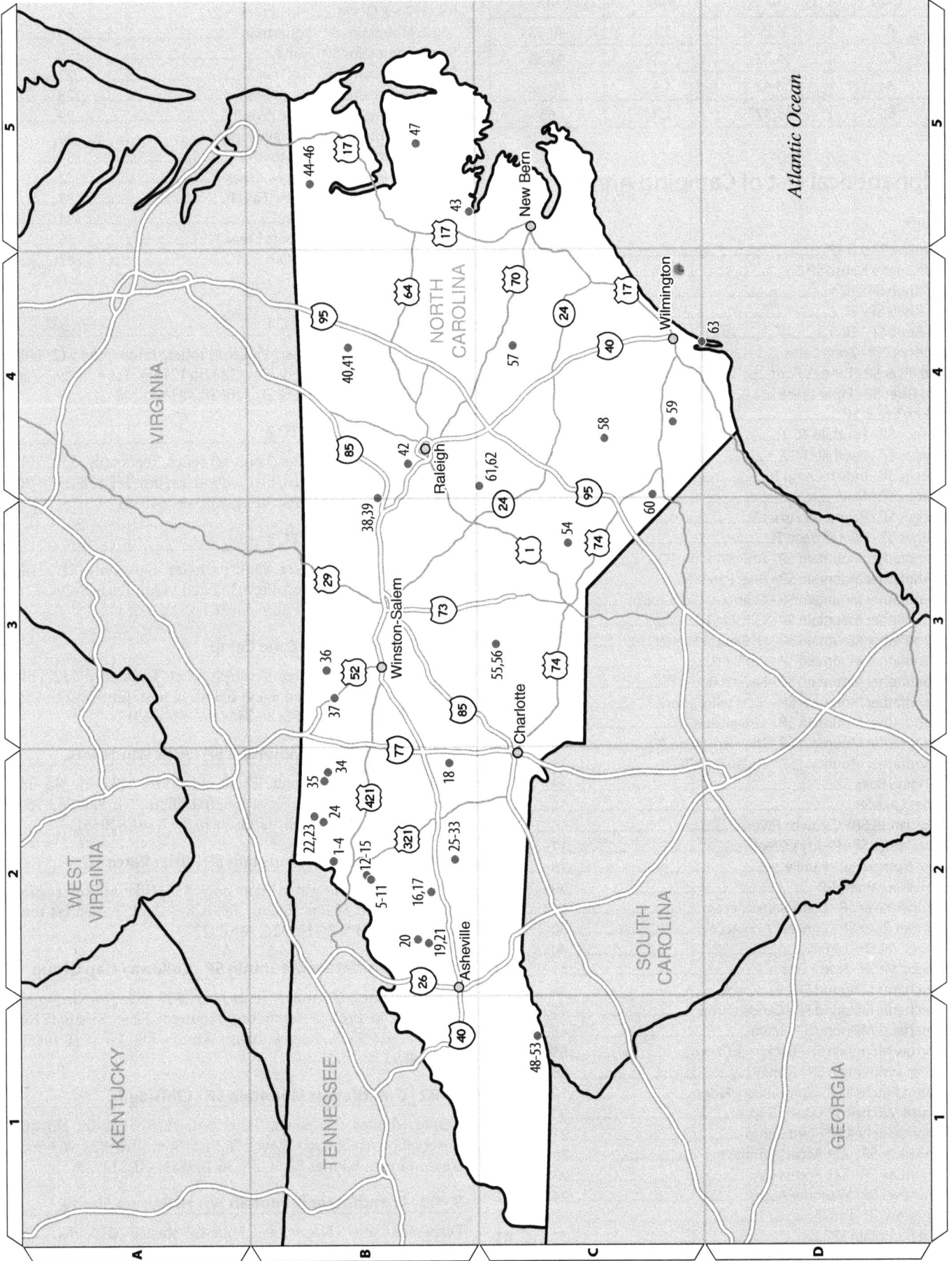

Atlantic Ocean

VIRGINIA

WEST VIRGINIA

KENTUCKY

TENNESSEE

SOUTH CAROLINA

GEORGIA

NORTH CAROLINA

New Bern

Wilmington

Raleigh

Winston-Salem

Charlotte

Asheville

47

44-46

17

43

17

17

64

70

24

95

40

17

63

40,41

57

58

59

42

85

61,62

38,39

24

95

60

29

1

54

74

73

55,56

74

52

36

37

85

77

35

34

18

24

421

22,23

1-4

321

25-33

12-15

5-11

16,17

20

19,21

26

40

48-53

Map	ID	Map	ID
B2	1-35	C1	48-53
B3	36-37	C3	54-56
B4	38-42	C4	57-62
B5	43-47	D4	63

Alphabetical List of Camping Areas

1 • B2 | Elk Knob SP - TC 1

Dispersed sites, No water, Vault/pit toilet, Tents only: $12, Hike-in, Reservations accepted, Elev: 3997ft/1218m, Tel: 828-297-7261, Nearest town: Todd. GPS: 36.340538, -81.681202

2 • B2 | Elk Knob SP - TC 2

Dispersed sites, No water, Vault/pit toilet, Tents only: $12, Hike-in, Reservations accepted, Elev: 3806ft/1160m, Tel: 828-297-7261, Nearest town: Todd. GPS: 36.342533, -81.678391

3 • B2 | Elk Knob SP - TC 3

Dispersed sites, No water, Vault/pit toilet, Tents only: $12, Hike-in, Reservations accepted, Elev: 3739ft/1140m, Tel: 828-297-7261, Nearest town: Todd. GPS: 36.346861, -81.670561

4 • B2 | Elk Knob SP - Zone Camp

Dispersed sites, No water, Vault/pit toilet, Tents only: $12, Hike-in, Reservations accepted, Elev: 4034ft/1230m, Tel: 828-297-7261, Nearest town: Todd. GPS: 36.346269, -81.676315

5 • B2 | Grandfather Mountain SP - Attic Window TC

Dispersed sites, No water, Tents only: $15, Hike-in, No fires, Reservations required, Elev: 5862ft/1787m, Tel: 828-963-9522, Nearest town: Banner Elk. GPS: 36.102957, -81.820351

6 • B2 | Grandfather Mountain SP - Briar Patch TC

Dispersed sites, No water, Tents only: $15, Hike-in, Reservations required, Elev: 5520ft/1682m, Tel: 828-963-9522, Nearest town: Banner Elk. GPS: 36.109316, -81.802775

7 • B2 | Grandfather Mountain SP - Calloway Gap Group

Dispersed sites, No water, Tents only: $15, Hike-in, Group site: $28-$35, No fires, Reservations required, Elev: 5635ft/1718m, Tel: 828-963-9522, Nearest town: Banner Elk. GPS: 36.108829, -81.814693

8 • B2 | Grandfather Mountain SP - Cliffside TC

Dispersed sites, No water, Tents only: $15, Hike-in, No fires, Reservations required, Elev: 5762ft/1756m, Tel: 828-963-9522, Nearest town: Banner Elk. GPS: 36.109881, -81.812726

9 • B2 | Grandfather Mountain SP - Hi Balsam Shelter

Dispersed sites, No water, Hike-to shelter: $15, No fires,

Reservations required, Elev: 5714ft/1742m, Tel: 828-963-9522, Nearest town: Banner Elk. GPS: 36.110713, -81.807873

10 • B2 | Grandfather Mountain SP - Profile TC

Dispersed sites, No water, Tents only: $15, Hike-in, Reservations required, Elev: 4810ft/1466m, Tel: 828-963-9522, Nearest town: Banner Elk. GPS: 36.117733, -81.815016

11 • B2 | Grandfather Mountain SP - Ravens Roost TC

Dispersed sites, No water, Tents only: $15, Hike-in, No fires, Reservations required, Elev: 5730ft/1747m, Tel: 828-963-9522, Nearest town: Banner Elk. GPS: 36.111252, -81.808606

12 • B2 | Grandfather Mountain SP - Storyteller's Rock TC

Dispersed sites, No water, Tents only: $15, Hike-in, Reservations required, Elev: 4447ft/1355m, Tel: 828-963-9522, Nearest town: Banner Elk. GPS: 36.119494, -81.794421

13 • B2 | Grandfather Mountain SP - Streamside TC

Dispersed sites, No water, Tents only: $15, Hike-in, Stream water, Reservations required, Elev: 4318ft/1316m, Tel: 828-963-9522, Nearest town: Banner Elk. GPS: 36.117847, -81.792072

14 • B2 | Grandfather Mountain SP - The Hermitage TC

Dispersed sites, No water, Tents only: $15, Hike-in, Stream water, Reservations required, Elev: 4452ft/1357m, Tel: 828-963-9522, Nearest town: Banner Elk. GPS: 36.117033, -81.794482

15 • B2 | Grandfather Mountain SP - The Refuge TC

Dispersed sites, No water, Tents only: $15, Hike-in, Reservations required, Elev: 4432ft/1351m, Tel: 828-963-9522, Nearest town: Banner Elk. GPS: 36.120183, -81.793749

16 • B2 | Lake James SP - Catawba River

Total sites: 20, RV sites: 0, Central water, Flush toilet, Free showers, No RV dump, Tents only: $23, Walk-to sites, Open Mar-Nov, Reservations accepted, Elev: 1230ft/375m, Tel: 828-584-7728, Nearest town: Nebo. GPS: 35.732371, -81.899602

17 • B2 | Lake James SP - Paddy's Creek

Total sites: 33, RV sites: 0, Central water, Flush toilet, Free showers, No RV dump, Tents only: $10-23, Open Mar-Nov, Max Length: 20ft, Reservations accepted, Elev: 1293ft/394m, Tel: 828-584-7728, Nearest town: Nebo. GPS: 35.756983, -81.875082

18 • B2 | Lake Norman SP - Family

Total sites: 33, RV sites: 33, Elec sites: 1, Central water, Flush toilet, Free showers, RV dump, Tents: $19-23/RVs: $19-33, $6 senior/military discount, Generator hours: 0700-2200, Open Mar-Nov, Max Length: 70ft, Reservations accepted, Elev: 846ft/258m, Tel: 704-528-6350, Nearest town: Troutman. GPS: 35.646011, -80.943006

19 • B2 | Mount Mitchell SP - Commissary Ridge

Dispersed sites, No water, No toilets, Tents only: Fee unk, Walk-to sites, 1.8 mi, Location approximate, Open all year, Reservations not accepted, Elev: 6396ft/1950m, Tel: 828-675-4611, Nearest town: Asheville. GPS: 35.760145, -82.258795

20 • B2 | Mount Mitchell SP - Deep Gap

Dispersed sites, No water, No toilets, Tents only: Fee unk, Walk-to sites, 4.5 mi, Open all year, Reservations not accepted, Elev: 5919ft/1804m, Tel: 828-675-4611, Nearest town: Asheville. GPS: 35.814144, -82.251287

21 • B2 | Mount Mitchell SP - Tent Camp

Total sites: 9, Central water, No toilets, No showers, No RV dump, Tents only: $23, Walk-to sites, $6 senior/military discount, Open all year, Reservations accepted, Elev: 6312ft/1924m, Tel: 828-675-4611, Nearest town: Asheville. GPS: 35.760131, -82.271353

22 • B2 | New River SP - 221 Access Primitive

Total sites: 14, Central water, Flush toilet, Free showers, Tents only: $19-23, Walk-to/boat-in/group sites, $6 senior/military discount, Fee: $48, Open all year, Max Length: 62ft, Reservations accepted, Elev: 2570ft/783m, Tel: 336-982-2587, Nearest town: Laurel Springs. GPS: 36.458148, -81.339184

23 • B2 | New River SP - 221 Access RV

Total sites: 20, RV sites: 20, Elec sites: 20, Water at site, Flush toilet, Free showers, RV dump, Tent & RV camping: $22-33, 10 Full hookups, $6 senior/military discount, Open all year, Max Length: 65ft, Reservations accepted, Elev: 2776ft/846m, Tel: 336-982-2587, Nearest town: Laurel Springs. GPS: 36.465682, -81.343307

24 • B2 | New River SP - Wagoner Access

Total sites: 10, Central water, Flush toilet, Free showers, Tents only: $19-23, Walk-to/boat-in/group sites, Group site: $70-$80, $6 senior/military discount, Fee: $48, Open all year, Reservations accepted, Elev: 2644ft/806m, Tel: 336-982-2587, Nearest town: Laurel Springs. GPS: 36.413932, -81.384535

25 • B2 | South Mountains SP - Equestrian

Total sites: 14, RV sites: 14, Elec sites: 14, Central water, Flush toilet, Free showers, No RV dump, Tent & RV camping: $19-23, Equestrian facility, Open all year, Reservations accepted, Elev: 1238ft/377m, Tel: 828-433-4772, Nearest town: Connelly Springs. GPS: 35.594973, -81.610456

26 • B2 | South Mountains SP - Family

Total sites: 18, RV sites: 18, Elec sites: 2, Central water, Vault/pit toilet, No showers, No RV dump, Tents: $19-23/RVs: $19-28, Open all year, Max Length: 70ft, Reservations accepted, Elev: 1401ft/427m, Tel: 828-433-4772, Nearest town: Connelly Springs. GPS: 35.597456, -81.622971

27 • B2 | South Mountains SP - Fox Trail TC

Dispersed sites, Vault/pit toilet, Tents only: $12, Hike-in, Open all year, Reservations accepted, Elev: 2440ft/744m, Tel: 828-433-4772, Nearest town: Connelly Springs. GPS: 35.595514, -81.677292

28 • B2 | South Mountains SP - Jacob Branch TC

Dispersed sites, Vault/pit toilet, Tents only: $12, Hike-in, Open all year, Reservations accepted, Elev: 2243ft/684m, Tel: 828-433-4772, Nearest town: Connelly Springs. GPS: 35.599654, -81.669126

29 • B2 | South Mountains SP - Little River TC

Dispersed sites, Vault/pit toilet, Tents only: $12, Hike-in, Open all year, Reservations accepted, Elev: 1967ft/600m, Tel: 828-433-4772, Nearest town: Connelly Springs. GPS: 35.607959, -81.626148

30 • B2 | South Mountains SP - Murray Branch TC

Dispersed sites, Vault/pit toilet, Tents only: $12, Hike-in, Open all year, Reservations accepted, Elev: 2427ft/740m, Tel: 828-433-4772, Nearest town: Connelly Springs. GPS: 35.592313, -81.683232

31 • B2 | South Mountains SP - Sawtooth TC

Dispersed sites, Vault/pit toilet, Tents only: $12, Hike-in, Open all year, Reservations accepted, Elev: 2055ft/626m, Tel: 828-433-4772, Nearest town: Connelly Springs. GPS: 35.618565, -81.632871

32 • B2 | South Mountains SP - Shinny Creek TC

Dispersed sites, Vault/pit toilet, Tents only: $12, Hike-in, Open all year, Reservations accepted, Elev: 1565ft/477m, Tel: 828-433-4772, Nearest town: Connelly Springs. GPS: 35.603994, -81.643686

33 • B2 | South Mountains SP - Upper Falls TC

Dispersed sites, Vault/pit toilet, Tents only: $12, Hike-in, Open all year, Reservations accepted, Elev: 1785ft/544m, Tel: 828-433-4772, Nearest town: Connelly Springs. GPS: 35.593852, -81.638251

34 • B2 | Stone Mountain SP - Main

Total sites: 88, RV sites: 88, Elec sites: 41, Water at site, Flush toilet, Free showers, RV dump, Tents: $19-23/RVs: $24-33, 4 group sites: $52-$62, $6 senior/military discount, Open all year, Max Length: 95ft, Reservations accepted, Elev: 1932ft/589m, Tel: 336-957-8185, Nearest town: Roaring Gap. GPS: 36.382311, -81.020469

35 • B2 | Stone Mountain SP - Widow's Creek TC

Total sites: 6, No water, No toilets, Tents only: $12, Hike-in, 1.5-3 mi, Open all year, Reservations not accepted, Elev: 1677ft/511m, Tel: 336-957-8185, Nearest town: Roaring Gap. GPS: 36.404045, -81.084915

36 • B3 | Hanging Rock SP

Total sites: 73, RV sites: 73, Central water, Flush toilet, Free showers, No RV dump, Tent & RV camping: $19-23, Group site: $28-$32, $6 senior/military discount, $13 in winter, Open all year, Max Length: 60ft, Reservations accepted, Elev: 1818ft/554m, Tel: 336-593-8480, Nearest town: Danbury. GPS: 36.389669, -80.276224

37 • B3 | Pilot Mountain SP

Total sites: 49, RV sites: 49, Central water, Flush toilet, Free showers, No RV dump, Tent & RV camping: $19-23, $6 senior/military discount, Open Mar-Nov, Max Length: 38ft, Reservations accepted, Elev: 1378ft/420m, Tel: 336-325-2355, Nearest town: Pinnacle. GPS: 36.347749, -80.471408

38 • B4 | Eno River SP - Fanny's Ford

Total sites: 5, RV sites: 0, Vault/pit toilet, Tents only: $12, Hike-in, Reservations accepted, Elev: 435ft/133m, Tel: 919-383-1686, Nearest town: Eno. GPS: 36.082051, -79.005609

39 • B4 | Eno River SP - Piper Creek

Total sites: 5, RV sites: 0, Vault/pit toilet, Tents only: $12, Hike-in, 1.2 mi, Reservations accepted, Elev: 371ft/113m, Tel: 919-383-1686, Nearest town: Eno. GPS: 36.052346, -78.986672

40 • B4 | Medoc Mt SP - Family

Total sites: 34, RV sites: 34, Elec sites: 12, Water at site, Flush toilet, Free showers, No RV dump, Tents: $12-23/RVs: $22-28, 4 group sites: $52-$62, $6 senior/military discount, Open all year, Max Length: 80ft, Reservations accepted, Elev: 203ft/62m, Tel: 252-586-6588, Nearest town: Hollister. GPS: 36.245655, -77.891972

41 • B4 | Medoc Mt SP - Horse Camp

Total sites: 5, RV sites: 5, No water, Vault/pit toilet, No showers, No RV dump, Tents: $12-23/RVs: $22-28, $6 senior/military discount, Open all year, Reservations accepted, Elev: 169ft/52m, Tel: 252-586-6588, Nearest town: Hollister. GPS: 36.234661, -77.893578

42 • B4 | William B. Umstead SP - Main

Total sites: 28, RV sites: 0, Central water, Flush toilet, Free showers, No RV dump, Tents only: $19-23, Also group site & cabins, Group sites, $6 senior/military discount, Open Apr-Nov, Max Length: 30ft, Reservations accepted, Elev: 446ft/136m, Tel: 919-571-4170, Nearest town: Raleigh. GPS: 35.889762, -78.756177

43 • B5 | Goose Creek SP

Total sites: 14, Central water, Vault/pit toilet, No showers, No RV dump, Tents only: $12, 2 group sites: $46-$52, $6 daily entrance fee, Open all year, Reservations accepted, Elev: 46ft/14m, Tel: 252-923-2191, Nearest town: Washington. GPS: 35.475095, -76.925552

44 • B5 | Merchants Millpond SP - Backpack

Total sites: 5, No water, Vault/pit toilet, Tents only: $12, Hike-in, Open all year, Reservations accepted, Elev: 33ft/10m, Tel: 252-357-1191, Nearest town: Gatesville. GPS: 36.442538, -76.673111

45 • B5 | Merchants Millpond SP - Canoe Camp

Total sites: 10, No water, Vault/pit toilet, Tents only: $12, Hike-in/boat-in, Open all year, Reservations accepted, Elev: 8ft/2m, Tel: 252-357-1191, Nearest town: Gatesville. GPS: 36.429942, -76.689616

46 • B5 | Merchants Millpond SP - Main

Total sites: 20, RV sites: 20, Central water, Flush toilet, Free showers, No RV dump, Tent & RV camping: $19-23, $6 senior/military discount, Open all year, Max Length: 60ft, Reservations accepted, Elev: 37ft/11m, Tel: 252-357-1191, Nearest town: Gatesville. GPS: 36.445157, -76.694061

47 • B5 | Pettigrew SP - Family

Total sites: 13, RV sites: 13, Central water, Flush toilet, Free showers, No RV dump, Tent & RV camping: $19-23, Do not rely on GPS - see park website, $6 senior/military discount, Winter rate $13 (washhouse closed), Open all year, Max Length: 75ft,

Reservations accepted, Elev: 26ft/8m, Tel: 252-797-4475, Nearest town: Creswell. GPS: 35.790338, -76.407953

48 • C1 | Gorges SP - Foothills TC 1

Dispersed sites, No water, Tents only: Free, Hike-in, Open all year, Reservations not accepted, Elev: 1147ft/350m, Tel: 828-966-9099, Nearest town: Sapphire. GPS: 35.071301, -82.884325

49 • C1 | Gorges SP - Foothills TC 2

Dispersed sites, No water, Tents only: Free, Hike-in, Open all year, Reservations not accepted, Elev: 1574ft/480m, Tel: 828-966-9099, Nearest town: Sapphire. GPS: 35.059209, -82.920483

50 • C1 | Gorges SP - Indian Camp TC

Dispersed sites, No water, Tents only: Free, Hike-in, Open all year, Reservations not accepted, Elev: 2211ft/674m, Tel: 828-966-9099, Nearest town: Sapphire. GPS: 35.086674, -82.917299

51 • C1 | Gorges SP - Main

Total sites: 31, RV sites: 14, Elec sites: 14, Water at site, Flush toilet, Tent & RV camping: Fee unk, Also cabins, 14 Full hookups, Elev: 3265ft/995m, Tel: 828-966-9099. GPS: 35.097153, -82.951358

52 • C1 | Gorges SP - Raymond Fisher TC

Total sites: 8, No water, Vault/pit toilet, Tents only: $12, Hike-in, 1.5 mi, Open all year, Reservations required, Elev: 2733ft/833m, Tel: 828-966-9099, Nearest town: Sapphire. GPS: 35.084356, -82.948673

53 • C1 | Gorges SP - Wintergreen TC

Dispersed sites, No water, Tents only: Free, Hike-in, Open all year, Reservations not accepted, Elev: 1619ft/493m, Tel: 828-966-9099, Nearest town: Sapphire. GPS: 35.090967, -82.915869

54 • C3 | Lumber River SP - Chalk Banks Access

Total sites: 14, RV sites: 14, Central water, Vault/pit toilet, No showers, No RV dump, Tent & RV camping: $12, Group site: $10-$42, Open all year, Max Length: 75ft, Reservations accepted, Elev: 233ft/71m, Tel: 910-628-4564, Nearest town: Orrum. GPS: 34.915204, -79.353371

55 • C3 | Morrow Mountain SP - Backpack Camp

Total sites: 4, No water, Vault/pit toilet, Tents only: $12, Hike-in, Open all year, Reservations accepted, Elev: 325ft/99m, Tel: 704-982-4402, Nearest town: Albemarle. GPS: 35.356003, -80.076745

56 • C3 | Morrow Mountain SP - Family

Total sites: 106, RV sites: 106, Elec sites: 22, Central water, Flush toilet, Free showers, RV dump, Tents: $19-23/RVs: $22-28, $6 senior/military discount, Open all year, Max Length: 55ft, Reservations accepted, Elev: 420ft/128m, Tel: 704-982-4402, Nearest town: Albemarle. GPS: 35.372925, -80.068301

57 • C4 | Cliffs of the Neuse SP

Total sites: 32, RV sites: 32, Elec sites: 12, Water at site, Flush toilet, Free showers, RV dump, Tents: $19-23/RVs: $24-30, Also group sites & cabins, Group site: $70-$80, Open all year, Reservations accepted, Elev: 151ft/46m, Tel: 919-778-6234, Nearest town: Goldsboro. GPS: 35.240564, -77.887617

58 • C4 | Jones Lake SP

Total sites: 20, RV sites: 20, Elec sites: 1, Water at site, Flush toilet, Free showers, No RV dump, Tents: $19-23/RVs: $24-30, 6 Full hookups, Group site: $52-$62, $6 senior/military discount, Open all year, Max Length: 60ft, Reservations accepted, Elev: 85ft/26m, Tel: 910-588-4550, Nearest town: Elizabethtown. GPS: 34.680857, -78.598342

59 • C4 | Lake Waccamaw SP

Total sites: 5, No water, Vault/pit toilet, No showers, No RV dump, Tents only: $12-32, Walk-to sites, $6 senor/military discount, Reservations accepted, Elev: 52ft/16m, Tel: 910-646-4748, Nearest town: Lake Waccamaw. GPS: 34.260003, -78.478014

60 • C4 | Lumber River SP - Princess Ann Access

Total sites: 9, Central water, Vault/pit toilet, No showers, No RV dump, Tents only: $12, Walk-to sites, 2 group sites: $10-$42, Open all year, Reservations accepted, Elev: 144ft/44m, Tel: 910-628-4564, Nearest town: Orrum. GPS: 34.387991, -79.001372

61 • C4 | Raven Rock SP - Campbell Creek TC

Total sites: 5, No water, Vault/pit toilet, Tents only: $12, Hike-in, Elev: 255ft/78m, Tel: 910-893-4888, Nearest town: Lillington. GPS: 35.475349, -78.934537

62 • C4 | Raven Rock SP - Moccasin Branch

Total sites: 24, RV sites: 9, Elec sites: 9, Water at site, Flush toilet, Free showers, Tents: $23/RVs: $33, 9 Full hookups, Reservations accepted, Elev: 342ft/104m, Tel: 910-893-4888, Nearest town: Lillington. GPS: 35.457515, -78.906537

63 • D4 | Carolina Beach SP

Total sites: 83, RV sites: 83, Elec sites: 9, Water at site, Flush toilet, Free showers, RV dump, Tents: $23/RVs: $23-33, Also group sites & cabins, Group sites: $42-$52,9 Full hookups, $6 senior/military discount, Open all year, Max Length: 90ft, Reservations accepted, Elev: 39ft/12m, Tel: 910-458-8206, Nearest town: Carolina Beach. GPS: 34.050668, -77.908212

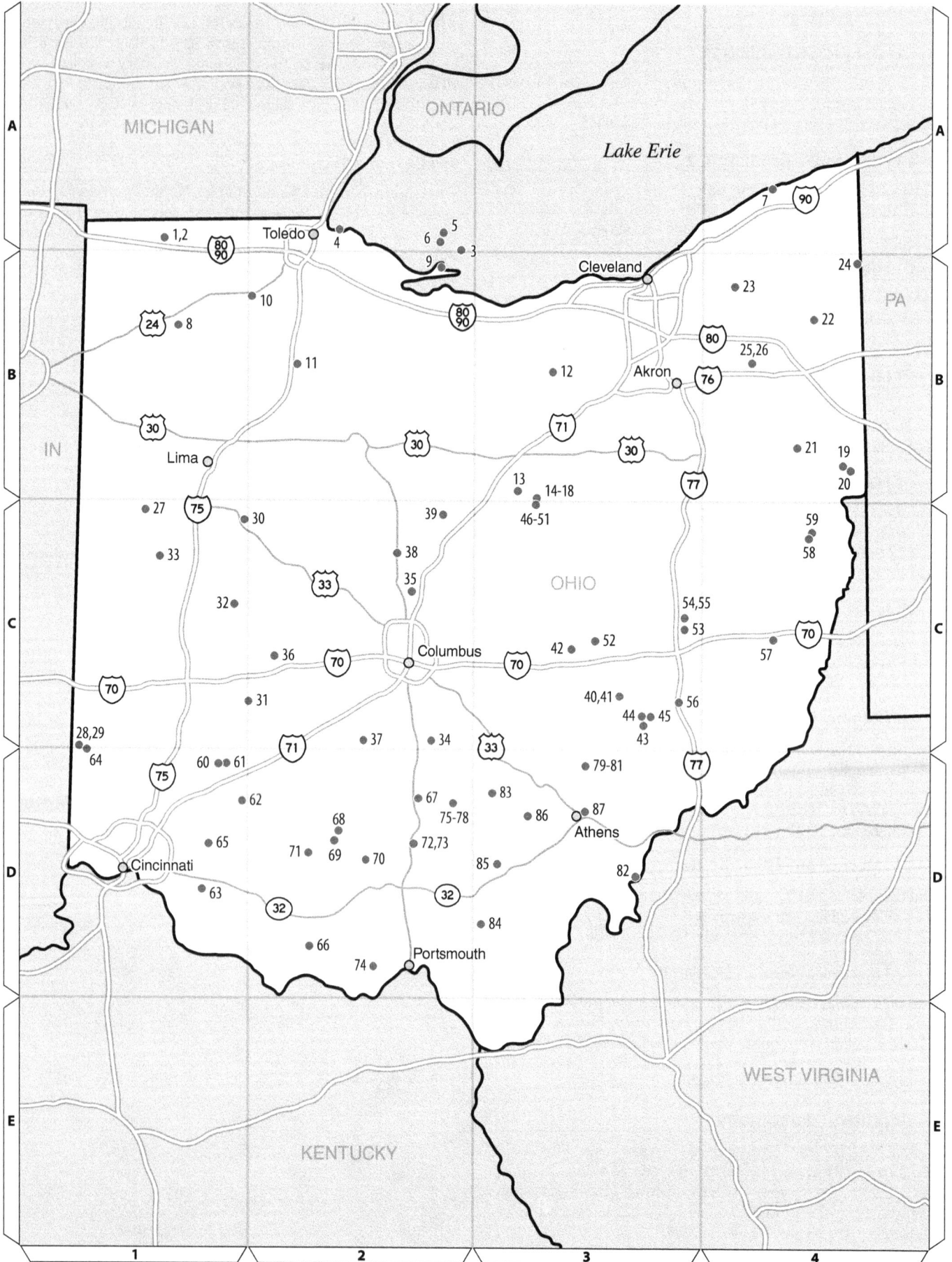

Ohio

MICHIGAN

ONTARIO

Lake Erie

PA

IN

OHIO

WEST VIRGINIA

KENTUCKY

Toledo

Cleveland

Akron

Lima

Columbus

Athens

Cincinnati

Portsmouth

1,2
4
5
6
3
9
7
90
24
23
22
10
24
8
11
12
25,26
80
76
30
30
30
71
77
13
14-18
21
19
20
46-51
39
27
75
30
59
58
33
38
35
54,55
53
33
42
52
70
57
32
36
70
56
31
40,41
70
70
28,29
44
45
64
43
75
71
37
34
33
79-81
77
60
61
67
83
62
75-78
86
87
65
68
72,73
69
70
85
82
63
32
32
84
66
74

90
80
90

Map	ID	Map	ID
A1	1-2	C1	27-33
A2	3-6	C2	34-39
A4	7	C3	40-56
B1	8	C4	57-59
B2	9-11	D1	60-65
B3	12-18	D2	66-78
B4	19-26	D3	79-87

Alphabetical List of Camping Areas

Name	ID	Map
A.W. Marion SP	34	C2
Adams Lake SP	66	D2
Alum Creek SP	35	C2
Barkcamp SP	57	C4
Beaver Creek SP	19	B4
Beaver Creek SP - Horseman's Camp	20	B4
Blue Rock SP	40	C3
Blue Rock SP - Horse Camp	41	C3
Buck Creek SP	36	C2
Burr Oak SP - Dock 2 CG	79	D3
Burr Oak SP - Dock 3 CG	80	D3
Burr Oak SP - Main CG	81	D3
Caesar Creek SP - Horseman's Camp	60	D1
Caesar Creek SP - Main CG	61	D1
Cowan Lake SP	62	D1
Deer Creek SP	37	C2
Delaware SP	38	C2
Dillon SP	42	C3
East Fork SP	63	D1
East Harbor SP	9	B2
Findley SP	12	B3
Forked Run SP	82	D3
Geneva SP	7	A4
Grand Lake-St. Marys SP	27	C1
Great Seal SP	67	D2
Guilford Lake SP	21	B4
Harrison Lake SP - North	1	A1
Harrison Lake SP - South	2	A1
Hocking Hills SP	83	D3
Hueston Woods SP - Area 1-2	28	C1
Hueston Woods SP - Area 3-4	29	C1
Hueston Woods SP - Horseman's Camp	64	D1
Independence Dam SP	8	B1
Indian Lake SP	30	C1
Jackson Lake SP	84	D3
Jefferson Lake SP - Horseman's Camp	58	C4
Jefferson Lake SP - Main CG	59	C4
Jesse Owens SP - Maple Grove	43	C3
Jesse Owens SP - Sand Hollow	44	C3
Jesse Owens SP - Sawmill	45	C3
John Bryan SP	31	C1
Kelleys Island SP	3	A2
Kiser Lake SP	32	C1
Lake Alma SP	85	D3
Lake Hope SP	86	D3
Lake Loramie SP	33	C1
Malabar Farm SP	13	B3
Mary Jane Thurston SP	10	B2
Maumee Bay SP	4	A2
Middle Bass Island SP	5	A2
Mohican SP - Blue TC 1	46	C3
Mohican SP - Blue TC 2	47	C3
Mohican SP - Blue TC 3	48	C3
Mohican SP - Hemlock Grove	14	B3
Mohican SP - Main	15	B3
Mohican SP - Mohican Mt TC 1	16	B3
Mohican SP - Mohican Mt TC 2	17	B3
Mohican SP - Mohican Mt TC 3	18	B3
Mohican SP - Red TC	49	C3
Mohican SP - Yellow TC 1	50	C3
Mohican SP - Yellow TC 2	51	C3
Mosquito Lake SP	22	B4
Mount Gilead SP	39	C2
Muskingum River Parkway SP - Ellis Lock 11	52	C3
Paint Creek SP	68	D2
Paint Creek SP - Horseman's Camp	69	D2
Pike Lake SP	70	D2
Punderson SP	23	B4
Pymatuning SP	24	B4
Rocky Fork SP	71	D2
Salt Fork SP	53	C3
Salt Fork SP - Horseman's Camp	54	C3
Salt Fork SP - White Loop A	55	C3
Scioto Trail SP - Caldwell Lake	72	D2
Scioto Trail SP - Stewart Lake	73	D2
Shawnee SP	74	D2
South Bass Island SP	6	A2
Stonelick Lake SP	65	D1
Strouds Run SP	87	D3
Tar Hollow SP - Logan Hollow	75	D2
Tar Hollow SP - North Ridge	76	D2
Tar Hollow SP - Pine Lake	77	D2
Tar Hollow SP - Ross Hollow	78	D2
Van Buren SP	11	B2
West Branch SP	25	B4
West Branch SP - Equestrian Camp	26	B4
Wolf Run SP	56	C3

1 • A1 | Harrison Lake SP - North

Total sites: 126, RV sites: 126, Elec sites: 126, Central water, Flush toilet, Free showers, RV dump, Tent & RV camping: $28, Also cabins, Limited services in winter, $1 less Sun-Thu/$2 more holidays Apr-Oct/$3 less Nov-Mar, Open all year, Reservations accepted, Elev: 794ft/242m, Tel: 419-237-2593, Nearest town: Fayette. GPS: 41.642647, -84.362804

2 • A1 | Harrison Lake SP - South

Total sites: 59, RV sites: 59, Elec sites: 26, Central water, Vault/pit toilet, No showers, No RV dump, Tents: $24/RVs: $27, Limited services in winter, $1 less Sun-Thu/$2 more holidays Apr-Oct/$3 less Nov-Mar, Open all year, Reservations accepted, Elev: 784ft/239m, Tel: 419-237-2593, Nearest town: Fayette. GPS: 41.637726, -84.362615

3 • A2 | Kelleys Island SP

Total sites: 124, RV sites: 124, Elec sites: 81, Central water, Flush toilet, Free showers, RV dump, Tents: $28/RVs: $30-43, 35 Full hookups, $1 less Sun-Thu/$2 more holidays Apr-Oct/$3 less Nov-Mar, Open Apr-Oct, Reservations accepted, Elev: 577ft/176m, Tel: 419-746-2546, Nearest town: Lakeside-Marblehead. GPS: 41.613226, -82.704919

4 • A2 | Maumee Bay SP

Total sites: 252, RV sites: 252, Elec sites: 252, Central water, Flush toilet, Free showers, RV dump, Tent & RV camping: $30, Also cabins, Limited services in winter, $1 less Sun-Thu/$2 more holidays Apr-Oct/$3 less Nov-Mar, Open all year, Reservations accepted, Elev: 574ft/175m, Tel: 419-836-8828, Nearest town: Oregon. GPS: 41.683752, -83.394945

5 • A2 | Middle Bass Island SP

Total sites: 20, RV sites: 0, Central water, Flush toilet, Free showers, No RV dump, Tents only: $20, Walk-to sites, Access by ferry, $1 less Sun-Thu/$2 more holidays Apr-Oct/$3 less Nov-Mar, Open May-Oct, Reservations accepted, Elev: 580ft/177m, Nearest town: Middle Bass Island. GPS: 41.672868, -82.808868

6 • A2 | South Bass Island SP

Total sites: 128, RV sites: 70, Elec sites: 61, Water at site, Flush toilet, Free showers, Tents: $30/RVs: $34-43, 10 Full hookups, Access by ferry, $1 less Sun-Thu/$2 more holidays Apr-Oct/$3 less Nov-Mar, Open Apr-Oct, Reservations accepted, Elev: 606ft/185m, Tel: 419-285-2112, Nearest town: Put-In-Bay. GPS: 41.644078, -82.837548

7 • A4 | Geneva SP

Total sites: 100, RV sites: 100, Elec sites: 93, Water at site, Flush toilet, Free showers, RV dump, Tents: $26/RVs: $30-39, Also cabins, 19 Full hookups, Limited services in winter, $1 less Sun-Thu/$2 more holidays Apr-Oct/$3 less Nov-Mar, Open all year, Elev: 594ft/181m, Tel: 440-466-8400, Nearest town: Geneva. GPS: 41.850998, -80.986859

8 • B1 | Independence Dam SP

Total sites: 25, RV sites: 0, No water, Vault/pit toilet, No showers, No RV dump, Tents only: $20, Open Apr-Oct, Reservations not accepted, Elev: 664ft/202m, Tel: 419-956-1368, Nearest town: Defiance. GPS: 41.291973, -84.275918

9 • B2 | East Harbor SP

Total sites: 540, RV sites: 533, Elec sites: 340, Water at site, Flush toilet, Free showers, RV dump, Tents: $28/RVs: $32-43, Also cabins, 51 Full hookups, Limited services in winter, $1 less Sun-Thu/$2 more holidays Apr-Oct/$3 less Nov-Mar, Generator hours: 0700-2200, Open all year, Max Length: 50ft, Reservations accepted, Elev: 610ft/186m, Tel: 419-734-5857, Nearest town: Lakeside-Marblehead. GPS: 41.545443, -82.812472

10 • B2 | Mary Jane Thurston SP

Total sites: 43, RV sites: 27, Elec sites: 27, Water at site, Flush toilet, No showers, RV dump, Tents: $22/RVs: $26-30, Also cabins, Limited services in winter, $1 less Sun-Thu/$2 more holidays Apr-Oct/$3 less Nov-Mar, Open all year, Reservations accepted, Elev: 663ft/202m, Tel: 419-832-7662, Nearest town: McClure. GPS: 41.410324, -83.877874

11 • B2 | Van Buren SP

Total sites: 66, RV sites: 66, Elec sites: 13, Central water, Vault/pit toilet, No showers, RV dump, Tents: $20/RVs: $24, Limited services in winter, $1 less Sun-Thu/$2 more holidays Apr-Oct/$3 less Nov-Mar, Stay limit: 14 days, Open all year, Reservations accepted, Elev: 784ft/239m, Tel: 419-832-7662, Nearest town: Van Buren. GPS: 41.136755, -83.619569

12 • B3 | Findley SP

Total sites: 271, RV sites: 271, Elec sites: 90, Water at site, Flush toilet, Free showers, RV dump, Tents: $26/RVs: $30-39, Also cabins, 15 Full hookups, Limited services in winter, $1 less Sun-Thu/$2 more holidays Apr-Oct/$3 less Nov-Mar, Open all year, Reservations accepted, Elev: 942ft/287m, Tel: 440-647-4490, Nearest town: Wellington. GPS: 41.123947, -82.208771

13 • B3 | Malabar Farm SP

Total sites: 15, RV sites: 15, Central water, Vault/pit toilet, No showers, No RV dump, Tent & RV camping: $20, $1 less Sun-Thu/$2 more holidays Apr-Oct/$3 less Nov-Mar, Open Apr-Nov, Elev: 1286ft/392m, Tel: 419-892-2784, Nearest town: Lucas. GPS: 40.642724, -82.401118

14 • B3 | Mohican SP - Hemlock Grove

Total sites: 24, RV sites: 24, Vault/pit toilet, Tent & RV camping: $24, Open all year, Elev: 984ft/300m, Tel: 419-994-4290, Nearest town: Loudonville. GPS: 40.611499, -82.308621

15 • B3 | Mohican SP - Main

Total sites: 149, RV sites: 139, Elec sites: 114, Central water, Flush toilet, Free showers, RV dump, Tents: $28/RVs: $32-43, Also cabins, 51 Full hookups, Limited services in winter, $1 less Sun-Thu/$2 more holidays Apr-Oct/$3 less Nov-Mar, Open all year, Reservations accepted, Elev: 939ft/286m, Tel: 419-994-4290, Nearest town: Loudonville. GPS: 40.609903, -82.266139

16 • B3 | Mohican SP - Mohican Mt TC 1

Dispersed sites, Tents only: Free, Hike-in, Open all year, Reservations not accepted, Elev: 1221ft/372m, Tel: 419-994-5125, Nearest town: Loudonville. GPS: 40.616400, -82.285000

17 • B3 | Mohican SP - Mohican Mt TC 2

Dispersed sites, Tents only: Free, Hike-in, Open all year, Reservations not accepted, Elev: 1210ft/369m, Tel: 419-994-5125, Nearest town: Loudonville. GPS: 40.617100, -82.280200

18 • B3 | Mohican SP - Mohican Mt TC 3

Dispersed sites, Tents only: Free, Hike-in, Open all year, Reservations not accepted, Elev: 1209ft/369m, Tel: 419-994-5125, Nearest town: Loudonville. GPS: 40.616100, -82.276900

19 • B4 | Beaver Creek SP

Total sites: 50, RV sites: 50, Elec sites: 6, Central water, Vault/pit toilet, No showers, RV dump, Tents: $19/RVs: $19-24, $1 less Sun-Thu/$2 more holidays Apr-Oct/$3 less Nov-Mar, Open all year, Reservations accepted, Elev: 1106ft/337m, Tel: 330-385-3091, Nearest town: East Liverpool. GPS: 40.729845, -80.622751

20 • B4 | Beaver Creek SP - Horseman's Camp

Total sites: 59, RV sites: 59, No water, Vault/pit toilet, No showers, No RV dump, Tent & RV camping: $19, $1 less Sun-Thu/$2 more holidays Apr-Oct/$3 less Nov-Mar, Open all year, Reservations accepted, Elev: 1000ft/305m, Tel: 330-385-3091, Nearest town: Calcutta. GPS: 40.713771, -80.581890

21 • B4 | Guilford Lake SP

Total sites: 41, RV sites: 41, Elec sites: 41, Central water, Flush toilet, Free showers, RV dump, Tent & RV camping: $28, Limited services in winter, $1 less Sun-Thu/$2 more holidays Apr-Oct/$3 less Nov-Mar, Open all year, Reservations accepted, Elev: 1168ft/356m, Tel: 330-222-1712, Nearest town: Lisbon. GPS: 40.806763, -80.878081

22 • B4 | Mosquito Lake SP

Total sites: 232, RV sites: 232, Elec sites: 216, Central water, Flush toilet, Free showers, RV dump, Tents: $24/RVs: $28-37, 18 Full hookups, Limited services in winter, $1 less Sun-Thu/$2 more holidays Apr-Oct/$3 less Nov-Mar, Open all year, Reservations accepted, Elev: 925ft/282m, Tel: 330-638-5700, Nearest town: Cortland. GPS: 41.316315, -80.771439

23 • B4 | Punderson SP

Total sites: 200, RV sites: 188, Elec sites: 197, Central water, Flush toilet, Free showers, RV dump, Tent & RV camping: $28-37, Also cabins, 20 Full hookups, Limited services in winter, $1 less Sun-Thu/$2 more holidays Apr-Oct/$3 less Nov-Mar, Open all year, Reservations accepted, Elev: 1214ft/370m, Tel: 440-564-1195, Nearest town: Newbury. GPS: 41.456637, -81.204123

24 • B4 | Pymatuning SP

Total sites: 352, RV sites: 352, Elec sites: 331, Water at site, Flush toilet, Free showers, RV dump, Tents: $23/RVs: $23-36, Also cabins, 20 Full hookups, Limited services in winter, $1 less Sun-Thu/$2 more holidays Apr-Oct/$3 less Nov-Mar, Open all year, Reservations accepted, Elev: 1027ft/313m, Tel: 440-293-6684, Nearest town: Andover. GPS: 41.547602, -80.528856

25 • B4 | West Branch SP

Total sites: 198, RV sites: 198, Elec sites: 184, Water at site, Flush toilet, Free showers, RV dump, Tents: $26/RVs: $30-39, 29 Full hookups, Limited services in winter, $1 less Sun-Thu/$2 more holidays Apr-Oct/$3 less Nov-Mar, Open all year, Reservations accepted, Elev: 1043ft/318m, Tel: 330-296-3239, Nearest town: Ravenna. GPS: 41.142061, -81.114085

26 • B4 | West Branch SP - Equestrian Camp

Total sites: 9, RV sites: 9, No water, Vault/pit toilet, Tent & RV camping: $20, Limited services in winter, $1 less Sun-Thu/$2 more holidays Apr-Oct/$3 less Nov-Mar, Open all year, Reservations accepted, Elev: 1043ft/318m, Tel: 330-296-3239, Nearest town: Ravenna. GPS: 41.150335, -81.112294

27 • C1 | Grand Lake-St. Marys SP

Total sites: 191, RV sites: 191, Elec sites: 181, Water at site, Flush toilet, Free showers, RV dump, Tents: $26/RVs: $30-39, Also cabins, 34 Full hookups, Limited services in winter, $1 less Sun-Thu/$2 more holidays Apr-Oct/$3 less Nov-Mar, Open all year, Reservations accepted, Elev: 889ft/271m, Tel: Info: 419-394-2774/ Res: 866-644-6727, Nearest town: St. Marys. GPS: 40.546985, -84.441046

28 • C1 | Hueston Woods SP - Area 1-2

Total sites: 141, RV sites: 108, Elec sites: 3, Central water, No toilets, No showers, No RV dump, Tents: $24/RVs: $24-28, Limited services in winter, $1 less Sun-Thu/$2 more holidays Apr-Oct/$3 less Nov-Mar, Open all year, Reservations accepted, Elev: 889ft/271m, Tel: 513-523-1060, Nearest town: College Corner. GPS: 39.589163, -84.772629

29 • C1 | Hueston Woods SP - Area 3-4

Total sites: 246, RV sites: 187, Elec sites: 246, Central water, Flush toilet, Free showers, RV dump, Tent & RV camping: $28, Limited services in winter, $1 less Sun-Thu/$2 more holidays Apr-Oct/$3 less Nov-Mar, Open all year, Reservations accepted, Elev: 951ft/290m, Tel: 513-523-1060, Nearest town: College Corner. GPS: 39.583122, -84.771166

30 • C1 | Indian Lake SP

Total sites: 438, RV sites: 438, Elec sites: 438, Central water, Flush toilet, Free showers, RV dump, Tent & RV camping: $30-39, Also cabins, 43 Full hookups, Limited services in winter, $1 less Sun-Thu/$2 more holidays Apr-Oct/$3 less Nov-Mar, Open all year, Reservations accepted, Elev: 1017ft/310m, Tel: 937-843-3553, Nearest town: Lakeview. GPS: 40.514219, -83.898614

31 • C1 | John Bryan SP

Total sites: 60, RV sites: 60, Elec sites: 10, Central water, Vault/pit toilet, No showers, RV dump, Tents: $22/RVs: $26, Limited services in winter, $1 less Sun-Thu/$2 more holidays Apr-Oct/$3 less Nov-Mar, Open all year, Reservations accepted, Elev: 1014ft/309m, Tel: 937-767-1274, Nearest town: Yellow Springs. GPS: 39.787896, -83.867002

32 • C1 | Kiser Lake SP

Total sites: 118, RV sites: 118, Elec sites: 10, Central water, Vault/pit toilet, No showers, RV dump, Tents: $22/RVs: $26, Also cabins, Limited services in winter, $1 less Sun-Thu/$2 more holidays Apr-Oct/$3 less Nov-Mar, Open all year, Reservations accepted, Elev: 1152ft/351m, Tel: 937-362-3565, Nearest town: Conover. GPS: 40.180728, -83.948519

33 • C1 | Lake Loramie SP

Total sites: 175, RV sites: 175, Elec sites: 160, Central water, Flush toilet, Free showers, RV dump, Tents: $28/RVs: $28-37, Also cabins, Some Full hookups, Limited services in winter, $1 less Sun-Thu/$2 more holidays Apr-Oct/$3 less Nov-Mar, Open all year, Reservations accepted, Elev: 974ft/297m, Tel: 937-295-3900, Nearest town: Minster. GPS: 40.357297, -84.355483

34 • C2 | A.W. Marion SP

Total sites: 60, RV sites: 52, Elec sites: 28, Central water, No toilets, No showers, RV dump, Tents: $22/RVs: $26, Also walk-to sites, Limited services in winter, $1 less Sun-Thu/$2 more holidays Apr-Oct/$3 less Nov-Mar, Open all year, Max Length: 50ft, Reservations accepted, Elev: 900ft/274m, Tel: 740-869-3124, Nearest town: Circleville. GPS: 39.634257, -82.874719

35 • C2 | Alum Creek SP

Total sites: 286, RV sites: 286, Elec sites: 286, Water at site, Flush toilet, Free showers, RV dump, Tent & RV camping: $32-43, Also cabins, 24 Full hookups, $1 less Sun-Thu/$2 more holidays Apr-Oct/$3 less Nov-Mar, Open Apr-Oct, Max Length: 50ft, Reservations accepted, Elev: 906ft/276m, Tel: 740-548-4039, Nearest town: Delaware. GPS: 40.236091, -82.982817

36 • C2 | Buck Creek SP

Total sites: 111, RV sites: 111, Elec sites: 89, Central water, Flush toilet, Free showers, RV dump, Tents: $26/RVs: $30, Also cabins, Limited services in winter, $1 less Sun-Thu/$2 more holidays Apr-Oct/$3 less Nov-Mar, Open all year, Reservations accepted, Elev: 1024ft/312m, Tel: 937-322-5284, Nearest town: Springfield. GPS: 39.968688, -83.726523

37 • C2 | Deer Creek SP

Total sites: 227, RV sites: 227, Elec sites: 227, Water at site, Flush toilet, Free showers, RV dump, Tent & RV camping: $30, Also cabins, Limited services in winter, $1 less Sun-Thu/$2 more holidays Apr-Oct/$3 less Nov-Mar, Open all year, Reservations accepted, Elev: 866ft/264m, Tel: 740-869-3508, Nearest town: Mt. Sterling. GPS: 39.637568, -83.241704

38 • C2 | Delaware SP

Total sites: 211, RV sites: 211, Elec sites: 211, Central water, Flush toilet, Free showers, RV dump, Tent & RV camping: $30, Limited services in winter, $1 less Sun-Thu/$2 more holidays Apr-Oct/$3 less Nov-Mar, Open all year, Max Length: 50ft, Reservations accepted, Elev: 942ft/287m, Tel: 740-363-4561, Nearest town: Delaware. GPS: 40.397376, -83.063056

39 • C2 | Mount Gilead SP

Total sites: 59, RV sites: 59, Elec sites: 59, Water at site, No toilets, No showers, RV dump, Tents: $26/RVs: $26-33, 22 Full hookups, Limited services in winter, $1 less Sun-Thu/$2 more holidays Apr-Oct/$3 less Nov-Mar, Open all year, Reservations accepted, Elev: 1207ft/368m, Tel: 419-946-1961, Nearest town: Mt. Gilead. GPS: 40.547474, -82.809778

40 • C3 | Blue Rock SP

Total sites: 117, RV sites: 97, Central water, Flush toilet, Free showers, RV dump, Tent & RV camping: $20-24, Also cabins, $1 less Sun-Thu/$2 more holidays Apr-Oct/$3 less Nov-Mar, Open Apr-Oct, Reservations accepted, Elev: 876ft/267m, Tel: 740-453-4377, Nearest town: Blue Rock. GPS: 39.818048, -81.851401

41 • C3 | Blue Rock SP - Horse Camp

Total sites: 21, RV sites: 21, Central water, Vault/pit toilet, No showers, No RV dump, Tent & RV camping: $20-24, $1 less Sun-Thu/$2 more holidays Apr-Oct/$3 less Nov-Mar, Open Apr-Oct, Reservations accepted, Elev: 938ft/286m, Tel: 740-453-4377, Nearest town: Blue Rock. GPS: 39.815555, -81.851864

42 • C3 | Dillon SP

Total sites: 195, RV sites: 195, Elec sites: 183, Water at site, Flush toilet, Free showers, RV dump, Tent & RV camping: $28-37, Also cabins, 10 Full hookups, Limited services in winter, $1 less Sun-Thu/$2 more holidays Apr-Oct/$3 less Nov-Mar, Open all year, Reservations accepted, Elev: 919ft/280m, Tel: 740-453-4377, Nearest town: Nashport. GPS: 40.008287, -82.106932

43 • C3 | Jesse Owens SP - Maple Grove

Dispersed sites, No water, Vault/pit toilet, Tent & RV camping: Free, Generator hours: 0700-2300, Open all year, Elev: 945ft/288m, Tel: 740-439-3521, Nearest town: McConnelsville. GPS: 39.706694, -81.725105

44 • C3 | Jesse Owens SP - Sand Hollow

Dispersed sites, Central water, Vault/pit toilet, No showers, No RV dump, Tent & RV camping: Free, Stay limit: 14 days, Generator hours: 0700-2300, Open May-Nov, Elev: 928ft/283m, Tel: 740-439-3521, Nearest town: McConnelsville. GPS: 39.737098, -81.732638

45 • C3 | Jesse Owens SP - Sawmill

Dispersed sites, Central water, Vault/pit toilet, No showers, No RV dump, Tent & RV camping: Free, Stay limit: 14 days, Generator hours: 0700-2300, Open May-Nov, Elev: 820ft/250m, Tel: 740-439-3521, Nearest town: McConnelsville. GPS: 39.734991, -81.688525

46 • C3 | Mohican SP - Blue TC 1

Dispersed sites, Tents only: Free, Hike-in, Open all year, Reservations not accepted, Elev: 1274ft/388m, Tel: 419-994-5125, Nearest town: Loudonville. GPS: 40.590021, -82.287978

47 • C3 | Mohican SP - Blue TC 2

Dispersed sites, Tents only: Free, Hike-in, Open all year, Reservations not accepted, Elev: 1136ft/346m, Tel: 419-994-5125, Nearest town: Loudonville. GPS: 40.586019, -82.288997

48 • C3 | Mohican SP - Blue TC 3

Dispersed sites, Tents only: Free, Hike-in, Open all year, Reservations not accepted, Elev: 1154ft/352m, Tel: 419-994-5125, Nearest town: Loudonville. GPS: 40.592384, -82.320569

49 • C3 | Mohican SP - Red TC

Dispersed sites, Tents only: Free, Hike-in, Open all year, Reservations not accepted, Elev: 1303ft/397m, Tel: 419-994-5125, Nearest town: Loudonville. GPS: 40.591023, -82.304997

50 • C3 | Mohican SP - Yellow TC 1

Dispersed sites, Tents only: Free, Hike-in, Open all year, Reservations not accepted, Elev: 1127ft/344m, Tel: 419-994-5125, Nearest town: Loudonville. GPS: 40.591022, -82.313012

51 • C3 | Mohican SP - Yellow TC 2

Dispersed sites, Tents only: Free, Hike-in, Open all year, Reservations not accepted, Elev: 1108ft/338m, Tel: 419-994-5125, Nearest town: Loudonville. GPS: 40.590033, -82.307008

52 • C3 | Muskingum River Parkway SP - Ellis Lock 11

Total sites: 19, RV sites: 19, Central water, Vault/pit toilet, No showers, No RV dump, Tent & RV camping: $20, $1 less Sun-Thu/$2 more holidays Apr-Oct/$3 less Nov-Mar, Open Apr-Oct, Reservations accepted, Elev: 712ft/217m, Tel: 740-453-4377, Nearest town: McConnelsville. GPS: 40.044164, -81.977267

53 • C3 | Salt Fork SP

Total sites: 192, RV sites: 192, Elec sites: 192, Water at site, Flush toilet, Free showers, RV dump, Tent & RV camping: $26-39, Also cabins, 40 Full hookups, Limited services in winter, $1 less Sun-Thu/$2 more holidays Apr-Oct/$3 less Nov-Mar, Open all year, Reservations accepted, Elev: 991ft/302m, Tel: 740-439-3521, Nearest town: Lore City. GPS: 40.095209, -81.498509

54 • C3 | Salt Fork SP - Horseman's Camp

Total sites: 14, RV sites: 14, Central water, Vault/pit toilet, No showers, No RV dump, Tent & RV camping: $26, Limited services in winter, $1 less Sun-Thu/$2 more holidays Apr-Oct/$3 less Nov-Mar, Open all year, Reservations accepted, Elev: 1102ft/336m, Tel: 740-439-3521, Nearest town: Lore City. GPS: 40.121094, -81.494953

55 • C3 | Salt Fork SP - White Loop A

Dispersed sites, No water, Vault/pit toilet, Tents only: $19, Limited services in winter, $1 less Sun-Thu/$2 more holidays Apr-Oct/$3 less Nov-Mar, Open all year, Reservations accepted, Elev: 1030ft/314m, Tel: 740-439-3521, Nearest town: Lore City. GPS: 40.123983, -81.507701

56 • C3 | Wolf Run SP

Total sites: 138, RV sites: 138, Elec sites: 71, Central water, Flush toilet, Free showers, RV dump, Tents: $22/RVs: $22-26, $1 less Sun-Thu/$2 more holidays Apr-Oct/$3 less Nov-Mar, Open all year, Reservations accepted, Elev: 856ft/261m, Tel: 740-732-5035, Nearest town: Caldwell. GPS: 39.792107, -81.538905

57 • C4 | Barkcamp SP

Total sites: 146, RV sites: 132, Elec sites: 146, Water at site, Flush toilet, Free showers, RV dump, Tents: $26/RVs: $26-33, Also group sites & cabins, 19 Full hookups, Group site, No pets in C Loop, Limited services in winter, $1 less Sun-Thu/$2 more holidays Apr-Oct/$3 less Nov-Mar, Open all year, Max Length: 55ft, Reservations accepted, Elev: 1214ft/370m, Tel: 740-484-4064, Nearest town: Belmont. GPS: 40.038381, -81.020301

58 • C4 | Jefferson Lake SP - Horseman's Camp

Total sites: 30, RV sites: 30, Central water, Vault/pit toilet, No showers, No RV dump, Tent & RV camping: $20, Showers at beach, $1 less Sun-Thu/$2 more holidays Apr-Oct/$3 less Nov-Mar, Open all year, Elev: 1286ft/392m, Tel: 740-765-4459, Nearest town: Richmond. GPS: 40.446768, -80.819069

59 • C4 | Jefferson Lake SP - Main CG

Total sites: 97, RV sites: 97, Elec sites: 5, Central water, Vault/pit toilet, No showers, RV dump, Tents: $20/RVs: $24, Showers at beach, $1 less Sun-Thu/$2 more holidays Apr-Oct/$3 less Nov-Mar, Open all year, Reservations accepted, Elev: 1237ft/377m, Tel: 740-765-4459, Nearest town: Richmond. GPS: 40.466229, -80.807141

60 • D1 | Caesar Creek SP - Horseman's Camp

Total sites: 30, RV sites: 30, Central water, Flush toilet, Free showers, RV dump, Tent & RV camping: $20, Also cabins, $1 less Sun-Thu/$2 more holidays Apr-Oct/$3 less Nov-Mar, Open Apr-Oct, Reservations not accepted, Elev: 869ft/265m, Tel: 937-488-4595, Nearest town: Waynesville. GPS: 39.536241, -84.013073

61 • D1 | Caesar Creek SP - Main CG

Total sites: 283, RV sites: 229, Elec sites: 239, Water at site, Flush toilet, Free showers, RV dump, Tents: $30/RVs: $30-41, Also cabins, 35 Full hookups, $1 less Sun-Thu/$2 more holidays Apr-Oct/$3 less Nov-Mar, Open Apr-Oct, Reservations accepted, Elev: 909ft/277m, Tel: 937-488-4595, Nearest town: Waynesville. GPS: 39.536377, -83.980469

62 • D1 | Cowan Lake SP

Total sites: 254, RV sites: 254, Elec sites: 237, Central water, Flush toilet, Free showers, RV dump, Tents: $26/RVs: $30, Also cabins, Limited services in winter, $1 less Sun-Thu/$2 more holidays Apr-Oct/$3 less Nov-Mar, Open all year, Reservations accepted, Elev: 1037ft/316m, Tel: 937-383-3751, Nearest town: Wilmington. GPS: 39.391462, -83.891563

63 • D1 | East Fork SP

Total sites: 389, RV sites: 389, Elec sites: 389, Central water, Flush toilet, Free showers, RV dump, Tents: $30/RVs: $30-39, Also cabins, 23 Full hookups, Limited services in winter, $1 less Sun-Thu/$2 more holidays Apr-Oct/$3 less Nov-Mar, Open all year, Reservations accepted, Elev: 863ft/263m, Tel: 513-724-6521, Nearest town: Bethel. GPS: 39.035281, -84.094658

64 • D1 | Hueston Woods SP - Horseman's Camp

Total sites: 25, RV sites: 25, Elec sites: 20, Central water, Tents: $20/RVs: $20-24, $1 less Sun-Thu/$2 more holidays Apr-Oct/$3 less Nov-Mar, Open all year, Reservations accepted, Elev: 1030ft/314m, Tel: 513-523-1060, Nearest town: College Corner. GPS: 39.580629, -84.736196

65 • D1 | Stonelick Lake SP

Total sites: 114, RV sites: 114, Elec sites: 108, Central water, Flush toilet, Free showers, RV dump, Tents: $22/RVs: $26-28, Limited services in winter, $1 less Sun-Thu/$2 more holidays Apr-Oct/$3 less Nov-Mar, Open all year, Reservations accepted, Elev: 925ft/282m, Tel: 513-734-4323, Nearest town: Pleasant Plain. GPS: 39.217164, -84.059538

66 • D2 | Adams Lake SP

Total sites: 10, RV sites: 5, Central water, Vault/pit toilet, No showers, No RV dump, Tent & RV camping: Free, Max Length: 18ft, Reservations not accepted, Elev: 779ft/237m, Nearest town: West Union. GPS: 38.813311, -83.522106

67 • D2 | Great Seal SP

Total sites: 15, RV sites: 15, Central water, Vault/pit toilet, No showers, No RV dump, Tent & RV camping: $20, $1 less Sun-Thu/$2 more holidays Apr-Oct/$3 less Nov-Mar, Open Mar-Nov, Reservations accepted, Elev: 889ft/271m, Tel: 740-887-4818, Nearest town: Chillicothe. GPS: 39.402453, -82.941223

68 • D2 | Paint Creek SP

Total sites: 197, RV sites: 197, Elec sites: 197, Central water, Flush toilet, Free showers, RV dump, Tent & RV camping: $28-30, Also cabins, Limited services in winter, $1 less Sun-Thu/$2 more holidays Apr-Oct/$3 less Nov-Mar, Open all year, Reservations accepted, Elev: 889ft/271m, Tel: 937-981-7061, Nearest town: Bainbridge. GPS: 39.265556, -83.379081

69 • D2 | Paint Creek SP - Horseman's Camp

Total sites: 12, RV sites: 12, Central water, Vault/pit toilet, No showers, No RV dump, No tents/RVs: $20, $1 less Sun-Thu/$2 more holidays Apr-Oct/$3 less Nov-Mar, Open all year, Elev: 902ft/275m, Tel: 937- 981-7061, Nearest town: Bainbridge. GPS: 39.245855, -83.386532

70 • D2 | Pike Lake SP

Total sites: 79, RV sites: 79, Elec sites: 79, Central water, Vault/pit toilet, No showers, RV dump, Tent & RV camping: $24, Also cabins, Limited services in winter, $1 less Sun-Thu/$2 more holidays Apr-Oct/$3 less Nov-Mar, Open all year, Reservations accepted, Elev: 830ft/253m, Tel: 740-493-2212, Nearest town: Bainbridge. GPS: 39.157999, -83.219293

71 • D2 | Rocky Fork SP

Total sites: 341, RV sites: 341, Elec sites: 140, Water at site, Flush toilet, Free showers, RV dump, Tents: $24/RVs: $26-37, 19 Full hookups, $1 less Sun-Thu/$2 more holidays Apr-Oct/$3 less Nov-Mar, Reservations accepted, Elev: 886ft/270m, Tel: 937-393-3210, Nearest town: Hillsboro. GPS: 39.188232, -83.530762

72 • D2 | Scioto Trail SP - Caldwell Lake

Total sites: 55, RV sites: 55, Elec sites: 55, Central water, Vault/pit toilet, No showers, RV dump, Tent & RV camping: $26, Also cabins, Limited services in winter, $1 less Sun-Thu/$2 more holidays Apr-Oct/$3 less Nov-Mar, Open all year, Reservations accepted, Elev: 734ft/224m, Tel: 740-887-4818, Nearest town: Chillicothe. GPS: 39.230181, -82.955979

73 • D2 | Scioto Trail SP - Stewart Lake

Total sites: 18, Central water, Vault/pit toilet, No showers, RV dump, Tents only: $22, Walk-to sites, Limited services in winter, $1 less Sun-Thu/$2 more holidays Apr-Oct/$3 less Nov-Mar, Open all year, Reservations not accepted, Elev: 750ft/229m, Tel: 740-887-4818, Nearest town: Chillicothe. GPS: 39.219691, -82.962135

74 • D2 | Shawnee SP

Total sites: 107, RV sites: 107, Elec sites: 95, Central water, Flush toilet, Free showers, RV dump, Tents: $22/RVs: $22-26, Also cabins, Limited services in winter, $1 less Sun-Thu/$2 more holidays Apr-Oct/$3 less Nov-Mar, Open all year, Reservations accepted, Elev: 718ft/219m, Tel: 740-858-4561, Nearest town: Portsmouth. GPS: 38.728772, -83.180945

75 • D2 | Tar Hollow SP - Logan Hollow

Total sites: 42, RV sites: 42, Elec sites: 42, Flush toilet, Free showers, RV dump, Tents: $24/RVs: $28, Limited services in winter, $1 less Sun-Thu/$2 more holidays Apr-Oct/$3 less Nov-Mar, Stay limit: 14 days, Open all year, Reservations accepted, Elev: 948ft/289m, Tel: 740-887-4818, Nearest town: Laurelville. GPS: 39.392724, -82.748556

76 • D2 | Tar Hollow SP - North Ridge

Total sites: 12, RV sites: 0, Flush toilet, Free showers, RV dump, Tents only: $24, Walk-to sites, Limited services in winter, $1 less Sun-Thu/$2 more holidays Apr-Oct/$3 less Nov-Mar, Stay limit: 14 days, Open all year, Reservations accepted, Elev: 1083ft/330m,

Tel: 740-887-4818, Nearest town: Laurelville. GPS: 39.391450, -82.757190

77 • D2 | Tar Hollow SP - Pine Lake

Total sites: 9, RV sites: 0, Flush toilet, Free showers, RV dump, Tents only: $24, Walk-to sites, Limited services in winter, $1 less Sun-Thu/$2 more holidays Apr-Oct/$3 less Nov-Mar, Stay limit: 14 days, Open all year, Reservations accepted, Elev: 873ft/266m, Tel: 740-887-4818, Nearest town: Laurelville. GPS: 39.382714, -82.746585

78 • D2 | Tar Hollow SP - Ross Hollow

Total sites: 28, RV sites: 28, Elec sites: 28, Flush toilet, Free showers, RV dump, Tent & RV camping: $28, Limited services in winter, $1 less Sun-Thu/$2 more holidays Apr-Oct/$3 less Nov-Mar, Stay limit: 14 days, Open all year, Reservations accepted, Elev: 961ft/293m, Tel: 740-887-4818, Nearest town: Laurelville. GPS: 39.393524, -82.755536

79 • D3 | Burr Oak SP - Dock 2 CG

Total sites: 13, RV sites: 13, Vault/pit toilet, Tent & RV camping: $20, Limited services in winter, $1 less Sun-Thu/$2 more holidays Apr-Oct/$3 less Nov-Mar, Open all year, Elev: 814ft/248m, Tel: 740-767-3570, Nearest town: Glouster. GPS: 39.521945, -82.040005

80 • D3 | Burr Oak SP - Dock 3 CG

Total sites: 8, RV sites: 8, Vault/pit toilet, Tent & RV camping: $20, Limited services in winter, $1 less Sun-Thu/$2 more holidays Apr-Oct/$3 less Nov-Mar, Open all year, Elev: 781ft/238m, Tel: 740-767-3570, Nearest town: Glouster. GPS: 39.551431, -82.024582

81 • D3 | Burr Oak SP - Main CG

Total sites: 99, RV sites: 82, Elec sites: 17, Central water, Flush toilet, Free showers, RV dump, Tents: $22/RVs: $22-26, Also cabins, Limited services in winter, $1 less Sun-Thu/$2 more holidays Apr-Oct/$3 less Nov-Mar, Open all year, Elev: 768ft/234m, Tel: 740-767-3570, Nearest town: Glouster. GPS: 39.537933, -82.035157

82 • D3 | Forked Run SP

Total sites: 143, RV sites: 143, Elec sites: 79, Central water, Flush toilet, Free showers, RV dump, Tents: $22/RVs: $22-26, Also cabins, Limited services in winter, $1 less Sun-Thu/$2 more holidays Apr-Oct/$3 less Nov-Mar, Open all year, Reservations accepted, Elev: 659ft/201m, Tel: 740-378-6206, Nearest town: Reedsville. GPS: 39.091516, -81.773204

83 • D3 | Hocking Hills SP

Total sites: 169, RV sites: 169, Elec sites: 156, Water at site, Flush toilet, Free showers, RV dump, Tents: $24-28/RVs: $32-43, Also cabins, 47 Full hookups, Limited services in winter, $1 less Sun-Thu/$2 more holidays Apr-Oct/$3 less Nov-Mar, Open all year, Reservations accepted, Elev: 1060ft/323m, Tel: 740-385-6842, Nearest town: Logan. GPS: 39.433828, -82.536093

84 • D3 | Jackson Lake SP

Total sites: 34, RV sites: 25, Elec sites: 34, Central water, No toilets, No showers, RV dump, Tent & RV camping: $26, Limited services in winter, $1 less Sun-Thu/$2 more holidays Apr-Oct/$3 less Nov-Mar, Open Apr-Dec, Reservations accepted, Elev: 725ft/221m,

Tel: 740-682-6197, Nearest town: Oak Hill. GPS: 38.903167, -82.595864

85 • D3 | Lake Alma SP

Total sites: 81, RV sites: 81, Elec sites: 71, Central water, Vault/pit toilet, No showers, RV dump, Tents: $22/RVs: $22-33, 6 Full hookups, Limited services in winter, $1 less Sun-Thu/$2 more holidays Apr-Oct/$3 less Nov-Mar, Open all year, Reservations accepted, Elev: 758ft/231m, Tel: 740-384-4474, Nearest town: Wellston. GPS: 39.146943, -82.507691

86 • D3 | Lake Hope SP

Total sites: 187, RV sites: 187, Elec sites: 46, Central water, Flush toilet, Free showers, RV dump, Tents: $22/RVs: $22-26, Also cabins, Limited services in winter, $1 less Sun-Thu/$2 more holidays Apr-Oct/$3 less Nov-Mar, Open all year, Reservations accepted, Elev: 961ft/293m, Tel: 740-596-4938, Nearest town: McArthur. GPS: 39.341539, -82.344119

87 • D3 | Strouds Run SP

Total sites: 78, RV sites: 78, No water, Vault/pit toilet, No showers, No RV dump, Tents: $20/RVs: $29, $1 less Sun-Thu/$2 more holidays Apr-Oct/$3 less Nov-Mar, Open all year, Reservations accepted, Elev: 732ft/223m, Tel: 740-594-2628, Nearest town: Athens. GPS: 39.357218, -82.041451

Pennsylvania

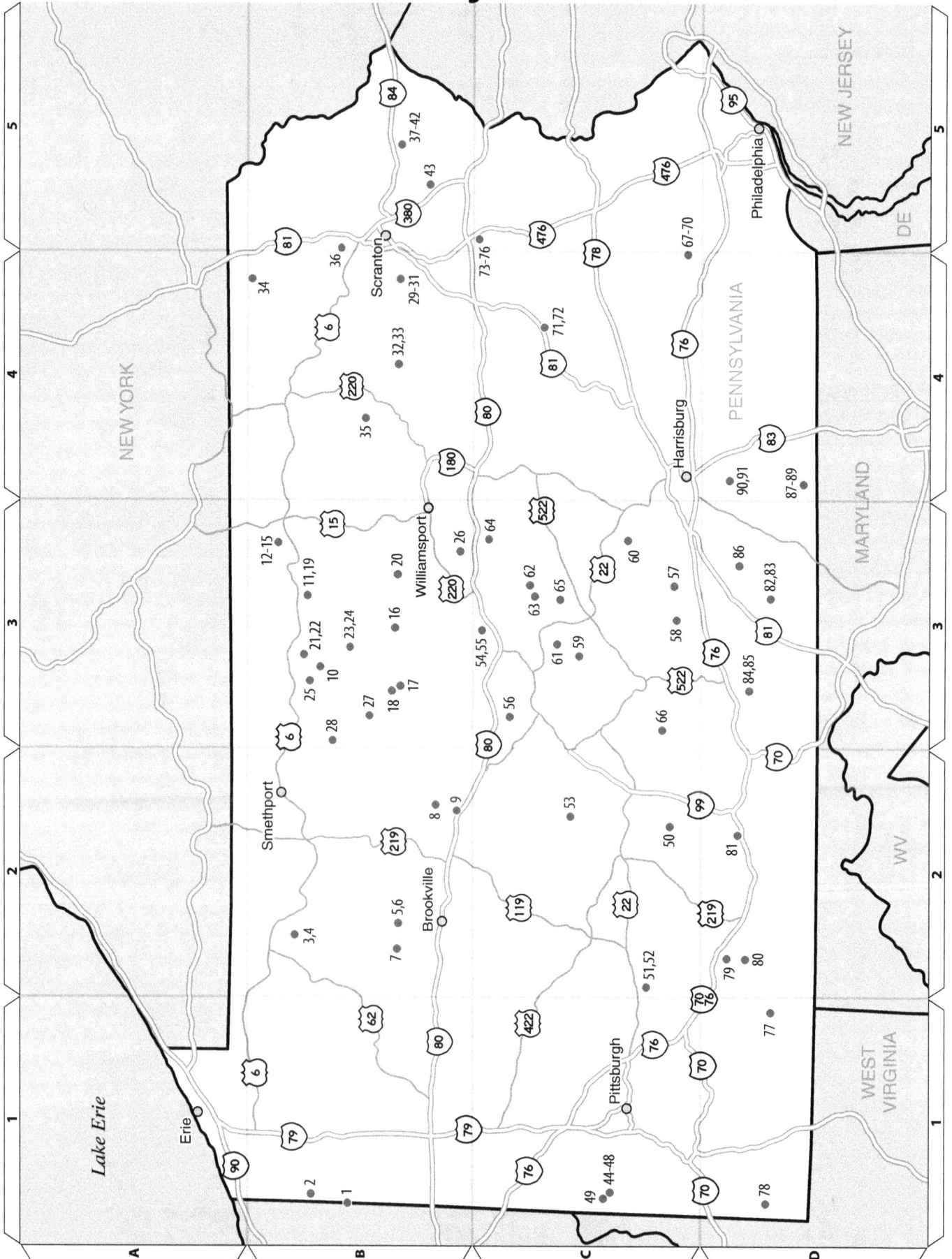

Map	ID	Map	ID
B1	1-2	C3	54-66
B2	3-9	C4	67-72
B3	10-28	C5	73-76
B4	29-35	D1	77-78
B5	36-43	D2	79-81
C1	44-49	D3	82-86
C2	50-53	D4	87-91

Alphabetical List of Camping Areas

1 • B1 | Pymatuning SP - Jamestown

Total sites: 324, RV sites: 324, Elec sites: 182, Water at site, Flush toilet, Free showers, RV dump, Tents: $24/RVs: $31-44, Also cabins, Pet Fee $2, $4 weekend/holiday premium, PA residents: $4.75 discount, Stay limit: 14-21 days, Open Apr-Oct, Max Length: 65ft, Reservations accepted, Elev: 1020ft/311m, Tel: 724-932-3142, Nearest town: Jamestown. GPS: 41.519047, -80.503237

2 • B1 | Pymatuning SP - Linesville

Total sites: 96, RV sites: 96, Elec sites: 73, Central water, Flush toilet, Free showers, RV dump, Tents: $24/RVs: $31, Also cabins, No pets, $4 weekend/holiday premium, PA residents: $4.75 discount, Stay limit: 14-21 days, Open Apr-Oct, Max Length: 65ft, Reservations accepted, Elev: 1027ft/313m, Tel: 724-932-3142, Nearest town: Jamestown. GPS: 41.659953, -80.463453

["

Open Apr-Oct, Max Length: 50ft, Reservations accepted, Elev: 971ft/296m, Tel: 570-923-6004, Nearest town: Renovo. GPS: 41.367375, -77.936444

19 • B3 | Leonard Harrison SP

Total sites: 28, RV sites: 28, Elec sites: 7, Central water, Flush toilet, Free showers, RV dump, Tents: $24/RVs: $31, Pet Fee $2, $4 weekend/holiday premium, PA residents: $4.75 discount, Open Apr-Oct, Max Length: 75ft, Reservations accepted, Elev: 1844ft/562m, Tel: 570-724-3061, Nearest town: Wellsboro. GPS: 41.697510, -77.450195

20 • B3 | Little Pine SP

Total sites: 99, RV sites: 93, Elec sites: 71, Central water, Flush toilet, Free showers, RV dump, Tents: $24/RVs: $31, Also cabins, Pet Fee $2, $4 weekend/holiday premium, PA residents: $4.75 discount, Open Apr-Dec, Max Length: 72ft, Reservations accepted, Elev: 778ft/237m, Tel: 570-753-6000, Nearest town: Waterville. GPS: 41.352507, -77.354284

21 • B3 | Lyman Run SP - Daggett Run

Total sites: 19, RV sites: 17, Elec sites: 17, Central water, Flush toilet, Free showers, No RV dump, Tents: $24/RVs: $31, Pet Fee $2, $4 weekend/holiday premium, PA residents: $4.75 discount, Open Apr-Nov, Max Length: 60ft, Reservations accepted, Elev: 1791ft/546m, Tel: 814-435-5010, Nearest town: Galeton. GPS: 41.728641, -77.762246

22 • B3 | Lyman Run SP - Lower

Total sites: 17, RV sites: 13, Elec sites: 13, Central water, Flush toilet, Free showers, RV dump, Tents: $24/RVs: $31, Pet Fee $2, $4 weekend/holiday premium, PA residents: $4.75 discount, Open Apr-Dec, Max Length: 60ft, Reservations accepted, Elev: 1676ft/511m, Tel: 814-435-5010, Nearest town: Galeton. GPS: 41.716045, -77.745505

23 • B3 | Ole Bull SP - CG 1

Total sites: 47, RV sites: 47, Elec sites: 32, Central water, Flush toilet, Free showers, RV dump, Tents: $24/RVs: $31, Also cabins, No pets, $4 weekend/holiday premium, PA residents: $4.75 discount, Open all year, Max Length: 64ft, Reservations accepted, Elev: 1217ft/371m, Tel: 814-435-5000, Nearest town: Cross Fork. GPS: 41.540394, -77.715636

24 • B3 | Ole Bull SP - CG 2

Total sites: 32, RV sites: 32, Elec sites: 24, Central water, Flush toilet, Free showers, RV dump, Tents: $24/RVs: $31, Also cabins, Pet Fee $2, $4 weekend/holiday premium, PA residents: $4.75 discount, Open all year, Max Length: 62ft, Reservations accepted, Elev: 1209ft/369m, Tel: 814-435-5000, Nearest town: Cross Fork. GPS: 41.536357, -77.715575

25 • B3 | Patterson SP

Dispersed sites, Central water, Vault/pit toilet, Tent & RV camping: $20, Pet Fee $2, $4 weekend/holiday premium, PA residents: $4.75 discount, Open Apr-Dec, Reservations not accepted, Elev: 2513ft/766m, Tel: 814-435-5010, Nearest town: Galeton. GPS: 41.696224, -77.893335

26 • B3 | Ravensburg SP

Total sites: 21, RV sites: 0, Central water, Flush toilet, Free showers, No RV dump, Tents only: $24, Pet Fee $2, $4 weekend/holiday premium, PA residents: $4.75 discount, Open May-Sep, Reservations not accepted, Elev: 1076ft/328m, Tel: 570-966-1455, Nearest town: Mifflinburg. GPS: 41.110107, -77.242920

27 • B3 | Sinnemahoning SP

Total sites: 35, RV sites: 33, Elec sites: 33, Central water, Flush toilet, Free showers, RV dump, Tents: $24/RVs: $31, Also walk-to sites/cabins, Pet Fee $2, $4 weekend/holiday premium, PA residents: $4.75 discount, Open Apr-Dec, Max Length: 85ft, Reservations accepted, Elev: 1027ft/313m, Tel: 814-647-8401, Nearest town: Austin. GPS: 41.459697, -78.061578

28 • B3 | Sizerville SP

Total sites: 23, RV sites: 23, Elec sites: 18, Central water, Flush toilet, Free showers, RV dump, Tents: $24/RVs: $31, Pet Fee $2, $4 weekend/holiday premium, PA residents: $4.75 discount, Stay limit: 14-21 days, Open Apr-Dec, Max Length: 60ft, Reservations accepted, Elev: 1352ft/412m, Tel: 814-486-5605, Nearest town: Emporium. GPS: 41.607155, -78.186537

29 • B4 | Frances Slocum SP - Hemlock Hill

Total sites: 31, RV sites: 31, Central water, Flush toilet, Free showers, RV dump, Tent & RV camping: $24, Pet Fee $2, $4 weekend/holiday premium, PA residents: $4.75 discount, Generator hours: 0800-2100, Open Apr-Oct, Max Length: 64ft, Reservations accepted, Elev: 1131ft/345m, Tel: 570-696-3525, Nearest town: Wyoming. GPS: 41.337275, -75.882174

30 • B4 | Frances Slocum SP - Rocky Knoll

Total sites: 15, RV sites: 0, Central water, Flush toilet, Free showers, RV dump, Tents only: $24, Walk-to sites, Pet Fee $2, $4 weekend/holiday premium, PA residents: $4.75 discount, Generator hours: 0800-2100, Open Apr-Oct, Reservations accepted, Elev: 1225ft/373m, Tel: 570-696-3525, Nearest town: Wyoming. GPS: 41.339471, -75.880744

31 • B4 | Frances Slocum SP - Stony Point

Total sites: 54, RV sites: 54, Elec sites: 54, Central water, Flush toilet, Free showers, RV dump, Tent & RV camping: $31, Pet Fee $2, $4 weekend/holiday premium, PA residents: $4.75 discount, Generator hours: 0800-2100, Open Apr-Oct, Max Length: 64ft, Reservations accepted, Elev: 1119ft/341m, Tel: 570-696-3525, Nearest town: Wyoming. GPS: 41.335493, -75.882494

32 • B4 | Ricketts Glen SP - Big Loop

Total sites: 73, RV sites: 73, Central water, Flush toilet, Free showers, RV dump, Tent & RV camping: $24, Also cabins, Pet Fee $2, $4 weekend/holiday premium, PA residents: $4.75 discount, Open Apr-Oct, Max Length: 50ft, Reservations accepted, Elev: 2242ft/683m, Tel: 570-477-5675, Nearest town: Benton. GPS: 41.341528, -76.298608

33 • B4 | Ricketts Glen SP - Small Loop

Total sites: 47, RV sites: 47, Central water, Flush toilet, Free showers, RV dump, Tent & RV camping: $24, Pet Fee $2, $4 weekend/holiday premium, PA residents: $4.75 discount, Open all year, Max Length: 50ft, Reservations accepted, Elev: 2250ft/

686m, Tel: 570-477-5675, Nearest town: Benton. GPS: 41.337629, -76.293616

34 • B4 | Salt Springs SP

Dispersed sites, Central water, Vault/pit toilet, Tent & RV camping: $20, Also cabins, Pet Fee $2, $4 weekend/holiday premium, PA residents: $4.75 discount, Stay limit: 14 days, Reservations accepted, Elev: 1174ft/358m, Tel: 570-945-3239, Nearest town: Dalton. GPS: 41.911711, -75.865209

35 • B4 | Worlds End SP

Total sites: 70, RV sites: 62, Elec sites: 32, Central water, Flush toilet, Free showers, RV dump, Tents: $24/RVs: $31, Also walk-to sites/cabins, Pet Fee $2, $4 weekend/holiday premium, PA residents: $4.75 discount, Open Apr-Dec, Max Length: 74ft, Reservations accepted, Elev: 1230ft/375m, Tel: 570-924-3287, Nearest town: Forksville. GPS: 41.470112, -76.569408

36 • B5 | Lackawanna SP

Total sites: 91, RV sites: 66, Elec sites: 56, Central water, Flush toilet, Free showers, RV dump, Tents: $24/RVs: $31, Pet Fee $2, $4 weekend/holiday premium, PA residents: $4.75 discount, Stay limit: 14-21 days, Open Apr-Oct, Max Length: 48ft, Reservations accepted, Elev: 1138ft/347m, Tel: 570-945-3239, Nearest town: Dalton. GPS: 41.561744, -75.715445

37 • B5 | Promised Land SP - Beechwood

Total sites: 102, RV sites: 102, Elec sites: 102, Central water, Flush toilet, Free showers, RV dump, Tents: $24/RVs: $31, Pet Fee $2, $4 weekend/holiday premium, PA residents: $4.75 discount, Stay limit: 14-21 days, Open Apr-Oct, Max Length: 80ft, Reservations accepted, Elev: 1745ft/532m, Tel: 570-676-3428, Nearest town: Greentown. GPS: 41.316951, -75.235148

38 • B5 | Promised Land SP - Deerfield

Total sites: 34, RV sites: 34, Central water, Flush toilet, Pay showers, No RV dump, Tent & RV camping: $24, Showers at Pickerel Point, Pet Fee $2, $4 weekend/holiday premium, PA residents: $4.75 discount, Stay limit: 14-21 days, Open May-Sep, Max Length: 55ft, Reservations accepted, Elev: 1785ft/544m, Tel: 570-676-3428, Nearest town: Greentown. GPS: 41.301182, -75.193811

39 • B5 | Promised Land SP - Northwoods

Total sites: 48, RV sites: 48, Elec sites: 48, Central water, Flush toilet, Free showers, RV dump, Tent & RV camping: $31, Pet Fee $2, $4 weekend/holiday premium, PA residents: $4.75 discount, Stay limit: 14-21 days, Open Apr-Oct, Max Length: 80ft, Reservations accepted, Elev: 1784ft/544m, Tel: 570-676-3428, Nearest town: Greentown. GPS: 41.319175, -75.230729

40 • B5 | Promised Land SP - Pickerel Point

Total sites: 75, RV sites: 37, Elec sites: 37, Water at site, Flush toilet, Free showers, RV dump, Tents: $24/RVs: $31-44, Pet Fee $2, $4 weekend/holiday premium, PA residents: $4.75 discount, Stay limit: 14-21 days, Open May-Sep, Max Length: 55ft, Reservations accepted, Elev: 1772ft/540m, Tel: 570-676-3428, Nearest town: Greentown. GPS: 41.306787, -75.193769

41 • B5 | Promised Land SP - Rhododenron

Total sites: 66, RV sites: 66, Elec sites: 17, Central water, Flush toilet, Free showers, RV dump, Tents: $24/RVs: $31, No pets, $4 weekend/holiday premium, PA residents: $4.75 discount, Stay limit: 14-21 days, Open Apr-Oct, Max Length: 80ft, Reservations accepted, Elev: 1730ft/527m, Tel: 570-676-3428, Nearest town: Greentown. GPS: 41.318178, -75.227635

42 • B5 | Promised Land SP - The Pines

Total sites: 58, RV sites: 58, Central water, Flush toilet, Pay showers, No RV dump, Tent & RV camping: $19-24, Showers at picnic area, Pet Fee $2, $4 weekend/holiday premium, PA residents: $4.75 discount, Stay limit: 14-21 days, Open May-Sep, Max Length: 87ft, Reservations accepted, Elev: 1818ft/554m, Tel: 570-676-3428, Nearest town: Greentown. GPS: 41.321832, -75.207907

43 • B5 | Tobyhanna SP

Total sites: 140, RV sites: 140, Elec sites: 21, Central water, Flush toilet, Free showers, RV dump, Tents: $24/RVs: $31, Pet Fee $2, $4 weekend/holiday premium, PA residents: $4.75 discount, Open Apr-Oct, Max Length: 40ft, Reservations accepted, Elev: 1998ft/609m, Tel: 570-894-8336, Nearest town: Tobyhanna. GPS: 41.210312, -75.404995

44 • C1 | Raccoon Creek SP - Loop C

Total sites: 40, RV sites: 40, Central water, Flush toilet, Free showers, RV dump, Tent & RV camping: $24, Pet Fee $2, $4 weekend/holiday premium, PA residents: $4.75 discount, Open May-Sep, Max Length: 78ft, Reservations accepted, Elev: 1112ft/339m, Tel: 724-899-2200, Nearest town: Hookstown. GPS: 40.499654, -80.410221

45 • C1 | Raccoon Creek SP - Loop D

Total sites: 26, RV sites: 0, Central water, Flush toilet, Free showers, RV dump, Tents only: $24, No pets, $4 weekend/holiday premium, PA residents: $4.75 discount, Open May-Sep, Max Length: 78ft, Reservations accepted, Elev: 1109ft/338m, Tel: 724-899-2200, Nearest town: Hookstown. GPS: 40.502524, -80.410028

46 • C1 | Raccoon Creek SP - Loop E

Total sites: 31, RV sites: 31, Elec sites: 23, Central water, Flush toilet, Free showers, RV dump, Tents: $24/RVs: $31, No pets, $4 weekend/holiday premium, PA residents: $4.75 discount, Open Apr-Oct, Max Length: 78ft, Reservations accepted, Elev: 1155ft/352m, Tel: 724-899-2200, Nearest town: Hookstown. GPS: 40.497286, -80.413653

47 • C1 | Raccoon Creek SP - Loop F

Total sites: 35, RV sites: 35, Elec sites: 14, Central water, Flush toilet, Free showers, RV dump, Tents: $24/RVs: $31, Pet Fee $2, $4 weekend/holiday premium, PA residents: $4.75 discount, Open Apr-Oct, Max Length: 78ft, Reservations accepted, Elev: 1134ft/346m, Tel: 724-899-2200, Nearest town: Hookstown. GPS: 40.498016, -80.410606

48 • C1 | Raccoon Creek SP - Loops A-B

Total sites: 40, RV sites: 40, Elec sites: 26, Central water, Flush toilet, Free showers, RV dump, Tents: $24/RVs: $31, Also cabins, No pets, $4 weekend/holiday premium, PA residents: $4.75 discount, Open May-Sep, Max Length: 78ft, Reservations accepted, Elev: 1127ft/344m, Tel: 724-899-2200, Nearest town: Hookstown. GPS: 40.498851, -80.415369

49 • C1 | Raccoon Creek SP - Sioux

Dispersed sites, Central water, Vault/pit toilet, No showers, No RV dump, Tent & RV camping: $20, Pet Fee $2, $4 weekend/holiday premium, PA residents: $4.75 discount, Open all year, Reservations accepted, Elev: 1198ft/365m, Tel: 724-899-2200, Nearest town: Hookstown. GPS: 40.515594, -80.436111

50 • C2 | Blue Knob SP

Total sites: 50, RV sites: 48, Elec sites: 48, Central water, Flush toilet, Free showers, RV dump, Tents: $24/RVs: $31, Pet Fee $2, $4 weekend/holiday premium, PA residents: $4.75 discount, Open Apr-Oct, Max Length: 65ft, Reservations accepted, Elev: 2431ft/741m, Tel: 814-276-3576, Nearest town: Imler. GPS: 40.290295, -78.592896

51 • C2 | Keystone SP - Hillside

Total sites: 59, RV sites: 59, Elec sites: 46, Central water, Flush toilet, Free showers, RV dump, Tents: $24/RVs: $31, Pet Fee $2, $4 weekend/holiday premium, PA residents: $4.75 discount, Open Apr-Oct, Max Length: 55ft, Reservations accepted, Elev: 1056ft/322m, Tel: 724-668-2939, Nearest town: Derry. GPS: 40.372244, -79.396558

52 • C2 | Keystone SP - Lakeside

Total sites: 42, RV sites: 42, Elec sites: 16, Central water, Flush toilet, Free showers, RV dump, Tents: $24/RVs: $31, No pets, $4 weekend/holiday premium, PA residents: $4.75 discount, Open Apr-Oct, Max Length: 40ft, Reservations accepted, Elev: 1066ft/325m, Tel: 724-668-2939, Nearest town: Derry. GPS: 40.372070, -79.383057

53 • C2 | Prince Gallitzin SP

Total sites: 398, RV sites: 398, Elec sites: 190, Water at site, Flush toilet, Free showers, RV dump, Tents: $24/RVs: $31-44, Also cabins, 28 Full hookups, Pet Fee $2, $4 weekend/holiday premium, PA residents: $4.75 discount, Open Apr-Oct, Reservations accepted, Elev: 1499ft/457m, Tel: 814-674-1000, Nearest town: Patton. GPS: 40.674496, -78.558514

54 • C3 | Bald Eagle SP - Primitive

Total sites: 70, RV sites: 35, Central water, Vault/pit toilet, No showers, RV dump, Tent & RV camping: $20, Pet Fee $2, $4 weekend/holiday premium, PA residents: $4.75 discount, Open Apr-Dec, Max Length: 48ft, Reservations accepted, Elev: 735ft/224m, Tel: 814-625-2775, Nearest town: Howard. GPS: 41.018651, -77.639716

55 • C3 | Bald Eagle SP - Russell P. Letterman CG

Total sites: 96, RV sites: 96, Elec sites: 87, Central water, Flush toilet, Free showers, RV dump, Tents: $24/RVs: $31-44, Also cabins, 18 Full hookups, Pet Fee $2, $4 weekend/holiday premium, PA residents: $4.75 discount, Open Apr-Dec, Max Length: 50ft, Reservations accepted, Elev: 659ft/201m, Tel: 814-625-2775, Nearest town: Howard. GPS: 41.037075, -77.643447

56 • C3 | Black Moshannon SP

Total sites: 74, RV sites: 74, Elec sites: 58, Water at site, Flush toilet, Free showers, RV dump, Tents: $24/RVs: $31-44, Also cabins, 10 Full hookups, Pet Fee $2, $4 weekend/holiday premium, PA residents: $4.75 discount, Open Apr-Dec, Max Length: 73ft, Reservations accepted, Elev: 1992ft/607m, Tel: 814-342-5960, Nearest town: Philipsburg. GPS: 40.916717, -78.064281

57 • C3 | Colonel Denning SP

Total sites: 52, RV sites: 46, Elec sites: 32, Central water, Vault/pit toilet, No showers, RV dump, Tents: $24/RVs: $31, Pets in sites 1-11 only, Pet Fee $2, $4 weekend/holiday premium, PA residents: $4.75 discount, Open May-Dec, Max Length: 50ft, Reservations accepted, Elev: 837ft/255m, Tel: 717-776-5272, Nearest town: Newville. GPS: 40.280952, -77.416481

58 • C3 | Fowlers Hollow SP

Total sites: 18, RV sites: 12, Elec sites: 12, Central water, Flush toilet, No showers, RV dump, Tents: $20/RVs: $27, Pet Fee $2, $4 weekend/holiday premium, PA residents: $4.75 discount, Reservations accepted, Elev: 945ft/288m, Tel: 717-776-5272, Nearest town: Newville. GPS: 40.270209, -77.583399

59 • C3 | Greenwood Furnace SP

Total sites: 53, RV sites: 51, Elec sites: 48, Central water, Flush toilet, Free showers, RV dump, Tents: $24/RVs: $31, Pet Fee $2, $4 weekend/holiday premium, PA residents: $4.75 discount, Stay limit: 14-21 days, Open Apr-Nov, Max Length: 92ft, Reservations accepted, Elev: 1056ft/322m, Tel: 814-667-1800, Nearest town: Huntingdon. GPS: 40.646240, -77.761963

60 • C3 | Little Buffalo SP

Total sites: 40, RV sites: 40, Elec sites: 28, Water at site, Flush toilet, Free showers, RV dump, Tents: $24/RVs: $31-44, Also cabins, 2 Full hookups, Pet Fee $2, $4 weekend/holiday premium, PA residents: $4.75 discount, Open Apr-Oct, Max Length: 45ft, Reservations accepted, Elev: 699ft/213m, Tel: 717-567-9255, Nearest town: Newport. GPS: 40.460801, -77.192064

61 • C3 | Penn Roosevelt SP

Total sites: 18, RV sites: 0, Central water, Vault/pit toilet, No showers, No RV dump, Tents only: $20, Pet Fee $2, $4 weekend/holiday premium, PA residents: $4.75 discount, Open all year, Reservations not accepted, Elev: 1696ft/517m, Tel: 814-667-1800, Nearest town: Huntingdon. GPS: 40.727195, -77.700594

62 • C3 | Poe Paddy SP

Total sites: 38, RV sites: 38, Central water, Vault/pit toilet, No showers, No RV dump, Tent & RV camping: $20, Pet fee $2, $4 weekend premium, Dump and shower at Poe Valley SP, Lower fee is for PA residents, Open Apr-Dec, Reservations accepted, Elev: 1001ft/305m, Tel: 717-667-3622, Nearest town: Milroy. GPS: 40.835007, -77.417279

63 • C3 | Poe Valley SP

Total sites: 45, RV sites: 45, Elec sites: 27, Central water, Flush toilet, Free showers, RV dump, Tents: $24/RVs: $31, Also cabins, Pet Fee $2, $4 weekend/holiday premium, PA residents: $4.75 discount, Open Apr-Dec, Reservations accepted, Elev: 1302ft/397m, Tel: 814-349-2460, Nearest town: Milroy. GPS: 40.822462, -77.467087

64 • C3 | Raymond B Winter SP

Total sites: 61, RV sites: 61, Elec sites: 49, Central water, Flush toilet, Free showers, RV dump, Tents: $24/RVs: $31, Also walk-to sites/cabins, Pet Fee $2, $4 weekend/holiday premium, PA residents: $4.75 discount, Open Apr-Dec, Max Length: 50ft, Reservations accepted, Elev: 1598ft/487m, Tel: 570-966-1455, Nearest town: Mifflinburg. GPS: 40.992572, -77.185413

65 • C3 | Reeds Gap SP

Total sites: 14, RV sites: 0, Central water, Flush toilet, Free showers, No RV dump, Tents only: $24, Pet Fee $2, $4 weekend/holiday premium, PA residents: $4.75 discount, Open Apr-Oct, Reservations accepted, Elev: 879ft/268m, Tel: 717-667-3622, Nearest town: Milroy. GPS: 40.720371, -77.476245

66 • C3 | Trough Creek SP

Total sites: 29, RV sites: 24, Elec sites: 29, Central water, Vault/pit toilet, No showers, RV dump, Tent & RV camping: $27, Also cabins, Pet Fee $2, $4 weekend/holiday premium, PA residents: $4.75 discount, Open Apr-Dec, Max Length: 60ft, Reservations accepted, Elev: 965ft/294m, Tel: 814-658-3847, Nearest town: James Creek. GPS: 40.324855, -78.127197

67 • C4 | French Creek SP - Loop A

Total sites: 55, RV sites: 55, Central water, Flush toilet, Free showers, RV dump, Tent & RV camping: $24, Also cabins, No pets, $4 weekend/holiday premium, PA residents: $4.75 discount, Open Apr-Oct, Max Length: 45ft, Reservations accepted, Elev: 893ft/272m, Tel: 610-582-9680, Nearest town: Elverson. GPS: 40.214373, -75.784042

68 • C4 | French Creek SP - Loop B

Total sites: 48, RV sites: 48, Elec sites: 31, Central water, Flush toilet, Free showers, RV dump, Tents: $24/RVs: $31, Also cabins, No pets, $4 weekend/holiday premium, PA residents: $4.75 discount, Open Apr-Oct, Max Length: 45ft, Reservations accepted, Elev: 901ft/275m, Tel: 610-582-9680, Nearest town: Elverson. GPS: 40.216811, -75.783863

69 • C4 | French Creek SP - Loop C

Total sites: 47, RV sites: 47, Elec sites: 29, Central water, Flush toilet, Free showers, RV dump, Tents: $24/RVs: $31-44, Also cabins, 17 Full hookups, Pet Fee $2, $4 weekend/holiday premium, PA residents: $4.75 discount, Open all year, Max Length: 45ft, Reservations accepted, Elev: 902ft/275m, Tel: 610-582-9680, Nearest town: Elverson. GPS: 40.216124, -75.785526

70 • C4 | French Creek SP - Loop D

Total sites: 51, RV sites: 51, Central water, Flush toilet, Free showers, RV dump, Tent & RV camping: $24, Also cabins, No pets, $4 weekend/holiday premium, PA residents: $4.75 discount, Open Apr-Oct, Max Length: 45ft, Reservations accepted, Elev: 903ft/275m, Tel: 610-582-9680, Nearest town: Elverson. GPS: 40.217934, -75.782933

71 • C4 | Locust Lake SP - RV

Total sites: 213, RV sites: 213, Elec sites: 80, Central water, Flush toilet, Free showers, RV dump, Tents: $24/RVs: $31, Pet Fee $2, $4 weekend/holiday premium, PA residents: $4.75 discount, Open Mar-Oct, Max Length: 68ft, Reservations accepted, Elev: 1299ft/396m, Tel: 570-467-2404, Nearest town: Barnesville. GPS: 40.779171, -76.125947

72 • C4 | Locust Lake SP - Tent

Total sites: 69, RV sites: 0, Central water, Flush toilet, Free showers, RV dump, Tents only: $24, Pet Fee $2, $4 weekend/holiday premium, PA residents: $4.75 discount, Open Mar-Oct, Reservations accepted, Elev: 1285ft/392m, Tel: 570-467-2404, Nearest town: Barnesville. GPS: 40.784097, -76.126083

73 • C5 | Hickory Run SP - East Loop

Total sites: 104, RV sites: 104, Elec sites: 19, Water at site, Flush toilet, Free showers, RV dump, Tents: $24/RVs: $31-44, 18 Full hookups, Pet Fee $2, $4 weekend/holiday premium, PA residents: $4.75 discount, Open Apr-Dec, Reservations accepted, Elev: 1590ft/485m, Tel: 570-443-0400, Nearest town: White Haven. GPS: 41.021997, -75.680439

74 • C5 | Hickory Run SP - Sites 1-164

Total sites: 164, RV sites: 153, Elec sites: 2, Central water, Flush toilet, Free showers, RV dump, Tents: $24/RVs: $31, No pets, $4 weekend/holiday premium, PA residents: $4.75 discount, Open Apr-Oct, Max Length: 90ft, Reservations accepted, Elev: 1407ft/429m, Tel: 570-443-0400, Nearest town: White Haven. GPS: 41.022754, -75.696908

75 • C5 | Hickory Run SP - Sites 165-228

Total sites: 64, RV sites: 64, Elec sites: 64, Central water, Flush toilet, Free showers, RV dump, Tents: $24/RVs: $31, Pet Fee $2, $4 weekend/holiday premium, PA residents: $4.75 discount, Open Apr-Oct, Max Length: 90ft, Reservations accepted, Elev: 1495ft/456m, Tel: 570-443-0400, Nearest town: White Haven. GPS: 41.022308, -75.692183

76 • C5 | Hickory Run SP - Sites 229-277

Total sites: 48, RV sites: 48, Elec sites: 48, Central water, Flush toilet, Free showers, RV dump, Tents: $24/RVs: $31, No pets, $4 weekend/holiday premium, PA residents: $4.75 discount, Open Apr-Oct, Max Length: 90ft, Reservations accepted, Elev: 1519ft/463m, Tel: 570-443-0400, Nearest town: White Haven. GPS: 41.022527, -75.690207

77 • D1 | Ohiopyle SP - Kentuck CG

Total sites: 224, RV sites: 197, Elec sites: 57, Central water, Flush toilet, Free showers, RV dump, Tents: $24/RVs: $31, Also cabins, Pet Fee $2, $4 weekend/holiday premium, PA residents: $4.75 discount, Open Apr-Dec, Max Length: 50ft, Reservations accepted, Elev: 1611ft/491m, Tel: 724-329-8591, Nearest town: Ohiopyle. GPS: 39.885959, -79.493119

78 • D1 | Ryerson Station SP

Total sites: 46, RV sites: 46, Elec sites: 22, Water at site, Flush toilet, Free showers, RV dump, Tents: $24/RVs: $31-44, Also cabins, 7 Full hookups, Pet Fee $2, $4 weekend/holiday premium, PA residents: $4.75 discount, Stay limit: 14-21 days, Open all year, Reservations accepted, Elev: 1306ft/398m, Tel: 724-428-4254, Nearest town: Wind Ridge. GPS: 39.888822, -80.440115

79 • D2 | Kooser SP

Total sites: 35, RV sites: 35, Elec sites: 28, Water at site, Flush toilet, Free showers, RV dump, Tents: $24/RVs: $31-44, 4 Full hookups, Pet Fee $2, $4 weekend/holiday premium, PA residents: $4.75 discount, Open Apr-Dec, Max Length: 100ft, Reservations accepted, Elev: 2369ft/722m, Tel: 814-445-8673, Nearest town: Somerset. GPS: 40.064089, -79.241288

80 • D2 | Laurel Hill SP

Total sites: 264, RV sites: 264, Elec sites: 149, Water at site, Flush toilet, Free showers, RV dump, Tents: $24/RVs: $31-44, Also cabins, 12 Full hookups, Pet Fee $2, $4 weekend/holiday premium, PA residents: $4.75 discount, Stay limit: 14 days, Open Apr-Oct, Max Length: 45ft, Reservations accepted, Elev: 1988ft/606m, Tel: 814-445-7725, Nearest town: Somerset. GPS: 39.992972, -79.243086

81 • D2 | Shawnee SP

Total sites: 293, RV sites: 293, Elec sites: 98, Central water, Flush toilet, Free showers, RV dump, Tents: $24/RVs: $31, Also cabins, Pet Fee $2, $4 weekend/holiday premium, PA residents: $4.75 discount, Open Apr-Dec, Max Length: 65+ft, Reservations accepted, Elev: 1260ft/384m, Tel: 814-733-4218, Nearest town: Schellsburg. GPS: 40.021424, -78.638368

82 • D3 | Caledonia SP - Chinquapin Hill

Total sites: 123, RV sites: 123, Elec sites: 10, Water at site, Flush toilet, Free showers, No RV dump, Tents: $24/RVs: $31-44, 17 Full hookups, Pet Fee $2, $4 weekend/holiday premium, PA residents: $4.75 discount, Open May-Oct, Max Length: 60ft, Reservations accepted, Elev: 1004ft/306m, Tel: 717-352-2161, Nearest town: Fayetteville. GPS: 39.910400, -77.478760

83 • D3 | Caledonia SP - Hosack Run

Total sites: 54, RV sites: 54, Elec sites: 35, Water at site, Flush toilet, Free showers, RV dump, Tents: $24/RVs: $31-44, 12 Full hookups, Pet Fee $2, $4 weekend/holiday premium, PA residents: $4.75 discount, Open Apr-Dec, Max Length: 50ft, Reservations accepted, Elev: 1030ft/314m, Tel: 717-352-2161, Nearest town: Fayetteville. GPS: 39.915354, -77.469397

84 • D3 | Cowans Gap SP - Camp Area A

Total sites: 177, RV sites: 177, Elec sites: 133, Flush toilet, Free showers, RV dump, Tents: $24/RVs: $31, Pet fee $2, $4 weekend premium, Lower fee is for PA residents, Open Apr-Dec, Max Length: 82ft, Reservations accepted, Elev: 1306ft/398m, Tel: 717-485-3948, Nearest town: Fort Loudon. GPS: 39.988016, -77.931352

85 • D3 | Cowans Gap SP - Camp Area B

Total sites: 34, RV sites: 27, Elec sites: 18, Flush toilet, Free showers, RV dump, Tents: $24/RVs: $31, Also walk-to sites, Pet fee $2, $4 weekend premium, Lower fee is for PA residents, Open Apr-Oct, Max Length: 70ft, Reservations accepted, Elev: 1257ft/383m, Tel: 717-485-3948, Nearest town: Fort Loudon. GPS: 40.000425, -77.926067

86 • D3 | Pine Grove Furnace SP - Charcoal Hearth

Total sites: 70, RV sites: 70, Elec sites: 47, Central water, Flush toilet, Free showers, RV dump, Tents: $24/RVs: $31, Also cabins, Pet Fee $2, $4 weekend/holiday premium, PA residents: $4.75 discount, Open Mar-Dec, Max Length: 60ft, Reservations accepted, Elev: 938ft/286m, Tel: 717-486-7174, Nearest town: Gardners. GPS: 40.026052, -77.311888

87 • D4 | Codorus SP - Loop A

Total sites: 42, RV sites: 42, Central water, Flush toilet, Free showers, RV dump, Tent & RV camping: $24, Pet Fee $2, $4 weekend/holiday premium, PA residents: $4.75 discount, Stay limit: 14 days, Open Apr-Oct, Max Length: 54ft, Reservations accepted, Elev: 714ft/218m, Tel: 717-637-2816, Nearest town: Hanover. GPS: 39.775047, -76.916067

88 • D4 | Codorus SP - Loops B,C,D

Total sites: 143, RV sites: 143, Elec sites: 120, Central water, Flush toilet, Free showers, RV dump, Tents: $24/RVs: $26-31, Pet Fee $2, $4 weekend/holiday premium, PA residents: $4.75 discount, Stay limit: 14 days, Open Apr-Oct, Max Length: 54ft, Reservations accepted, Elev: 728ft/222m, Tel: 717-637-2816, Nearest town: Hanover. GPS: 39.777347, -76.917807

89 • D4 | Codorus SP - Timberdoodle Tent Area

Total sites: 15, RV sites: 0, Central water, Vault/pit toilet, Free showers, No RV dump, Tents only: $24, Pet Fee $2, $4 weekend/holiday premium, PA residents: $4.75 discount, Stay limit: 14 days, Open Apr-Oct, Reservations accepted, Elev: 682ft/208m, Tel: 717-637-2816, Nearest town: Hanover. GPS: 39.780593, -76.922266

90 • D4 | Gifford Pinchot SP - East Side

Total sites: 192, RV sites: 192, Elec sites: 89, Central water, Flush toilet, Free showers, RV dump, Tents: $24/RVs: $31, Also cabins, 22 Full hookups, Pet Fee $2, $4 weekend/holiday premium, PA residents: $4.75 discount, Open Apr-Oct, Max Length: 55ft, Reservations accepted, Elev: 480ft/146m, Tel: 717-432-5011, Nearest town: Lewisberry. GPS: 40.064024, -76.896806

91 • D4 | Gifford Pinchot SP - West Side

Total sites: 148, RV sites: 148, Elec sites: 57, Water at site, Flush toilet, Free showers, RV dump, Tents: $24/RVs: $31-44, Also cabins, Pet Fee $2, $4 weekend/holiday premium, PA residents: $4.75 discount, Open Apr-Oct, Max Length: 55ft, Reservations accepted, Elev: 478ft/146m, Tel: 717-432-5011, Nearest town: Lewisberry. GPS: 40.063475, -76.899915

Rhode Island

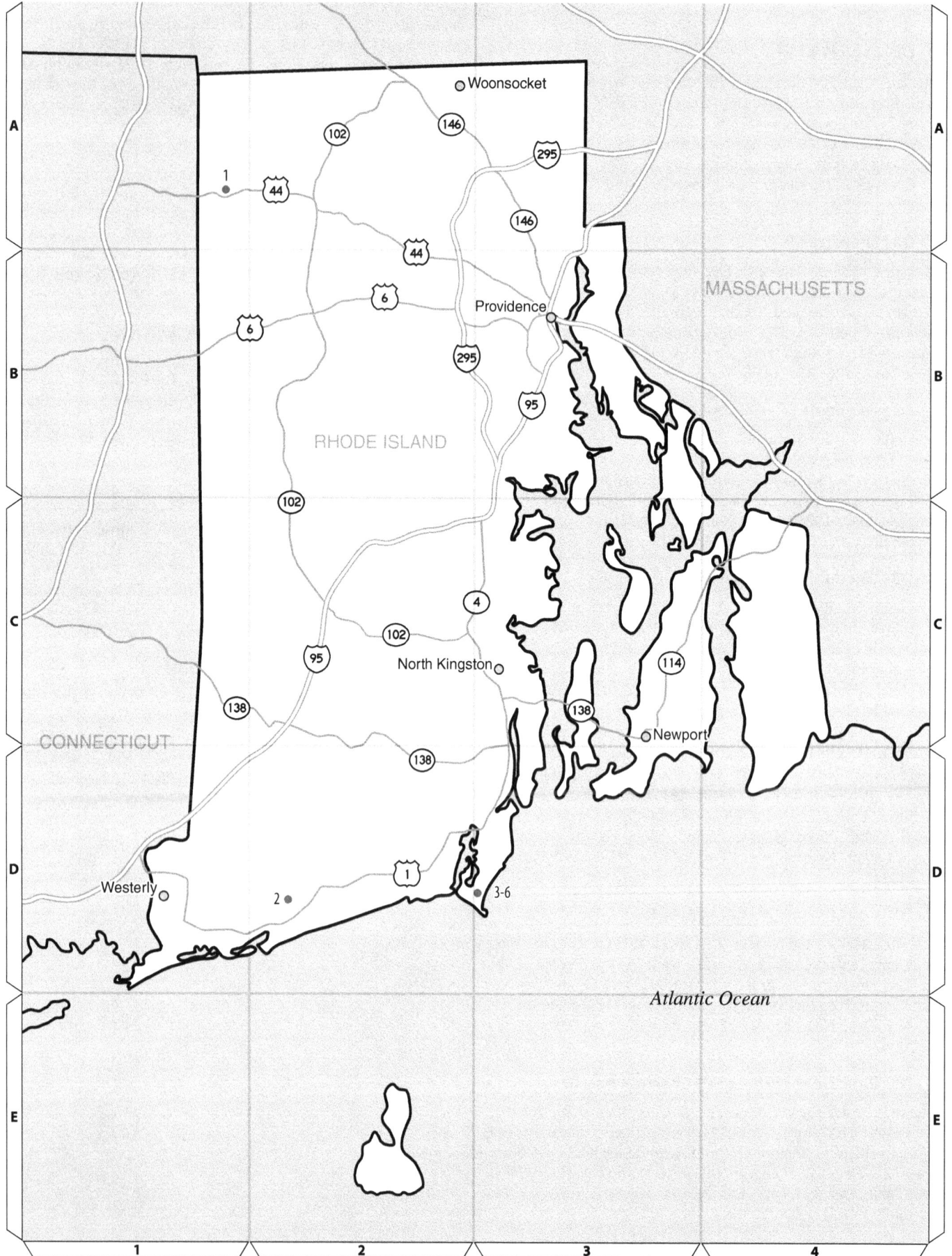

Map	ID	Map	ID
A1	1	D3	3-6
D2	2		

Alphabetical List of Camping Areas

1 • A1 | George Washington SP - Angell Loop

Dispersed sites, No water, Vault/pit toilet, Tents only: $36, Hike-in, .6 mi, 7 sites, RI residents: $18, Stay limit: 14 days, Reservations accepted, Elev: 593ft/181m, Tel: 401-568-6700, Nearest town: Chepachet. GPS: 41.921064, -71.765776

2 • D2 | Burlingame SP

Total sites: 692, RV sites: 692, Central water, Flush toilet, Free showers, RV dump, Tent & RV camping: $36, RI residents: $18, Stay limit: 14 days, Open Apr-Oct, Max Length: 102ft, Reservations accepted, Elev: 94ft/29m, Tel: 401-322-7337, Nearest town: Charlestown. GPS: 41.374879, -71.695753

3 • D3 | Fishermen's Memorial SP - Area 1

Total sites: 40, RV sites: 40, Elec sites: 40, Water at site, Flush toilet, Pay showers, RV dump, No tents/RVs: $55, 40 Full hookups, RI residents $18-$20, Open Apr-Oct, Max Length: 50ft, Reservations accepted, Elev: 22ft/7m, Tel: 401-789-8374, Nearest town: Narragansett. GPS: 41.380505, -71.496611

4 • D3 | Fishermen's Memorial SP - Area 2

Total sites: 65, RV sites: 65, Elec sites: 65, Water at site, Flush toilet, Pay showers, RV dump, Tent & RV camping: $45, RI residents $24, Open Apr-Oct, Max Length: 50ft, Reservations accepted, Elev: 43ft/13m, Tel: 401-789-8374, Nearest town: Narragansett. GPS: 41.379823, -71.493731

5 • D3 | Fishermen's Memorial SP - Area 3

Total sites: 35, RV sites: 0, Central water, Flush toilet, Pay showers, RV dump, Tents only: $36, RI residents $18, Open Apr-Oct, Max Length: 20ft, Reservations accepted, Elev: 39ft/12m, Tel: 401-789-8374, Nearest town: Narragansett. GPS: 41.381049, -71.492953

6 • D3 | Fishermen's Memorial SP - Area 4

Total sites: 42, RV sites: 42, Elec sites: 42, Water at site, Flush toilet, Pay showers, RV dump, Tent & RV camping: $45, RI residents $24, Stay limit: 14 days, Open Apr-Oct, Max Length: 50ft, Reservations accepted, Elev: 47ft/14m, Tel: 401-789-8374, Nearest town: Narragansett. GPS: 41.379273, -71.489705

South Carolina

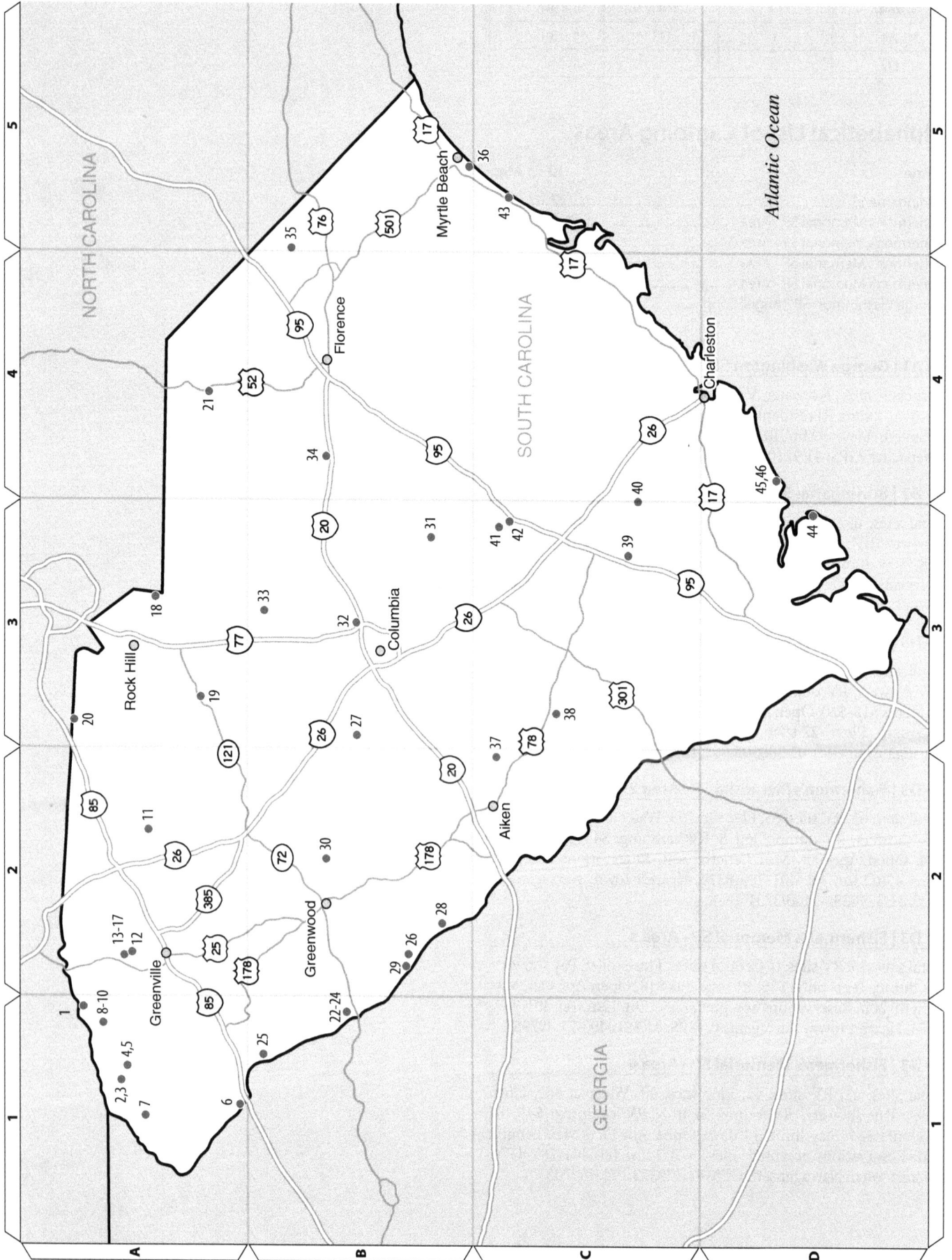

Map	ID	Map	ID
A1	1-10	B4	34
A2	11-17	B5	35-36
A3	18-20	C2	37
A4	21	C3	38-42
B1	22-25	C5	43
B2	26-32	D3	44
B3	33	D4	45-46

Alphabetical List of Camping Areas

1 • A1 | Caesars Head SP

Dispersed sites, Central water, Vault/pit toilet, No showers, No RV dump, Tents only: $14-30, Walk-to sites, 19 back-country sites, Dynamic pricing/fees can vary from day to day, Stay limit: 14 days, Reservations required, Elev: 3180ft/969m, Tel: 864-836-6115, Nearest town: Cleveland. GPS: 35.106034, -82.626030

2 • A1 | Devils Fork SP

Total sites: 59, RV sites: 59, Elec sites: 59, Water at site, Flush toilet, Free showers, RV dump, Tent & RV camping: $25-45, Also walk-to sites/cabins, Dynamic pricing/fees can vary from day to day, Stay limit: 14 days, Open Mar-Dec, Max Length: 40ft, Reservations accepted, Elev: 1148ft/350m, Tel: 864-944-2639, Nearest town: Salem. GPS: 34.955997, -82.951194

3 • A1 | Devils Fork SP - Walk-in

Total sites: 25, Central water, Flush toilet, No showers, No RV dump, Tents only: $25-47, Walk-to sites, Dynamic pricing/fees can vary from day to day, Stay limit: 14 days, Open Mar-Dec, Reservations accepted, Elev: 1139ft/347m, Tel: 864-944-2639, Nearest town: Salem. GPS: 34.958078, -82.949955

4 • A1 | Keowee-Toxaway SP - Main

Total sites: 24, RV sites: 10, Elec sites: 10, Water at site, Flush toilet, Free showers, RV dump, Tent & RV camping: $18-28, Dynamic pricing/fees can vary from day to day, Stay limit: 14 days, Open all year, Max Length: 40ft, Reservations accepted, Elev: 1092ft/333m, Tel: 864-868-2605, Nearest town: Sunset. GPS: 34.932047, -82.887114

5 • A1 | Keowee-Toxaway SP - Primitive

Total sites: 3, No water, Vault/pit toilet, Tents only: $10-20, Hike-in, Dynamic pricing/fees can vary from day to day, Stay limit: 14 days, Open all year, Reservations accepted, Elev: 919ft/280m, Tel: 864-868-2605, Nearest town: Sunset. GPS: 34.941671, -82.887087

6 • A1 | Lake Hartwell SP

Total sites: 128, RV sites: 115, Elec sites: 115, Water at site, Flush toilet, Free showers, RV dump, Tents: $19-25/RVs: $22-40, Also walk-to sites/cabins, 13 walk-to sites, Dynamic pricing/fees can vary from day to day, Stay limit: 14 days, Open all year, Max Length: 40ft, Reservations accepted, Elev: 722ft/220m, Tel: 864-972-3352, Nearest town: Fair Play. GPS: 34.497907, -83.040811

7 • A1 | Oconee SP

Total sites: 155, RV sites: 140, Elec sites: 140, Water at site, Flush toilet, Free showers, RV dump, Tents: $16/RVs: $20-50, Also cabins, Dynamic pricing/fees can vary from day to day, Stay limit: 14 days, Open all year, Reservations accepted, Elev: 1772ft/540m, Tel: 864-638-5353, Nearest town: Mountain Rest. GPS: 34.863758, -83.105606

8 • A1 | Table Rock SP - Main

Total sites: 69, RV sites: 69, Elec sites: 69, Water at site, Flush toilet, Free showers, RV dump, Tent & RV camping: $23-48, Also cabins, Dynamic pricing/fees can vary from day to day, Stay limit: 14 days, Open all year, Max Length: 40ft, Reservations accepted, Elev: 1250ft/381m, Tel: 864-878-9813, Nearest town: Pickens. GPS: 35.026559, -82.704729

9 • A1 | Table Rock SP - Pine Point Trailside

Total sites: 6, RV sites: 0, No water, Vault/pit toilet, Tents only: $17, Walk-to sites, Stay limit: 14 days, Open all year, Reservations accepted, Elev: 1172ft/357m, Tel: 864-878-9813, Nearest town: Pickens. GPS: 35.021941, -82.689897

10 • A1 | Table Rock SP - White Oak

Total sites: 25, RV sites: 25, Elec sites: 25, Water at site, Flush toilet, Free showers, RV dump, Tent & RV camping: $23-48, Also cabins, Dynamic pricing/fees can vary from day to day, Stay limit: 14 days, Open all year, Max Length: 40ft, Reservations accepted, Elev: 1339ft/408m, Tel: 864-878-9813, Nearest town: Pickens. GPS: 35.036798, -82.695853

11 • A2 | Croft SP

Total sites: 50, RV sites: 50, Elec sites: 50, Water at site, Flush toilet, Free showers, RV dump, Tent & RV camping: $25-39, Dynamic pricing/fees can vary from day to day, Stay limit: 14 days, Open all year, Max Length: 40ft, Reservations accepted, Elev: 574ft/175m, Tel: 864-585-1283, Nearest town: Spartanburg. GPS: 34.866584, -81.838596

12 • A2 | Paris Mountain SP

Total sites: 39, RV sites: 39, Elec sites: 39, Water at site, Flush toilet, Free showers, RV dump, Tent & RV camping: $30-40, Also cabins, Dynamic pricing/fees can vary from day to day, Stay limit: 14 days, Open all year, Max Length: 40ft, Reservations accepted, Elev: 1092ft/333m, Tel: 864-244-5565, Nearest town: Greenville. GPS: 34.925139, -82.374678

13 • A2 | Paris Mountain SP - TC 1

Total sites: 2, No water, Vault/pit toilet, Tents only: $17, Hike-in, Stay limit: 14 days, Open all year, Reservations accepted, Elev: 1221ft/372m, Tel: 864-244-5565, Nearest town: Greenville. GPS: 34.951793, -82.391842

14 • A2 | Paris Mountain SP - TC 2

Total sites: 2, No water, Vault/pit toilet, Tents only: $17, Hike-in, Stay limit: 14 days, Open all year, Reservations accepted, Elev: 1200ft/366m, Tel: 864-244-5565, Nearest town: Greenville. GPS: 34.952113, -82.394639

15 • A2 | Paris Mountain SP - TC 3

Total sites: 2, No water, Vault/pit toilet, Tents only: $17, Hike-in, Stay limit: 14 days, Open all year, Reservations accepted, Elev: 1245ft/379m, Tel: 864-244-5565, Nearest town: Greenville. GPS: 34.949892, -82.397656

16 • A2 | Paris Mountain SP - TC 4

Total sites: 2, No water, Vault/pit toilet, Tents only: $17, Hike-in, Stay limit: 14 days, Open all year, Reservations accepted, Elev: 1253ft/382m, Tel: 864-244-5565, Nearest town: Greenville. GPS: 34.949506, -82.396595

17 • A2 | Paris Mountain SP - TC 5

Total sites: 2, No water, Vault/pit toilet, Tents only: $17, Hike-in, Stay limit: 14 days, Open all year, Reservations accepted, Elev: 1240ft/378m, Tel: 864-244-5565, Nearest town: Greenville. GPS: 34.950369, -82.394431

18 • A3 | Andrew Jackson SP

Total sites: 25, RV sites: 25, Elec sites: 25, Water at site, Flush toilet, Free showers, RV dump, Tent & RV camping: $22-25, Dynamic pricing/fees can vary from day to day, Stay limit: 14 days, Open all year, Max Length: 36ft, Reservations accepted, Elev: 568ft/173m, Tel: 803-285-3344, Nearest town: Lancaster. GPS: 34.845481, -80.805196

19 • A3 | Chester SP

Total sites: 25, RV sites: 25, Elec sites: 25, Water at site, Flush toilet, Free showers, RV dump, Tent & RV camping: $28-39, Dynamic pricing/fees can vary from day to day, Stay limit: 14 days, Open all year, Reservations accepted, Elev: 472ft/144m, Tel: 803-385-2680, Nearest town: Chester. GPS: 34.680299, -81.243645

20 • A3 | Kings Mountain SP

Total sites: 125, RV sites: 115, Elec sites: 115, Water at site, Flush toilet, Free showers, RV dump, Tents: $15-25/RVs: $19-38, Dynamic pricing/fees can vary from day to day, Stay limit: 14 days, Open all year, Max Length: 40ft, Reservations accepted, Elev: 824ft/251m, Tel: 803-222-3209, Nearest town: Blacksburg. GPS: 35.151055, -81.348352

21 • A4 | Cheraw SP

Total sites: 17, RV sites: 17, Elec sites: 17, Water at site, Flush toilet, Free showers, RV dump, Tent & RV camping: $30-35, Dynamic pricing/fees can vary from day to day, Stay limit: 14 days, Open all year, Reservations accepted, Elev: 128ft/39m, Tel: 843-537-9656, Nearest town: Cheraw. GPS: 34.640261, -79.893599

22 • B1 | Calhoun Falls SP - CG 1

Total sites: 45, RV sites: 45, Elec sites: 45, Water at site, Flush toilet, Free showers, RV dump, Tent & RV camping: $25-45, Dynamic pricing/fees can vary from day to day, Stay limit: 14 days, Open Mar-Dec, Max Length: 40ft, Elev: 594ft/181m, Tel: 864-447-8267, Nearest town: Calhoun Falls. GPS: 34.107481, -82.620191

23 • B1 | Calhoun Falls SP - CG 2

Total sites: 41, RV sites: 41, Elec sites: 41, Water at site, Flush toilet, Free showers, RV dump, Tent & RV camping: $25-45, Dynamic pricing/fees can vary from day to day, Stay limit: 14 days, Open Mar-Dec, Max Length: 40ft, Reservations accepted, Elev: 526ft/160m, Tel: 864-447-8267, Nearest town: Calhoun Falls. GPS: 34.112203, -82.618957

24 • B1 | Calhoun Falls SP - Primitive

Total sites: 14, Central water, Flush toilet, Free showers, No RV dump, Tents only: $17, Walk-to sites, Dynamic pricing/fees can vary from day to day, Stay limit: 14 days, Open Mar-Dec, Reservations accepted, Elev: 500ft/152m, Tel: 864-447-8267, Nearest town: Calhoun Falls. GPS: 34.103225, -82.623197

25 • B1 | Sadlers Creek SP

Total sites: 66, RV sites: 52, Elec sites: 52, Water at site, Flush toilet, Free showers, RV dump, Tents: $15-24/RVs: $20-46, Dynamic pricing/fees can vary from day to day, Stay limit: 14 days, Open all year, Max Length: 40ft, Reservations accepted, Elev: 692ft/211m, Tel: 864-226-8950, Nearest town: Anderson. GPS: 34.421726, -82.818255

26 • B2 | Baker Creek SP

Total sites: 50, RV sites: 50, Elec sites: 50, Water at site, Flush toilet, Free showers, RV dump, Tent & RV camping: $21-30, Dynamic pricing/fees can vary from day to day, Open Mar-Sep, Max Length: 40ft, Reservations accepted, Elev: 381ft/116m, Tel: 864-443-2457, Nearest town: McCormick. GPS: 33.879855, -82.365099

27 • B2 | Dreher Island SP

Total sites: 112, RV sites: 97, Elec sites: 97, Water at site, Flush toilet, Free showers, RV dump, Tents: $35-45/RVs: $40-50, Dynamic pricing/fees can vary from day to day, Stay limit: 14 days, Open all year, Max Length: 45ft, Reservations accepted, Elev: 358ft/109m, Tel: 803-364-4152, Nearest town: Prosperity. GPS: 34.088444, -81.409278

28 • B2 | Hamilton Branch SP

Total sites: 184, RV sites: 173, Elec sites: 173, Water at site, Flush toilet, Free showers, RV dump, Tents: $20/RVs: $23-50, Dynamic pricing/fees can vary from day to day, Stay limit: 14 days, Open all year, Max Length: 40ft, Reservations accepted, Elev: 410ft/125m, Tel: 864-333-2223, Nearest town: Plum Branch. GPS: 33.753890, -82.218060

29 • B2 | Hickory Knob SRP

Total sites: 44, RV sites: 44, Elec sites: 44, Water at site, Flush toilet, Free showers, RV dump, Tent & RV camping: $21-24, Also cabins, Dynamic pricing/fees can vary from day to day, Stay limit: 14 days, Open all year, Max Length: 30ft, Elev: 420ft/128m, Tel: 864-391-2450, Nearest town: McCormick. GPS: 33.883063, -82.423952

30 • B2 | Lake Greenwood SP

Total sites: 125, RV sites: 125, Elec sites: 125, Water at site, Flush toilet, Free showers, RV dump, Tent & RV camping: $20-45, Full hookups sites, Dynamic pricing/fees can vary from day to day, Stay limit: 14 days, Open all year, Max Length: 40ft, Reservations accepted, Elev: 505ft/154m, Tel: 864-543-3535, Nearest town: Ninety Six. GPS: 34.197426, -81.950133

31 • B2 | Poinsett SP

Total sites: 50, RV sites: 24, Elec sites: 24, Water at site, Flush toilet, Free showers, RV dump, Tents: $14-23/RVs: $18-45, Also cabins, Dynamic pricing/fees can vary from day to day, Stay limit: 14 days, Open all year, Max Length: 40ft, Reservations accepted, Elev: 236ft/72m, Tel: 803-494-8177, Nearest town: Wedgefield. GPS: 33.806701, -80.542226

32 • B2 | Sesquicentennial SP

Total sites: 84, RV sites: 84, Elec sites: 84, Water at site, Flush toilet, Free showers, RV dump, Tent & RV camping: $25-40, Also group sites & cabins, Group site available, Dynamic pricing/fees can vary from day to day, Stay limit: 14 days, Open all year, Max Length: 35ft, Reservations accepted, Elev: 289ft/88m, Tel: 803-788-2706, Nearest town: Columbia. GPS: 34.087298, -80.910397

33 • B3 | Lake Wateree SP

Total sites: 72, RV sites: 72, Elec sites: 72, Water at site, Flush toilet, Free showers, RV dump, Tent & RV camping: $25-65, Dynamic pricing/fees can vary from day to day, Stay limit: 14 days, Open all year, Max Length: 40ft, Elev: 256ft/78m, Tel: 803-482-6401, Nearest town: Winnsboro. GPS: 34.435887, -80.864102

34 • B4 | Lee SP

Total sites: 48, RV sites: 48, Elec sites: 48, Water at site, Flush toilet, Free showers, RV dump, Tent & RV camping: $20-35, 23 equestrian sites, Dynamic pricing/fees can vary from day to day, Stay limit: 14 days, Open all year, Max Length: 36ft, Reservations accepted, Elev: 194ft/59m, Tel: 803-428-5307, Nearest town: Bishopville. GPS: 34.199379, -80.186717

35 • B5 | Little Pee Dee SP

Total sites: 50, RV sites: 32, Elec sites: 32, Water at site, Flush toilet, Free showers, RV dump, Tents: $13-20/RVs: $18-30, Dynamic pricing/fees can vary from day to day, Stay limit: 14 days, Open all year, Reservations accepted, Elev: 134ft/41m, Tel: 843-774-8872, Nearest town: Dillon. GPS: 34.331744, -79.264856

36 • B5 | Myrtle Beach SP

Total sites: 270, RV sites: 270, Elec sites: 270, Water at site, Flush toilet, Free showers, RV dump, Tent & RV camping: $24-60, Also cabins, 66 Full hookups, Dynamic pricing/fees can vary from day to day, Stay limit: 14 days, Open all year, Max Length: 40ft, Reservations accepted, Elev: 15ft/5m, Tel: 843-238-5325, Nearest town: Myrtle Beach. GPS: 33.653920, -78.926530

37 • C2 | Aiken SP - Main CG

Total sites: 25, RV sites: 25, Elec sites: 25, Water at site, Flush toilet, Free showers, RV dump, Tent & RV camping: $22-30, Group site for youth/church use: $15-$40, Stay limit: 14 days, Max Length: 55ft, Reservations accepted, Elev: 312ft/95m, Tel: 803-649-2857, Nearest town: Windsor. GPS: 33.553493, -81.496999

38 • C3 | Barnwell SP

Total sites: 25, RV sites: 25, Elec sites: 25, Water at site, Flush toilet, Free showers, RV dump, Tent & RV camping: $19-28, Also cabins, 8 Full hookups, Dynamic pricing/fees can vary from day to day, Stay limit: 14 days, Open all year, Max Length: 36ft, Reservations accepted, Elev: 302ft/92m, Tel: 803-284-2212, Nearest town: Blackville. GPS: 33.334768, -81.307536

39 • C3 | Colleton SP

Total sites: 25, RV sites: 25, Elec sites: 25, Water at site, Flush toilet, Free showers, RV dump, Tent & RV camping: $23-42, Dynamic pricing/fees can vary from day to day, Stay limit: 14 days, Open all year, Max Length: 40ft, Reservations accepted, Elev: 144ft/44m, Tel: 843-538-8206, Nearest town: Walterboro. GPS: 33.062744, -80.615967

40 • C3 | Givhans Ferry SP

Total sites: 25, RV sites: 13, Elec sites: 25, Water at site, Flush toilet, Free showers, RV dump, Tents: $17-32/RVs: $22-47, Also cabins, 6 Full hookups, Dynamic pricing/fees can vary from day to day, Stay limit: 14 days, Open all year, Max Length: 40ft, Reservations accepted, Elev: 79ft/24m, Tel: 843-873-0692, Nearest town: Ridgeville. GPS: 33.030633, -80.387459

41 • C3 | Santee SP - Cypress View

Total sites: 50, RV sites: 50, Elec sites: 50, Water at site, Flush toilet, Free showers, RV dump, Tent & RV camping: $18-45, Also cabins, Dynamic pricing/fees can vary from day to day, Stay limit: 14 days, Open all year, Max Length: 40ft, Reservations accepted, Elev: 112ft/34m, Tel: 803-854-2408, Nearest town: Santee. GPS: 33.549617, -80.496795

42 • C3 | Santee SP - Lakeshore

Total sites: 108, RV sites: 108, Elec sites: 108, Water at site, Flush toilet, Free showers, RV dump, Tent & RV camping: $18-45, Dynamic pricing/fees can vary from day to day, Stay limit: 14 days, Open all year, Max Length: 40ft, Reservations accepted, Elev: 82ft/25m, Tel: 803-854-2408, Nearest town: Santee. GPS: 33.508797, -80.471575

43 • C5 | Huntington Beach SP

Total sites: 137, RV sites: 131, Elec sites: 131, Water at site, Flush toilet, Free showers, RV dump, Tent & RV camping: $38-65, 24 Full hookups, Dynamic pricing/fees can vary from day to day, Stay limit: 14 days, Open all year, Max Length: 40ft, Reservations accepted, Elev: 15ft/5m, Tel: 843-237-4440, Nearest town: Murrels Inlet. GPS: 33.506271, -79.063941

44 • D3 | Hunting Island SP

Total sites: 181, RV sites: 171, Elec sites: 171, Water at site, Flush toilet, Free showers, RV dump, Tents: $28-48/RVs: $36-65, Dynamic pricing/fees can vary from day to day, Stay limit: 14 days, Open all year, Max Length: 40ft, Reservations accepted, Elev: 76ft/23m, Tel: 843-838-2011, Nearest town: Beaufort. GPS: 32.369873, -80.444580

45 • D4 | Edisto Beach SP - Beach

Total sites: 75, RV sites: 70, Elec sites: 63, Water at site, Flush toilet, Free showers, RV dump, Tent & RV camping: $38-72, Dynamic pricing/fees can vary from day to day, Stay limit: 14 days, Open all year, Max Length: 40ft, Elev: 10ft/3m, Tel: , Nearest town: Edisto Beach. GPS: 32.507199, -80.292355

46 • D4 | Edisto Beach SP - Live Oak

Total sites: 55, RV sites: 50, Elec sites: 50, Water at site, Flush toilet, Free showers, RV dump, Tent & RV camping: $38-72, Also walk-to sites, Dynamic pricing/fees can vary from day to day, Stay limit: 14 days, Open all year, Max Length: 40ft, Elev: 56ft/17m, Tel: 843-869-2156, Nearest town: Edisto Beach. GPS: 32.511774, -80.301458

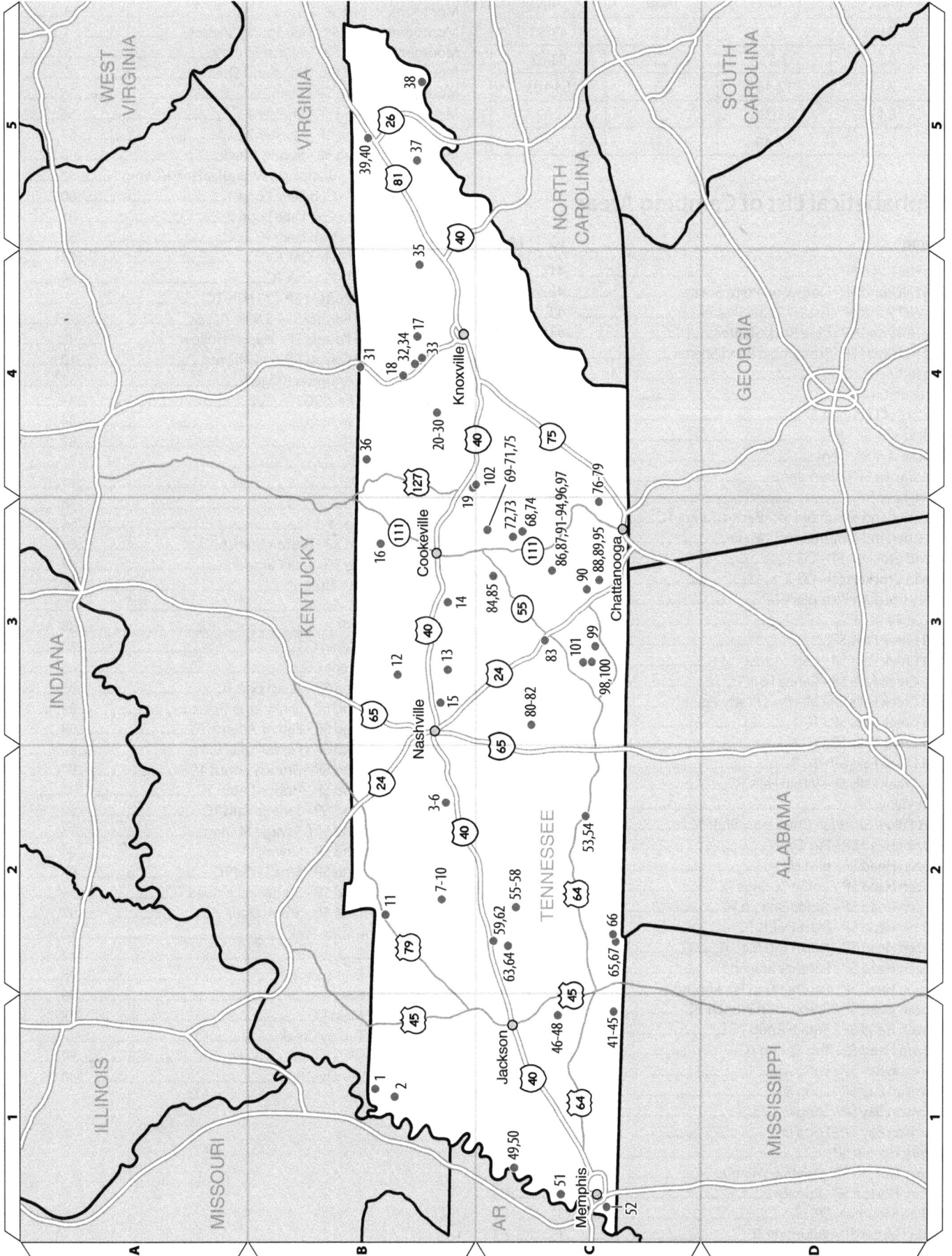

Tennessee

WEST VIRGINIA

VIRGINIA

NORTH CAROLINA

SOUTH CAROLINA

GEORGIA

KENTUCKY

INDIANA

ILLINOIS

MISSOURI

TENNESSEE

ALABAMA

MISSISSIPPI

AR

Knoxville

Cookeville

Nashville

Chattanooga

Jackson

Memphis

26

81

40

38

39,40

37

35

31

18

32,34

17

33

36

20-30

127

40

75

111

16

19

102

69-71,75

72,73

68,74

111

86,87,91-94,96,97

88,89,95

90

76-79

14

84,85

55

40

13

83

101

99

98,100

12

24

15

65

80-82

65

24

3-6

40

53,54

7-10

55-58

64

11

59,62

66

79

63,64

65,67

45

46-48

41-45

45

1

2

40

64

49,50

51

52

Map	ID	Map	ID
B1	1-2	C1	41-52
B2	3-11	C2	53-67
B3	12-16	C3	68-101
B4	17-36	C4	102
B5	37-40		

Alphabetical List of Camping Areas

1 • B1 | Reelfoot Lake SP - Airpark

Total sites: 24, RV sites: 14, Elec sites: 14, Water at site, Flush toilet, Free showers, RV dump, Tents: $16-18/RVs: $26-28, Also cabins, Open all year, Max Length: 35ft, Reservations accepted, Elev: 282ft/86m, Tel: 731-253-9652, Nearest town: Tiptonville. GPS: 36.474682, -89.343597

2 • B1 | Reelfoot Lake SP - South

Total sites: 86, RV sites: 86, Elec sites: 86, Water at site, Flush toilet, Free showers, RV dump, Tent & RV camping: $26-36, Also cabins, Open all year, Max Length: 60ft, Reservations accepted, Elev: 305ft/93m, Tel: 731-253-9652, Nearest town: Tiptonville. GPS: 36.354427, -89.398029

3 • B2 | Montgomery Bell SP

Total sites: 109, RV sites: 87, Elec sites: 87, Water at site, Flush toilet, Free showers, RV dump, Tents: $16-18/RVs: $27-37, Also cabins, 40 Full hookups, Generator hours: 0600-2200, Open all year, Max Length: 60ft, Reservations accepted, Elev: 663ft/202m, Tel: 615-797-9052, Nearest town: Burns. GPS: 36.096875, -87.287008

4 • B2 | Montgomery Bell SP - Hall Spring Shelter

Dispersed sites, No water, Vault/pit toilet, Hike-to shelter: $9-10, No tents - use shelter, Permit required, Reservations accepted, Elev: 742ft/226m, Tel: 615-797-9052, Nearest town: Burns. GPS: 36.073543, -87.290988

5 • B2 | Montgomery Bell SP - Wildcat Shelter

Dispersed sites, No water, Vault/pit toilet, Hike-to shelter: $9-10, No tents - use shelter, Permit required, Reservations accepted, Elev: 727ft/222m, Tel: 615-797-9052, Nearest town: Burns. GPS: 36.101975, -87.266166

6 • B2 | Montgomery Bell SP - Woodland Shelter

Dispersed sites, No water, Vault/pit toilet, Hike-to shelter: $9-10, No tents - use shelter, Permit required, Reservations accepted, Elev: 788ft/240m, Tel: 615-797-9052, Nearest town: Burns. GPS: 36.076355, -87.274701

7 • B2 | Nathan Bedford Forrest SP - 20 Mile TC

Dispersed sites, No water, Vault/pit toilet, Tents only: $9-10, Hike-in, 4.5 mi, Open all year, Reservations accepted, Elev: 630ft/192m, Tel: 800-714-7305, Nearest town: Eva. GPS: 36.120159, -87.960187

8 • B2 | Nathan Bedford Forrest SP - 5 Mile TC

Dispersed sites, No water, Vault/pit toilet, Tents only: $9-10, Hike-in, 2.95 mi, Open all year, Reservations accepted, Elev: 546ft/166m, Tel: 800-714-7305, Nearest town: Eva. GPS: 36.107091, -87.969788

9 • B2 | Nathan Bedford Forrest SP - Happy Hollow

Total sites: 37, RV sites: 37, Elec sites: 37, Water at site, Flush toilet, Free showers, RV dump, Tent & RV camping: $24, Also cabins, Open all year, Max Length: 50ft, Reservations accepted, Elev: 525ft/160m, Tel: 800-714-7305, Nearest town: Eva. GPS: 36.092919, -87.986874

10 • B2 | Nathan Bedford Forrest SP - Lakefront

Total sites: 13, RV sites: 13, Central water, Vault/pit toilet, Tent & RV camping: $16-18, Open all year, Max Length: 25ft, Reservations accepted, Elev: 379ft/116m, Tel: 800-714-7305, Nearest town: Eva. GPS: 36.087947, -87.971429

11 • B2 | Paris Landing SP

Total sites: 57, RV sites: 57, Elec sites: 39, Water at site, Flush toilet, Free showers, RV dump, Tents: $16-18/RVs: $26-32, Also cabins, Open all year, Max Length: 60ft, Reservations accepted, Elev: 404ft/123m, Tel: 800-250-8614, Nearest town: Buchanan. GPS: 36.440432, -88.086749

12 • B3 | Bledsoe Creek SP

Total sites: 77, RV sites: 58, Elec sites: 58, Water at site, Flush toilet, Free showers, RV dump, Tents: $16-17/RVs: $26-37, Open all year, Max Length: 40ft, Reservations accepted, Elev: 495ft/151m, Tel: 615-452-3706, Nearest town: Gallatin. GPS: 36.375576, -86.355306

13 • B3 | Cedars of Lebanon SP

Total sites: 117, RV sites: 87, Elec sites: 117, Water at site, Flush toilet, Free showers, RV dump, Tent & RV camping: $26-35, Stay limit: 14 days, Open all year, Max Length: 40ft, Reservations accepted, Elev: 666ft/203m, Tel: 800-713-5180, Nearest town: Lebanon. GPS: 36.083092, -86.321663

14 • B3 | Edgar Evins SP

Total sites: 69, RV sites: 60, Elec sites: 60, Water at site, Flush toilet, Free showers, RV dump, Tents: $12-14/RVs: $26-36, Also walk-to sites/cabins, 9 walk-to sites, Open all year, Max Length: 40ft, Reservations accepted, Elev: 692ft/211m, Tel: 800-250-8619, Nearest town: Silver Point. GPS: 36.081219, -85.832188

15 • B3 | Long Hunter SP - Volunteer TC

Total sites: 2, No water, No toilets, Tents only: $9-12, Hike-in, 6 mi, Open all year, Reservations required, Elev: 530ft/162m, Tel: 615-885-2422, Nearest town: Hermitage. GPS: 36.124146, -86.556634

16 • B3 | Standing Stone State Park

Total sites: 36, RV sites: 36, Elec sites: 36, Water at site, Flush toilet, Free showers, RV dump, Tent & RV camping: $26-35, Also cabins, 1 Full hookups, Vehicles over 30' must enter via Hwy 52, Stay limit: 14 days, Open all year, Max Length: 45ft, Reservations accepted, Elev: 978ft/298m, Tel: 931-823-6347, Nearest town: Hilham. GPS: 36.474905, -85.412234

17 • B4 | Big Ridge SP

Total sites: 50, RV sites: 50, Elec sites: 50, Water at site, Flush toilet, Free showers, RV dump, Tent & RV camping: $26-29, Also cabins, Open all year, Max Length: 35ft, Reservations accepted, Elev: 1079ft/329m, Tel: 865-992-5523, Nearest town: Maynardville. GPS: 36.241489, -83.933542

18 • B4 | Cove Lake SP

Total sites: 100, RV sites: 100, Elec sites: 100, Water at site, Flush toilet, Free showers, RV dump, Tent & RV camping: $26-31, Open all year, Max Length: 50ft, Reservations accepted, Elev: 1043ft/318m, Tel: 423-566-9701, Nearest town: Caryville. GPS: 36.314469, -84.213807

19 • B4 | Cumberland Mountain SP - Back-country TC

Dispersed sites, No water, Tents only: $9-10, Hike-in, Open all year, Reservations accepted, Elev: 1813ft/553m, Tel: 800-250-8618, Nearest town: Crossville. GPS: 35.916683, -85.019652

20 • B4 | Frozen Head SP - Big Cove

Total sites: 20, RV sites: 20, Central water, Flush toilet, Free showers, No RV dump, Tent & RV camping: $16-20, Group site: $32, Open Mar-Oct, Max Length: 32ft, Reservations required, Elev: 1512ft/461m, Tel: 423-346-3318, Nearest town: Wartburg. GPS: 36.132646, -84.497027

21 • B4 | Frozen Head SP - Bird Mt TC

Dispersed sites, No water, No toilets, Tents only: $9-10, Hike-in, Registration required, Elev: 2937ft/895m, Tel: 931-456-6259. GPS: 36.149484, -84.488193

22 • B4 | Frozen Head SP - Coffin Springs TC

Dispersed sites, No water, Tents only: $9-10, Hike-in, Reservations required, Elev: 2941ft/896m, Tel: 423-346-3318, Nearest town: Wartburg. GPS: 36.150841, -84.449902

23 • B4 | Frozen Head SP - Judge Branch TC

Dispersed sites, No water, Tents only: $9-10, Hike-in, Reservations required, Elev: 1573ft/479m, Tel: 423-346-3318, Nearest town: Wartburg. GPS: 36.124841, -84.488794

24 • B4 | Frozen Head SP - Mart Fields TC

Dispersed sites, No water, Tents only: $9-10, Hike-in, Reservations required, Elev: 3008ft/917m, Tel: 423-346-3318, Nearest town: Wartburg. GPS: 36.107478, -84.470671

25 • B4 | Frozen Head SP - North Old Mac TC

Dispersed sites, No water, Tents only: $9-10, Hike-in, Reservations required, Elev: 2405ft/733m, Tel: 423-346-3318, Nearest town: Wartburg. GPS: 36.134499, -84.474242

26 • B4 | Frozen Head SP - Panther Branch TC

Dispersed sites, No water, Tents only: $9-10, Hike-in, Reservations required, Elev: 1821ft/555m, Tel: 423-346-3318, Nearest town: Wartburg. GPS: 36.139491, -84.472917

27 • B4 | Frozen Head SP - Panther Gap Rockhouse TC

Dispersed sites, No water, Tents only: $9-10, Hike-in, Reservations required, Elev: 2806ft/855m, Tel: 423-346-3318, Nearest town: Wartburg. GPS: 36.129191, -84.457139

28 • B4 | Frozen Head SP - Spicewood Branch TC

Dispersed sites, No water, Tents only: $9-10, Hike-in, Reservations required, Elev: 1672ft/510m, Tel: 423-346-3318, Nearest town: Wartburg. GPS: 36.118757, -84.488974

29 • B4 | Frozen Head SP - Squire Knob TC

Dispersed sites, No water, Tents only: $9-10, Hike-in, Reservations required, Elev: 3148ft/960m, Tel: 423-346-3318, Nearest town: Wartburg. GPS: 36.152834, -84.457437

30 • B4 | Frozen Head SP - Tub Spring TC

Dispersed sites, No water, Tents only: $9-10, Hike-in, Reservations required, Elev: 3063ft/934m, Tel: 423-346-3318, Nearest town: Wartburg. GPS: 36.126571, -84.458388

31 • B4 | Indian Mountain SP

Total sites: 47, RV sites: 47, Elec sites: 47, Water at site, Flush toilet, Free showers, RV dump, Tent & RV camping: $34-36, Open all year, Reservations accepted, Elev: 968ft/295m, Tel: 423-784-7958, Nearest town: Jellico. GPS: 36.589465, -84.139858

32 • B4 | Norris Dam SP - Andrews Ridge TC

Dispersed sites, No water, Vault/pit toilet, Tents only: $8, Hike-in, Open all year, Reservations accepted, Elev: 1274ft/388m, Tel: 865-426-7461, Nearest town: Lake City. GPS: 36.255659, -84.119699

33 • B4 | Norris Dam SP - East CG

Total sites: 35, RV sites: 25, Elec sites: 25, Water at site, Flush toilet, Free showers, RV dump, Tents: $15/RVs: $26-29, Open all year, Max Length: 40ft, Reservations accepted, Elev: 1201ft/366m, Tel: 865-426-7461, Nearest town: Lake City. GPS: 36.221905, -84.082989

34 • B4 | Norris Dam SP - West CG

Total sites: 50, RV sites: 50, Elec sites: 50, Water at site, Flush toilet, Free showers, RV dump, Tent & RV camping: $27-29, Open all year, Max Length: 40ft, Reservations accepted, Elev: 1414ft/431m, Tel: 865-426-7461, Nearest town: Lake City. GPS: 36.242175, -84.120469

35 • B4 | Panther Creek SP

Total sites: 50, RV sites: 50, Elec sites: 50, Water at site, Flush toilet, Free showers, RV dump, Tent & RV camping: $28-38, 8 Full hookups, Stay limit: 14 days, Open all year, Max Length: 65ft, Reservations accepted, Elev: 1155ft/352m, Tel: 423-587-7046, Nearest town: Morristown. GPS: 36.214395, -83.402721

36 • B4 | Pickett CCC SP

Total sites: 27, RV sites: 27, Elec sites: 20, Water at site, Flush toilet, Free showers, RV dump, Tents: $16-18/RVs: $22-24, Also cabins, Dark Sky park, Stay limit: 14 days, Open all year, Max Length: 24ft, Reservations accepted, Elev: 1600ft/488m, Tel: 931-879-5821, Nearest town: Jamestown. GPS: 36.552108, -84.798245

37 • B5 | Davy Crockett Birthplace SP

Total sites: 88, RV sites: 71, Elec sites: 71, Water at site, Flush toilet, Free showers, RV dump, Tents: $16-18/RVs: $26-36, 54 Full hookups, Stay limit: 14-28 days, Open all year, Max Length: 40ft, Reservations accepted, Elev: 1404ft/428m, Tel: 423-257-2167, Nearest town: Limestone. GPS: 36.210001, -82.659001

38 • B5 | Roan Mountain SP

Total sites: 106, RV sites: 86, Elec sites: 86, Water at site, Flush toilet, Free showers, RV dump, Tents: $17-19/RVs: $26-32, 4 group sites, Open all year, Max Length: 70ft, Reservations accepted, Elev: 2887ft/880m, Tel: 423-772-0190, Nearest town: Roan Mountain. GPS: 36.163555, -82.098615

39 • B5 | Warrior's Path SP

Total sites: 94, RV sites: 94, Elec sites: 94, Water at site, Flush toilet, Free showers, RV dump, Tent & RV camping: $26-31, Stay limit: 14 days, Open all year, Max Length: 40ft, Reservations accepted,

Elev: 1312ft/400m, Tel: 423-239-8531, Nearest town: Kingsport. GPS: 36.497534, -82.480508

40 • B5 | Warrior's Path SP - Overflow

Total sites: 40, RV sites: 40, Central water, Flush toilet, Free showers, RV dump, Tent & RV camping: $26, Stay limit: 14 days, Open May-Sep, Max Length: 40ft, Reservations accepted, Elev: 1320ft/402m, Tel: 423-239-8531, Nearest town: Kingsport. GPS: 36.498472, -82.483466

41 • C1 | Big Hill Pond SP

Total sites: 28, RV sites: 28, Central water, Flush toilet, Free showers, No RV dump, Tent & RV camping: $16-17, Generator hours: 0800-2200, Open all year, Reservations accepted, Elev: 535ft/163m, Tel: 731-645-7967, Nearest town: Pocahontas. GPS: 35.065938, -88.722718

42 • C1 | Big Hill Pond SP - Dogwood Point Shelter

Dispersed sites, No water, Vault/pit toilet, Hike-to shelter: Free, No pets, Open all year, Reservations not accepted, Elev: 474ft/144m, Tel: 731-645-7967, Nearest town: Pocahontas. GPS: 35.023112, -88.740573

43 • C1 | Big Hill Pond SP - Grassy Point Shelter

Dispersed sites, No water, Vault/pit toilet, Hike-to shelter: Free, No pets, Open all year, Reservations not accepted, Elev: 516ft/157m, Tel: 731-645-7967, Nearest town: Pocahontas. GPS: 35.060853, -88.731985

44 • C1 | Big Hill Pond SP - Pipe Rock Shelter

Dispersed sites, No water, Vault/pit toilet, Hike-to shelter: Free, No pets, Open all year, Reservations not accepted, Elev: 517ft/158m, Tel: 731-645-7967, Nearest town: Pocahontas. GPS: 35.032668, -88.730669

45 • C1 | Big Hill Pond SP - Tuscumbia Bend Shelter

Dispersed sites, No water, Vault/pit toilet, Hike-to shelter: Free, No pets, Open all year, Reservations not accepted, Elev: 464ft/141m, Tel: 731-645-7967, Nearest town: Pocahontas. GPS: 35.052388, -88.747959

46 • C1 | Chickasaw SP - RV

Total sites: 52, RV sites: 52, Elec sites: 52, Water at site, Flush toilet, Free showers, Tents: $27-36/RVs: $25-35, Also cabins, 22 Full hookups, Open all year, Max Length: 50ft, Reservations accepted, Elev: 538ft/164m, Tel: 800-458-1752, Nearest town: Henderson. GPS: 35.390437, -88.782405

47 • C1 | Chickasaw SP - Tent

Total sites: 29, RV sites: 0, Central water, Flush toilet, Free showers, No RV dump, Tents only: $17-18, Open all year, Max Length: 50ft, Reservations accepted, Elev: 538ft/164m, Tel: 800-458-1752, Nearest town: Henderson. GPS: 35.387273, -88.768933

48 • C1 | Chickasaw SP - Wrangler

Total sites: 32, RV sites: 32, Elec sites: 32, Water at site, Flush toilet, Free showers, Tent & RV camping: $27-28, Open all year, Max Length: 50ft, Reservations accepted, Elev: 522ft/159m, Tel: 800-458-1752, Nearest town: Henderson. GPS: 35.388782, -88.773764

49 • C1 | Fort Pillow SP

Total sites: 30, RV sites: 30, Elec sites: 21, Central water, Flush toilet, Free showers, No RV dump, Tents: $12-13/RVs: $16-29, Open all year, Max Length: 60ft, Reservations accepted, Elev: 407ft/124m, Tel: 731-738-5581, Nearest town: Henning. GPS: 35.627539, -89.858013

50 • C1 | Fort Pillow SP - Blue Chickasaw Bluff TC

Dispersed sites, No water, Vault/pit toilet, Tents only: $9-10, Hike-in, Open all year, Reservations accepted, Elev: 359ft/109m, Tel: 731-738-5581, Nearest town: Henning. GPS: 35.622673, -89.866489

51 • C1 | Meeman-Shelby Forest SP

Total sites: 49, RV sites: 49, Elec sites: 49, Water at site, Flush toilet, Free showers, RV dump, Tent & RV camping: $27-30, Stay limit: 14 days, Open all year, Max Length: 40ft, Reservations accepted, Elev: 404ft/123m, Tel: 800-471-5293, Nearest town: Millington. GPS: 35.345762, -90.045486

52 • C1 | T.O. Fuller SP

Total sites: 45, RV sites: 45, Elec sites: 45, Water at site, Flush toilet, Free showers, RV dump, Tent & RV camping: $26-28, Open all year, Max Length: 85ft, Reservations accepted, Elev: 318ft/97m, Tel: 901-543-7581, Nearest town: Memphis. GPS: 35.059288, -90.127296

53 • C2 | David Crockett SP - CG 1

Total sites: 55, RV sites: 45, Elec sites: 45, Water at site, Flush toilet, Free showers, RV dump, Tents: $12-13/RVs: $26-36, Also cabins, Open Mar-Nov, Max Length: 50ft, Reservations accepted, Elev: 840ft/256m, Tel: 931-762-9408, Nearest town: Lawrenceburg. GPS: 35.247567, -87.348945

54 • C2 | David Crockett SP - CG 2

Total sites: 53, RV sites: 52, Elec sites: 52, Water at site, Flush toilet, Free showers, RV dump, Tent & RV camping: $34-37, Also cabins, Open all year, Max Length: 52ft, Reservations accepted, Elev: 988ft/301m, Tel: 931-762-9408, Nearest town: Lawrenceburg. GPS: 35.259049, -87.362196

55 • C2 | Mousetail Landing SP - Main

Total sites: 25, RV sites: 25, Elec sites: 19, Water at site, Flush toilet, Free showers, RV dump, Tents: $16-18/RVs: $26-30, Open all year, Max Length: 37ft, Reservations accepted, Elev: 640ft/195m, Tel: 731-847-0841, Nearest town: Linden. GPS: 35.665578, -88.004719

56 • C2 | Mousetail Landing SP - Shelter 1

Dispersed sites, No water, Vault/pit toilet, Hike-to shelter: $8, Permit required, Reservations not accepted, Elev: 464ft/141m, Nearest town: Linden. GPS: 35.675693, -88.003257

57 • C2 | Mousetail Landing SP - Shelter 2

Dispersed sites, No water, Vault/pit toilet, Hike-to shelter: $8, Permit required, Reservations not accepted, Elev: 520ft/158m, Nearest town: Linden. GPS: 35.676717, -88.014228

58 • C2 | Mousetail Landing SP - Spring Creek

Total sites: 21, RV sites: 5, Central water, Tent & RV camping:

$16-18, Open all year, Max Length: 37ft, Reservations accepted, Elev: 368ft/112m, Tel: 731-847-0841, Nearest town: Linden. GPS: 35.651211, -88.019322

59 • C2 | Natchez Trace SP - Bucksnort Wrangler Horse Camp

Total sites: 62, RV sites: 62, Elec sites: 62, Water at site, Flush toilet, Free showers, RV dump, Tent & RV camping: $26-27, Also cabins, Open all year, Max Length: 20ft, Reservations accepted, Elev: 699ft/213m, Tel: 800-250-8616, Nearest town: Wildersville. GPS: 35.792247, -88.272047

60 • C2 | Natchez Trace SP - Cub Lake Loop 1

Total sites: 23, RV sites: 23, Elec sites: 23, Water at site, Flush toilet, Free showers, RV dump, Tent & RV camping: $26-29, Also cabins, Open all year, Max Length: 25ft, Reservations accepted, Elev: 518ft/158m, Tel: 800-250-8616, Nearest town: Wildersville. GPS: 35.778391, -88.253311

61 • C2 | Natchez Trace SP - Cub Lake Loop 2

Total sites: 46, RV sites: 46, Central water, Flush toilet, Free showers, RV dump, Tent & RV camping: $16-17, Also cabins, Open May-Oct, Max Length: 20ft, Reservations accepted, Elev: 508ft/155m, Tel: 800-250-8616, Nearest town: Wildersville. GPS: 35.774528, -88.255038

62 • C2 | Natchez Trace SP - Cub Lake TC

Dispersed sites, No water, Vault/pit toilet, Tents only: $9-10, Hike-in, Open May-Oct, Reservations accepted, Elev: 549ft/167m, Tel: 800-250-8616, Nearest town: Wildersville. GPS: 35.782322, -88.246766

63 • C2 | Natchez Trace SP - Pin Oak RV

Total sites: 77, RV sites: 77, Elec sites: 77, Water at site, Flush toilet, Free showers, RV dump, Tent & RV camping: $34-37, Also cabins, 77 Full hookups, Open all year, Max Length: 80ft, Reservations accepted, Elev: 468ft/143m, Tel: 800-250-8616, Nearest town: Wildersville. GPS: 35.692215, -88.290981

64 • C2 | Natchez Trace SP - Pin Oak TC

Dispersed sites, No water, Vault/pit toilet, Tents only: $9-10, Hike-in, Open May-Oct, Reservations accepted, Elev: 558ft/170m, Tel: 800-250-8616, Nearest town: Wildersville. GPS: 35.714039, -88.286353

65 • C2 | Pickwick Landing SP

Total sites: 48, RV sites: 48, Elec sites: 48, Water at site, Flush toilet, Free showers, RV dump, Tent & RV camping: $22-26, Also cabins, Open all year, Max Length: 70ft, Reservations accepted, Elev: 495ft/151m, Tel: 731-689-3129, Nearest town: Savannah. GPS: 35.053788, -88.225721

66 • C2 | Pickwick Landing SP - Bruton Branch

Total sites: 33, RV sites: 33, Central water, Flush toilet, Free showers, No RV dump, Tent & RV camping: $16-20, Open Apr-Oct, Max Length: 50ft, Reservations accepted, Elev: 425ft/130m, Tel: 800-250-8615, Nearest town: Savannah. GPS: 35.069047, -88.190483

67 • C2 | Pickwick Landing SP - Trail Camps

Total sites: 4, RV sites: 0, No water, Tents only: $9-10, Walk-to sites, .3 mi-.5 mi, Open Apr-Oct, Reservations accepted, Elev: 509ft/155m, Tel: 800-250-8615, Nearest town: Savannah. GPS: 35.057831, -88.227465

68 • C3 | Fall Creek Falls SP

Total sites: 238, RV sites: 222, Elec sites: 222, Water at site, Flush toilet, Free showers, RV dump, Tents: $15/RVs: $25-32, Also cabins, 92 Full hookups, Open all year, Max Length: 65ft, Reservations accepted, Elev: 1706ft/520m, Tel: 800-250-8611, Nearest town: Pikeville. GPS: 35.658151, -85.350162

69 • C3 | Fall Creek Falls SP - Cable Crossing TC

Total sites: 2, RV sites: 0, No water, Tents only: $9-10, Hike-in, 1.5 mi, Open all year, Reservations accepted, Elev: 1626ft/496m, Tel: 800-250-8611, Nearest town: Pikeville. GPS: 35.850147, -85.301908

70 • C3 | Fall Creek Falls SP - Caney Fork TC

Total sites: 4, RV sites: 0, No water, Tents only: $9-12, Hike-in, 4.5 mi, Open all year, Reservations accepted, Elev: 935ft/285m, Tel: 800-250-8611, Nearest town: Pikeville. GPS: 35.833984, -85.326731

71 • C3 | Fall Creek Falls SP - Martha's Pretty Point TC

Total sites: 4, RV sites: 0, No water, Tents only: $9-10, Hike-in, Open all year, Reservations accepted, Elev: 1768ft/539m, Tel: 800-250-8611, Nearest town: Pikeville. GPS: 35.848038, -85.307308

72 • C3 | Fall Creek Falls SP - TC 1

Dispersed sites, No water, Vault/pit toilet, Tents only: $9-10, Hike-in, Open all year, Elev: 1700ft/518m, Tel: 800-250-8611, Nearest town: Pikeville. GPS: 35.693735, -85.353838

73 • C3 | Fall Creek Falls SP - TC 2

Dispersed sites, No water, Vault/pit toilet, Tents only: $9-10, Hike-in, Open all year, Elev: 1759ft/536m, Tel: 800-250-8611, Nearest town: Pikeville. GPS: 35.689906, -85.385415

74 • C3 | Fall Creek Falls SP - TC 3

Dispersed sites, No water, Vault/pit toilet, Tents only: $9-10, Hike-in, Open all year, Elev: 1670ft/509m, Tel: 800-250-8611, Nearest town: Pikeville. GPS: 35.628598, -85.330641

75 • C3 | Fall Creek Falls SP - Virgin Falls TC

Total sites: 3, RV sites: 0, No water, Tents only: $9-10, Hike-in, 4.3 mi, Open all year, Reservations accepted, Elev: 1164ft/355m, Tel: 800-250-8611, Nearest town: Pikeville. GPS: 35.838787, -85.330817

76 • C3 | Harrison Bay SP - Loop A

Total sites: 47, RV sites: 47, Elec sites: 47, Water at site, Flush toilet, Free showers, RV dump, Tent & RV camping: $27-34, Max Length: 65ft, Reservations accepted, Elev: 700ft/213m, Tel: 423-344-6214, Nearest town: Harrison. GPS: 35.172726, -85.126965

77 • C3 | Harrison Bay SP - Loop B

Total sites: 48, RV sites: 48, Elec sites: 48, Water at site, Flush toilet, Free showers, RV dump, Tent & RV camping: $22-24, Max Length: 65ft, Reservations accepted, Elev: 713ft/217m, Tel: 423-344-6214, Nearest town: Harrison. GPS: 35.170613, -85.124233

78 • C3 | Harrison Bay SP - Loop C

Total sites: 40, RV sites: 40, Elec sites: 40, Water at site, Flush toilet, Free showers, RV dump, Tent & RV camping: $26-29, Max Length: 65ft, Reservations accepted, Elev: 743ft/226m, Tel: 423-344-6214, Nearest town: Harrison. GPS: 35.168741, -85.125819

79 • C3 | Harrison Bay SP - Loop D

Total sites: 27, RV sites: 27, Central water, Flush toilet, Free showers, No RV dump, Tents only: $16-17, Reservations accepted, Elev: 770ft/235m, Tel: 423-344-6214, Nearest town: Harrison. GPS: 35.168822, -85.129206

80 • C3 | Henry Horton SP

Total sites: 75, RV sites: 56, Elec sites: 56, Water at site, Flush toilet, Free showers, Tents: $16-17/RVs: $33-38, Also cabins, 6 hammock sites: $11-$13, Trap, Skeet, Open all year, Max Length: 40ft, Reservations accepted, Elev: 682ft/208m, Tel: 800-250-8612, Nearest town: Chapel Hill. GPS: 35.590326, -86.702029

81 • C3 | Henry Horton SP - Adeline Wilhoite TC

Total sites: 3, RV sites: 0, Central water, Vault/pit toilet, Tents only: $9-10, Hike-in, Open all year, Reservations accepted, Elev: 702ft/214m, Tel: 800-250-8612, Nearest town: Chapel Hill. GPS: 35.583652, -86.709486

82 • C3 | Henry Horton SP - Primitive

Total sites: 9, RV sites: 0, Central water, Vault/pit toilet, No showers, Tents only: $12-13, Reservations accepted, Elev: 688ft/210m, Tel: 800-250-8612, Nearest town: Chapel Hill. GPS: 35.593281, -86.703183

83 • C3 | Old Stone Fort SP

Total sites: 50, RV sites: 50, Elec sites: 50, Water at site, Flush toilet, Free showers, RV dump, Tent & RV camping: $26-34, Open all year, Max Length: 50ft, Reservations accepted, Elev: 1010ft/308m, Tel: 931-723-5073, Nearest town: Manchester. GPS: 35.490861, -86.106216

84 • C3 | Rock Island SP - Main CG

Total sites: 50, RV sites: 50, Elec sites: 50, Water at site, Flush toilet, Free showers, RV dump, Tent & RV camping: $34-40, Also cabins, Open all year, Max Length: 50ft, Reservations accepted, Elev: 906ft/276m, Tel: 931-686-2471, Nearest town: Rock Island. GPS: 35.812276, -85.645959

85 • C3 | Rock Island SP - Tent CG

Total sites: 10, Water at site, Flush toilet, Free showers, No RV dump, Tents only: $22-26, 20A electric, Open Mar-Oct, Reservations accepted, Elev: 933ft/284m, Tel: 931-686-2471, Nearest town: Rock Island. GPS: 35.810564, -85.641788

86 • C3 | South Cumberland SP - Alum Gap TC

Total sites: 8, RV sites: 0, Central water, Vault/pit toilet, Tents only: $9-11, Hike-in, 2.9 mi, Group site: $35, Reservations required, Elev: 1910ft/582m, Tel: 931-924-2980, Nearest town: Sequatchie. GPS: 35.434698, -85.683192

87 • C3 | South Cumberland SP - Dinky Line TC

Total sites: 4, RV sites: 0, Central water, Vault/pit toilet, Tents only: $9-11, Hike-in, 3.6 mi, Reservations required, Elev: 1902ft/580m, Tel: 931-924-2980, Nearest town: Beersheba Springs. GPS: 35.459211, -85.566311

88 • C3 | South Cumberland SP - Father Adamz TC

Total sites: 8, RV sites: 0, No water, Vault/pit toilet, Tents only: $9-11, Walk-to sites, .5 mi, Reservations required, Elev: 1776ft/541m, Tel: 931-924-2980, Nearest town: Sequatchie. GPS: 35.181566, -85.677184

89 • C3 | South Cumberland SP - Foster Falls

Total sites: 26, RV sites: 26, Central water, Flush toilet, Free showers, No RV dump, Tent & RV camping: $18-23, No generators, Max Length: 18ft, Reservations required, Elev: 1778ft/542m, Tel: 931-924-2980, Nearest town: Sequatchie. GPS: 35.181205, -85.672862

90 • C3 | South Cumberland SP - Grundy Forest TC

Total sites: 5, RV sites: 0, Central water, Vault/pit toilet, Tents only: $9-11, Hike-in, Reservations required, Elev: 1751ft/534m, Tel: 931-924-2980, Nearest town: Sequatchie. GPS: 35.249943, -85.754206

91 • C3 | South Cumberland SP - Hobbs Cabin TC

Dispersed sites, Central water, Vault/pit toilet, Tents only: $9-11, Hike-in, Reservations required, Elev: 1910ft/582m, Tel: 931-924-2980, Nearest town: Beersheba Springs. GPS: 35.471246, -85.594475

92 • C3 | South Cumberland SP - Savage Falls TC

Total sites: 7, RV sites: 0, Central water, Vault/pit toilet, Tents only: $9-11, Hike-in, 1.8 mi, 1 group site: $15, Reservations required, Elev: 1914ft/583m, Tel: 931-924-2980, Nearest town: Beersheba Springs. GPS: 35.438185, -85.555362

93 • C3 | South Cumberland SP - Savage Station

Total sites: 7, RV sites: 0, Central water, Vault/pit toilet, Tents only: $9-11, Walk-to/group sites, 1 group site: $15, Reservations required, Elev: 1852ft/564m, Tel: 931-924-2980, Nearest town: Beersheba Springs. GPS: 35.435769, -85.541263

94 • C3 | South Cumberland SP - Sawmill TC

Total sites: 8, RV sites: 0, Central water, Vault/pit toilet, Tents only: $9-11, Hike-in, 5.0 mi, Reservations required, Elev: 1079ft/329m, Tel: 931-924-2980, Nearest town: Sequatchie. GPS: 35.450073, -85.617213

95 • C3 | South Cumberland SP - Small Wild TC

Dispersed sites, Central water, Vault/pit toilet, Tents only: $9-11, Hike-in, 2.5 mi, Reservations required, Elev: 1777ft/542m, Tel: 931-924-2980, Nearest town: Sequatchie. GPS: 35.182304, -85.690735

96 • C3 | South Cumberland SP - Stagecoach Road TC

Total sites: 9, RV sites: 0, Central water, Vault/pit toilet, Tents only: $9-11, Hike-in, 6 mi, 1 group site: $15, Reservations required, Elev: 1849ft/564m, Tel: 931-924-2980, Nearest town: Beersheba Springs. GPS: 35.447918, -85.593981

97 • C3 | South Cumberland SP - Stone Door

Total sites: 12, RV sites: 0, Central water, Vault/pit toilet, Tents only: $9-11, Walk-to/group sites, 3 group sites: $25-$45, Reservations required, Elev: 1894ft/577m, Tel: 931-924-2980, Nearest town: Beersheba Springs. GPS: 35.445258, -85.657993

98 • C3 | Tims Ford SP - Evans Loop TC

Dispersed sites, No water, Vault/pit toilet, Tents only: $9-10, Hike-in, Open all year, Reservations accepted, Elev: 905ft/276m, Tel: 931-962-1183, Nearest town: Winchester. GPS: 35.227286, -86.273393

99 • C3 | Tims Ford SP - Fairview

Total sites: 82, RV sites: 82, Elec sites: 82, Water at site, Flush toilet, Free showers, RV dump, Tent & RV camping: $33-38, 31 Full hookups, Stay limit: 14-28 days, Open Apr-Oct, Max Length: 60ft, Reservations accepted, Elev: 902ft/275m, Tel: 931-967-4230, Nearest town: Winchester. GPS: 35.199705, -86.159818

100 • C3 | Tims Ford SP - Main CG

Total sites: 52, RV sites: 52, Elec sites: 52, Water at site, Flush toilet, Free showers, RV dump, Tent & RV camping: $26-32, 4 Full hookups, Stay limit: 14-28 days, Open all year, Max Length: 40ft, Reservations accepted, Elev: 948ft/289m, Tel: 931-962-1183, Nearest town: Winchester. GPS: 35.219952, -86.250011

101 • C3 | Tims Ford SP - Turkey Creek

Total sites: 20, No water, Vault/pit toilet, No showers, No RV dump, Tents only: $12-14, Stay limit: 14-28 days, Open all year, Reservations required, Elev: 952ft/290m, Tel: 931-962-1183, Nearest town: Winchester. GPS: 35.269942, -86.275237

102 • C4 | Cumberland Mountain SP - Main

Total sites: 145, RV sites: 145, Elec sites: 145, Water at site, Flush toilet, Free showers, RV dump, Tent & RV camping: $32-35, Also cabins, Open all year, Max Length: 40ft, Reservations accepted, Elev: 1778ft/542m, Tel: 800-250-8618, Nearest town: Crossville. GPS: 35.900877, -84.994296

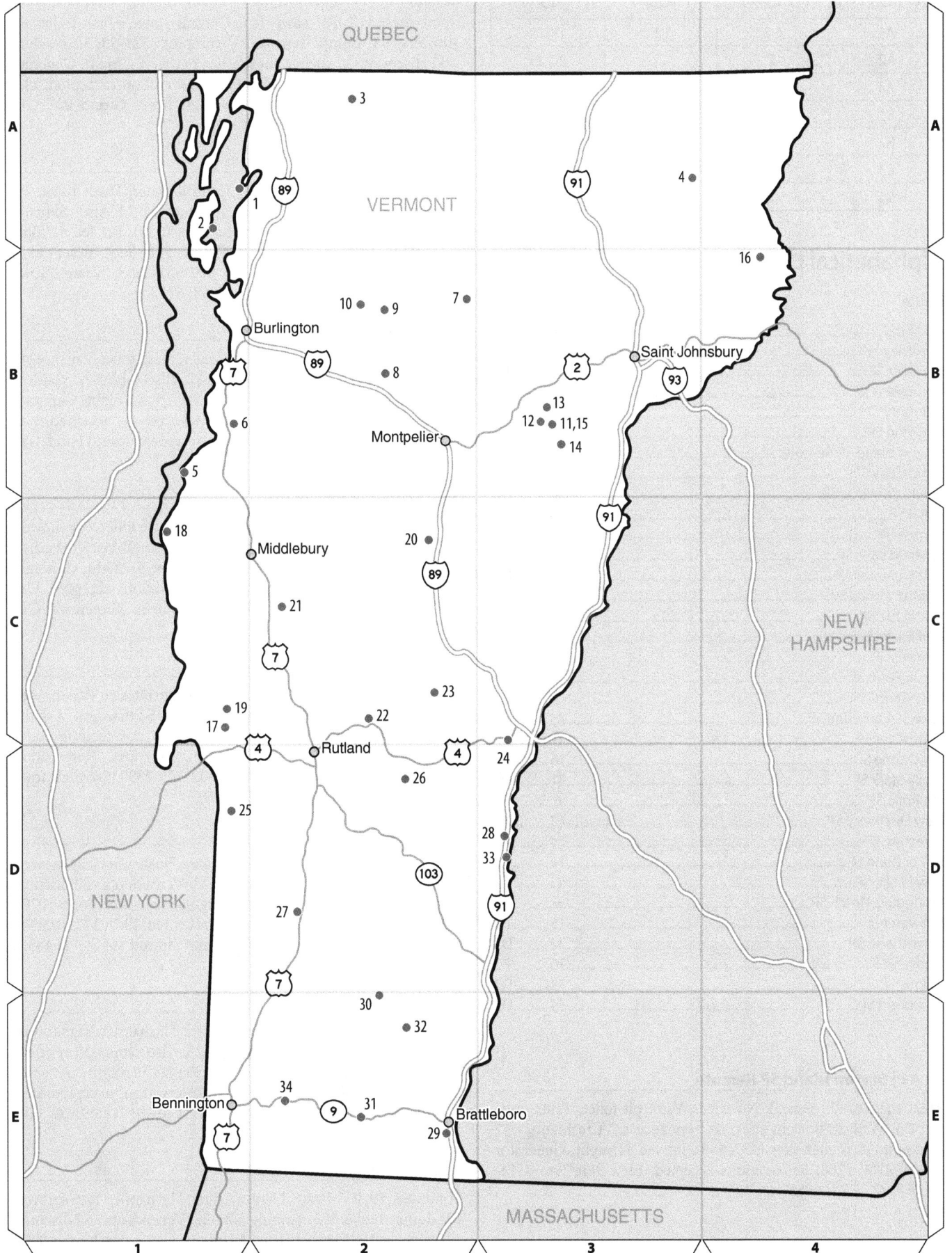

Vermont

QUEBEC

A

3

91

4

VERMONT

89

16

1

2

10 9

7

Burlington

89

8

Saint Johnsbury

2

7

93

B

6

13

12 11,15

Montpelier

14

5

18

Middlebury

20

89

21

NEW
HAMPSHIRE

C

7

23

19

22

17

4

Rutland

4

24

26

25

28

33

103

27

91

NEW YORK

D

7

30

32

34

Bennington

9 31

Brattleboro

7

29

E

MASSACHUSETTS

1   2   3   4

Map	ID	Map	ID
A1	1-2	C1	17-19
A2	3	C2	20-23
A3	4	C3	24
B1	5-6	D1	25
B2	7-10	D2	26-27
B3	11-15	D3	28-34
B4	16		

Alphabetical List of Camping Areas

1 • A1 | Burton Island SP Remote

Total sites: 4, RV sites: 0, No water, Vault/pit toilet, Tents only: $21-23, Walk-to/boat-in sites, or ferry access, Vt residents - $2 discount, 26 shelter sites ($37-$39), Pet fee $1/night, Generator hours: 0700-2200, Reservations accepted, Elev: 96ft/29m. GPS: 44.767592, -73.210983

2 • A1 | Grand Isle SP

Total sites: 117, RV sites: 117, Central water, Flush toilet, Pay showers, RV dump, Tent & RV camping: $21-23, Vt residents - $2 discount, 36 shelter sites ($30), Pet fee $1/night, Generator hours: 0700-2200, Open May-Oct, Reservations accepted, Elev: 141ft/43m, Tel: 802-372-4300, Nearest town: Grand Isle. GPS: 44.687256, -73.291260

3 • A2 | Lake Carmi SP

Total sites: 140, RV sites: 140, Central water, Flush toilet, Pay showers, RV dump, Tent & RV camping: $21-23, Also cabins, Vt residents - $2 discount, 35 shelter sites ($30), Pet fee $1/night, Generator hours: 0700-2200, Open May-Sep, Reservations accepted, Elev: 466ft/142m, Tel: 802-933-8383, Nearest town: Enosburg Falls. GPS: 44.954081, -72.876113

4 • A3 | Brighton SP

Total sites: 54, RV sites: 54, Central water, Flush toilet, Pay showers, RV dump, Tent & RV camping: $21-23, Also cabins, Vt residents - $2 discount, 23 shelter sites ($30), Pet fee $1/night, Generator hours: 0700-2200, Open May-Oct, Reservations accepted, Elev: 1204ft/367m, Tel: 802-723-4360, Nearest town: Island Pond. GPS: 44.797722, -71.853627

5 • B1 | Button Bay SP

Total sites: 56, RV sites: 56, Central water, Flush toilet, Pay showers, RV dump, Tent & RV camping: $21-23, Also cabins, Vt residents - $2 discount, 13 shelter sites ($30), Pet fee $1/night, Generator hours: 0700-2200, Open May-Oct, Reservations accepted, Elev: 118ft/36m, Tel: 802-475-2377, Nearest town: Vergennes. GPS: 44.181396, -73.357910

6 • B1 | Mt. Philo SP

Total sites: 7, RV sites: 7, Central water, Flush toilet, Pay showers, Tent & RV camping: $21-23, Vt residents - $2 discount, 3 shelter sites ($25-$27), Pet fee $1/night, Trailers not recommended, Generator hours: 0700-2200, Open May-Oct, Reservations accepted, Elev: 768ft/234m, Tel: 802-425-2390, Nearest town: Charlotte. GPS: 44.279967, -73.214607

7 • B2 | Elmore SP

Total sites: 45, RV sites: 45, Central water, Flush toilet, Pay showers, RV dump, Tent & RV camping: $21-23, Vt residents - $2 discount, 15 shelter sites ($30), Pet fee $1/night, Generator hours: 0700-2200, Open May-Oct, Reservations accepted, Elev: 1211ft/369m, Tel: 802-888-2982, Nearest town: Lake Elmore. GPS: 44.544521, -72.530809

8 • B2 | Little River SP

Total sites: 81, RV sites: 81, Central water, Flush toilet, Pay showers, RV dump, Tent & RV camping: $21-23, Also cabins, Vt residents - $2 discount, 20 shelter sites ($30), Pet fee $1/night, Generator hours: 0700-2200, Open May-Oct, Reservations accepted, Elev: 715ft/218m, Tel: 802-244-7103, Nearest town: Waterbury. GPS: 44.390263, -72.766996

9 • B2 | Smugglers Notch SP

Total sites: 19, RV sites: 8, Central water, Flush toilet, Free showers, RV dump, Tent & RV camping: $21-23, Vt residents - $2 discount, 14 shelter sites ($30), Pet fee $1/night, Generator hours: 0700-

2200, Open May-Oct, Elev: 1565ft/477m, Tel: 802-253-4014, Nearest town: Stowe. GPS: 44.519701, -72.775562

10 • B2 | Underhill SP

Total sites: 2, RV sites: 0, Central water, No toilets, No showers, No RV dump, Tents only: $21-23, Vt residents - $2 discount, , Steep road, 7 shelter sites ($25-$27), Pet fee - $1/night, Generator hours: 0700-2200, Open May-Oct, Reservations accepted, Elev: 1896ft/578m, Tel: 802-899-3022, Nearest town: Underhill Center. GPS: 44.529241, -72.842853

11 • B3 | Big Deer SP

Total sites: 23, RV sites: 23, Flush toilet, Pay showers, RV dump, Tent & RV camping: $21-23, Vt residents - $2 discount, 5 shelter sites ($30), Pet fee $1/night, Generator hours: 0700-2200, Open May-Sep, Elev: 1191ft/363m, Tel: 802-584-3822, Nearest town: Groton. GPS: 44.287241, -72.268844

12 • B3 | Kettle Pond SP

Total sites: 26, RV sites: 0, No water, Vault/pit toilet, Shelter: $21-23, Vt residents - $2 discount, 6 remote sites, Pet fee $1/night, Generator hours: 0700-2200, Open May-Oct, Reservations accepted, Elev: 1473ft/449m, Tel: 802-426-3042, Nearest town: Marshfield. GPS: 44.294154, -72.309324

13 • B3 | New Discovery SP

Total sites: 46, RV sites: 46, Central water, Flush toilet, Pay showers, Tent & RV camping: $21-23, Vt residents - $2 discount, 15 shelter sites ($35-$27), 7 horse sites, Generator hours: 0700-2200, Open May-Oct, Reservations accepted, Elev: 1762ft/537m, Tel: 802-426-3042, Nearest town: Marshfield. GPS: 44.320742, -72.289444

14 • B3 | Ricker Pond SP

Total sites: 27, RV sites: 27, Central water, Flush toilet, Pay showers, RV dump, Tent & RV camping: $21-23, Also cabins, Vt residents - $2 discount, 23 shelter sites ($30), Pet fee $1/night, Generator hours: 0700-2200, Open May-Oct, Reservations accepted, Elev: 1040ft/317m, Tel: 802-584-3821, Nearest town: Groton. GPS: 44.247327, -72.248658

15 • B3 | Stillwater SP

Total sites: 62, RV sites: 62, Central water, Flush toilet, Pay showers, RV dump, Tent & RV camping: $21-23, Vt residents - $2 discount, 17 shelter sites ($30), Pet fee $1/night, Generator hours: 0700-2200, Open May-Sep, Reservations accepted, Elev: 1129ft/344m, Tel: 802-584-3822, Nearest town: Groton. GPS: 44.280838, -72.272993

16 • B4 | Maidstone SP

Total sites: 34, RV sites: 34, Central water, Flush toilet, Pay showers, RV dump, Tent & RV camping: $21-23, Vt residents - $2 discount, 37 shelter sites ($30), Pet fee $1/night, Generator hours: 0700-2200, Open May-Sep, Reservations accepted, Elev: 1352ft/412m, Tel: 802-676-3930, Nearest town: Guildhall. GPS: 44.636122, -71.646244

17 • C1 | Bomoseen SP

Total sites: 56, RV sites: 56, Central water, Flush toilet, Pay showers, RV dump, Tent & RV camping: $21-23, Vt residents - $2 discount, 10 shelter sites ($30), Pet fee $1/night, Generator hours: 0700-2200, Open May-Sep, Reservations accepted, Elev: 420ft/128m, Tel: 802-265-4242, Nearest town: Fair Haven. GPS: 43.655868, -73.228494

18 • C1 | D A R SP

Total sites: 47, RV sites: 47, Central water, Flush toilet, Pay showers, RV dump, Tent & RV camping: $21-23, Vt residents - $2 discount, 24 shelter sites ($25-$27), Pet fee $1/night, Open May-Sep, Reservations accepted, Elev: 171ft/52m, Tel: 802-759-2354, Nearest town: Addison. GPS: 44.055141, -73.413118

19 • C1 | Half Moon Pond SP

Total sites: 52, RV sites: 52, Central water, Flush toilet, Pay showers, RV dump, Tent & RV camping: $21-23, Vt residents - $2 discount, 11 shelter sites ($30), Pet fee $1/night, Generator hours: 0700-2200, Open May-Oct, Reservations accepted, Elev: 633ft/193m, Tel: 802-273-2848, Nearest town: Hubbardton. GPS: 43.695288, -73.221016

20 • C2 | Allis SP

Total sites: 16, RV sites: 16, Central water, Flush toilet, Pay showers, RV dump, Tent & RV camping: $21-23, Vt residents - $2 discount, 8 shelter sites ($30), Pet fee $1/night, Generator hours: 0700-2200, Open May-Sep, Reservations accepted, Elev: 1980ft/604m, Tel: 802-276-3175, Nearest town: Brookfield. GPS: 44.046165, -72.635926

21 • C2 | Branbury SP

Total sites: 37, RV sites: 37, Central water, Flush toilet, Pay showers, RV dump, Tent & RV camping: $21-23, Vt residents - $2 discount, 7 shelter sites ($30), Pet fee $1/night, Generator hours: 0700-2200, Open May-Oct, Reservations accepted, Elev: 597ft/182m, Tel: 802-247-5925, Nearest town: Salisbury. GPS: 43.906177, -73.069795

22 • C2 | Gifford Woods SP

Total sites: 22, RV sites: 22, Central water, Flush toilet, Pay showers, RV dump, Tent & RV camping: $21-23, Also cabins, Vt residents - $2 discount, 20 shelter sites ($25-$27), Pet fee $1/night, Generator hours: 0700-2200, Open May-Oct, Reservations accepted, Elev: 1627ft/496m, Tel: 802-775-5354, Nearest town: Killington. GPS: 43.673739, -72.811303

23 • C2 | Silver Lake SP

Total sites: 40, RV sites: 40, Central water, Flush toilet, Pay showers, RV dump, Tent & RV camping: $21-23, Vt residents - $2 discount, 7 shelter sites ($30), Pet fee $1/night, Generator hours: 0700-2200, Open May-Sep, Elev: 1381ft/421m, Tel: 802-234-9451, Nearest town: Bethel. GPS: 43.732910, -72.613770

24 • C3 | Quechee SP

Total sites: 45, RV sites: 45, Central water, Flush toilet, Pay showers, RV dump, Tent & RV camping: $21-23, Vt residents - $2 discount, 7 shelter sites ($30), Pet fee $1/night, Generator hours: 0700-2200, Open May-Oct, Reservations accepted, Elev: 673ft/205m, Tel: 802-295-2990, Nearest town: White River Jct. GPS: 43.636719, -72.401367

25 • D1 | Lake St. Catherine SP

Total sites: 50, RV sites: 50, Central water, Flush toilet, Pay showers, RV dump, Tent & RV camping: $21-23, Vt residents - $2 discount, 11 shelter sites ($30), Pet fee $1/night, Generator hours: 0700-2200, Open May-Sep, Reservations accepted, Elev: 518ft/158m, Tel: 802-287-9158, Nearest town: Poultney. GPS: 43.480469, -73.204834

26 • D2 | Calvin Coolidge SP

Total sites: 26, RV sites: 26, Central water, Flush toilet, Pay showers, RV dump, Tent & RV camping: $21-23, Vt residents - $2 discount, 36 shelter sites ($30), Pet fee $1/night, Generator hours: 0700-2200, Open May-Oct, Reservations accepted, Elev: 1676ft/511m, Tel: 802-672-3612, Nearest town: Plymouth. GPS: 43.551270, -72.698975

27 • D2 | Emerald Lake SP

Total sites: 67, RV sites: 67, Central water, Flush toilet, Pay showers, RV dump, Tent & RV camping: $21-23, Vt residents - $2 discount, 37 shelter sites ($25-$27), Pet fee $1/night, Generator hours: 0700-2200, Open May-Oct, Reservations accepted, Elev: 932ft/284m, Tel: 802-362-1655, Nearest town: East Dorset. GPS: 43.277588, -73.008789

28 • D3 | Ascutney SP

Total sites: 48, RV sites: 38, Central water, Flush toilet, Pay showers, RV dump, Tent & RV camping: $21-23, Vt residents - $2 discount, 10 shelter sites ($30), Pet fee $1/night, Generator hours: 0700-2200, Open May-Oct, Elev: 558ft/170m, Tel: 802-674-2060, Nearest town: Windsor. GPS: 43.437102, -72.406439

29 • D3 | Fort Dummer SP

Total sites: 50, RV sites: 50, Central water, Flush toilet, Pay showers, RV dump, Tent & RV camping: $21-23, Vt residents - $2 discount, 10 shelter sites ($25-$27), Pet fee $1/night, Generator hours: 0700-2200, Open May-Sep, Reservations accepted, Elev: 633ft/193m, Tel: 802-254-2610, Nearest town: Brattleboro. GPS: 42.823301, -72.565997

30 • D3 | Jamaica SP

Total sites: 41, RV sites: 41, Central water, Flush toilet, Pay showers, RV dump, Tent & RV camping: $21-23, Vt residents - $2 discount, 18 shelter sites ($30), Pet fee $1/night, Generator hours: 0700-2200, Open May-Oct, Reservations accepted, Elev: 764ft/233m, Tel: 802-874-4600, Nearest town: Jamaica. GPS: 43.106591, -72.772872

31 • D3 | Molly Stark SP

Total sites: 23, RV sites: 23, Central water, Flush toilet, Pay showers, RV dump, Tent & RV camping: $21-23, Vt residents - $2 discount, 11 shelter sites ($25-$27), Pet fee $1/night, Generator hours: 0700-2200, Open May-Oct, Reservations accepted, Elev: 1913ft/583m, Tel: 802-464-5460, Nearest town: Wilmington. GPS: 42.852327, -72.815048

32 • D3 | Townshend SP

Total sites: 30, RV sites: 8, Central water, Flush toilet, Free showers, No RV dump, Tent & RV camping: $21-23, Vt residents - $2 discount, 4 shelter sites ($30), Pet fee $1/night, Generator hours: 0700-2200, Open May-Sep, Reservations accepted, Elev: 459ft/140m, Tel: 802-365-7500, Nearest town: Townsend. GPS: 43.041501, -72.691689

33 • D3 | Wilgus SP

Total sites: 21, RV sites: 15, Central water, Flush toilet, Pay showers, RV dump, Tent & RV camping: $21-23, Also cabins, Vt residents - $2 discount, 6 shelter sites ($30), Pet fee - $1/night, Generator hours: 0700-2200, Open May-Oct, Reservations accepted, Elev: 368ft/112m, Tel: 802-674-5422, Nearest town: Ascutney. GPS: 43.390767, -72.405475

34 • D3 | Woodford SP

Total sites: 83, RV sites: 83, Central water, Flush toilet, Pay showers, RV dump, Tent & RV camping: $21-23, Vt residents - $2 discount, 20 shelter sites ($30), Pet fee - $1/night, Generator hours: 0700-2200, Open May-Oct, Reservations accepted, Elev: 2402ft/732m, Tel: 802-447-7169, Nearest town: Bennington. GPS: 42.886067, -73.036662

Virginia

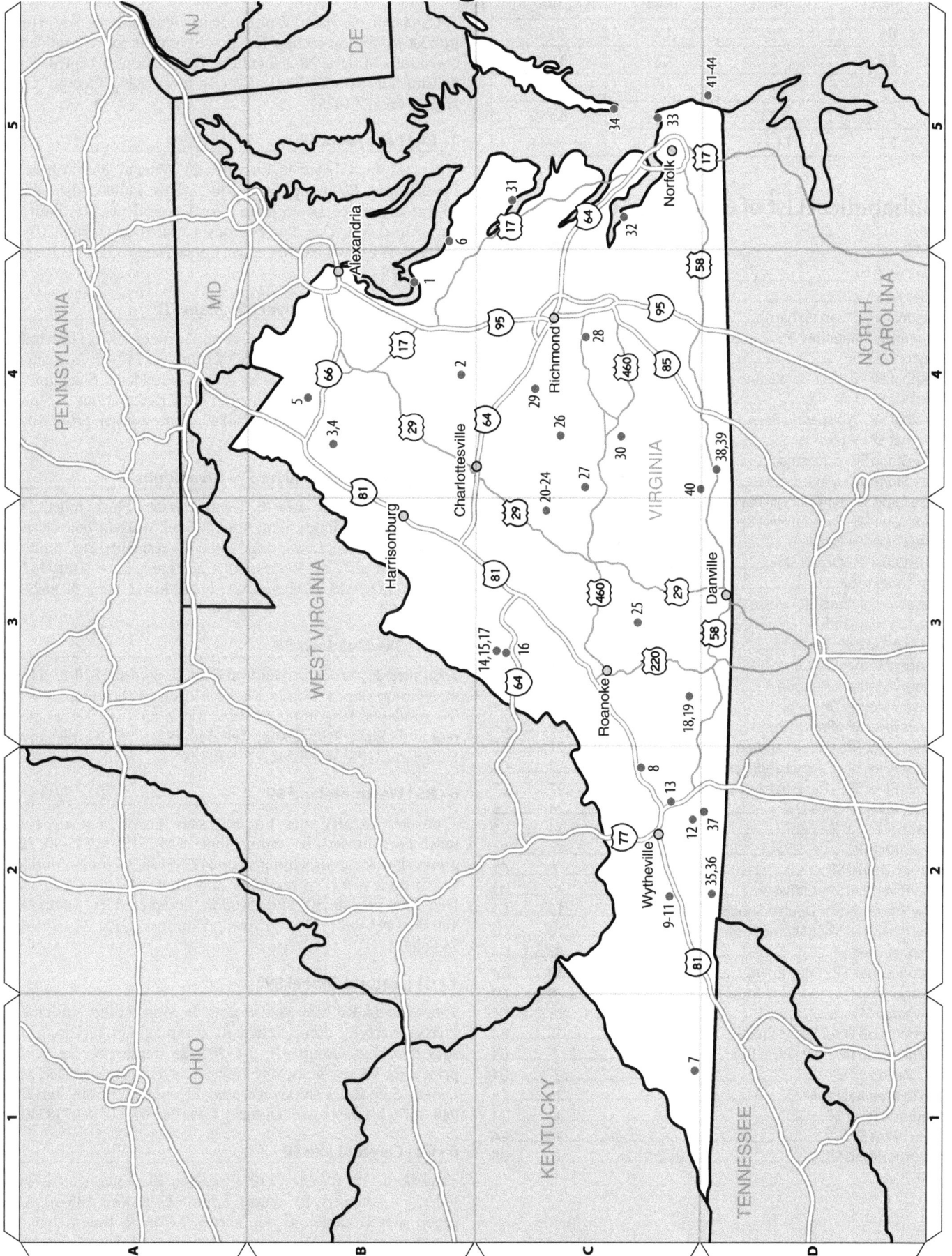

Map	ID	Map	ID
B4	1-5	C4	26-30
B5	6	C5	31-34
C1	7	D2	35-37
C2	8-13	D4	38-40
C3	14-25	D5	41-44

Alphabetical List of Camping Areas

1 • B4 | Caledon SP - Stuarts Wharf

Total sites: 6, No water, Vault/pit toilet, Tents only: $15-18, Hike-in/boat-in, $5 transaction fee, Lower price is for VA residents, Stay limit: 14 days, No generators, Reservations accepted, Elev: 8ft/2m, Tel: 540-663-3861, Nearest town: King George. GPS: 38.363766, -77.142526

2 • B4 | Lake Anna SP

Total sites: 46, RV sites: 46, Elec sites: 23, Water at site, Flush toilet, Free showers, RV dump, Tents: $30-35/RVs: $40-46, Also cabins, $5 transaction fee, Lower price is for VA residents, Stay limit: 14 days, Open Mar-Dec, Reservations accepted, Elev: 358ft/109m, Tel: 540-854-5503, Nearest town: Spotsylvania. GPS: 38.109819, -77.825829

3 • B4 | Shenendoah River SP - Main CG

Total sites: 32, RV sites: 32, Elec sites: 32, Water at site, Flush toilet, Free showers, RV dump, Tent & RV camping: $40-46, Also cabins, $5 transaction fee, Lower price is for VA residents, Stay limit: 14 days, Open all year, Max Length: 60ft, Reservations accepted, Elev: 569ft/173m, Tel: 540-622-6840, Nearest town: Front Royal. GPS: 38.849628, -78.310913

4 • B4 | Shenendoah River SP - River Right

Total sites: 10, RV sites: 0, Central water, Flush toilet, Free showers, No RV dump, Tents only: $25-30, Walk-to/boat-in sites, $5 transaction fee, Lower price is for VA residents, Stay limit: 14 days, Open all year, Reservations accepted, Elev: 549ft/167m, Tel: 540-622-6840, Nearest town: Front Royal. GPS: 38.862972, -78.302457

5 • B4 | Sky Meadows SP

Total sites: 15, No water, Vault/pit toilet, Tents only: $20-25, Hike-in, 3 Group sites: $70-$124, $5 transaction fee, Lower price is for VA residents, Stay limit: 14 days, Open all year, Reservations required, Elev: 919ft/280m, Tel: 540-592-3556, Nearest town: Delaplane. GPS: 38.990246, -77.974888

6 • B5 | Westmoreland SP

Total sites: 133, RV sites: 129, Elec sites: 42, Water at site, Flush toilet, Free showers, RV dump, Tents: $25-30/RVs: $35-40, Also group sites & cabins, Group sites: $125-$148, $5 transaction fee, Lower price is for VA residents, Stay limit: 14 days, Open Mar-Dec, Max Length: 40ft, Reservations accepted, Elev: 164ft/50m, Tel: 804-493-8821, Nearest town: Montross. GPS: 38.167915, -76.868321

7 • C1 | Natural Tunnel SP

Total sites: 34, RV sites: 34, Elec sites: 34, Water at site, Flush toilet, Free showers, RV dump, Tent & RV camping: $35-40, Also group sites & cabins, Group site: $70-$82, $5 transaction fee, Lower price is for VA residents, Stay limit: 14 days, Open Mar-Dec, Max Length: 50ft, Reservations accepted, Elev: 1824ft/556m, Tel: 276-940-2674, Nearest town: Duffield. GPS: 36.704560, -82.738230

8 • C2 | Claytor Lake SP

Total sites: 110, RV sites: 110, Elec sites: 40, Water at site, Flush toilet, Free showers, RV dump, Tents: $25-30/RVs: $35-40, Also group sites & cabins, Group site: $70-$82, $5 transaction fee, Lower price is for VA residents, Stay limit: 14 days, Open Mar-

Dec, Elev: 1949ft/594m, Tel: 540-643-2500, Nearest town: Dublin. GPS: 37.057443, -80.626173

9 • C2 | Hungry Mother SP - Camp Burson

Total sites: 50, RV sites: 50, Elec sites: 50, Water at site, Flush toilet, Free showers, RV dump, Tent & RV camping: $35-45, Also cabins, 30 Full hookups, $5 transaction fee, Lower price is for VA residents, Open Mar-Dec, Max Length: 30-39ft, Reservations accepted, Elev: 2185ft/666m, Tel: 276-781-7400, Nearest town: Marion. GPS: 36.868992, -81.526161

10 • C2 | Hungry Mother SP - Loop B

Total sites: 20, RV sites: 20, Elec sites: 20, Water at site, Flush toilet, Free showers, RV dump, Tent & RV camping: $35-40, Also cabins, $5 transaction fee, Lower price is for VA residents, Open Mar-Dec, Max Length: 35ft, Reservations accepted, Elev: 2241ft/683m, Tel: 276-781-7400, Nearest town: Marion. GPS: 36.890368, -81.519808

11 • C2 | Hungry Mother SP - Loop C

Total sites: 11, RV sites: 0, Central water, Flush toilet, Free showers, No RV dump, Tents only: $25-30, $5 transaction fee, Lower price is for VA residents, Open Mar-Dec, Reservations accepted, Elev: 2267ft/691m, Tel: 276-781-7400, Nearest town: Marion. GPS: 36.891635, -81.519495

12 • C2 | New River Trail SP - Double Shoals

Total sites: 2, No water, Vault/pit toilet, Tents only: $15-18, Hike-in/boat-in, $5 transaction fee, Lower price is for VA residents, Stay limit: 14 days, Reservations not accepted, Elev: 2089ft/637m, Tel: 276-699-6778, Nearest town: Fries. GPS: 36.759183, -80.962261

13 • C2 | New River Trail SP - Millrace/Foster Falls

Total sites: 21, Central water, Vault/pit toilet, Tents only: $20-25, Walk-to sites, Also 9 group sites, $5 transaction fee, Lower price is for VA residents, Stay limit: 14 days, Reservations required, Elev: 1922ft/586m, Tel: 276-699-6778, Nearest town: Max Meadows. GPS: 36.885107, -80.858552

14 • C3 | Douthat SP - Beaver Dam Equestrian

Total sites: 14, RV sites: 14, Elec sites: 14, Central water, Flush toilet, Free showers, RV dump, Tent & RV camping: $35-40, $5 transaction fee, Lower price is for VA residents, Stay limit: 14 days, Open Mar-Dec, Max Length: 40ft, Reservations accepted, Elev: 1532ft/467m, Tel: 540-862-8100, Nearest town: Millboro. GPS: 37.914962, -79.796914

15 • C3 | Douthat SP - Lakeside

Total sites: 19, RV sites: 19, Central water, Flush toilet, Free showers, RV dump, Tent & RV camping: $30-35, Also cabins, $5 transaction fee, Lower price is for VA residents, Stay limit: 14 days, No generators, Open Mar-Dec, Max Length: 40ft, Reservations accepted, Elev: 1496ft/456m, Tel: 540-862-8100, Nearest town: Millboro. GPS: 37.909269, -79.797721

16 • C3 | Douthat SP - Whispering Pines Horse Camp

Total sites: 20, RV sites: 20, Elec sites: 20, Water at site, Flush toilet, Free showers, RV dump, Tent & RV camping: $35-40, $5 transaction fee, Lower price is for VA residents, Stay limit: 14 days, Open Mar-Dec, Max Length: 50ft, Reservations accepted,

Elev: 1296ft/395m, Tel: 540-862-8100, Nearest town: Millboro. GPS: 37.862053, -79.815748

17 • C3 | Douthat SP - White Oak

Total sites: 31, RV sites: 31, Elec sites: 31, Water at site, Flush toilet, Free showers, RV dump, Tent & RV camping: $35-40, $5 transaction fee, Lower price is for VA residents, Stay limit: 14 days, Open Mar-Dec, Max Length: 40ft, Reservations accepted, Elev: 1457ft/444m, Tel: 540-862-8100, Nearest town: Millboro. GPS: 37.897219, -79.801716

18 • C3 | Fairy Stone SP - Equestrian

Total sites: 5, RV sites: 5, Elec sites: 5, Water at site, Vault/pit toilet, No showers, No RV dump, No tents/RVs: $25-30, $5 transaction fee, Lower price is for VA residents, Open Mar-Dec, Reservations accepted, Elev: 1150ft/351m, Tel: 276-930-2424, Nearest town: Stuart. GPS: 36.783469, -80.125904

19 • C3 | Fairy Stone SP - Main

Total sites: 50, RV sites: 50, Elec sites: 50, Flush toilet, Free showers, RV dump, Tent & RV camping: $35-40, Also cabins, $5 transaction fee, Lower price is for VA residents, Stay limit: 14 days, Open Mar-Dec, Reservations accepted, Elev: 1119ft/341m, Tel: 276-930-2424, Nearest town: Stuart. GPS: 36.794125, -80.108663

20 • C3 | James River SP - Branch Pond

Total sites: 7, No water, Vault/pit toilet, Tents only: $15-18, $5 transaction fee, Lower price is for VA residents, Stay limit: 14 days, Open all year, Reservations accepted, Elev: 541ft/165m, Tel: 434-933-4355, Nearest town: Gladstone. GPS: 37.633334, -78.796892

21 • C3 | James River SP - Canoe Landing

Total sites: 13, No water, Vault/pit toilet, Tents only: $15-18, $5 transaction fee, Lower price is for VA residents, Stay limit: 14 days, Open all year, Reservations accepted, Elev: 375ft/114m, Tel: 434-933-4355, Nearest town: Gladstone. GPS: 37.613951, -78.815131

22 • C3 | James River SP - Canoe Landing Equestrian

Total sites: 5, RV sites: 5, No water, Vault/pit toilet, Tents: $15-18/RVs: $13-15, Also cabins, $5 transaction fee, Lower price is for VA residents, Stay limit: 14 days, Open Mar-Dec, Max Length: 30ft, Reservations accepted, Elev: 376ft/115m, Tel: 434-933-4355, Nearest town: Gladstone. GPS: 37.614973, -78.814774

23 • C3 | James River SP - Horseshoe Equestrian

Total sites: 10, RV sites: 10, Elec sites: 10, Water at site, Flush toilet, Free showers, No tents/RVs: $35-40, $5 transaction fee, Lower price is for VA residents, Stay limit: 14 days, Open Mar-Dec, Max Length: 40ft, Reservations accepted, Elev: 551ft/168m, Tel: 434-933-4355, Nearest town: Gladstone. GPS: 37.622364, -78.806003

24 • C3 | James River SP - Red Oak

Total sites: 30, RV sites: 30, Elec sites: 30, Water at site, Flush toilet, Free showers, RV dump, Tent & RV camping: $35-40, Also cabins, $5 transaction fee, Lower price is for VA residents, Stay limit: 14 days, Open Mar-Dec, Reservations accepted, Elev: 518ft/158m, Tel: 434-933-4355, Nearest town: Gladstone. GPS: 37.625621, -78.812763

25 • C3 | Smith Mountain Lake SP

Total sites: 50, RV sites: 24, Elec sites: 24, Water at site, Flush toilet, Free showers, RV dump, Tents: $20-24/RVs: $30-35, Also cabins, $5 transaction fee, Lower price is for VA residents, Stay limit: 14 days, Open Mar-Dec, Max Length: 50ft, Reservations accepted, Elev: 925ft/282m, Tel: 540-297-6066, Nearest town: Huddleston. GPS: 37.083425, -79.594941

26 • C4 | Bear Creek SP

Total sites: 53, RV sites: 39, Elec sites: 39, Water at site, Flush toilet, Free showers, RV dump, Tents: $25-35/RVs: $35-40, Also cabins, Group site: $144, $5 transaction fee, Lower price is for VA residents, Stay limit: 14 days, Open Mar-Dec, Max Length: 35ft, Elev: 348ft/106m, Tel: 804-492-4410, Nearest town: Cumberland. GPS: 37.531978, -78.272137

27 • C4 | Holliday Lake SP

Total sites: 37, RV sites: 37, Elec sites: 37, Water at site, Flush toilet, Free showers, RV dump, Tent & RV camping: $35-40, Group site: $100-$117, $5 transaction fee, Lower price is for VA residents, Stay limit: 14 days, Open Mar-Dec, Max Length: 38ft, Reservations accepted, Elev: 574ft/175m, Tel: 434-248-6308, Nearest town: Appomattox. GPS: 37.399183, -78.641284

28 • C4 | Pocahontas SP

Total sites: 119, RV sites: 119, Elec sites: 119, Water at site, Flush toilet, Free showers, RV dump, Tent & RV camping: $35-40, Also cabins, $5 transaction fee, Lower fee is for VA residents, Stay limit: 14 days, Open Mar-Dec, Max Length: 40ft, Reservations accepted, Elev: 246ft/75m, Tel: 804-796-4255, Nearest town: Chesterfield. GPS: 37.378488, -77.575016

29 • C4 | Powhatan SP

Total sites: 35, RV sites: 29, Elec sites: 29, Water at site, Flush toilet, Free showers, Tents: $15-18/RVs: $35-40, $5 transaction fee, Lower fee is for VA residents, Stay limit: 14 days, Open Mar-Nov, Max Length: 60ft, Reservations accepted, Elev: 154ft/47m, Tel: 804-598-7148, Nearest town: Powhatan. GPS: 37.679333, -77.945847

30 • C4 | Twin Lakes SP

Total sites: 33, RV sites: 22, Elec sites: 33, Water at site, Flush toilet, Free showers, RV dump, Tent & RV camping: $35-40, Also cabins, $5 transaction fee, Lower price is for VA residents, Stay limit: 14 days, Open Mar-Dec, Max Length: 36ft, Reservations accepted, Elev: 492ft/150m, Tel: 434-392-3435, Nearest town: Green Bay. GPS: 37.176586, -78.279361

31 • C5 | Belle Isle SP

Total sites: 28, RV sites: 28, Elec sites: 28, Central water, Flush toilet, Free showers, RV dump, Tents: $15-18/RVs: $35-40, $5 transaction fee, Lower price is for VA residents, Stay limit: 14 days, Open Mar-Dec, Elev: 36ft/11m, Tel: 804-462-5030, Nearest town: Lancaster. GPS: 37.782085, -76.592485

32 • C5 | Chippokes Plantation SP

Total sites: 48, RV sites: 48, Elec sites: 48, Water at site, Flush toilet, Free showers, Tent & RV camping: $35-45, Also cabins, Group site: $70-$82, $5 transaction fee, Lower price is for VA residents, Stay limit: 14 days, Open Mar-Dec, Max Length: 50ft, Elev: 12ft/4m, Tel: 757-294-3625, Nearest town: Surry. GPS: 37.142488, -76.741065

33 • C5 | First Landing SP

Total sites: 190, RV sites: 190, Elec sites: 109, Water at site, Flush toilet, Free showers, RV dump, Tents: $30-35/RVs: $40-46, Also cabins, $5 transaction fee, Lower price is for VA residents, Stay limit: 14 days, Open Mar-Dec, Reservations accepted, Elev: 10ft/3m, Tel: 800-933-7275, Nearest town: Virginia Beach. GPS: 36.917845, -76.055114

34 • C5 | Kiptopeke SP

Total sites: 133, RV sites: 86, Elec sites: 86, Water at site, Flush toilet, Free showers, RV dump, Tents: $30-35/RVs: $40-47, Also cabins, 86 Full hookups sites, $5 transaction fee, Lower price is for VA residents, Stay limit: 14 days, Open Apr-Dec, Max Length: 40ft, Reservations accepted, Elev: 46ft/14m, Tel: 757-331-2267, Nearest town: Cape Charles. GPS: 37.170513, -75.981904

35 • D2 | Grayson Highlands SP - Horse Camp

Total sites: 23, RV sites: 23, Elec sites: 23, Water at site, Tents: $25-30/RVs: $35-40, $18 Nov/Mar/Apr - no water, $5 transaction fee, Lower price is for VA residents, Stay limit: 14 days, Open Mar-Dec, Max Length: 40ft, Reservations accepted, Elev: 4495ft/1370m, Tel: 276-579-7092, Nearest town: Mouth of Wilson. GPS: 36.628824, -81.515801

36 • D2 | Grayson Highlands SP - Main CG

Total sites: 69, RV sites: 69, Elec sites: 37, Water at site, Flush toilet, Free showers, RV dump, Tents: $25-30/RVs: $35-40, Group site: $70-$82$15-$18 Nov/Mar/Apr - no water, $5 transaction fee, Lower price is for VA residents, Stay limit: 14 days, Open Mar-Dec, Max Length: 40ft, Reservations accepted, Elev: 4285ft/1306m, Tel: 276-579-7092, Nearest town: Mouth of Wilson. GPS: 36.640113, -81.486058

37 • D2 | New River Trail SP - Cliffview

Total sites: 10, Central water, Vault/pit toilet, Tents only: $20-25, Walk-to sites, Ride-in, $5 transaction fee, Lower price is for VA residents, Stay limit: 14 days, Reservations required, Elev: 2293ft/699m, Tel: 276-699-6778, Nearest town: Galax. GPS: 36.695967, -80.915956

38 • D4 | Occoneechee SP

Total sites: 48, RV sites: 48, Elec sites: 39, Water at site, Flush toilet, Free showers, RV dump, Tents: $25-35/RVs: $35-45, Also cabins, $5 transaction fee, Lower price is for VA residents, Stay limit: 14 days, Open Mar-Dec, Reservations accepted, Elev: 394ft/120m, Tel: 434-374-2210, Nearest town: Clarksville. GPS: 36.628495, -78.531177

39 • D4 | Occoneechee SP - Equestrian

Total sites: 11, RV sites: 11, Elec sites: 11, Central water, Vault/pit toilet, No showers, No RV dump, Tent & RV camping: $20-25, Also cabins, $5 transaction fee, Lower price is for VA residents, Stay limit: 14 days, Open Mar-Dec, Max Length: 65ft, Reservations accepted, Elev: 346ft/105m, Tel: 434-374-2210, Nearest town: Clarksville. GPS: 36.618999, -78.507066

40 • D4 | Staunton River SP

Total sites: 48, RV sites: 34, Elec sites: 34, Water at site, Flush toilet, Free showers, RV dump, Tents: $25-30/RVs: $35-40, Also cabins, $5 transaction fee, Lower price is for VA residents, Stay limit: 14 days, Open Mar-Dec, Reservations accepted, Elev: 374ft/114m, Tel: 434-572-4623, Nearest town: Scottsburg. GPS: 36.702321, -78.666403

41 • D5 | False Cape SP - Barbour Hill Bay Side

Total sites: 3, No water, Vault/pit toilet, Tents only: $20-25, Hike-in/boat-in, $5 transaction fee, VA resident discount: $5, Bike-in, Stay limit: 14 days, Open all year, Reservations required, Elev: 3ft/1m, Tel: 757-426-7128, Nearest town: Virginia Beach. GPS: 36.619985, -75.908977

42 • D5 | False Cape SP - Barbour Hill Ocean Side

Total sites: 3, No water, Vault/pit toilet, Tents only: $20-25, Hike-in/boat-in, $5 transaction fee, VA resident discount: $5, Bike-in, Stay limit: 14 days, Open all year, Reservations required, Elev: 14ft/4m, Tel: 757-426-7128, Nearest town: Virginia Beach. GPS: 36.623284, -75.891039

43 • D5 | False Cape SP - Bay Side

Total sites: 3, No water, Vault/pit toilet, Tents only: $20-25, Hike-in/boat-in, $5 transaction fee, VA resident discount: $5, Bike-in, Stay limit: 14 days, Open all year, Reservations required, Elev: 5ft/2m, Tel: 757-426-7128, Nearest town: Virginia Beach. GPS: 36.596489, -75.886789

44 • D5 | False Cape SP - Ocean Side

Total sites: 3, No water, Vault/pit toilet, Tents only: $20-25, Hike-in/boat-in, $5 transaction fee, VA resident discount: $5, Bike-in, Stay limit: 14 days, Open all year, Reservations required, Elev: 9ft/3m, Tel: 757-426-7128, Nearest town: Virginia Beach. GPS: 36.598627, -75.881243

West Virginia

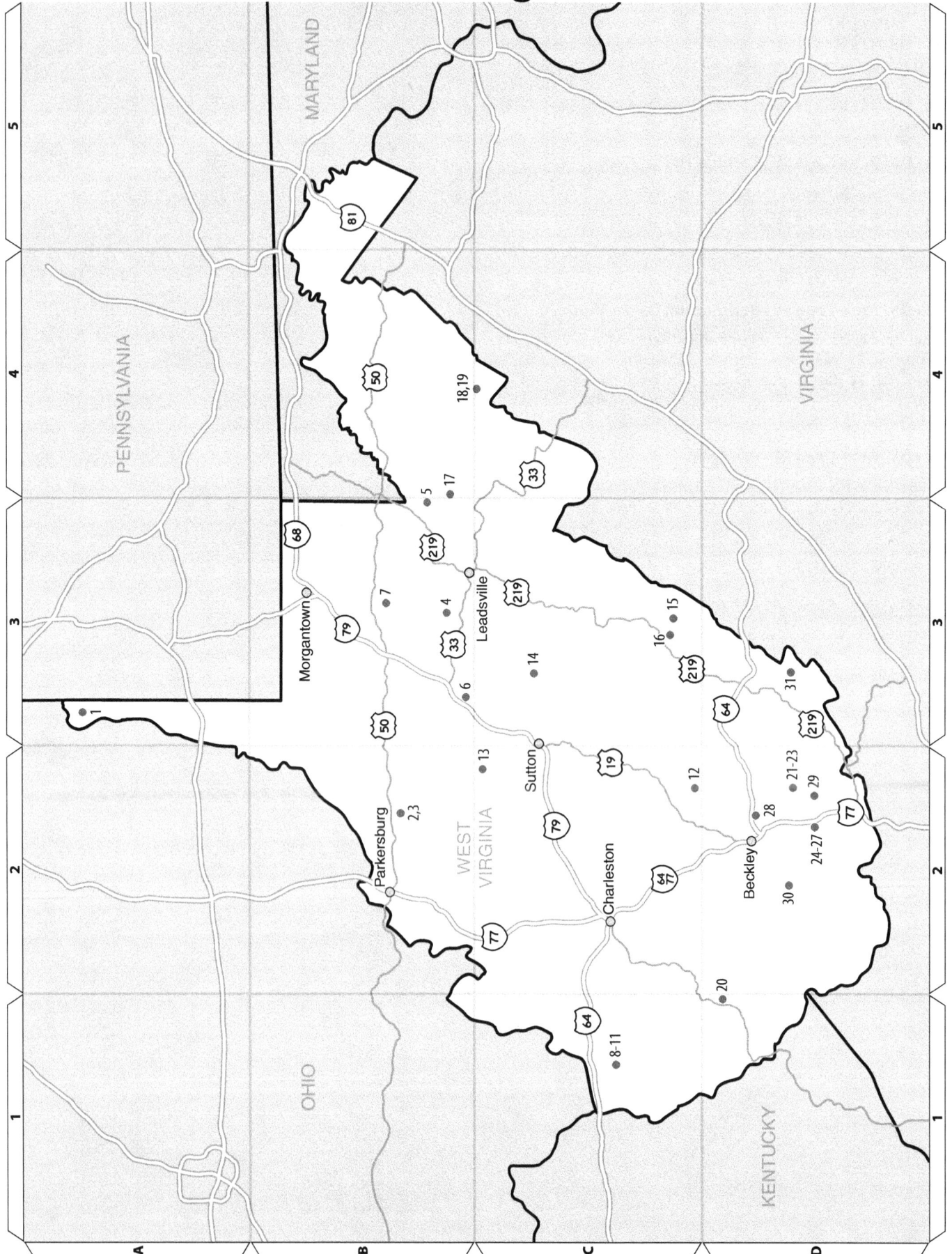

Map	ID	Map	ID
A3	1	C3	14-16
B2	2-3	C4	17-19
B3	4-7	D1	20
C1	8-11	D2	21-30
C2	12-13	D3	31

Alphabetical List of Camping Areas

1 • A3 | Tomlinson Run SP

Total sites: 54, RV sites: 54, Elec sites: 39, Central water, Flush toilet, Free showers, RV dump, Tents: $25/RVs: $29, Also cabins, Stay limit: 14 days, Open Apr-Oct, Reservations accepted, Elev: 1191ft/363m, Tel: 304-564-3651, Nearest town: New Manchester. GPS: 40.548234, -80.579468

2 • B2 | North Bend SP - Cokeley

Total sites: 28, RV sites: 28, Elec sites: 28, Water at site, Flush toilet, Free showers, Tent & RV camping: $31, Stay limit: 14 days, Open May-Oct, Reservations not accepted, Elev: 791ft/241m, Tel: 304-643-2931, Nearest town: Cairo. GPS: 39.218638, -81.078261

3 • B2 | North Bend SP - River Run

Total sites: 49, RV sites: 49, Elec sites: 26, Central water, Flush toilet, Free showers, Tents: $25/RVs: $31, Stay limit: 14 days, Open Apr-Oct, Reservations accepted, Elev: 771ft/235m, Tel: 304-643-2931, Nearest town: Cairo. GPS: 39.224757, -81.103619

4 • B3 | Audra SP

Total sites: 67, RV sites: 67, Elec sites: 13, Central water, Flush toilet, Free showers, RV dump, Tents: $27/RVs: $32, Stay limit: 14 days, Open Apr-Oct, Reservations accepted, Elev: 1707ft/520m, Tel: 304-457-1162, Nearest town: Buckhannon. GPS: 39.034963, -80.060775

5 • B3 | Blackwater Falls SP

Total sites: 65, RV sites: 65, Elec sites: 30, Central water, Flush toilet, Free showers, RV dump, Tents: $25/RVs: $28, Open Apr-Oct, Reservations accepted, Elev: 3123ft/952m, Tel: 304-259-5216, Nearest town: Davis. GPS: 39.112061, -79.495361

6 • B3 | Stonewall Resort SP - Briar Point

Total sites: 46, RV sites: 40, Elec sites: 40, Water at site, Flush toilet, Free showers, RV dump, Tents: $32/RVs: $57-72, 40 Full hookups, Stay limit: 14 days, Open all year, Reservations accepted, Elev: 1086ft/331m, Tel: 304-269-8889, Nearest town: Weston. GPS: 38.947889, -80.488719

7 • B3 | Tygart Lake SP

Total sites: 40, RV sites: 40, Elec sites: 14, Central water, Flush toilet, Free showers, RV dump, Tents: $25/RVs: $28, Stay limit: 14 days, Open Apr-Oct, Reservations accepted, Elev: 1371ft/418m, Tel: 304-265-6144, Nearest town: Grafton. GPS: 39.285675, -80.008514

8 • C1 | Beech Fork SP - Four Coves

Total sites: 88, RV sites: 88, Elec sites: 88, Central water, Flush toilet, Free showers, RV dump, Tent & RV camping: $31-33, Stay limit: 14 days, Open Apr-Oct, Reservations accepted, Elev: 598ft/182m, Tel: 304-528-5794, Nearest town: Barboursville. GPS: 38.308083, -82.357363

9 • C1 | Beech Fork SP - Lakeview

Total sites: 51, RV sites: 51, Elec sites: 51, Central water, Flush toilet, Free showers, RV dump, Tent & RV camping: $31-33, Stay limit: 14 days, Open Apr-Oct, Reservations accepted, Elev: 613ft/187m, Tel: 304-528-5794, Nearest town: Barboursville. GPS: 38.312352, -82.355146

10 • C1 | Beech Fork SP - Moxley Branch

Total sites: 87, RV sites: 87, Elec sites: 50, Central water, Flush toilet, Free showers, RV dump, Tents: $24/RVs: $33-40, Stay limit: 14 days, Open Apr-Oct, Reservations accepted, Elev: 598ft/182m, Tel: 304-528-5794, Nearest town: Barboursville. GPS: 38.306145, -82.351686

11 • C1 | Beech Fork SP - Old Orchard

Total sites: 49, RV sites: 49, Elec sites: 49, Central water, Flush toilet, Free showers, RV dump, Tent & RV camping: $35-38, 49 Full hookups, Stay limit: 14 days, Open all year, Reservations accepted, Elev: 600ft/183m, Tel: 304-528-5794, Nearest town: Barboursville. GPS: 38.307043, -82.348947

12 • C2 | Babcock SP

Total sites: 52, RV sites: 52, Elec sites: 28, Central water, Flush toilet, Free showers, RV dump, Tents: $28/RVs: $31, Open Apr-Oct, Reservations accepted, Elev: 2369ft/722m, Tel: 304-438-3004, Nearest town: Clifftop. GPS: 38.007021, -80.948752

13 • C2 | Cedar Creek SP

Total sites: 65, RV sites: 65, Elec sites: 65, Water at site, Flush toilet, Free showers, RV dump, Tent & RV camping: $33, 10 Group sites, Open Apr-Oct, Reservations accepted, Elev: 843ft/257m, Tel: 304-462-7158, Nearest town: Glenville. GPS: 38.878626, -80.868045

14 • C3 | Holly River SP

Total sites: 88, RV sites: 88, Elec sites: 88, Central water, Flush toilet, Free showers, RV dump, Tent & RV camping: $29-31, Also cabins, Stay limit: 14 days, Open Apr-Nov, Reservations accepted, Elev: 1732ft/528m, Tel: 304-493-6353, Nearest town: Hacker Valley. GPS: 38.668812, -80.373371

15 • C3 | Watoga SP - Beaver Creek CG

Total sites: 38, RV sites: 38, Elec sites: 12, Central water, Flush toilet, Free showers, Tents: $27/RVs: $31-33, Open Apr-Dec, Reservations not accepted, Elev: 2625ft/800m, Tel: 304-799-4087, Nearest town: Huntersville. GPS: 38.100885, -80.093655

16 • C3 | Watoga SP - Riverside CG

Total sites: 50, RV sites: 50, Elec sites: 38, Central water, Flush toilet, Free showers, Tents: $27/RVs: $31-33, Open Apr-Dec, Reservations accepted, Elev: 2142ft/653m, Tel: 304-799-4087, Nearest town: Seebert. GPS: 38.111447, -80.179108

17 • C4 | Canaan Valley Resort SP

Total sites: 34, RV sites: 34, Elec sites: 34, Water at site, Flush toilet, Free showers, RV dump, Tent & RV camping: $37, 34 Full hookups sites, $2/night resort fee, Nov-Apr: $32, Stay limit: 14 days, Open all year, Max Length: 45ft, Reservations accepted, Elev: 3274ft/998m, Tel: 304-866-4121, Nearest town: Canaan Valley. GPS: 39.017058, -79.458334

18 • C4 | Lost River SP - Ball Field

Total sites: 3, RV sites: 0, Flush toilet, Free showers, Tents only: $24, Stay limit: 14 days, Reservations required, Elev: 1997ft/609m, Tel: 304-897-5372, Nearest town: Mathias. GPS: 38.894569, -78.924913

19 • C4 | Lost River SP - Big Ridge Mt

Total sites: 2, RV sites: 0, No water, Vault/pit toilet, Tents only: $29, Hike-in, 1.5 mi, Stay limit: 14 days, Reservations required, Elev: 2955ft/901m, Tel: 304-897-5372, Nearest town: Mathias. GPS: 38.905101, -78.901253

20 • D1 | Chief Logan SP

Total sites: 26, RV sites: 26, Elec sites: 26, Water at site, Flush toilet, Free showers, RV dump, Tent & RV camping: $33-35, 14 Full hookups, Stay limit: 14 days, Open Apr-Oct, Reservations accepted, Elev: 800ft/244m, Tel: 304-792-7125, Nearest town: Logan. GPS: 37.884519, -82.018066

21 • D2 | Bluestone SP - Meador

Total sites: 32, RV sites: 32, Elec sites: 22, Water at site, Flush toilet, Free showers, RV dump, Tents: $27/RVs: $31-35, Stay limit: 14 days, Open Apr-Oct, Reservations accepted, Elev: 1507ft/459m, Tel: 304-466-2805, Nearest town: Hinton. GPS: 37.611271, -80.936249

22 • D2 | Bluestone SP - Old Mill

Total sites: 44, RV sites: 44, Central water, Flush toilet, Free showers, No RV dump, Tent & RV camping: $21, Cold showers, Stay limit: 14 days, Open Apr-Oct, Reservations accepted, Elev: 1430ft/436m, Tel: 304-466-2805, Nearest town: Hinton. GPS: 37.605198, -80.943695

23 • D2 | Bluestone SP - Tent

Total sites: 5, No water, Vault/pit toilet, Tents only: $19, Stay limit: 14 days, Open Apr-Oct, Reservations accepted, Elev: 1488ft/454m, Tel: 304-466-2805, Nearest town: Hinton. GPS: 37.610537, -80.939691

24 • D2 | Camp Creek SP - Almost Heaven Shelter

Dispersed sites, No water, Vault/pit toilet, Hike-to shelter: $20, First night: $20, Stay limit: 14 days, Open all year, Reservations accepted, Elev: 2505ft/764m, Tel: 304-425-9481, Nearest town: Camp Creek. GPS: 37.517794, -81.151882

25 • D2 | Camp Creek SP - Blue Jay

Total sites: 12, Central water, Vault/pit toilet, No showers, No RV dump, Tents only: $18, Stay limit: 14 days, Open Apr-Oct, Reservations not accepted, Elev: 2159ft/658m, Tel: 304-425-9481, Nearest town: Camp Creek. GPS: 37.513626, -81.130893

26 • D2 | Camp Creek SP - Double C Horse Camp

Total sites: 7, RV sites: 7, Central water, Vault/pit toilet, No showers, No RV dump, Tent & RV camping: $25, Stay limit: 14 days, Open May-Oct, Reservations required, Elev: 2297ft/700m, Tel: 304-425-9481, Nearest town: Camp Creek. GPS: 37.521741, -81.128987

27 • D2 | Camp Creek SP - Mash Fork

Total sites: 26, RV sites: 26, Elec sites: 26, Water at site, Flush toilet, Free showers, Tent & RV camping: $28-35, 9 Full hookups, Limited services Nov-Mar, Stay limit: 14 days, Open all year, Reservations accepted, Elev: 2064ft/629m, Tel: 304-425-9481, Nearest town: Camp Creek. GPS: 37.501769, -81.137438

28 • D2 | Little Beaver SP

Total sites: 46, RV sites: 46, Elec sites: 30, Water at site, Flush toilet, Free showers, Tents: $31/RVs: $33, Group site, Stay limit: 14 days, Reservations accepted, Elev: 2422ft/738m, Tel: 304-763-2494, Nearest town: Beaver. GPS: 37.755801, -81.080299

29 • D2 | Pipestem Resort SP

Total sites: 82, RV sites: 82, Elec sites: 50, Water at site, Flush toilet, Free showers, RV dump, Tents: $31/RVs: $35-39, 31 Full hookups, Stay limit: 14 days, Open all year, Reservations accepted, Elev: 2756ft/840m, Tel: 304-466-1800, Nearest town: Pipestem. GPS: 37.518827, -80.981888

30 • D2 | Twin Falls Resort SP

Total sites: 50, RV sites: 50, Elec sites: 25, Central water, Flush toilet, Free showers, RV dump, Tents: $25/RVs: $28, Also cabins, Stay limit: 14 days, Open all year, Reservations accepted, Elev: 2303ft/702m, Tel: 304-294-4000, Nearest town: Mullens. GPS: 37.619761, -81.429255

31 • D3 | Moncove Lake SP

Total sites: 48, RV sites: 48, Elec sites: 34, Central water, Flush toilet, Free showers, RV dump, Tents: $25/RVs: $28, Group site: $50, Stay limit: 14 days, Reservations accepted, Elev: 2523ft/769m, Tel: 304-772-3450, Nearest town: Gap Mills. GPS: 37.617751, -80.355229

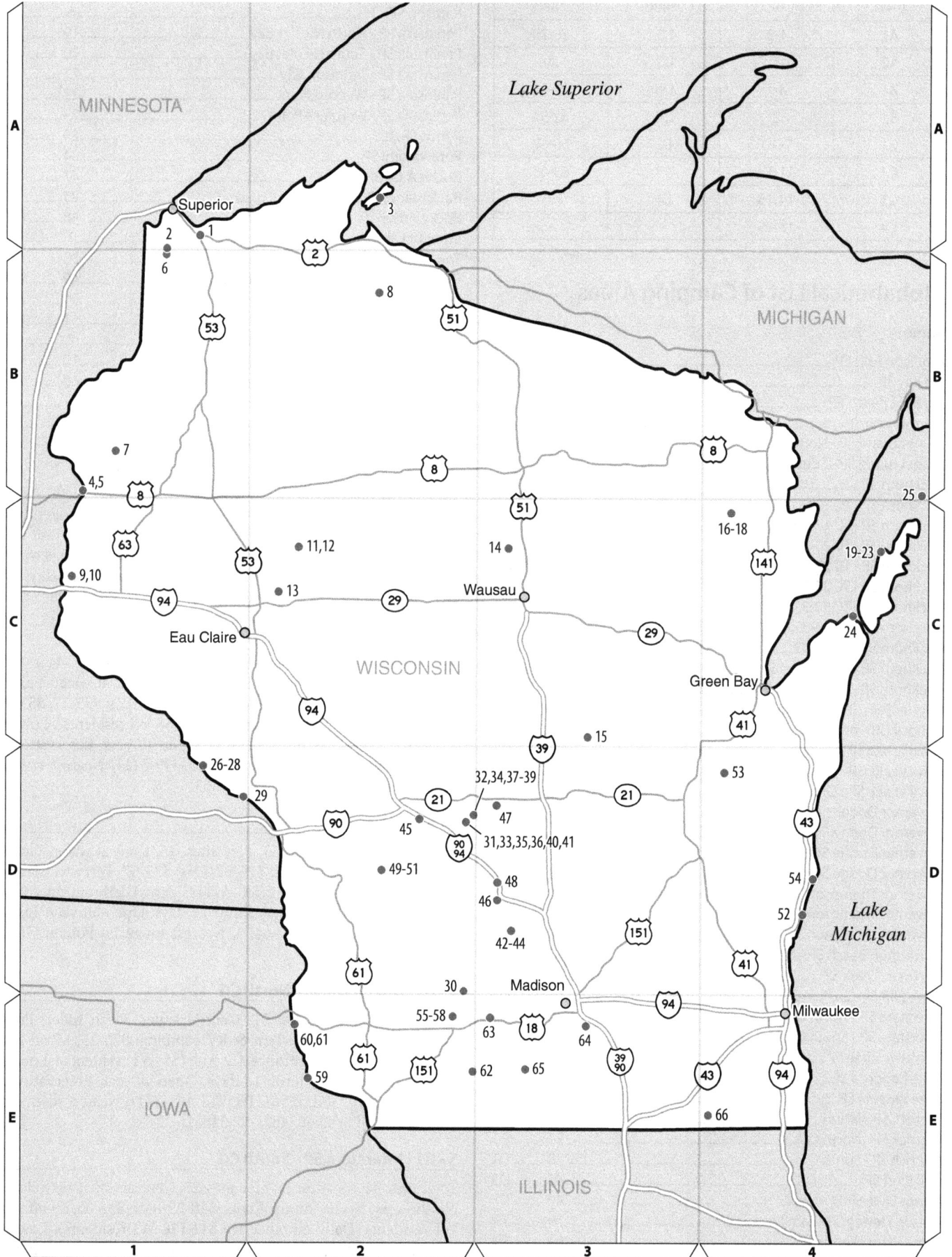

Wisconsin

MINNESOTA

Lake Superior

MICHIGAN

A

Superior

2
6
1

(2)

3

8

(51)

(53)

B

7

4,5

(8)

(63)

(8)

(8)

25

9,10

11,12

(53)

14

(51)

16-18

(141)

19-23

13

(94)

(29)

Wausau

24

Eau Claire

(29)

Green Bay

WISCONSIN

C

26-28

29

(90)

45

(21)

32,34,37-39

47

31,33,35,36,40,41

15

(39)

(21)

53

(41)

(43)

54

D

49-51

(90)(94)

48

46

52

Lake Michigan

42-44

(151)

61

30

Madison

(41)

55-58

63

(18)

64

(94)

Milwaukee

60,61

59

(61)

(151)

62

65

(39)(90)

(43)

(94)

66

E

IOWA

ILLINOIS

1   2   3   4

Map	ID	Map	ID
A1	1-2	D1	26-29
A2	3	D2	30
B1	4-7	D3	31-51
B2	8	D4	52-54
C1	9-10	E2	55-62
C2	11-13	E3	63-65
C3	14-15	E4	66
C4	16-25		

Alphabetical List of Camping Areas

1 • A1 | Amnicon Falls SP

Total sites: 36, RV sites: 34, Central water, Vault/pit toilet, No showers, No RV dump, Tent & RV camping: $21-23, $5 off for WI residents, Daily entrance fee $11 ($8 WI residents), Lower off-season rates, Stay limit: 14 days, No generators, Reservations accepted, Elev: 787ft/240m, Tel: 715-398-3000, Nearest town: South Range. GPS: 46.609009, -91.892461

2 • A1 | Pattison SP

Total sites: 59, RV sites: 59, Elec sites: 18, Central water, Flush toilet, Free showers, RV dump, Tents: $25-27/RVs: $35-37, $5 off for WI residents, Daily entrance fee $11 ($8 WI residents), Lower off-season rates, Stay limit: 14 days, Open all year, Reservations accepted, Elev: 1004ft/306m, Tel: 715-399-3111, Nearest town: Superior. GPS: 46.535872, -92.116465

3 • A2 | Big Bay SP

Total sites: 60, RV sites: 53, Elec sites: 15, Central water, Flush toilet, Free showers, Tents: $25-27/RVs: $35-37, Ferry to island, $5 off for WI residents, $11 ($8 - WI residents) daily entrance fee, Lower off-season rates, Stay limit: 14 days, Open all year, Elev: 663ft/202m, Tel: 715-747-6425, Nearest town: La Pointe. GPS: 46.795745, -90.673601

4 • B1 | Interstate SP - North CG

Total sites: 45, RV sites: 31, Central water, Flush toilet, Free showers, No RV dump, Tent & RV camping: $20-25, $5 off for WI residents, Daily entrance fee $11 ($8 WI residents), Lower off-season rates, Stay limit: 14 days, Open all year, Reservations accepted, Elev: 738ft/225m, Tel: 715-483-3747, Nearest town: St Croix Falls. GPS: 45.403457, -92.648316

5 • B1 | Interstate SP - South CG

Total sites: 34, RV sites: 25, Elec sites: 25, Central water, No toilets, No showers, No RV dump, Tents: $20-25/RVs: $33-35, $5 off for WI residents, Daily entrance fee $11 ($8 WI residents), Lower off-season rates, Stay limit: 14 days, Open all year, Reservations accepted, Elev: 718ft/219m, Tel: 715-483-3747, Nearest town: St Croix Falls. GPS: 45.389901, -92.661401

6 • B1 | Pattison SP - TC

Dispersed sites, No water, Vault/pit toilet, Tents only: $25-27, Hike-in, 1.6 mi, $5 off for WI residents, $11 ($8 - WI residents) daily entrance fee, Lower off-season rates, Stay limit: 14 days, Reservations accepted, Elev: 1119ft/341m, Tel: 715-399-3111, Nearest town: Superior. GPS: 46.520565, -92.125265

7 • B1 | Straight Lake SP

Total sites: 10, RV sites: 0, No water, Vault/pit toilet, Tents only: $20-23, Walk-to sites, $5 off for WI residents, Daily entrance fee $11 ($8 WI residents), Stay limit: 14 days, Reservations accepted, Elev: 1287ft/392m, Tel: 715-431-0724, Nearest town: Luck. GPS: 45.600704, -92.413893

8 • B2 | Copper Falls SP

Total sites: 56, RV sites: 56, Elec sites: 24, Central water, Flush toilet, Free showers, RV dump, Tents: $25-27/RVs: $35-37, $5 off for WI residents, Daily entrance fee $11 ($8 WI residents), Lower off-season rates, Stay limit: 14 days, Open all year, Reservations accepted, Elev: 1217ft/371m, Tel: 715-274-5123, Nearest town: Mellen. GPS: 46.359363, -90.647159

9 • C1 | Willow River SP - 100/200 Loops

Total sites: 80, RV sites: 80, Elec sites: 34, Central water, Flush toilet, Free showers, No RV dump, Tents: $25/RVs: $40, $5 off for WI residents, Daily entrance fee $11 ($8 WI residents), Stay limit: 14 days, Open all year, Reservations accepted, Elev: 889ft/271m, Tel: 715-386-5931, Nearest town: Hudson. GPS: 45.013912, -92.681349

10 • C1 | Willow River SP - 300 Loop

Total sites: 70, RV sites: 70, Elec sites: 20, Central water, Flush toilet, Free showers, RV dump, Tents: $25/RVs: $40, $5 off for WI residents, Daily entrance fee $11 ($8 WI residents), Stay limit: 14 days, Open all year, Reservations accepted, Elev: 735ft/224m, Tel: 715-386-5931, Nearest town: Hudson. GPS: 45.013322, -92.697418

11 • C2 | Brunet Island SP - North CG

Total sites: 45, RV sites: 45, Central water, Vault/pit toilet, No showers, RV dump, Tent & RV camping: $23-25, $5 off for WI residents, Daily entrance fee $11 ($8 WI residents), Lower off-season rates, Stay limit: 14 days, Open all year, Reservations accepted, Elev: 1017ft/310m, Tel: 715-239-6888, Nearest town: Cornell. GPS: 45.182023, -91.170479

12 • C2 | Brunet Island SP - South CG

Total sites: 24, RV sites: 24, Elec sites: 24, Central water, Vault/pit toilet, No showers, RV dump, Tent & RV camping: $33-35, $5 off for WI residents, Daily entrance fee $11 ($8 WI residents), Lower off-season rates, Stay limit: 14 days, Open all year, Reservations accepted, Elev: 1037ft/316m, Tel: 715-239-6888, Nearest town: Cornell. GPS: 45.176236, -91.172028

13 • C2 | Lake Wissota SP

Total sites: 116, RV sites: 116, Elec sites: 58, Central water, Flush toilet, Free showers, RV dump, Tents: $20-25/RVs: $33-35, Stay limit: 14 days, Open all year, Reservations accepted, Elev: 945ft/288m, Tel: 715-382-4574, Nearest town: Chippewa Falls. GPS: 44.969368, -91.299498

14 • C3 | Council Grounds SP

Total sites: 55, RV sites: 55, Elec sites: 19, Central water, Flush toilet, Free showers, RV dump, Tents: $20-25/RVs: $33-35, $5 off for WI residents, Daily entrance fee $11 ($8 WI residents), Lower off-season rates, Stay limit: 14 days, Open all year, Reservations accepted, Elev: 1345ft/410m, Tel: 715-536-8773, Nearest town: Merrill. GPS: 45.186035, -89.749512

15 • C3 | Hartman Creek SP

Total sites: 74, RV sites: 74, Elec sites: 23, Central water, Flush toilet, Free showers, RV dump, Tents: $23-25/RVs: $35, $5 off for WI residents, Daily entrance fee $11 ($8 WI residents), Lower off-season rates, Stay limit: 14 days, Open Apr-Nov, Reservations accepted, Elev: 961ft/293m, Tel: 715-258-2372, Nearest town: Waupaca. GPS: 44.323242, -89.217285

16 • C4 | Governor Thompson SP - East

Total sites: 30, RV sites: 30, Elec sites: 16, Central water, Flush toilet, Free showers, RV dump, Tents: $21-23/RVs: $33-35, $5 off for WI residents, Daily entrance fee $11 ($8 WI residents), Lower off-season rates, Stay limit: 14 days, Reservations accepted, Elev: 992ft/302m. GPS: 45.342234, -88.234633

17 • C4 | Governor Thompson SP - North

Total sites: 20, RV sites: 20, Central water, Flush toilet, Free showers, RV dump, Tent & RV camping: $21-23, $5 off for WI residents, Daily entrance fee $11 ($8 WI residents), Lower off-season rates, Stay limit: 14 days, Reservations accepted, Elev: 993ft/303m. GPS: 45.343515, -88.239025

18 • C4 | Governor Thompson SP - South

Total sites: 40, RV sites: 40, Central water, Flush toilet, Free showers, RV dump, Tent & RV camping: $21-23, $5 off for WI residents, Daily entrance fee $11 ($8 WI residents), Lower off-season rates, Stay limit: 14 days, Reservations accepted, Elev: 991ft/302m. GPS: 45.341363, -88.238416

19 • C4 | Peninsula SP - North Nicolet Bay

Total sites: 44, RV sites: 44, Central water, Flush toilet, Free showers, RV dump, Tent & RV camping: $25-27, $5 off for WI residents, Daily entrance fee $11 ($8 WI residents), Lower off-season rates, Stay limit: 14 days, Open all year, Reservations accepted, Elev: 600ft/183m, Tel: 920-868-3258, Nearest town: Fish Creek. GPS: 45.169386, -87.223177

20 • C4 | Peninsula SP - South Nicolet Bay

Total sites: 143, RV sites: 143, Elec sites: 54, Central water, Flush toilet, Free showers, RV dump, Tents: $25-27/RVs: $40-42, $5 off for WI residents, Daily entrance fee $11 ($8 WI residents), Lower off-season rates, Stay limit: 14 days, Open all year, Reservations accepted, Elev: 615ft/187m, Tel: 920-868-3258, Nearest town: Fish Creek. GPS: 45.163427, -87.219607

21 • C4 | Peninsula SP - Tennison Bay

Total sites: 188, RV sites: 188, Elec sites: 97, Central water, Flush toilet, Free showers, RV dump, Tents: $25-27/RVs: $40-42, $5 off for WI residents, Daily entrance fee $11 ($8 WI residents), Lower off-season rates, Stay limit: 14 days, Open all year, Reservations accepted, Elev: 610ft/186m, Tel: 920-868-3258, Nearest town: Fish Creek. GPS: 45.161085, -87.233839

22 • C4 | Peninsula SP - Weborg Point

Total sites: 12, RV sites: 12, Elec sites: 12, Central water, Flush toilet, Free showers, RV dump, Tent & RV camping: $40-42, $5 off for WI residents, Daily entrance fee $11 ($8 WI residents), Lower off-season rates, Stay limit: 14 days, Open all year, Reservations accepted, Elev: 581ft/177m, Tel: 920-868-3258, Nearest town: Fish Creek. GPS: 45.134639, -87.239509

23 • C4 | Peninsula SP - Welcker's Point

Total sites: 81, RV sites: 81, Central water, Flush toilet, Free showers, RV dump, Tent & RV camping: $25-27, $5 off for WI residents, Daily entrance fee $11 ($8 WI residents), Lower off-season rates, Stay limit: 14 days, Open all year, Reservations accepted, Elev: 564ft/172m, Tel: 920-868-3258, Nearest town: Fish Creek. GPS: 45.173204, -87.226972

24 • C4 | Potawatomi SP

Total sites: 123, RV sites: 123, Elec sites: 40, Central water, Flush toilet, Free showers, RV dump, Tents: $23-25/RVs: $35, $5 off for WI residents, Daily entrance fee $11 ($8 WI residents), Lower off-season rates, Stay limit: 14 days, Open all year, Reservations accepted, Elev: 627ft/191m, Tel: 920-746-2890, Nearest town: Sturgeon Bay. GPS: 44.864496, -87.413345

25 • C4 | Rock Island SP

Total sites: 40, RV sites: 0, Central water, Vault/pit toilet, Tents only: $25, Hike-in, Ferry to island (no vehicles), sites, $5 off for WI residents, $11 ($8 - WI residents) daily entrance fee, Stay limit: 14 days, Open all year, Elev: 574ft/175m, Tel: 920-847-2235, Nearest town: On Island. GPS: 45.408644, -86.828106

26 • D1 | Merrick SP - Island

Total sites: 5, Central water, Flush toilet, No showers, No RV dump, Tents only: $20-21, Walk-to sites, $5 off for WI residents, Daily entrance fee $11 ($8 WI residents), Lower off-season rates, Stay limit: 14 days, Open all year, Reservations accepted, Elev: 656ft/200m, Tel: 608-687-4936, Nearest town: Fountain City. GPS: 44.150369, -91.751845

27 • D1 | Merrick SP - North CG

Total sites: 25, RV sites: 25, Elec sites: 22, Central water, Flush toilet, Free showers, RV dump, Tents: $20-21/RVs: $31-35, $5 off for WI residents, Daily entrance fee $11 ($8 WI residents), Lower off-season rates, Stay limit: 14 days, Open all year, Reservations accepted, Elev: 686ft/209m, Tel: 608-687-4936, Nearest town: Fountain City. GPS: 44.159351, -91.762238

28 • D1 | Merrick SP - South CG

Total sites: 35, RV sites: 35, Central water, Vault/pit toilet, No showers, No RV dump, Tent & RV camping: $20-21, $5 off for WI residents, Daily entrance fee $11 ($8 WI residents), Lower off-season rates, Stay limit: 14 days, Open all year, Reservations accepted, Elev: 666ft/203m, Tel: 608-687-4936, Nearest town: Fountain City. GPS: 44.146238, -91.744139

29 • D1 | Perrot SP

Total sites: 102, RV sites: 102, Elec sites: 38, Central water, Flush toilet, Free showers, RV dump, Tents: $20-25/RVs: $33-35, $5 off for WI residents, Daily entrance fee $11 ($8 WI residents), Lower off-season rates, Stay limit: 14 days, Open all year, Reservations accepted, Elev: 712ft/217m, Tel: 608-534-6409, Nearest town: Trempealeau. GPS: 44.026932, -91.483656

30 • D2 | Tower Hill SP

Total sites: 11, RV sites: 11, Central water, Vault/pit toilet, No showers, No RV dump, Tent & RV camping: $20-21, $5 off for WI residents, Daily entrance fee $11 ($8 WI residents), Lower off-season rates, Stay limit: 14 days, Reservations accepted, Elev: 761ft/232m, Tel: 608-588-2116, Nearest town: Spring Green. GPS: 43.146725, -90.047702

31 • D3 | Buckhorn SP

Total sites: 60, RV sites: 60, Elec sites: 7, Central water, Flush toilet, Free showers, No RV dump, Tents: $20-25/RVs: $33-37, $5 off for WI residents, Daily entrance fee $11 ($8 WI residents), Lower off-season rates, Stay limit: 14 days, Open all year, Reservations accepted, Elev: 889ft/271m, Tel: 608-565-2789, Nearest town: Necedah. GPS: 43.941398, -90.016755

32 • D3 | Buckhorn SP - TC 1-3

Total sites: 3, No water, Vault/pit toilet, Tents only: $20-25, Walk-to/boat-in sites, $5 off for WI residents, Daily entrance fee $11 ($8 WI residents), Lower off-season rates, Stay limit: 14 days, Reservations accepted, Elev: 906ft/276m, Tel: 608-565-2789, Nearest town: Necedah. GPS: 43.956608, -89.978467

33 • D3 | Buckhorn SP - TC 17-19

Total sites: 3, No water, Vault/pit toilet, Tents only: $20-25, Hike-in/boat-in, 1.2 mi, $5 off for WI residents, Daily entrance fee $11 ($8 WI residents), Stay limit: 14 days, Reservations accepted, Elev: 894ft/272m, Tel: 608-565-2789, Nearest town: Necedah. GPS: 43.917445, -90.005496

34 • D3 | Buckhorn SP - TC 20-22

Total sites: 3, No water, Vault/pit toilet, Tents only: $20-25, Walk-to/boat-in sites, $5 off for WI residents, Daily entrance fee $11 ($8 WI residents), Lower off-season rates, Stay limit: 14 days, Reservations accepted, Elev: 910ft/277m, Tel: 608-565-2789, Nearest town: Necedah. GPS: 43.946655, -89.979967

35 • D3 | Buckhorn SP - TC 23-24

Total sites: 2, No water, Vault/pit toilet, Tents only: $20-25, Hike-in/boat-in, $5 off for WI residents, Daily entrance fee $11 ($8 WI residents), Lower off-season rates, Stay limit: 14 days, Reservations accepted, Elev: 899ft/274m, Tel: 608-565-2789, Nearest town: Necedah. GPS: 43.931793, -90.019173

36 • D3 | Buckhorn SP - TC 26-29

Total sites: 4, No water, Vault/pit toilet, Tents only: $20-25, Walk-to sites, $5 off for WI residents, Daily entrance fee $11 ($8 WI residents), Lower off-season rates, Stay limit: 14 days, Reservations accepted, Elev: 927ft/283m, Tel: 608-565-2789, Nearest town: Necedah. GPS: 43.936184, -90.017591

37 • D3 | Buckhorn SP - TC 30-33

Total sites: 4, No water, Vault/pit toilet, Tents only: $20-25, Walk-to sites, $5 off for WI residents, Daily entrance fee $11 ($8 WI residents), Lower off-season rates, Stay limit: 14 days, Reservations accepted, Elev: 914ft/279m, Tel: 608-565-2789, Nearest town: Necedah. GPS: 43.945319, -89.983622

38 • D3 | Buckhorn SP - TC 34-37,43-45

Total sites: 7, No water, Vault/pit toilet, Tents only: $20-25, Walk-to/boat-in sites, $5 off for WI residents, Daily entrance fee $11 ($8 WI residents), Lower off-season rates, Stay limit: 14 days, Reservations accepted, Elev: 933ft/284m, Tel: 608-565-2789, Nearest town: Necedah. GPS: 43.939203, -89.980548

39 • D3 | Buckhorn SP - TC 39-42

Total sites: 4, No water, Vault/pit toilet, Tents only: $20-25, Walk-to sites, $5 off for WI residents, Daily entrance fee $11 ($8 WI residents), Lower off-season rates, Stay limit: 14 days, Reservations accepted, Elev: 892ft/272m, Tel: 608-565-2789, Nearest town: Necedah. GPS: 43.943649, -89.983786

40 • D3 | Buckhorn SP - TC 4-7,13-15

Total sites: 7, No water, Vault/pit toilet, Tents only: $20-25, Hike-in/boat-in, $5 off for WI residents, Daily entrance fee $11 ($8 WI residents), Lower off-season rates, Stay limit: 14 days, Reservations accepted, Elev: 887ft/270m, Tel: 608-565-2789, Nearest town: Necedah. GPS: 43.921153, -90.008869

41 • D3 | Buckhorn SP - TC 8-12, 16, 25

Total sites: 7, No water, Vault/pit toilet, Tents only: $20-25, Hike-in/boat-in, $5 off for WI residents, Daily entrance fee $11 ($8 WI residents), Lower off-season rates, Stay limit: 14 days, Reservations accepted, Elev: 916ft/279m, Tel: 608-565-2789, Nearest town: Necedah. GPS: 43.926231, -90.014945

42 • D3 | Devil's Lake SP - Ice Age

Total sites: 194, RV sites: 194, Central water, Flush toilet, Free showers, RV dump, Tent & RV camping: $25-27, $5 off for WI residents, Daily entrance fee $16 ($13 WI residents), Stay limit: 14 days, Open all year, Reservations accepted, Elev: 1050ft/320m, Tel: 608-356-8301, Nearest town: Wisconsin Dells. GPS: 43.435359, -89.724338

43 • D3 | Devil's Lake SP - Northern Lights

Total sites: 133, RV sites: 133, Elec sites: 55, Central water, Flush toilet, Free showers, Tents: $25-27/RVs: $40-42, $5 off for WI residents, Daily entrance fee $11 ($8 WI residents), Stay limit: 14 days, Open all year, Reservations accepted, Elev: 1030ft/314m, Tel: 608-356-8301, Nearest town: Wisconsin Dells. GPS: 43.431743, -89.728402

44 • D3 | Devil's Lake SP - Quartzite

Total sites: 80, RV sites: 80, Elec sites: 46, Central water, Flush toilet, Free showers, RV dump, Tents: $25-27/RVs: $40-42, $5 off for WI residents, Daily entrance fee $11 ($8 WI residents), Stay limit: 14 days, Open all year, Reservations accepted, Elev: 965ft/294m, Tel: 608-356-8301, Nearest town: Wisconsin Dells. GPS: 43.432102, -89.734808

45 • D3 | Mill Bluff SP

Total sites: 21, RV sites: 21, Elec sites: 6, Central water, Vault/pit toilet, No showers, No RV dump, Tents: $20-21/RVs: $31-33, $5 off for WI residents, Daily entrance fee $11 ($8 WI residents), Stay limit: 14 days, Open May-Sep, Reservations accepted, Elev: 1007ft/307m, Tel: 608-427-6692, Nearest town: Camp Douglas. GPS: 43.940918, -90.319092

46 • D3 | Mirror Lake SP

Total sites: 151, RV sites: 151, Elec sites: 47, Central water, Flush toilet, Free showers, RV dump, Tents: $25-27/RVs: $35-37, $5 off for WI residents, Daily entrance fee $11 ($8 WI residents), Lower off-season rates, Stay limit: 14 days, Open all year, Reservations accepted, Elev: 942ft/287m, Tel: 608-254-2333, Nearest town: Wisconsin Dells. GPS: 43.570072, -89.804666

47 • D3 | Roche A Cri SP

Total sites: 40, RV sites: 40, Elec sites: 4, Central water, Vault/pit toilet, No showers, RV dump, Tents: $20-21/RVs: $31-33, $5 off for WI residents, Daily entrance fee $11 ($8 WI residents), Lower off-season rates, Stay limit: 14 days, Open May-Oct, Reservations accepted, Elev: 1007ft/307m, Tel: 608-339-6881, Nearest town: Friendship. GPS: 44.001709, -89.817871

48 • D3 | Rocky Arbor SP

Total sites: 89, RV sites: 78, Elec sites: 19, Central water, Flush toilet, Free showers, RV dump, Tents: $20-25/RVs: $31-35, Stay limit: 14 days, Open May-Sep, Reservations accepted, Elev: 971ft/296m, Tel: 608-254-8001, Nearest town: Wisconsin Dells. GPS: 43.642842, -89.808607

49 • D3 | Wildcat Mountain SP - Cart-in Sites

Total sites: 20, RV sites: 0, Central water, Vault/pit toilet, No showers, No RV dump, Tents only: $20-25, Walk-to sites, $5 off for WI residents, Daily entrance fee $11 ($8 WI residents), Lower off-season rates, Open all year, Reservations accepted, Elev: 1231ft/375m, Tel: 608-337-4775, Nearest town: Ontario. GPS: 43.699012, -90.571838

50 • D3 | Wildcat Mountain SP - Family

Total sites: 25, RV sites: 25, Central water, Flush toilet, Free showers, RV dump, Tent & RV camping: $20-25, $5 off for WI residents, Daily entrance fee $11 ($8 WI residents), Lower off-season rates, Stay limit: 14 days, Open all year, Reservations accepted, Elev: 1260ft/384m, Nearest town: Ontario. GPS: 43.698854, -90.574713

51 • D3 | Wildcat Mountain SP - Horse Camp

Total sites: 24, RV sites: 24, Central water, Vault/pit toilet, No showers, No RV dump, Tent & RV camping: $20-25, $5 off for WI residents, Daily entrance fee $11 ($8 WI residents), Lower off-season rates, Stay limit: 14 days, Open May-Nov, Reservations accepted, Elev: 971ft/296m, Tel: 608-337-4775, Nearest town: Ontario. GPS: 43.710969, -90.563942

52 • D4 | Harrington Beach SP - Main CG

Total sites: 69, RV sites: 64, Elec sites: 31, Central water, Flush toilet, Free showers, RV dump, Tents: $23-25/RVs: $35-37, Also walk-to sites, 5 walk-to sites, $5 off for WI residents, $11 ($8 - WI residents) daily entrance fee, Stay limit: 14 days, Open May-

Oct, Reservations accepted, Elev: 654ft/199m, Tel: Info: 262-285-3015/Res: 888-947-2757, Nearest town: Belgium. GPS: 43.489046, -87.805542

53 • D4 | High Cliff SP

Total sites: 112, RV sites: 112, Elec sites: 32, Central water, Flush toilet, Free showers, RV dump, Tents: $25/RVs: $40, $5 off for WI residents, Daily entrance fee $11 ($8 WI residents), Stay limit: 14 days, Open all year, Reservations accepted, Elev: 1010ft/308m, Tel: 920-989-1106, Nearest town: Sherwood. GPS: 44.150594, -88.296874

54 • D4 | Kohler-Andrae SP

Total sites: 137, RV sites: 137, Elec sites: 52, Central water, Flush toilet, Free showers, RV dump, Tents: $25/RVs: $40, $5 off for WI residents, Daily entrance fee $11 ($8 WI residents), Lower off-season rates, Stay limit: 14 days, Open all year, Reservations accepted, Elev: 617ft/188m, Tel: 920-451-4080, Nearest town: Sheboygan. GPS: 43.655775, -87.725352

55 • E2 | Governor Dodge SP - Cox Hollow

Total sites: 118, RV sites: 116, Elec sites: 3, Central water, Flush toilet, Free showers, RV dump, Tents: $25/RVs: $35, $5 off for WI residents, Daily entrance fee $11 ($8 WI residents), Lower off-season rates, Stay limit: 14 days, Open all year, Reservations accepted, Elev: 1125ft/343m, Tel: 608-935-2315, Nearest town: Dodgeville. GPS: 43.019856, -90.115812

56 • E2 | Governor Dodge SP - Hickory Ridge TC

Total sites: 6, No water, Vault/pit toilet, Tents only: $25, Hike-in, $5 off for WI residents, Daily entrance fee $11 ($8 WI residents), Lower off-season rates, Stay limit: 14 days, Reservations accepted, Elev: 1085ft/331m, Tel: 608-935-2315, Nearest town: Dodgeville. GPS: 43.043521, -90.091879

57 • E2 | Governor Dodge SP - Trails End Horse Camp

Total sites: 11, RV sites: 11, Central water, Tent & RV camping: $25, $5 off for WI residents, Daily entrance fee $11 ($8 WI residents), Lower off-season rates, Stay limit: 14 days, Open Apr-Nov, Reservations accepted, Elev: 1120ft/341m, Tel: 608-935-2315, Nearest town: Dodgeville. GPS: 43.017695, -90.107018

58 • E2 | Governor Dodge SP - Twin Valley

Total sites: 150, RV sites: 146, Elec sites: 77, Central water, Flush toilet, Free showers, RV dump, Tents: $25/RVs: $35, $5 off for WI residents, Daily entrance fee $11 ($8 WI residents), Lower off-season rates, Stay limit: 14 days, Open all year, Reservations accepted, Elev: 1122ft/342m, Tel: 608-935-2315, Nearest town: Dodgeville. GPS: 43.024771, -90.103039

59 • E2 | Nelson Dewey SP - Family

Total sites: 45, RV sites: 45, Elec sites: 18, Central water, Flush toilet, Free showers, RV dump, Tents: $20-21/RVs: $31-33, Not plowed in winter - can walk in, $5 off for WI residents, Daily entrance fee $11 ($8 WI residents), Lower off-season rates, Stay limit: 14 days, Open all year, Reservations accepted, Elev: 951ft/290m, Tel: 608-725-5374, Nearest town: Cassville. GPS: 42.739902, -91.025465

60 • E2 | Wyalusing SP - Homestead

Total sites: 55, RV sites: 55, Elec sites: 9, Central water, Flush toilet, Free showers, RV dump, Tents: $23/RVs: $35, $5 off for WI residents, Daily entrance fee $11 ($8 WI residents), Stay limit: 14 days, Open all year, Reservations accepted, Elev: 1076ft/328m, Tel: 608-996-2261, Nearest town: Bagley. GPS: 42.978793, -91.122882

61 • E2 | Wyalusing SP - Wisconsin Ridge

Total sites: 55, RV sites: 55, Elec sites: 25, Central water, Flush toilet, Free showers, RV dump, Tents: $23/RVs: $35, $5 off for WI residents, Daily entrance fee $11 ($8 WI residents), Stay limit: 14 days, Open all year, Reservations accepted, Elev: 928ft/283m, Tel: 608-996-2261, Nearest town: Bagley. GPS: 42.993971, -91.118151

62 • E2 | Yellowstone SP

Total sites: 128, RV sites: 128, Elec sites: 38, Central water, Flush toilet, Free showers, RV dump, Tents: $20-25/RVs: $33-35, $5 off for WI residents, Daily entrance fee $11 ($8 WI residents), Stay limit: 14 days, Open Apr-Nov, Reservations accepted, Elev: 1024ft/312m, Tel: 608-523-4427, Nearest town: Blanchardville. GPS: 42.773756, -89.969506

63 • E3 | Blue Mound SP

Total sites: 89, RV sites: 77, Elec sites: 2, Central water, Flush toilet, Free showers, RV dump, Tents: $20-23/RVs: $33-35, 12 Bike-in sites, $5 off for WI residents, $11 ($8 - WI residents) daily entrance fee, Lower off-season rates, Stay limit: 14 days, Open all year, Reservations accepted, Elev: 1529ft/466m, Tel: 608-437-5711, Nearest town: Blue Mounds. GPS: 43.021747, -89.853328

64 • E3 | Lake Kegonsa SP

Total sites: 96, RV sites: 96, Elec sites: 29, Central water, Flush toilet, Free showers, RV dump, Tents: $20-27/RVs: $35-37, $5 off for WI residents, Daily entrance fee $11 ($8 WI residents), Lower off-season rates, Stay limit: 14 days, Open May-Oct, Reservations accepted, Elev: 932ft/284m, Tel: 608-873-9695, Nearest town: Stoughton. GPS: 42.980508, -89.234834

65 • E3 | New Glarus Woods SP

Total sites: 32, RV sites: 18, Elec sites: 18, Central water, Vault/pit toilet, No showers, No RV dump, Tents: $20-23/RVs: $31-33, $5 off for WI residents, Daily entrance fee $11 ($8 WI residents), Stay limit: 14 days, Open May-Oct, Max Length: 20ft, Reservations accepted, Elev: 1070ft/326m, Tel: 608-527-2335, Nearest town: New Glarus. GPS: 42.786976, -89.633709

66 • E4 | Big Foot Beach SP

Total sites: 100, RV sites: 100, Elec sites: 14, Central water, Flush toilet, Free showers, RV dump, Tents: $20-25/RVs: $33-35, $5 off for WI residents, Daily entrance fee $11 ($8 WI residents), Lower off-season rates, Stay limit: 14 days, Open all year, Reservations accepted, Elev: 934ft/285m, Tel: 262-248-2528, Nearest town: Lake Geneva. GPS: 42.571181, -88.425892

www.ingramcontent.com/pod-product-compliance
Lightning Source LLC
Chambersburg PA
CBHW050352100426
42739CB00015BB/3370